BOTANICAL
SKETCHBOOKS

AN ARTIST'S GUIDE TO PLANT STUDIES

I0729668

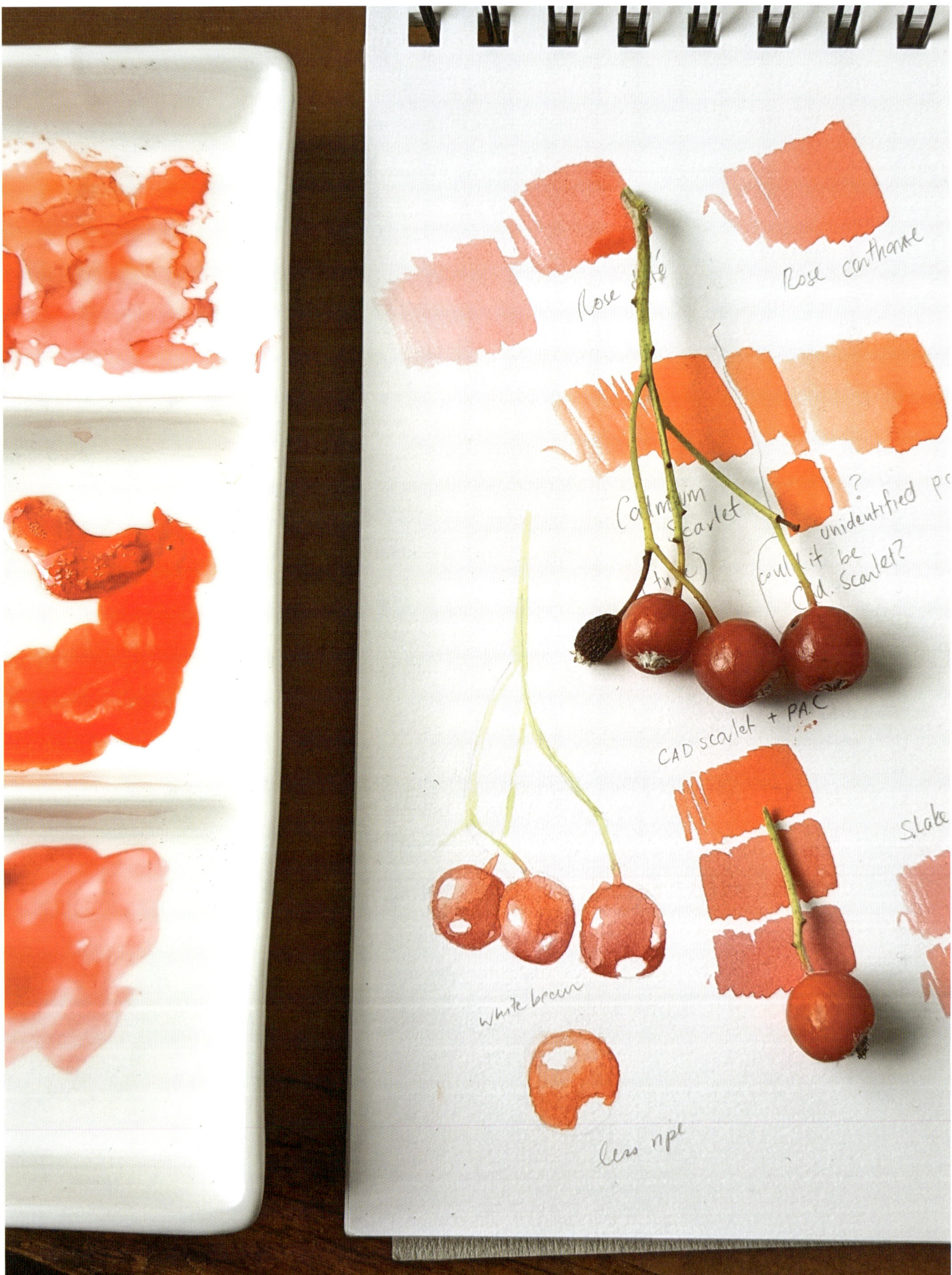

Rose doré
Rose carthame
Cadmium Scarlet
?
unidentified p
could it be
Cad. Scarlet?
CAD scarlet + PA.C
S.Lake
white brown
less ripe

Lucy T Smith

BOTANICAL SKETCHBOOKS

AN ARTIST'S GUIDE TO PLANT STUDIES

THE CROWOOD PRESS

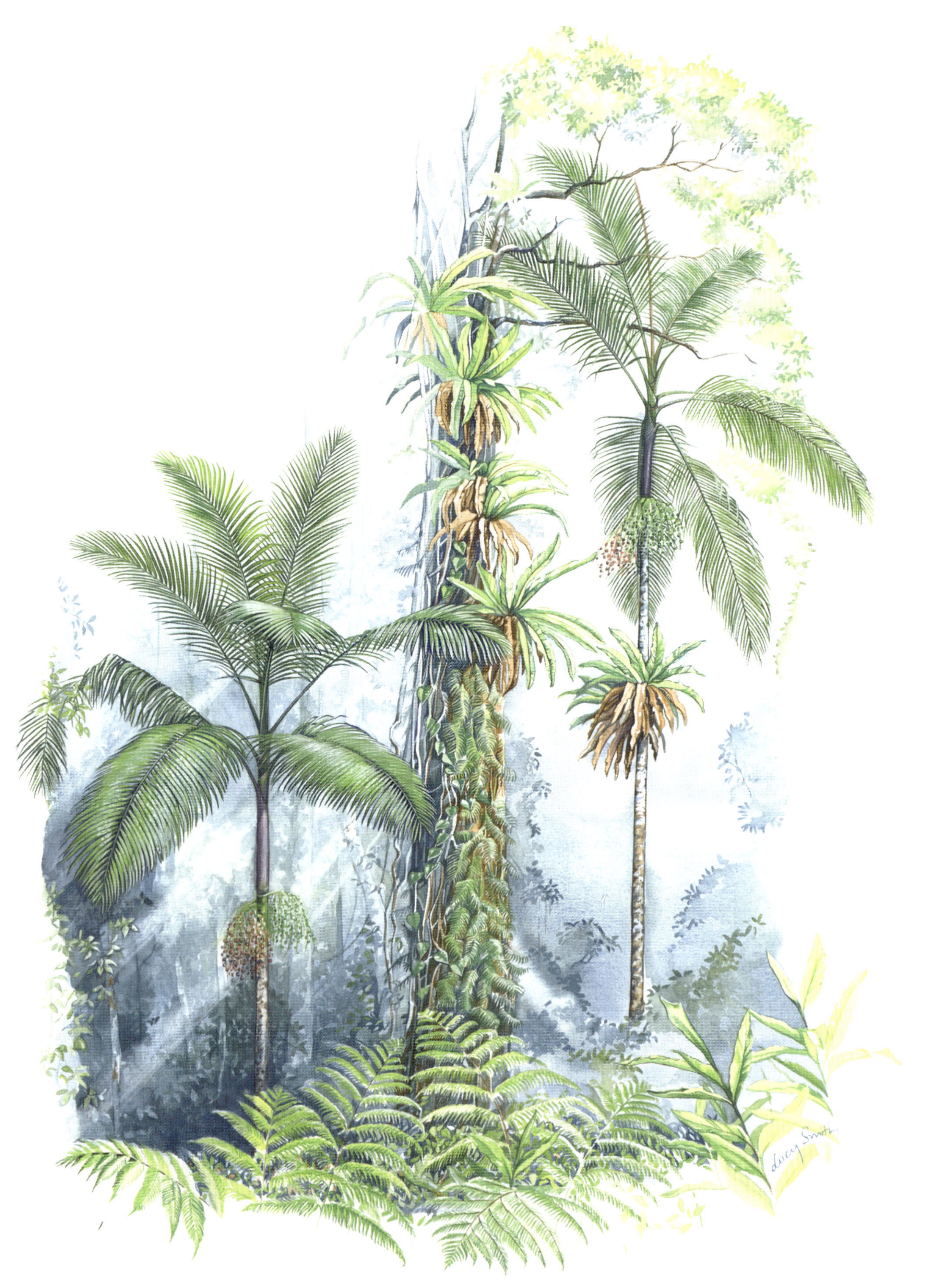

CONTENTS

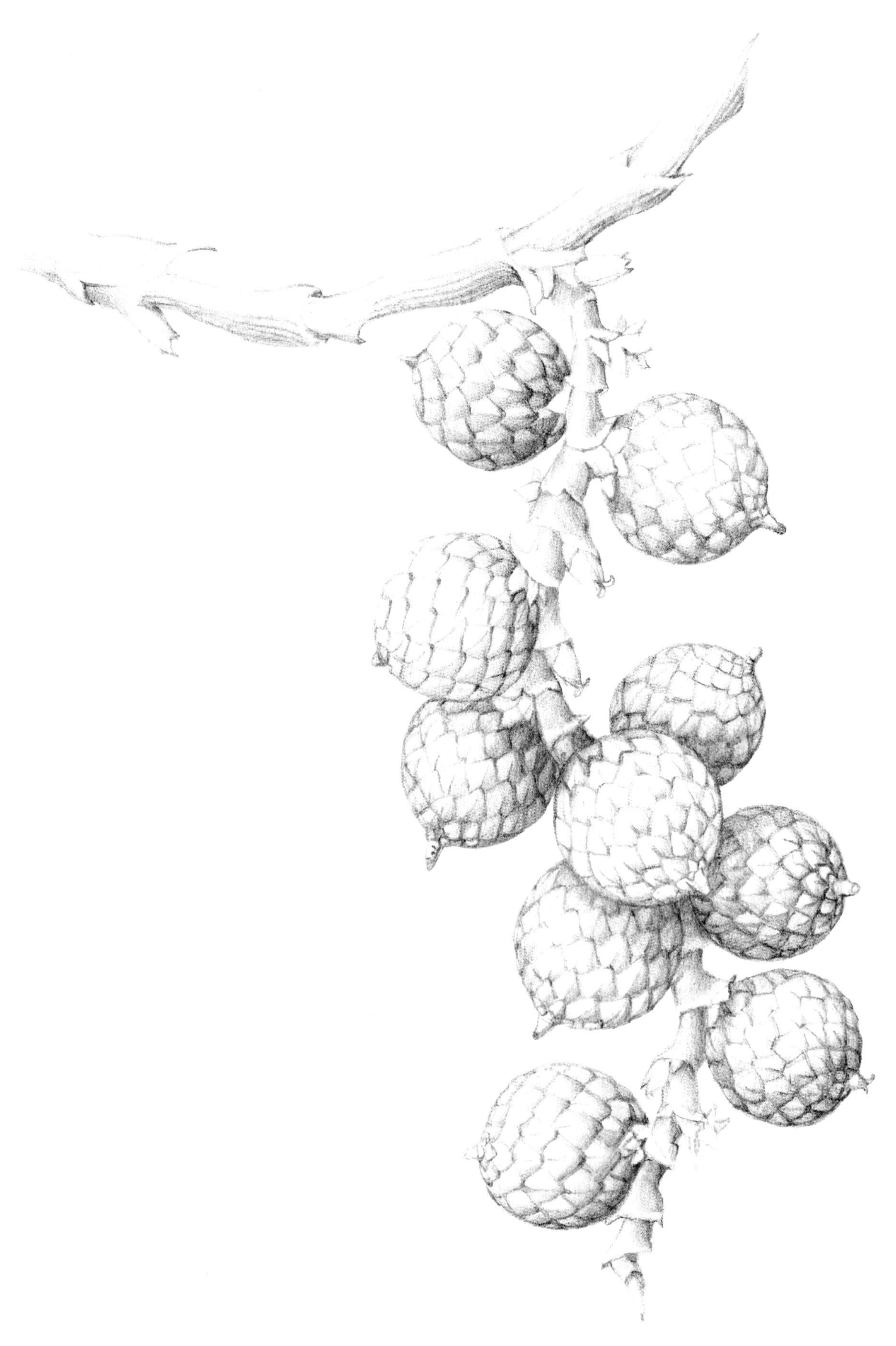

INTRODUCTION

Structured or organic, neat or messy, each study in my botanical sketchbooks has a unique story and a purpose behind it.

A botanical sketchbook can take many forms and hold different meanings for different people. It is a place where a botanical artist or illustrator studies plants through drawing and painting, capturing them using a variety of media. Whether they are preliminary works for final pieces, experiments in colour, or explorations of plant anatomy, the studies in a sketchbook can be made away from the pressures of achieving the perfection and polish of the finished artwork. But the sketchbook is not only for preliminary and exploratory work; it can also exist for its own sake, as a curated space in which an artist draws and records plants over a period of time, or in a particular place.

My sketchbook practice has evolved over the decades of my career as a professional botanical artist and illustrator. Some of my earliest working drawings were not bound by a book at all, but drawn on loose sheets of paper that were covered in notes and tiny pressed specimens, hastily curated into loose-leaf folders. I eventually became more organised, seeing the benefits of keeping my work in the more ordered space of a bound pad or book. Since then, I have never looked back and I now have a stack of sketchbooks in all shapes and sizes.

My sketchbooks hold drawings in pencil; some are loose and sketchy, others tight and highly detailed. Some show plants drawn quickly in the field or objects at my desk. In contrast, others are covered with the painstakingly detailed results of highly ordered flower dissections executed for scientific illustrations. Whilst pencil work predominates, watercolour also features – and often the two appear together. Pen and ink also make an appearance. It is very satisfying to look at all my sketchbooks produced over the years and see the progression of my skills, the beginnings of ideas for large projects, and the experiments that led to successful finished pieces.

All the examples and projects described here are illustrated either with work taken from sketchbook studies made over the past 30 years of my career as a botanical artist, or with work made specifically for this book. The process of reviewing my archive has proven that even an old hand like me can still be open to new ideas. In creating fresh artwork for the book, I took the time to try out some techniques and approaches that were less familiar to me. I found it all hugely inspiring and hope to incorporate some of them into my art practice in the future. My hope is that this book will do the same for you!

Sketching takes our appreciation of plants to a new level through the observation and depiction of their complex and beautiful forms. There are so many layers to explore and draw: form, structure, pattern and detail.

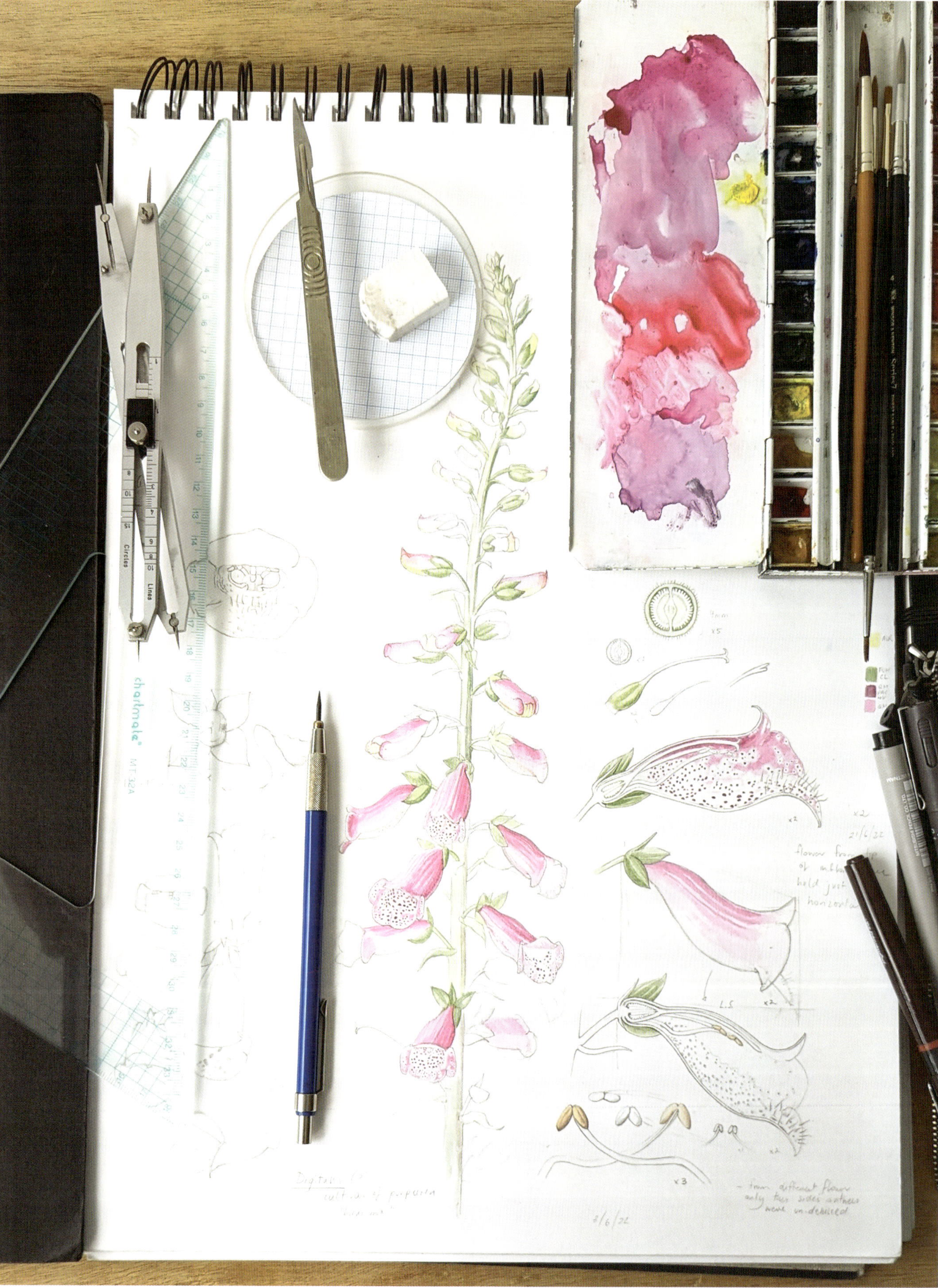

CHAPTER 1

MATERIALS

Capturing plants in a botanical sketchbook is as much about the process as it is about the end product. Drawing and painting plants brings a joy that comes not only from the artist's connection with their subjects, but also from the practical, physical and tactile aspects of the materials used to create the work. I have yet to meet an artist of any kind who does not derive great pleasure from their use of art materials. During my career as a botanical artist, I have discovered what works best for me, but I also like to try new things from time to time.

My sketchbooks fall in a number of loose categories. Some are for very specific types of work, while others contain a variety of different approaches. The type of sketchbook I use for scientific drawing may not be suitable for a study that uses watercolour, for example. Some sketchbooks are so beautifully made that I am inspired to fill them with studies that become works of art in their own right, creating a kind of curated piece.

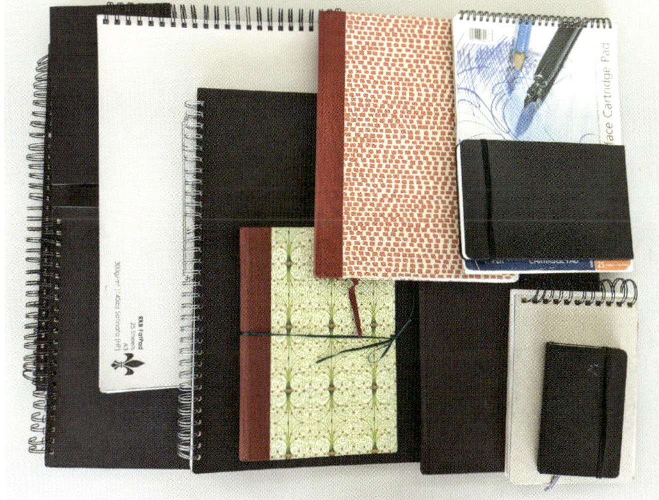

The sketchbooks I have used, both in the past and currently, range in size from A5 to A3. They are bound in different ways and contain many different paper types.

TYPES OF SKETCHBOOK WORK

Before detailing the types of books and materials I like to use, it is useful to categorise the type of work I do in my various sketchbooks. Each type has specific needs, although they do overlap sometimes.

Preparatory Work Sketchbook

This type of sketchbook contains the working drawings for my work as a scientific botanical illustrator and artist. The pages will also be used for notes, ideas and preliminary sketches for figuring out the composition of the final work.

The spiral binding of my scientific illustration sketchbook allows it to be laid flat on a desk or easel – perfect for resting my hand on the page to work on detail. The heavier paper can withstand the repeated erasure needed to get scientific drawings just right. I use this sketchbook in both horizontal and vertical formats.

The right tools for the job: enjoying the look, feel and quality of the materials we use to capture our botanical subjects is at least as important as appreciating the plants themselves.

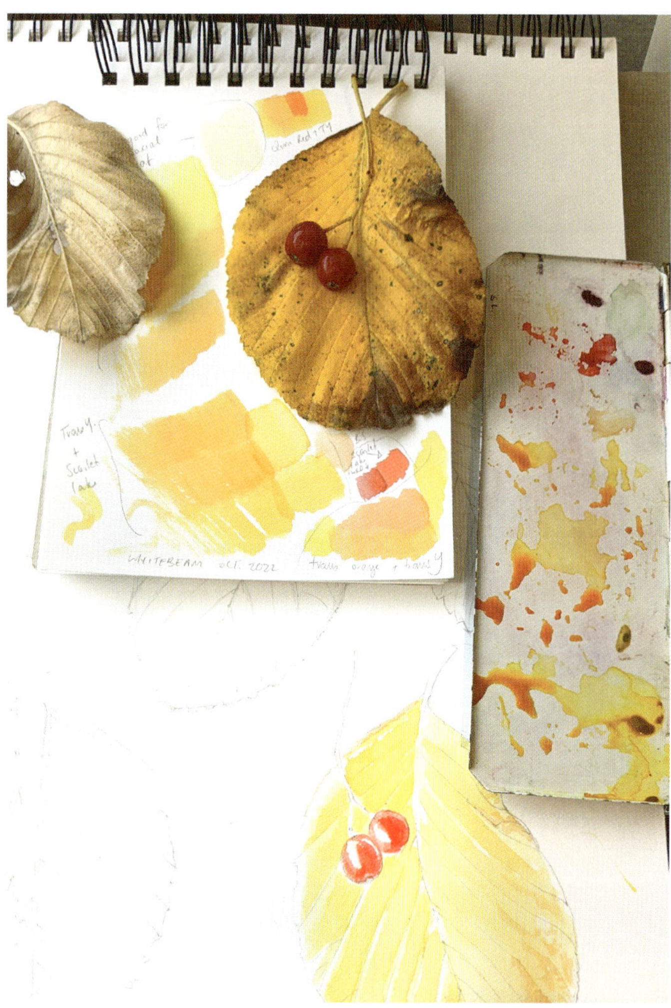

In this type of sketchbook, there will be many drawings of parts of plants, including dissections. As the work is mostly done in pencil, the book usually contains cartridge paper. I also use this sketchbook when making preparatory drawings for watercolour paintings, especially those of plants with complex forms. Sometimes I add colour to these studies, although the amount of paint that can be applied is limited by the paper type. Ideally, this sketchbook will be made up of a heavy paper (at least 160gsm) with a smooth surface, although it should not be too smooth, as some grain texture is needed for the pencil to grip on to.

When I know that I will need to add a little more watercolour, I will use a sketchbook containing heavyweight, smooth-surfaced watercolour paper. Conveniently, the paper that I use for my final watercolours, Fabriano 5, is available in spiral-bound pads of different sizes. This allows me to test techniques and colour in the sketchbooks, so that I can see exactly how the watercolour paint will work on the paper when I come to create the final version.

I use a larger size of pad or sketchbook for graphite drawings and watercolour studies, and a smaller size for making quick colour notes and colour sketches. The latter is especially useful for studying subjects in situ, as it is the most portable. This paper is suitable for working on in all media but is also quite expensive, so I would not use it for everyday scientific studies.

Spiral-bound R. K. Burt Fabriano 5 watercolour sketchbooks in A5 and A3 sizes. The 300gsm watercolour paper is designed to take wet media without buckling, so I can experiment with techniques such as wet-in-wet watercolour with these autumn leaves.

This small Moleskine sketchbook containing watercolour papers became my sketching and note-taking book for some aspects of the giant *Victoria* water lily illustration project. As a seed of *Victoria amazonica* germinated and grew in a fish tank, I recorded the changes each day across two pages.

Explorative Sketchbook

Sometimes, I make sketchbook studies simply for the pleasure of delighting in the drawing process. This type of sketchbook is a place for the activities of observation, drawing and painting for their own sake, and the studies in them may or may not be used as preparatory work for a final piece. There is a wide variety of approaches, from an investigation of form, which may include some dissection, to the documentation of a time and place through plants. Whilst the intention in these books is not to prepare for finished pieces of work, these studies often do result in ideas for projects. As this reflects an open-ended approach, they are my most creative sketchbooks. The paper in these books must be versatile enough to take a variety of media and styles.

SKETCHBOOKS AND PAPER

Size

Ready-made sketchbooks come in a wide variety of sizes, from small A6 through to larger A3 and above. There are several factors to take into consideration when choosing which size to buy. Do you want a portable sketchbook that fits in a pocket or bag, or will you be working in your sketchbook at a desk or easel? Are you drawing large or small objects? It is a simple matter to choose the most practical format for your needs; in reality, you will probably end up with a range of sketchbooks in different sizes.

My collection of sketchbooks comes in a variety of sizes, most of which are the standard 'A' formats used in the UK, but my preferred size is A3. I find I am most comfortable drawing on a surface where my hand can rest without falling off the edge. An A3 book is still portable, but not as portable as the A5-sized version that I use when making quick colour studies of plants in the field.

The smallest sketchbook in my possession is an A6 one (9 × 14cm), which I bought to try to develop a pocket-sketchbook habit; however, its small size did not work for me. The smallest sketchbook I do get on with is A5 (14 × 21cm) in size and is suitable for small sketches and colour studies. The next size up is A4 (19.5 × 29cm). This is the most popular size of sketchbook available and is the standard size of paper used in correspondence and stationery. Many of my older sketchbooks are A4-sized, but in more recent years I have settled on A3 (29.5 × 42cm) as my favourite. The A3 sketchbook allows for larger parts of plants to be drawn, and I enjoy the sensation of drawing without feeling cramped or crowded by the edge of the

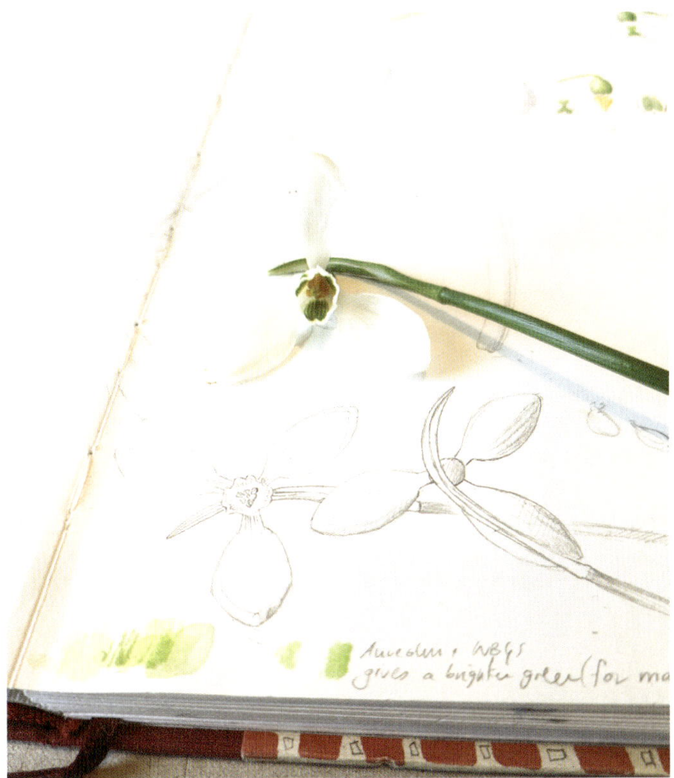

Exploring the flowers of *Galanthus elwesii* from a bee's viewpoint. As a professional botanical illustrator, many of my sketchbook studies are for specific projects and there is a pressure to draw to rigid guidelines and time frames. In my exploratory sketchbooks, I enjoy taking the time to draw and paint without an agenda. Drawing a snowdrop flower from this angle may be scientifically unconventional but I like the resulting shapes, patterns, and information it provides.

paper. My larger watercolour paper sketchbook is also A3 in size, providing me with plenty of room on the page to draw larger subjects and add many separate details to a single page.

Binding and Opening

Sketchbooks are primarily bound in three ways: stapled, spiral-bound or sewn. Each type has advantages and disadvantages that influence the way they can be used.

Stapled books are made up of larger pieces of paper stacked and folded and then stapled in the centre. There is a limit to the number of pages that can be bound in this way, so stapled books tend to be thinner than other types. Because they have fewer pages, they are lighter and more portable and useful for travelling, but they are usually covered in less rigid cardboard so need more resting support.

Spiral-bound sketchbooks have pages perforated by holes along one edge of the paper and held together by a metal or plastic binding structure. This type of binding allows for a larger number of sheets to be bound together than stapling. A variety of paper sizes and weights can be

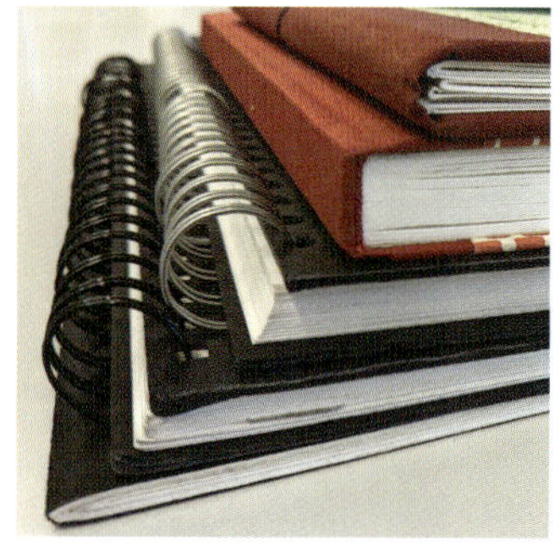

Various types of sketchbook binding: (bottom to top) stapled, spiral (plastic and metal), sewn, concertina.

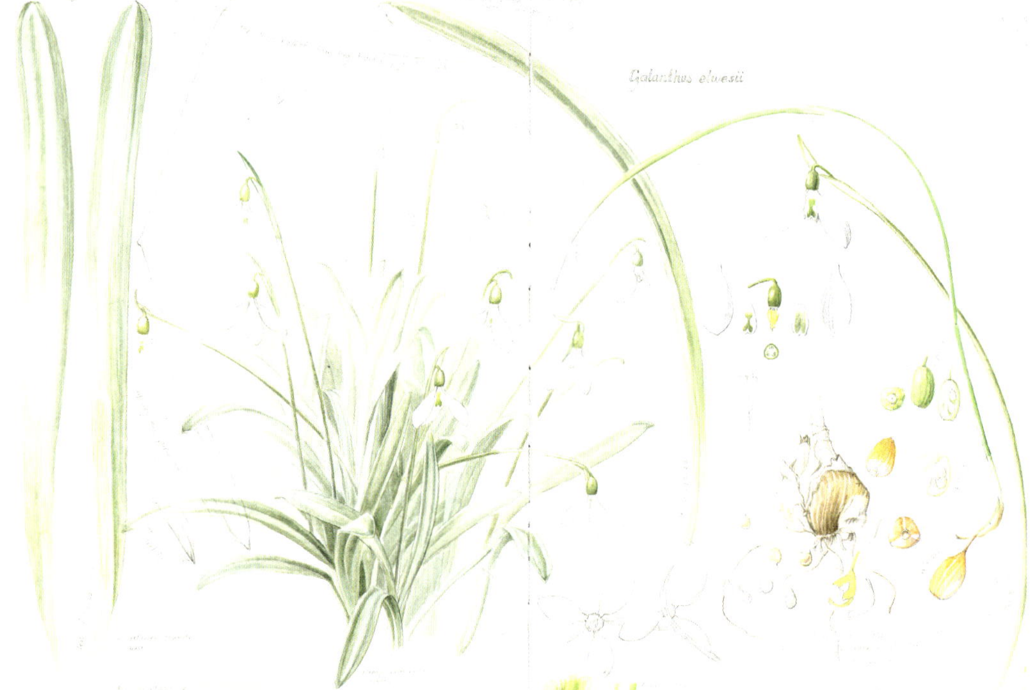

Because the Fabriano 'Venezia' sketchbook is sewn-bound, the user is able to work across a double-page spread. This study of the snowdrop *Galanthus elwesii* was developed over two growing seasons. As there was no plan, the composition spread organically across the two pages, starting on the right-hand side with the plant's fruit and seeds. The 200gsm paper is tough enough to take repeated erasure and accept some wet media. When working across two pages, I always choose a folded single page so that there is no gap between the two halves, only the binding thread.

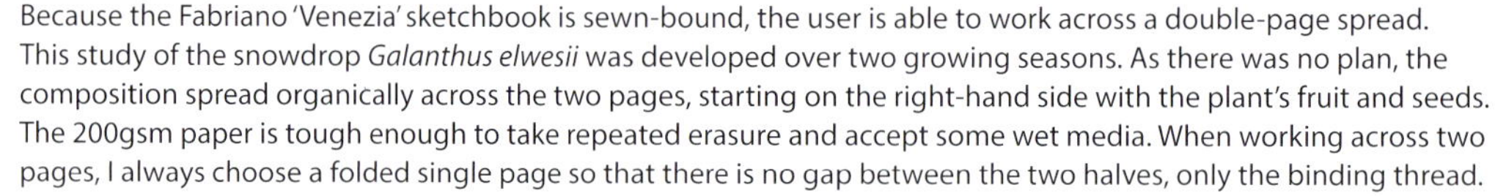

Spiral-bound A3 watercolour-paper sketchbook used in a horizontal (landscape) format to sketch hyacinth bulbs.

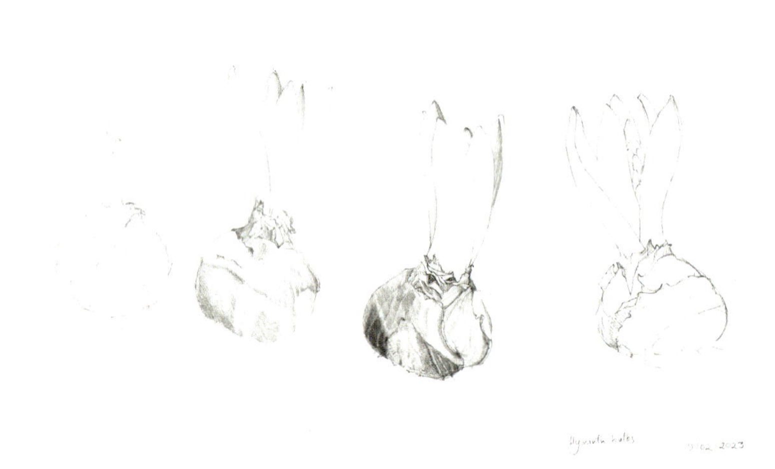

accommodated, and the paper is not folded. One significant advantage of a spiral-bound sketchbook is that it lies perfectly flat when opened out. A disadvantage is that the spiral binding can get in the way of the hand of the artist, especially a left-handed person. If the spiral binding is bothering you in this way, you can turn the book around and either use the paper in a horizontal position, or work in a vertical position but with the binding on the side opposite to your hand. Another disadvantage with a spiral-bound sketchbook is the tendency of the metal binding to disfigure and unravel itself after repeated openings.

Sewn binding, or thread-sewn binding, creates a book with a spine and represents the most secure way of holding paper in place. As the name suggests, thread is sewn through the fold of a folded sheet or sheets of paper. Bindings can take many forms. For example, multiple sheets of paper may be folded into bundles and sewn, or a single folded sheet may be bound individually before the lot are sewn together. One advantage of a sewn-bound sketchbook is that, unlike a spiral-bound book, it allows the artist to work across the fold between two pages. Only the stitching is in the way, and this can be worked over or even used as a feature of the artwork.

It is also important to consider how you would like your sketchbook to open. This is determined by the position of the binding, which will be either on the long or short edge of the paper. You can turn your sketchbook around to suit your need for a horizontal or vertical format.

Finally, a concertina sketchbook consists of a single folded piece of paper, or several pieces glued together to create a single, long piece of paper, folded into equal-sized pages, which create a continuous surface on which to draw. Each 'page' is interrupted only by the fold or valley on which you are working. You can potentially work on a continuous long piece that is revealed by extending the entire paper out of its end boards. One advantage of this type of sketchbook is that, as it has no binding, it is relatively easy to make yourself.

Paper Type

Sketchbooks are produced with many different types of paper. The choice can be slightly overwhelming, so the first step is to ask yourself what you want from the paper. Are you using predominantly dry media such as graphite pencil and pen and ink, or would you like to use wet media such as watercolour? Do you need a paper that will give you sharp lines for smaller details? The answers to these questions will help you start to choose. Sketchbooks suitable for botanical work contain both cartridge paper and watercolour paper.

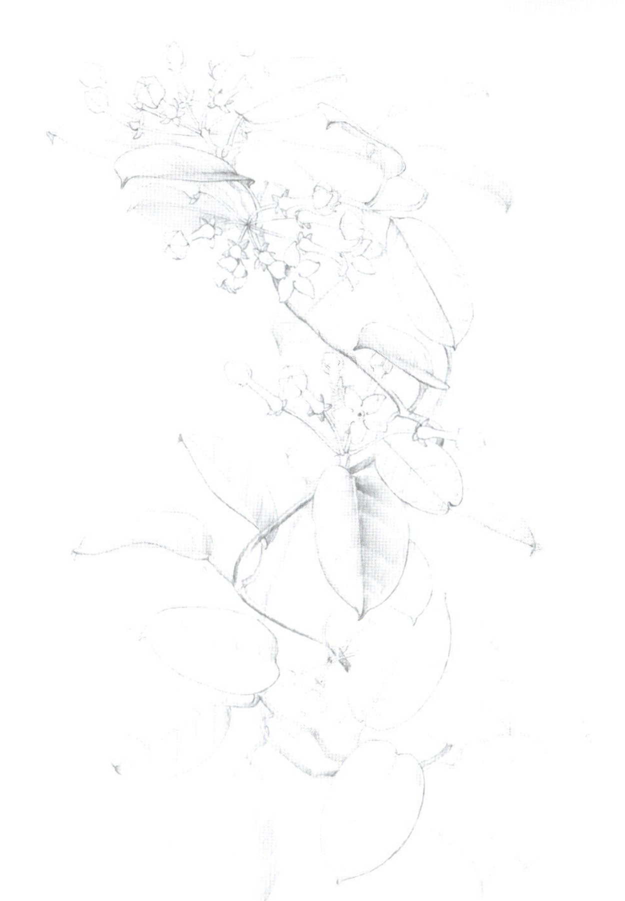

The spiral-bound A3 sketchbook used in a vertical (portrait) format. Any rectangular-shaped sketchbook can be used either horizontally or vertically, depending on the shape of the subject and how you prefer to work.

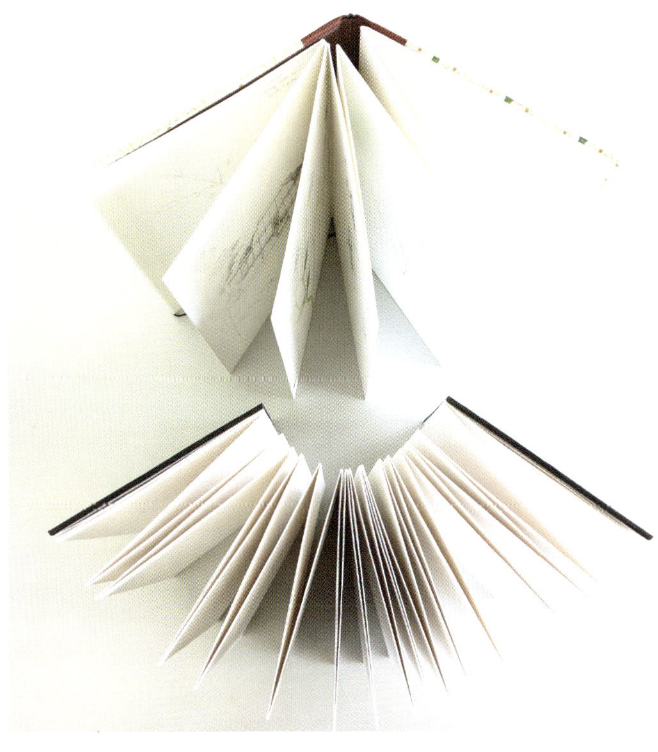

Concertina-style sketchbooks are popular, and fun to use. They are also the easiest type of sketchbook to make yourself, as they do not require stapling or sewn binding. This sketchbook (top) was handmade under the instruction of printmaker Frances Kiernan, while the one below was commercially manufactured. It is currently waiting to be drawn on.

Paper Weight

The first and most important aspect of the paper is its weight. Paper weight (which could also be described as 'thickness') is measured in 'gsm', or grams per square metre. The higher this number, the heavier the paper. A heavier paper will be stronger and take more erasure. If the cartridge paper is over around 150gsm, it may take a few layers of watercolour without buckling, but anything below that weight may suffer from the application of wet media. In that case, you may prefer a sketchbook that contains watercolour paper that is specifically designed to accept wet media. I use a combination of cartridge and watercolour paper sketchbooks, and prefer the paper weight to be at least 160gsm.

Paper Texture

The next important factor is the texture or surface of the paper. Do you want a very smooth surface, or do you prefer a bit of texture or 'tooth'? Working with graphite pencil on paper that is too smooth can result in a shiny line that smudges on the page. However, that surface may be perfect for your ink pens. A smoother texture is more suitable for work with very fine detail. The appearance of a rougher paper texture adds an element of interest to a piece of work. Each surface reacts differently to the same media: for example, pen applied to textured paper will give a line that is more feathered than the sharp line that will be achieved when the pen is applied to smooth paper.

I like to feel a paper's weight and texture with my own hands before purchasing a sketchbook. It is perfectly reasonable to approach a manufacturer or art supply shop (in person or online) to ask for paper samples. Aside from the practical considerations, there is an instinctual need to *enjoy* the paper with which you are working, and touch plays a huge part in this process. Once you have found a surface that you enjoy using, you may be inclined to stick with it. Be aware, though, that manufacturers sometimes change the type of paper used in a particular brand. In this case, you may need to seek out a replacement or an alternative.

Paper Colour

In terms of paper colour, you need to be aware that there are different types of white, ranging from warm and creamy to cool. A cooler white suits more technical botanical drawing, such as that for scientific botanical illustration, where visibility and clarity of detail are very important. A creamier white may be more appealing if you want your artwork to have a warmer feel to it.

Sketchbooks also come in a variety of tinted and coloured papers, including cream, tan, grey and solid black. A toned paper can lend a certain warmth to drawings. The background colour also provides a mid-tone to drawings, and highlights can be added using opaque pencil, pen or paint. On black paper, it may be necessary to use dry or wet media with a higher degree of opacity than for white paper. I would find it difficult to use a transparent medium such as watercolour on a toned paper without first laying down an opaque white layer, but I do find toned papers lovely for use with ink pens.

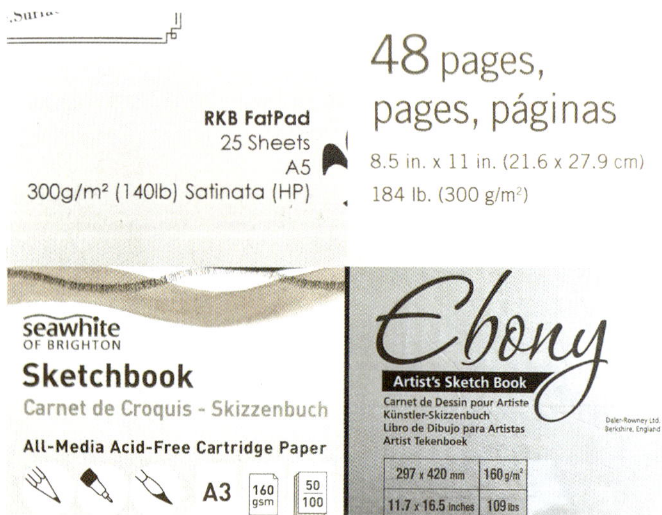

Manufacturers' labels showing paper weight in both metric and imperial. The weight indicates the thickness of the paper. Most of my sketchbooks are at least 160gsm.

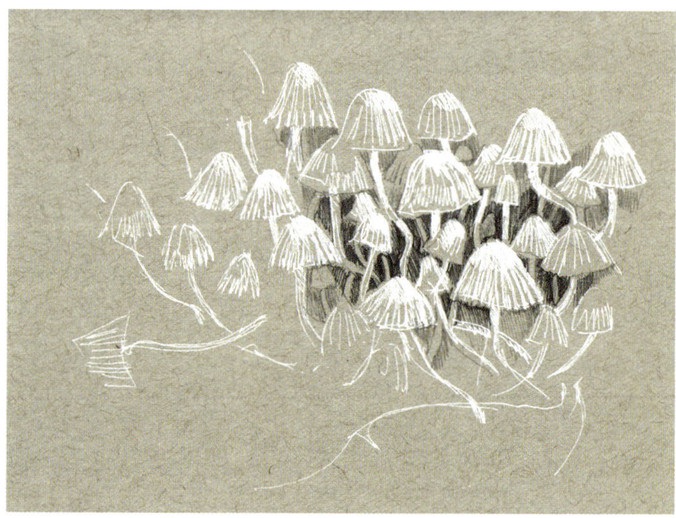

An A5 Strathmore sketchbook with warm grey paper was the perfect portable surface for capturing these tiny fungi, using white and grey pens.

OTHER TYPES OF PAPER

Tracing paper is useful in many ways. If a drawing in the sketchbook is becoming so overworked that you can no longer make sense of it, you can try placing a piece of tracing paper over the top of the drawing and drawing on it to help you rediscover the simple forms in the sketch. Tracing paper can also be used to transfer a drawing from one page to another. It can be folded to make small pockets for holding pressed plant material, or to protect the facing pages of a page where a pressed specimen has been mounted.

Graph paper can be used to observe small plant parts. By placing the parts on top of graph paper with 1mm squares, it is easy to read off measurements. You can also draw up a larger-scale grid to draw those parts at an enlarged size. Photographing small parts laid out on graph paper will provide accurate reference material.

Many artists like to make their own sketchbooks. The benefit of making your own is that you have control over the size of the book, what type of paper it contains, and what cover and binding you use. You can for example use the same type of watercolour paper for your sketchbook that you would normally use for finished pieces. You could also make a concertina-type sketchbook, which will allow you to stretch out multiple drawings over a continuous sheet of paper.

If you are documenting a singular project, such as plants from a particular place or time, a custom-made sketchbook will allow you to determine the exact size and shape required to fill the book for that unique project. Making your own sketchbook has never been easier, as there are plenty of how-to videos and instructions online.

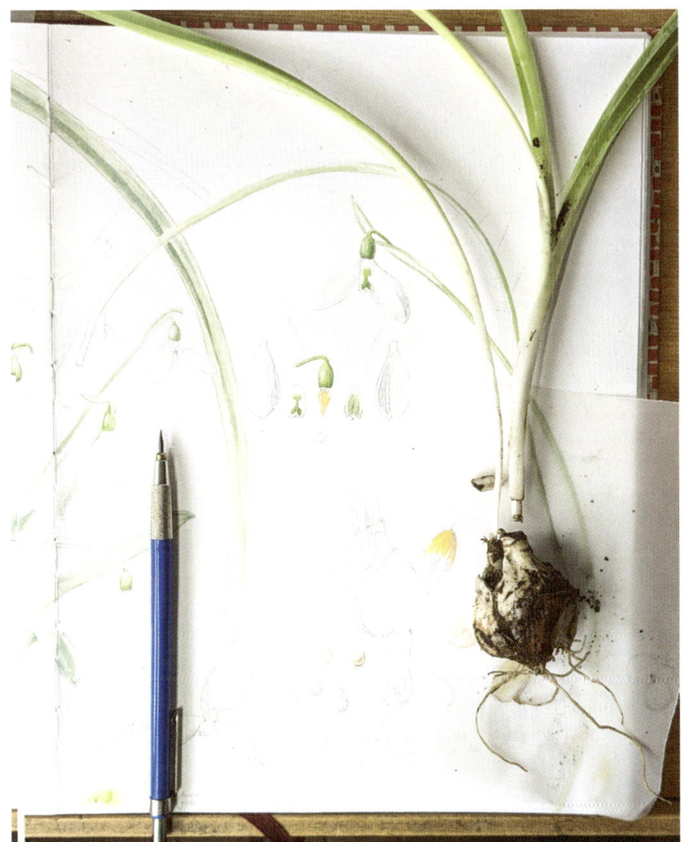

Tracing paper being used to protect the sketchbook paper surface from the damp, muddy snowdrop bulb while still seeing the drawing beneath it.

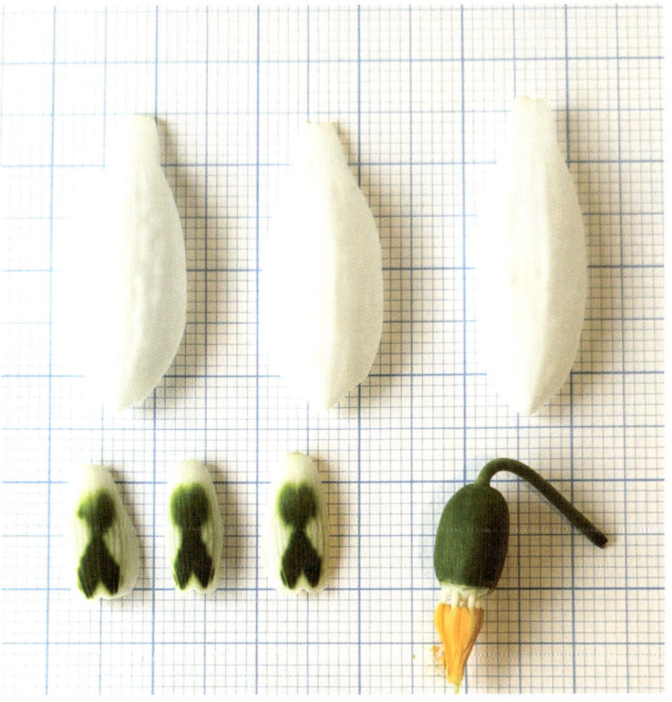

The outer and inner perianth segments, the ovary and stamens of the snowdrop *Galanthus elwesii* dissected and laid out on graph paper with 1mm squares – excellent reference for recording their height, width and shape.

DRAWING MATERIALS

Pencils

A graphite pencil is the most important drawing tool for a botanical sketchbook. Pencil work underlies many other techniques, such as watercolour and pen and ink. As they can be repeatedly erased and replaced, pencil lines are invaluable when developing a study from a rough sketch all the way through to a detailed drawing. A pencil is extremely versatile, as it can be used in different ways to create a wide variety of marks. With a highly sharpened point, it will capture the finest lines and detail. Laid on its side and applied gently in small ellipses, it will add smooth shading and tonal values. If drawing quickly and sketchily, the looser marks of a pencil can add character and life.

There are three types of pencil that are useful for botanical drawing: wooden pencils, lead holders (also known as clutch pencils) and clutch pencils with very small leads. I do not use the latter, as they cannot be sharpened in the same way as wooden pencils and 2mm lead holders.

Sharpening Pencils

Wooden pencils are best sharpened using a blade or scalpel, to achieve a long, sharp point that will be versatile for both line and shading work. Traditional wooden pencil sharpeners do not provide such a long point, although there are some specialised sharpeners that manage to mimic the blade-sharpened point quite well. A blade can also be used to sharpen a lead holder, but a 'lead pointer' sharpener is also very useful for keeping a point on these pencils.

My preferred pencil is a lead holder pencil with a 2mm lead. There are two main benefits to using this type of pencil. First, they are easy to sharpen – there is no need to carve away wood as on a wooden pencil. They can be sharpened with a blade, as above, or sharpened using a lead pointer designed specifically for them. Second, the sharpened lead can be retraced into the holder when not in use. This makes lead holder pencils very portable, as there is less chance of the lead breaking when carrying materials around.

Pencil Hardness

The two lead grades I use most are 2H and HB, but in addition I often use softer leads such as B and 2B. The darkness of a pencil line will vary according to the type of paper being used, so this is not a definitive rule or guide. Many people find that using a hard lead such as 2H causes them to draw more 'tightly' and dig into the paper. When this type of lead is being used for initial drawings, care must be taken to use it with a light hand to avoid hard lines and unerasable indentations. It is, however, invaluable for capturing very fine detail, as it provides a super sharp line.

Another benefit of the 2H pencil is that when used in under-drawing for wet media, it is less prone to bleeding into paint or pen and ink placed over it, so watercolour paint applied over the top will not be excessively tainted by the graphite grains.

Erasers

Erasers are an important editing tool. They are used not only to 'correct mistakes', but to erase lines and marks as a pencil drawing progresses from rough to finished stage. I use a white plastic eraser, as I like the cleanness of it. This type of eraser must be of high quality; a poorer-quality item can tear and damage the surface of the paper. Clean your eraser regularly by rubbing its surfaces on to a clean sheet of paper. This removes the previous deposits of rubbed graphite and minimises the risk of transferring smears of old graphite on to the drawing. Most erasers come in a protective cardboard covering to keep them clean. It is a good idea to keep this covering on the eraser, only exposing the part that is currently being used.

There are many other types of eraser available, including white plastic erasers that come in a pen-like form. Many botanical artists like to use an eraser of kneadable putty. Its soft, pliable texture allows you to make gentle erasures by rolling it over the surface of the paper. If using a putty eraser, be sure to keep it clean as it is not possible to remove excess graphite from its surface.

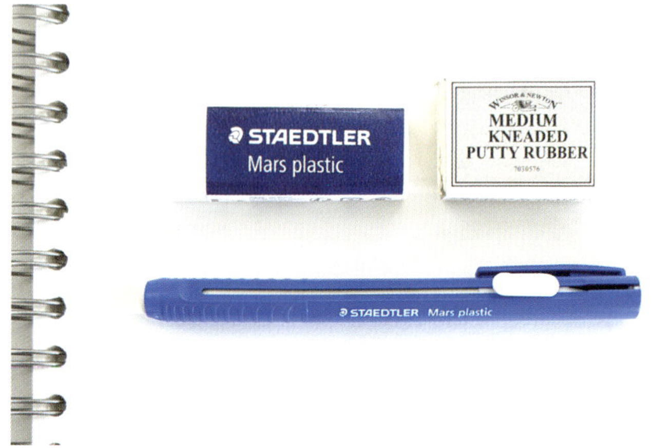

Types of eraser: white plastic block eraser and kneadable putty eraser (above), pen-style white eraser (below). Whichever type you prefer, the quality and texture are important. It must lift graphite without damaging the fibres of the paper, allowing successive layers of graphite or wet media to be added.

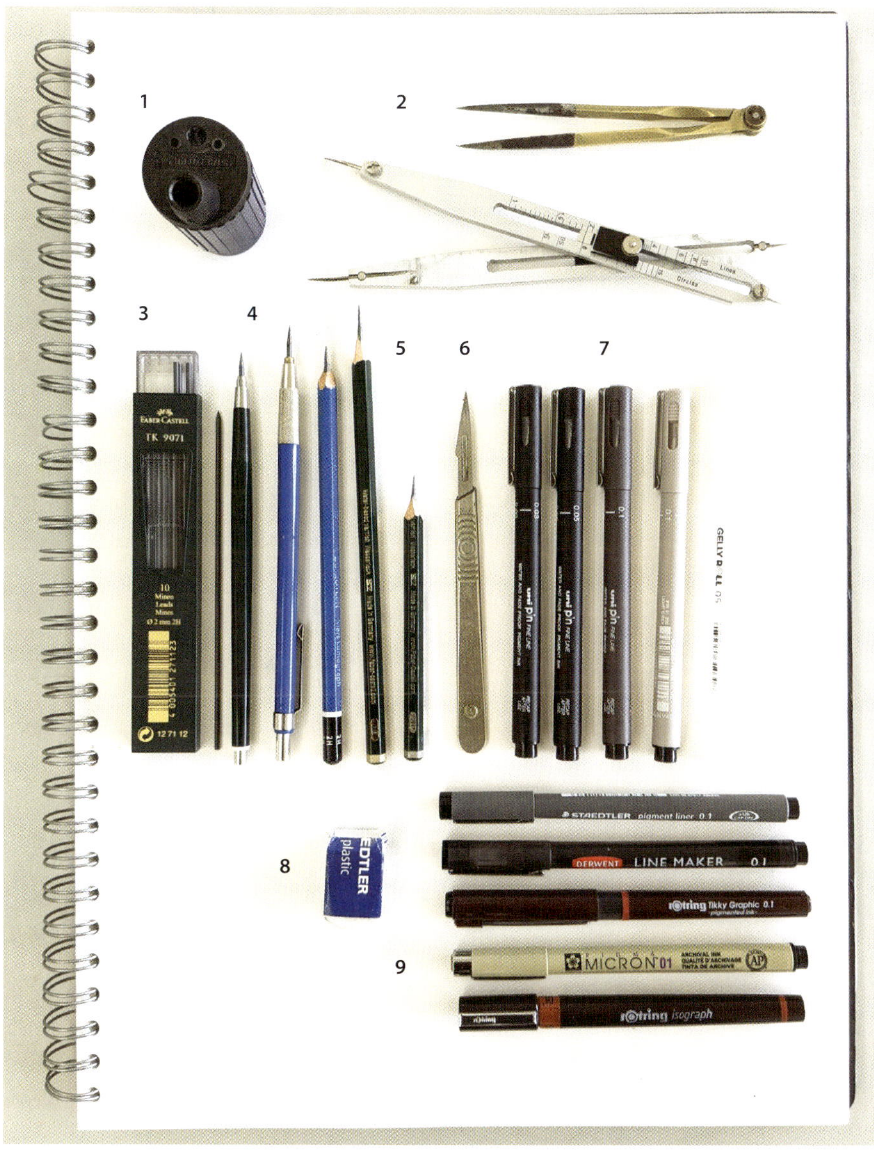

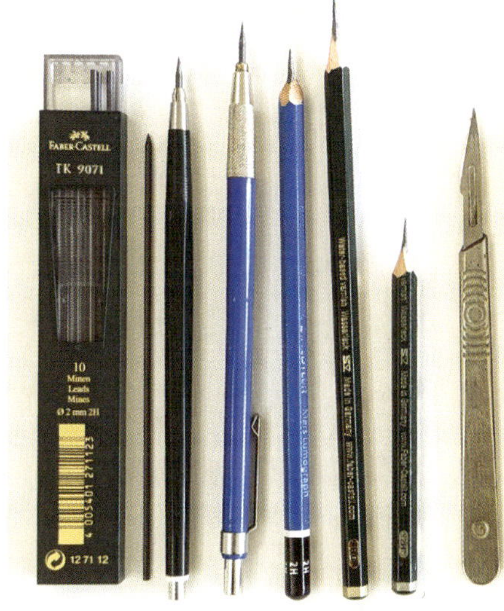

My green Staedtler lead holder carries an HB lead, and my blue Mars Technico a 2H lead. This was accidental but very convenient, as I can easily tell them apart when swapping between the two. The fine point of a wooden pencil can easily be broken in transit. Retracting a lead into a lead holder provides protection for a sharp tip.

Drawing equipment laid out on an A3 sketchbook pad: 1. A lead pointer sharpener. 2. Dividers and proportional dividers. 3. Spare 2mm leads. 4. 2mm lead holder clutch pencils. 5. Sharpened wooden pencils. 6. Scalpel blade for sharpening wooden pencils. 7. Fineliner ink pens in grey, black and white. 8. White plastic eraser. 9. Ink pens from various brands.

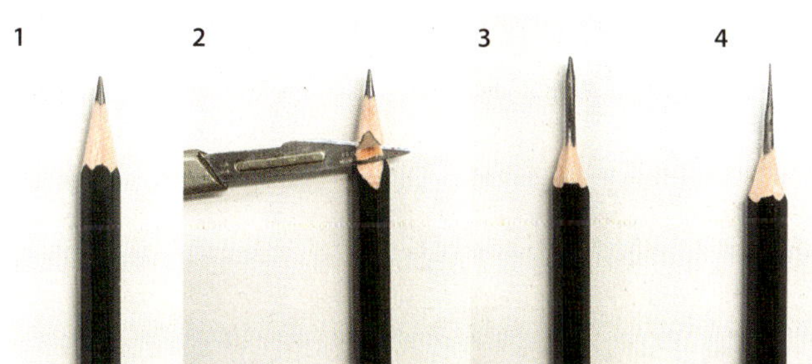

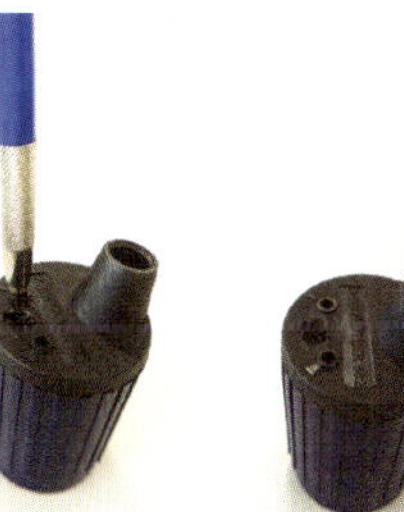

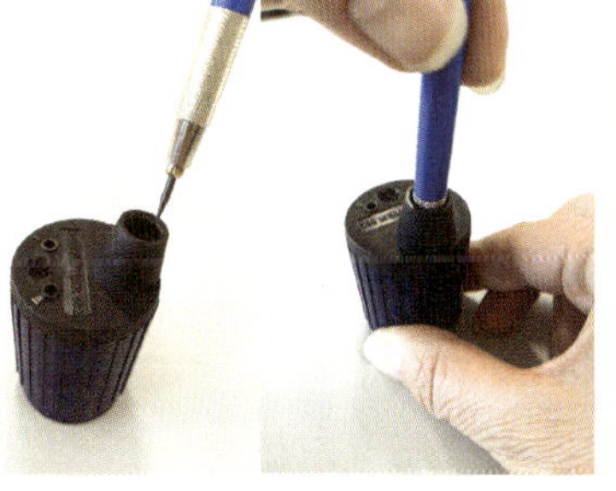

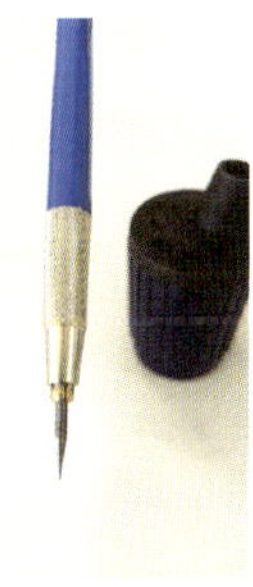

Sharpening a wooden pencil with a blade. 1: Traditional sharpener. 2: Carving away wood with a blade to expose a long lead tip (3). 4: The finessed point. On the final stage, be sure to sweep the blade gently past the tip, otherwise a lump of lead will accumulate there.

Sharpening a 2mm lead holder using a lead pointer tub: measure the tip to the required length using one of the guide holes marked with a triangle; insert it into the sharpening hole; keeping a steady, even pressure, move the pencil in a circular motion around the tub, so that the lead rubs against the metal cylinder inside. After sharpening, remove the pencil from the tub and wipe off excess graphite.

Ink Pens

A wide variety of ink pens and inks can be used in the botanical sketchbook. Ink can be used on its own to sketch free hand or placed over a pencil under-drawing. It can also be combined with watercolour. Whether you use dip pens (nib pens), technical drawing pens such as those in the Rotring 'isograph' range, or fineliners, the best and most versatile inks are those that are waterproof and light-fast. Waterproof ink will allow wet media to be applied on top of it without it dissolving. I use a selection of Rotring pens in sizes 0.10, 0.25 and 0.35, plus black fineliner pens from various brands, in sizes ranging from the smallest (0.03) to 0.2. In addition to the black ink pens, I also have some that carry grey ink, and a white Sakura 'Gelly Roll' pen for adding highlights to ink drawings on toned paper.

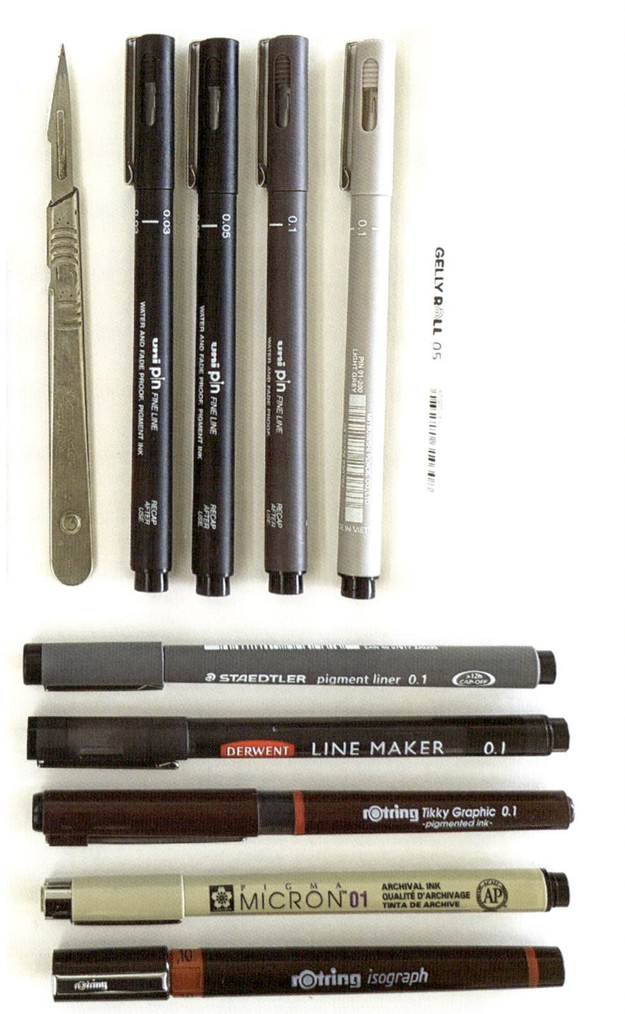

Fineliner pens are available in both black and grey, and I have a variety of them, including Uni Pin, Staedtler, Derwent, Sakura and Rotring 'Tikky graphic'. My Rotring pens are reserved mainly for scientific illustrations. The white Sakura 'Gelly Roll' pen is used to add highlights to ink work on toned paper.

DRAWING EQUIPMENT

Dividers and Proportional Dividers

Dividers allow you to take measurements directly from a plant specimen. This is very helpful in achieving accuracy in measured drawing. The length, width or angle of a part of the plant may be 'measured' by expanding the divider's points to match the observation and then transferring the dimensions to the paper via the dividers, so that the line may be drawn.

Proportional dividers go a step further, enabling a measurement to be enlarged or reduced immediately on transferral to the page, by use of a sliding scale. They have a sliding mechanism, which, when adjusted to the required number, allows the user to take a measurement and then either reduce it or enlarge it when transferring the measured line. For example, if the proportional dividers are set to '3', a dimension that is measured with the smaller opening of the points becomes tripled when it is transferred to the paper. The opposite result is obtained by measuring with the wider of the point openings. When transferred using the small opening, the measurement will be one-third.

Desk Easel or Drawing Board

When working in the field, you may simply hold the sketchbook on your lap, but on those days when you are based in the studio, it is advisable to work on a raised surface. This will be better both for the observation angles and for your posture. I work on a lightweight

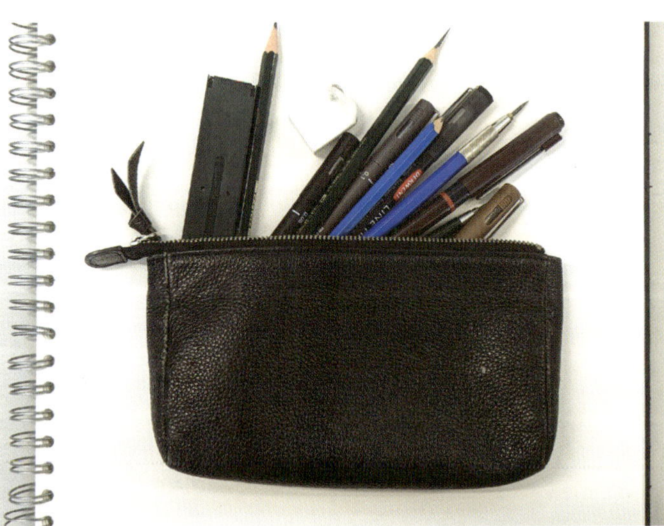

I carry my drawing pencils, pens and eraser in an old-school zipped pencil case. I carry only what I need at the time; everything else can stay in a drawer. This bag was actually designed as a make-up bag, but was of more use to me for carrying drawing equipment.

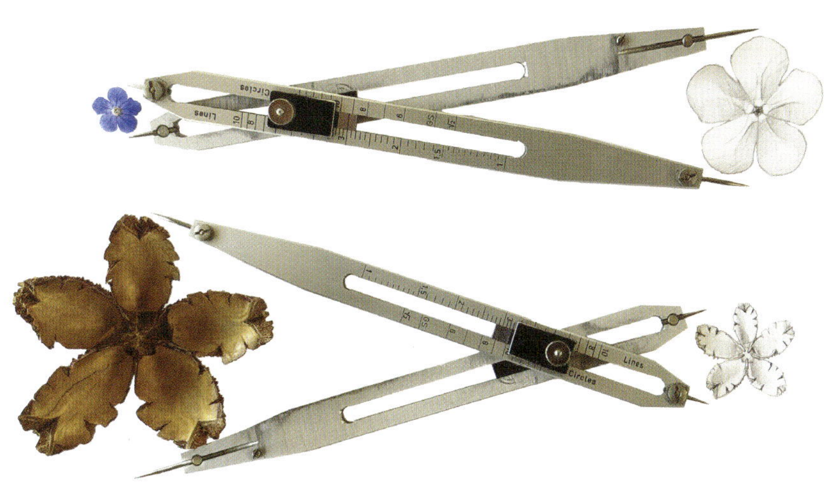

Enlarging and reducing with Ecobra proportional dividers: setting the dividers to '3' allows the flower (top) to be measured and enlarged to three times its size ('×3'). With the dividers still set to '3' but flipped the other way, the seed pod (below) has been measured and reduced to one third of its size.

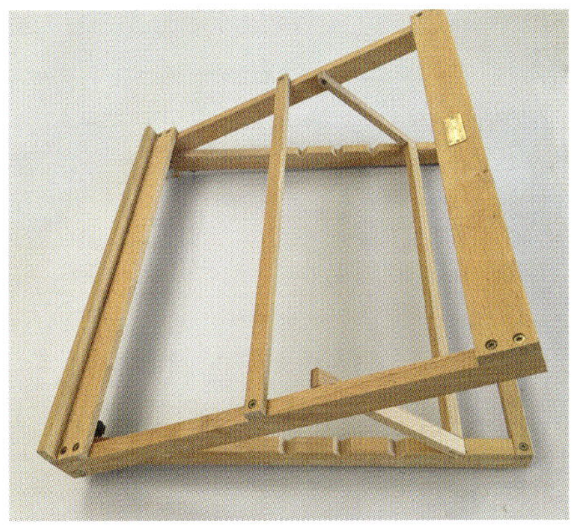

A lightweight wooden frame desk easel, which can be adjusted to four heights. Drawing boards of various sizes can sit on it, or a larger sketchbook can be laid directly on it. Drawing at an angle is beneficial for the posture, and it is also better for capturing live specimens, as the drawing surface is held at a similar height to the subject.

wooden-framed table easel, which can be raised and set at a few different angles. The frame easel will support a variety of drawing board sizes, or the sketchbook itself can sit directly on the easel. When working outdoors you may wish to take a wooden or cardboard drawing board to support the sketchbook and/or prop it against something to keep it raised.

PAINTING MATERIALS

Watercolour

Watercolour paint is the mostly commonly used colour medium in botanical art and illustration. There are other colour media, including coloured pencils, gouache, acrylic paint and oils, but watercolour paint is particularly well suited to use in a botanical sketchbook. This is because it tends to mimic the qualities of flowers with its translucency. The same translucency allows watercolour to be built up using layering, which permits controlled application and development of colours and tonal values. Not only can colour be applied quickly over large areas, but also, by reducing the dilution of the paint and using only the tip of the brush, very fine detail can be added. Just as observation of plant structure and form is ideally made from life, so too is the observation and replication of plant colour. Another benefit of using watercolour paint is that it is very portable, especially when used in pan form, and requires only a few brushes and the addition of water.

Over time, a botanical artist will build up their own unique preferred palette of colour choices and a repertoire of colour mixes, both remembered and documented. However, beginners may be overwhelmed at first by the range of pigments available. It is therefore helpful to have some understanding of where to start when buying watercolours. Generally, I work with a palette of primary colours and try to mix most of my final shades and tones from these. At times, however, this supposedly restricted palette expands, alongside some pigments that just need to come straight from the pan or tube, with minimal mixing!

I use a reasonably restricted palette of Winsor & Newton watercolour pigments in the 'Professional' range, and prefer to mix a colour than to try to match it with an exact pigment. This approach also avoids my having to carry too many different pigments. The pigments I use are those that are most light-fast and permanent. The 24 pigments currently in my watercolour tin include a range of cool and warm primary colours (yellows, reds and blues), plus some pinks, violets and earth colours. I occasionally try a new colour and fall in love with it, at which point it joins the rest of the long-standing collection in my tin.

Paint Types

Watercolour paints come in two forms, in tubes or pans. Tubes contain a liquid form of paint, made up of pigment and binder, which can be squeezed out in a small or large amount, depending on the quantity of paint needed. Paints in pan form contain pigment and binder in a solid, dried block, which can be reconstituted by adding water. Both forms come in large or small sizes, with pans being referred to as 'whole' or 'half'. Pans are the most portable form of watercolour paint and therefore the most practical for sketchbook work, especially when travelling with painting materials.

If you prefer to use tube watercolour paint, you can create your own portable travelling or sketching set by squeezing out small amounts on to a palette and allowing them to dry out. Alternatively, the tube paint can be squeezed into empty plastic half-pans and left to dry, to make it more portable. The paint can be reconstituted later with water in the same way as ready-made pan paint.

Paint Holders and Palettes

I use a Winsor & Newton tin palette made from enamelled metal. It contains compartments for two rows of twelve half-pan paints, with a central space for paintbrushes and other bits and pieces. I like to add a pencil, scalpel and eraser to this compartment when working in the field. There are two palette surfaces that fold out, one of which forms the outer lid of the kit. The inside of the lid contains four wells, which allow the creation of a pool of paint for washes, and the flat inner flap provides a smooth surface for making smaller, drier mixes of paint.

Most watercolour tin sets come with a preselected range of whole or half-pans, but some can be purchased empty. If you do not wish to use all the colours in a set, you can replace some with different pans or make your own by squeezing tube paint into empty pans, as described above.

I also have an ingenious smaller travel version of the paint tin, which contains everything you need for watercolour painting including paintbrush, water supply and water holder. Made from plastic, it includes space for fourteen half-pan paints, two fold-out palette

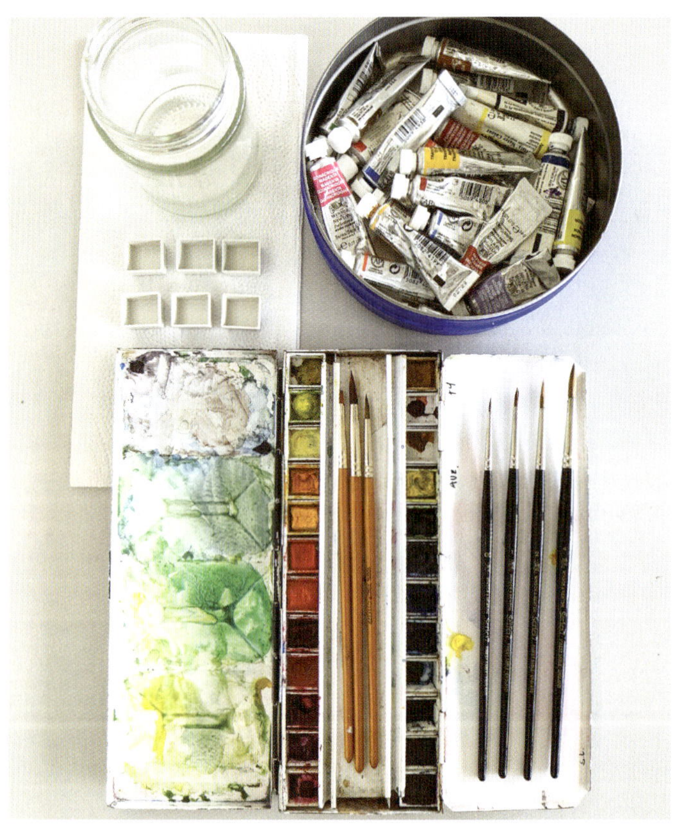

My watercolour kit. At the bottom is the tin containing 24 half-pan watercolours, all of which are movable and replaceable. The lid of the tin (left) becomes a palette with four wells, and there is another folding flat palette (right), where four of my sable brushes are arranged. There are synthetic brushes in the centre compartment. In the round tin are small tubes of watercolour paint, which I sometimes use when painting larger pieces. Empty half-pan containers can be filled with tube paint and left to dry and then transported in the same way as ready-made pan paints. Finally, there is a jar for water and a piece of paper towel for cleaning the palette and brushes, or mopping up excess paint.

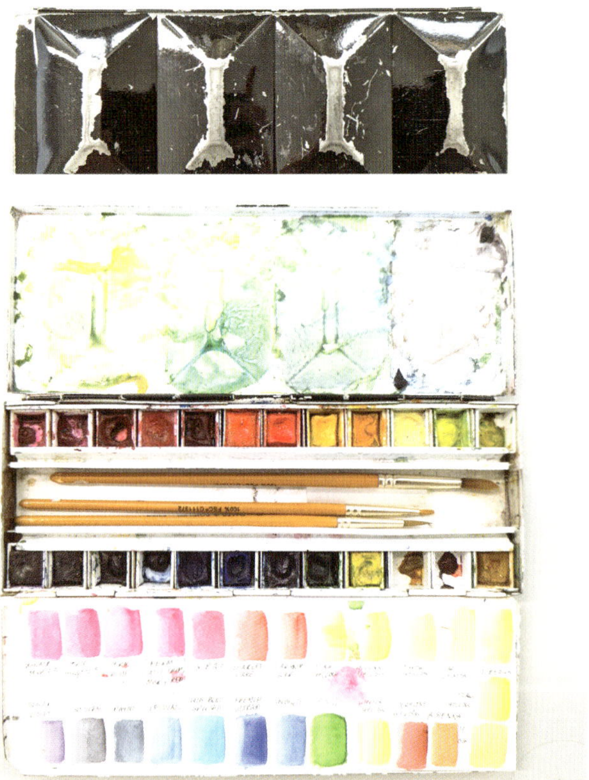

My Winsor & Newton watercolour tin closed (above) and open (below). I have owned this for 24 years, so it is a bit battered, but its strong metal construction has kept the half-pan watercolours inside safe. The four wells in the lid are used for mixing larger washes. The lower palette is flat and useful for smaller washes and dried mixes, which can be used for detail. Here the lower palette is covered by a piece of watercolour paper showing where the pigments are in the box. I change these occasionally or substitute other colours, depending on what I am going to paint.

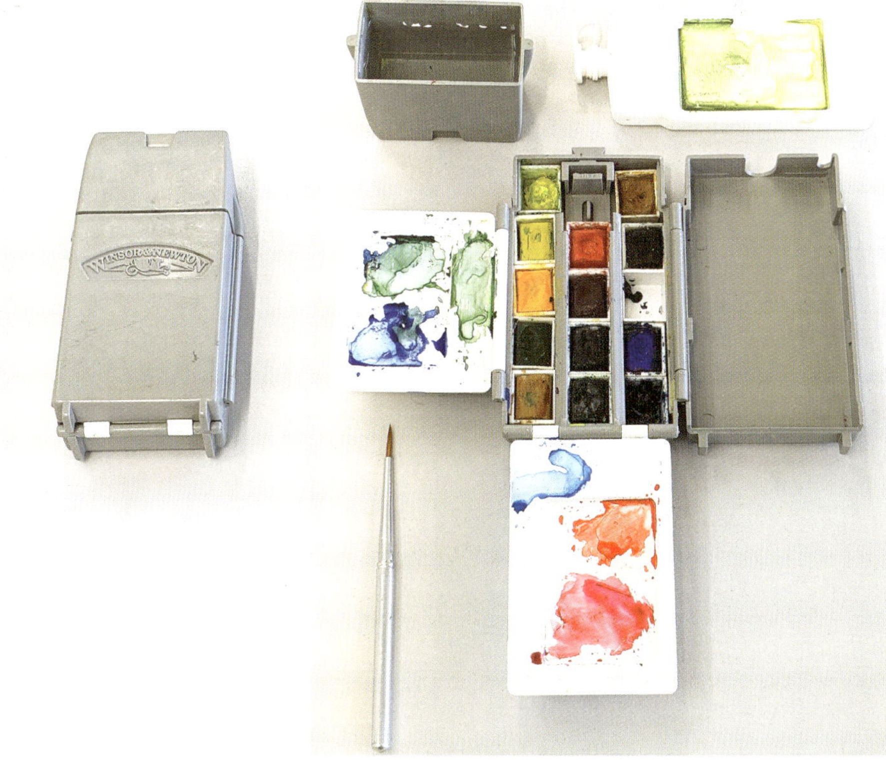
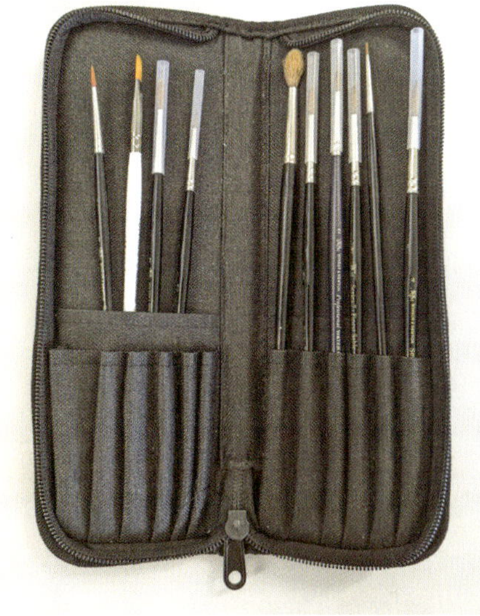

Zipped cases are perfect for transporting paintbrushes. Keep the plastic tubes that come with new sable-hair brushes, replacing them carefully over the brush head when not in use.

A watercolour travel kit, closed (left) and open (right). The kit opens to reveals space for fourteen half-pan watercolours, a water bottle, folding brush, water holder and three palettes (including one on the surface of the water bottle).

surfaces, a third fold-out palette surface recessed into a small water bottle, a travel brush and a lid that becomes a water-holding vessel.

Paintbrushes

I use a selection of round watercolour brushes that are made from both synthetic and natural materials, although the best are made from sable hair. I prefer to use the Winsor & Newton 'Series 7' range, which come in various sizes. For the type of work that I do in my sketchbooks, the 00, 1, 2 and 4 sizes in this range are all involved. I also carry synthetic Daler Rowney brushes in my paint tin, which I try to use when pulling paint from the dry pans. They are best for this, as it is necessary to be firm with the brush bristles when reconstituting the dried pan paint. This is likely to damage the more sensitive fibres of the expensive sable-hair brushes.

The bristles of paintbrushes can be protected by carrying them in a roll or zipped case. If the brushes are being carried in a paint tin, as they often are in my work, it is a good idea to re-cover the bristles in the protective plastic tubing that comes with the brush when it is purchased. To maintain the shape and sharp point of the brush, roll the damp bristles into a pointed shape on a piece of paper towel or cloth, dragging the bristles away from the tip.

If replacing the plastic tubing, do so carefully to avoid catching any hairs and bending them backwards. If this happens, snip the damaged hair off the brush with scissors or a scalpel blade.

Water Jars and Paper Towel

The final elements of my watercolour kit are pieces of paper towel and water jars. After the paint has been washed off a brush, the bristles can be rolled back into a point on a piece of paper towel before it is put away. When switching between pigment colours, it is possible to check that the brush is properly clean, as any pigment left on the brush will show up on the white paper towel.

Use a dampened piece of paper towel to wipe areas of the palette clean. A dry piece will also be useful for dabbing off excess paint if too much has been applied to the sketchbook page.

Finally, water jars are essential for adding water to pigments on the palette, and one for rinsing brushes, the other for adding water to pigment. Ideally you need two, one for rinsing brushes, the other for adding water to pigment but if space is limited, one will do. When working outdoors, make sure you have a lid for your jar and a water bottle for filling it.

PLANT EXAMINATION EQUIPMENT

Sometimes, the workplace of the botanical illustrator will seem more like a laboratory than an art studio! Alongside the usual equipment associated with making art there may be all sorts of pieces of equipment that are used for setting up plants for drawing and close examination.

Retort Stand

The retort stand is useful for positioning plants when drawing them in the studio. Pieces of plants such as small branches or flowers can be held in the clamp and lowered, lifted, tilted or rotated until they are in the perfect position for observation. If the clamp is adjusted to its widest setting, it can also support a small plant pot. Retort stands are easy to find on the websites of scientific or electrical equipment suppliers.

Plant-Dissecting Kit

Contained handily in a rolled-up bag with compartments, a dissecting kit holds several pairs of forceps (tweezers) for handling plant material, poking sticks, and a scalpel with spare blades.

Petri Dish

Plastic or glass petri dishes are useful for holding smaller pieces of plant material such as flowers, either whole or dissected. The dish allows for examination material to be moved with being disturbed, from the desk to the microscope, or simply moved while under the microscope. Lining a dish with damp paper towel can help keep a specimen fresh for longer, as can the addition of a clear lid. Plant material previously preserved in alcohol must be examined while immersed underwater, and a deeper dish will allow this too.

Ruler and Graph Paper

Both ruler and graph paper help when recording measurements of plant material. A clear plastic ruler works best, as you can hold it up to a plant and read through it. A set square (also known as a triangle) helps to ascertain angles when observing plants and can be used to draw horizontal and perpendicular lines in the sketchbook, to keep drawings straight and line up dissected plant parts.

Magnifiers and Microscopes

Hand-held magnifiers and hand-lenses may be sufficient for looking at some of the smaller details of plants. For more detailed examination such as scientific work, a microscope can be used. A stereo microscope with a zoom magnification setting is most appropriate for botanical examination and drawing. It should be possible to manipulate the specimen while it is under the lens.

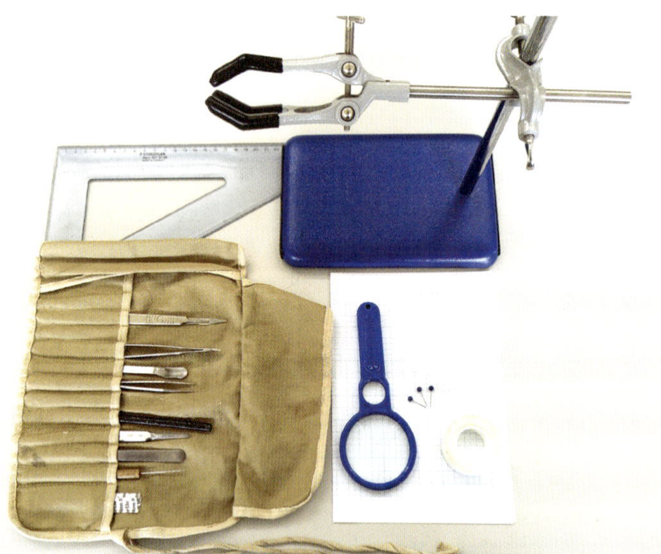

Equipment for examining and drawing plants. The retort stand (right) is used to position living plant material when drawing in the studio. The ruler is essential (along with dividers) for measuring specimens, and graph paper is helpful for measuring and drawing very small plant parts. A hand-held magnifier helps to see detail more closely, and a petri dish keeps tiny specimens safe and portable. The dissection kit contains everything I need to cut, poke and prod plant material. My dissection kit, containing forceps (tweezers) for handling plant material, scalpel and spare blades for dissection, and poking needles mounted on wooden handles.

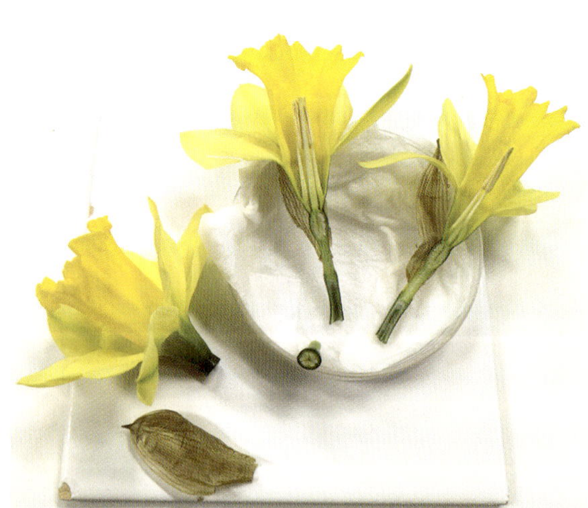

Narcissus flowers being dissected. Laying specimens on a petri dish allows them to be moved without being disturbed. A piece of damp paper towel extends the life of fresh material, and placing the petri dish lid (not shown here) over the specimen and putting it in the refrigerator can keep it fresher for longer.

A stereo microscope with zoom magnification. Newer microscopes are fitted with a digital lens that connects to a computer, allowing easy image capture. You should be able to examine and manipulate your plant material while looking down the lens. Professional scientific stereo microscopes also allow a camera lucida or 'drawing tube' to be attached to the scope, which makes drawing quicker and easier.

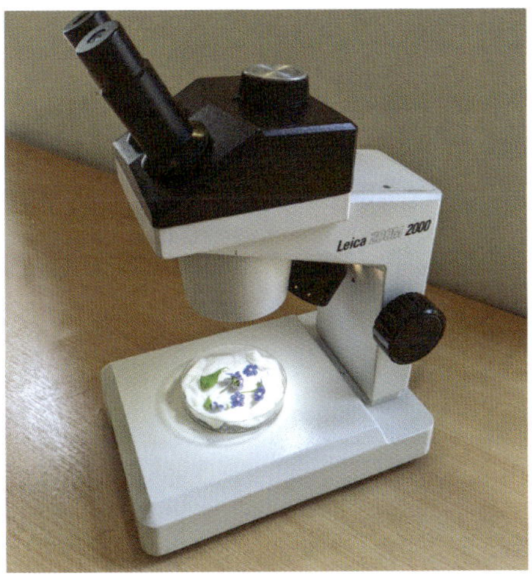

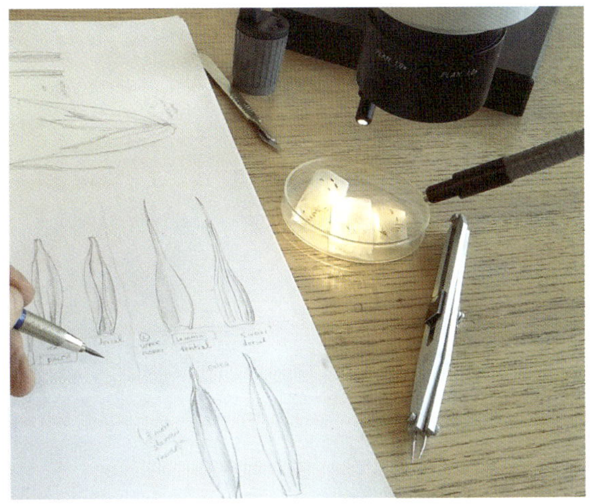

Tiny dried grass flowers held down in a petri dish using folded pieces of low-tack tape while being drawn under the microscope.

Pins and Blu Tack, Tape

Sometimes, small plant parts need to be held in place when they are being drawn. Pins can be used to hold dissected flowers down on foamboard or cardboard, while blu tack can stop items from moving around. I often use a low-tack tape such as 'magic tape' to hold down small parts of dried specimens, such as grasses, to prevent them from blowing away.

Cameras

Cameras are useful for recording plants that you are drawing and painting in your botanical sketchbook, to create photographs for reference and as a back-up resource. Usually, a combination of a digital SLR (single lens reflex) camera and a phone camera will be enough. Cameras have some disadvantages, such as the distortion in terms of imagery and colour that can be created by the lens. The benefit of a single-lens camera is that you can choose your lens size to match the human eye as closely as possible; wide-angle lenses will distort the most.

Phone cameras are very useful as they produce high-quality images and are usually close to hand. Phone cameras with good zoom functions and macro settings can also act as a magnifying tool when examining small details such as flower dissections.

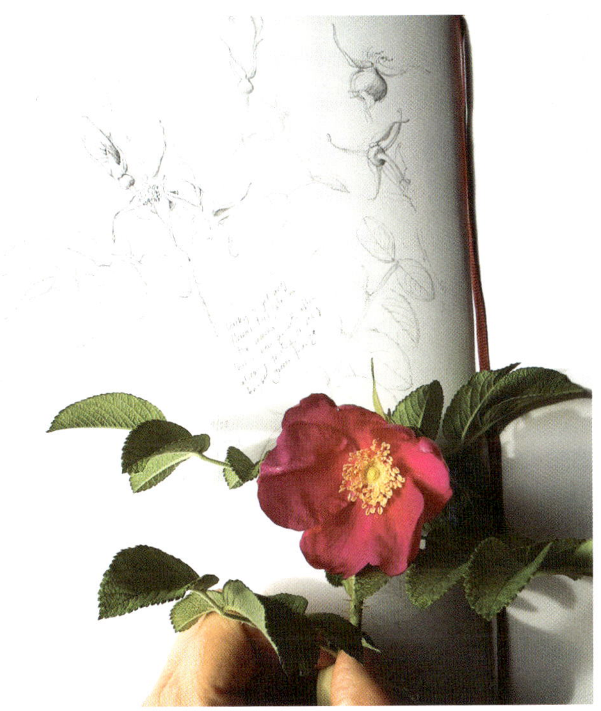

A rose, an open book, and a pencil. Time to get drawing!

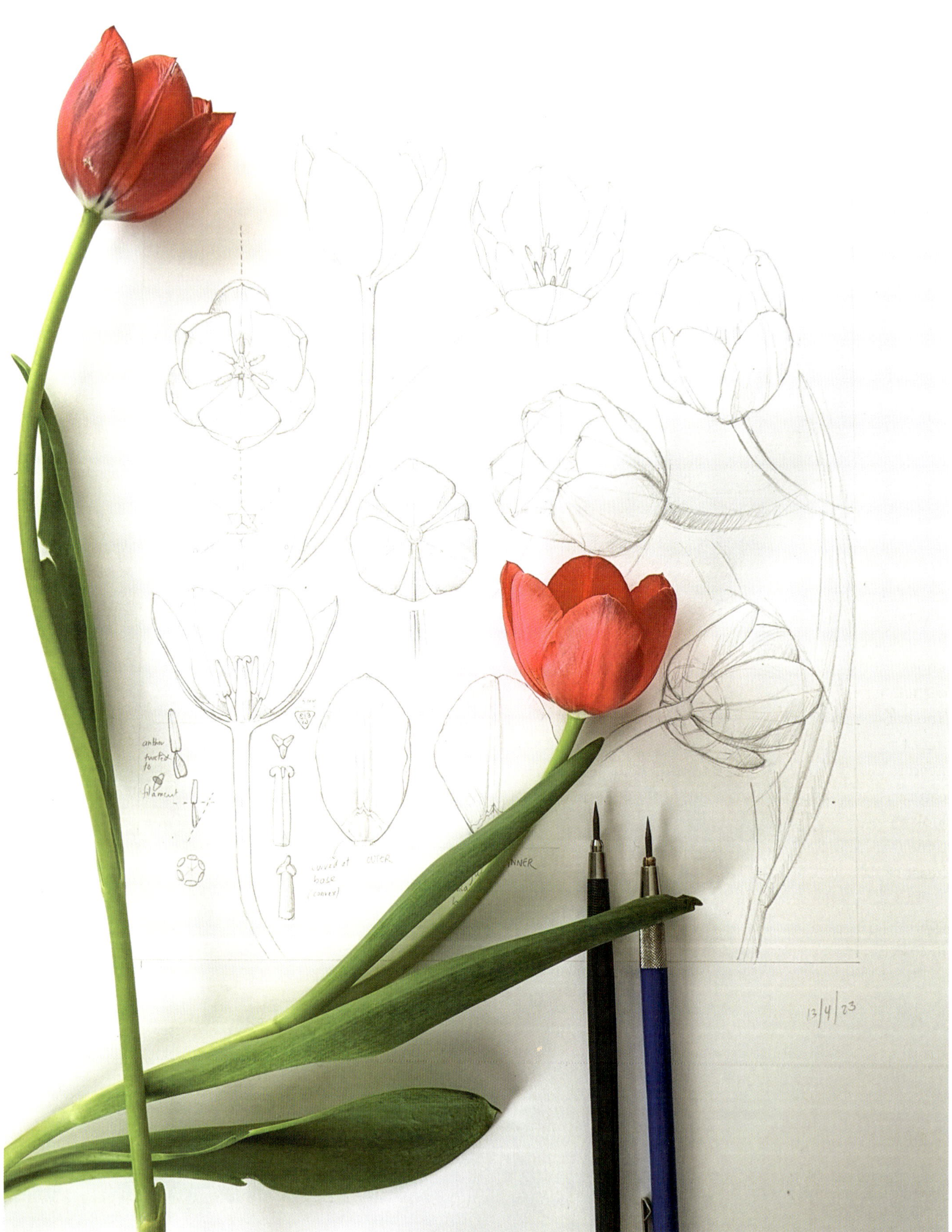

anther
fixed
to
filament
curved at
base
(convex)
OUTER
INNER
13/4/23

CHAPTER 2

METHODS AND TECHNIQUES

Once you have an idea of some of the types of sketchbooks and materials that are available, you can start to look at the ways in which they can be used to create interesting and informative sketchbook pages.

Sometimes, just getting started with a plant drawing or painting can be the hardest part. Some knowledge of basic techniques is helpful, and the botanical sketchbook is the best place to experiment with different media and approaches. Through practice, experimentation and repetition, you will discover what works best for you and begin to develop your own unique method and style.

The activity of drawing and painting plants requires several layers of skill. First come observation and understanding. Next comes the translation of that understanding into drawings that are accurate in terms of certain aspects, such as shape, structure, form and colour. The botanical artist also needs to possess an understanding of perspective, scale and composition. Finally, they need to be able to wrap all these elements together to capture the character and beauty of a plant and make it look alive on the page. It is these skills and abilities that underpin the marriage of art and science that lies at the heart of botanical art and illustration.

This chapter outlines some of the drawing and watercolour painting techniques that are used to depict plants in a sketchbook context, with an emphasis on drawing.

Many of the techniques described here will be familiar to anyone making general sketches. However, those who wish to make drawings of plants specifically will benefit from learning some additional drawing techniques that are especially relevant to the observation and recording of plant material.

General drawing practices will be covered first, before moving on to techniques that are specific to drawing plants. All the techniques outlined here will be demonstrated in the later chapters.

SETTING UP

Before you get started, it is vital to set up both your plant specimen and your drawing materials in a way that makes the process comfortable and successful.

Positioning the Subject

If you are drawing living plants indoors there are several options for setting up the plant material. Your plant may be growing in a pot, or you may have cut a branch or flower to bring inside. Either way, you need to consider the best angle at which to observe and draw the subject. Ideally, you will find the viewpoint that allows you to show the plant at its most natural, informative and aesthetically pleasing.

There are so many different ways in which we can capture plants in our botanical sketchbooks. At the heart of any plant study lies the desire to capture the essence of the plant before us, in an informed manner.

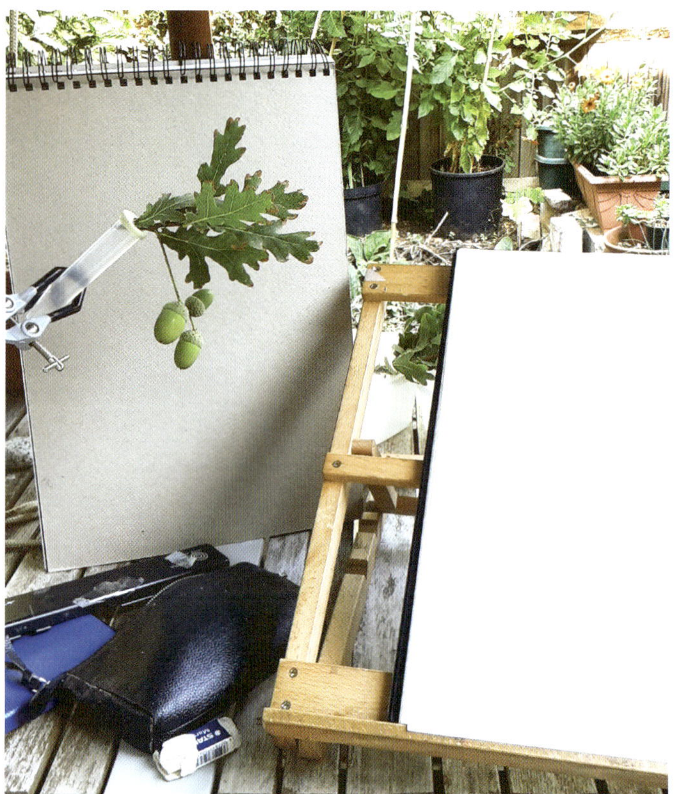

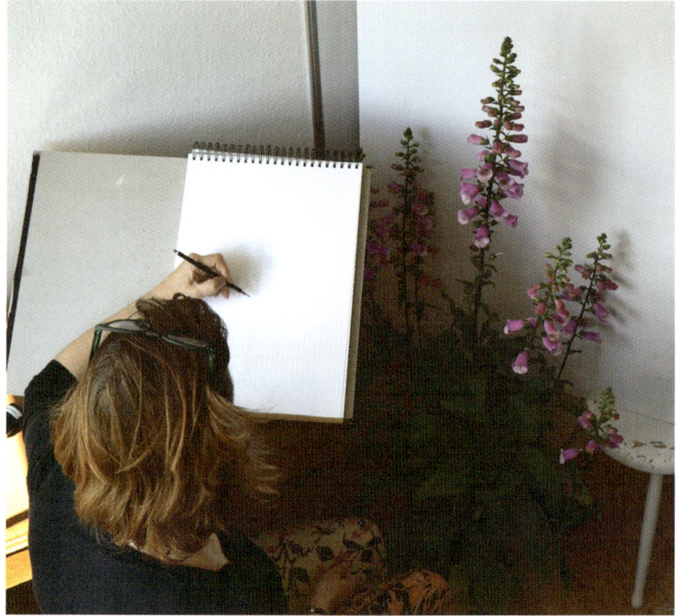

A specimen of oak branchlet with green acorns in a florist's tube, held in place by the clamp attached to the retort stand. The cardboard back of another sketchbook is placed behind it to hide distracting elements. The drawing sketchbook is held at an angle of 45 degrees by a wooden desk easel.

These potted *Digitalis* plants were quite tall, so it was easiest to place them on the floor and set my desk easel up at an angle to the desk. In this way I could arrange the inflorescence I wished to draw directly in front of me. A large sheet of foamboard was placed behind the plant to hide any distracting background elements.

To adjust the height and angle of your plant you may wish to raise or lower it relative to your drawing desk. A retort stand is very useful for holding smaller plant specimens at the right height and angle for drawing.

One of the challenges of working with live material is that it will change and grow while you are drawing it. For example, the leaves of a living plant that has been recently brought inside from outdoors will move as they look for the sunlight. Even cut material will change – flower buds will open, parts will extend, and flower heads will react to changes in temperature and may go over. You may need to work quickly.

Placing Plants on the Sketchbook

If your plants are small enough, you can place them directly on to the page and draw from them there. This method is only suitable if you are not trying to capture anything too three-dimensional; for example, it will work for a leaf laid on the paper to measure and draw its size and shape, but you will not be able to show it moving towards or away from you.

Plant parts laid directly on the page will drop nectar and sap. You can try to protect your sketchbook page from these using a loose piece of paper, but some marks and dirt may be unavoidable when using this method.

Light Source

It is important to get the light source right. Are you happy with the direction of the light and the way in which it is falling on your plant? Does it suit your drawing hand? Unless you want to have your hand cast a shadow over your subject, the light source will need to be on the opposite side.

If you are able to control the light source of what you are drawing, think about how the direction of the light will best show your object. It is traditional to light subjects from the upper left side, as this reflects the preference of a right-handed artist who does not want to work in their shadow. If you are left-handed, however, you may feel more comfortable reversing the lighting.

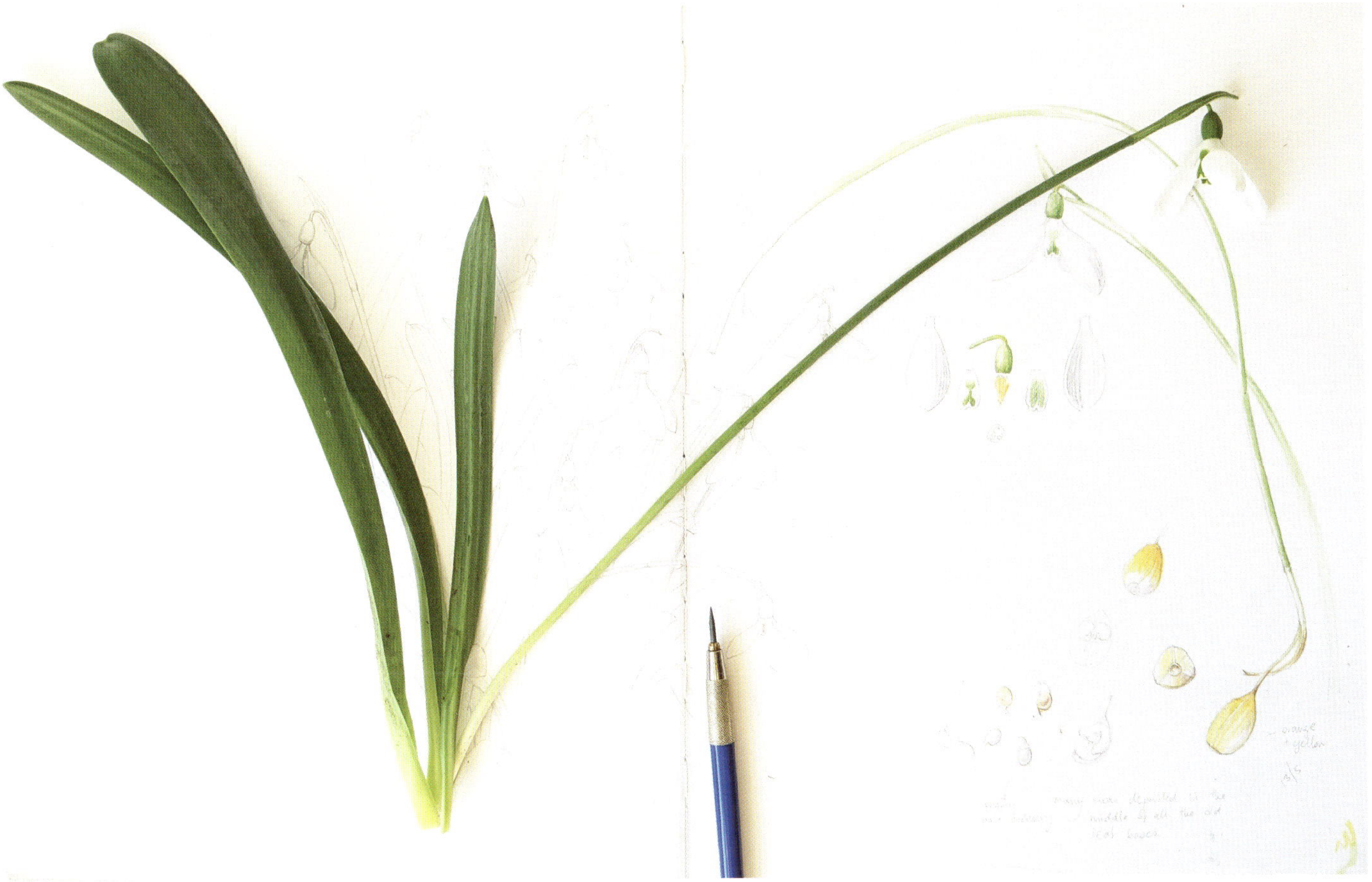

A *Galanthus elwesii* snowdrop flowering spike and two leaves removed from their bulb and laid directly on the double-page spread of the Fabriano 'Venezia' sketchbook. Laying the parts out like this helps when thinking about the composition of the study.

For the *Galanthus* study, I used one arching leaf and drew the other flat on the left-hand side of the page, showing its adaxial (upper) and abaxial (lower) surfaces as well as looking at the detail of the leaf at its tip. *See* page 12 for the finished double-page study.

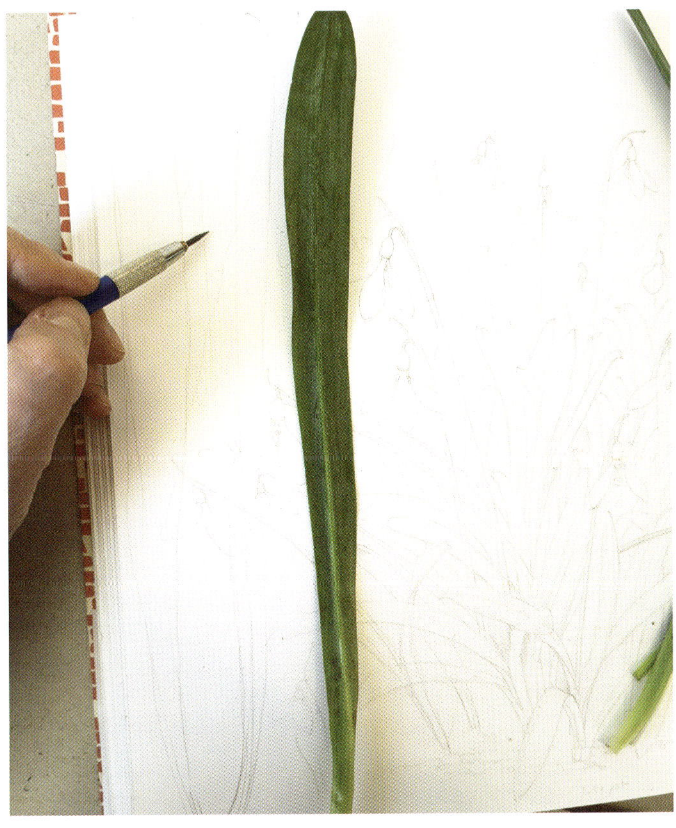

Positioning Yourself

Make sure you are sitting comfortably in a way that provides adequate postural support. This is easier to achieve if you work with your paper on a raised surface such as a desk easel. Have your drawing and painting materials close to hand so that you do not have to interrupt your work in order to go and find something.

A desk easel or other angled support for the sketchbook allows for hands-free, uninterrupted observation and drawing of the plant specimen at a comfortable and convenient angle. A wooden-framed desk easel is lightweight and reasonably portable. It can take a range of board sizes, or you can simply place your sketchbook directly on it. I use an easel when working in the studio or when travelling to work in a different place.

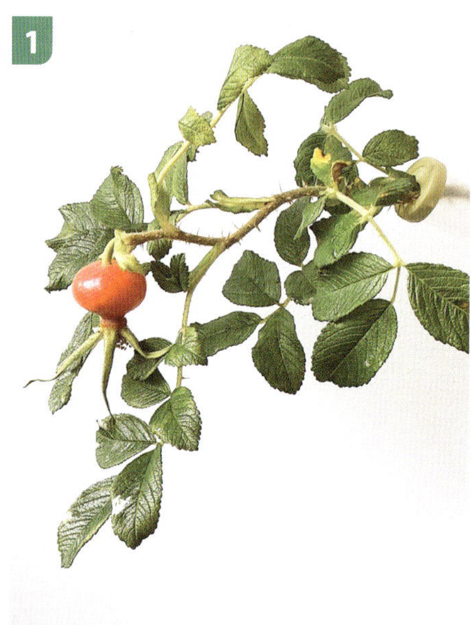

A plant specimen in a florist's tube is held by a clamp attached to a retort stand. It can be tilted into a desirable position and set at an appropriate height for drawing.

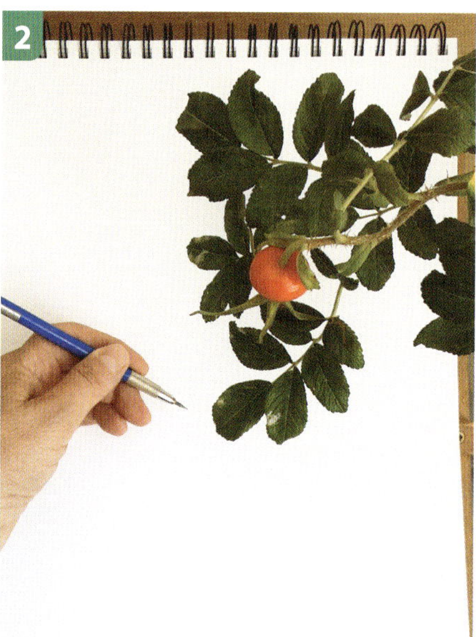

The specimen held on the stand can be positioned directly alongside the drawing surface. Raised up on a desk easel, the drawing surface is on almost the same plane as the specimen. Drawing can be done without losing sight of the specimen, avoiding the distortion that can arise when working on a flat surface. This also encourages better posture in the artist.

The final drawing with the specimen alongside. There is a satisfying immediacy to working directly from a piece of plant material in this way.

Drawing in the Field

When drawing plants outdoors, you will not have the luxury of controlling the environment or the plants in the way that you do indoors. The great benefit is that the plants you are observing behave more naturally, and you do not have to take a plant cutting or move a plant pot.

There are many particular challenges to working in the field; *see* Chapter 7 for more on this subject.

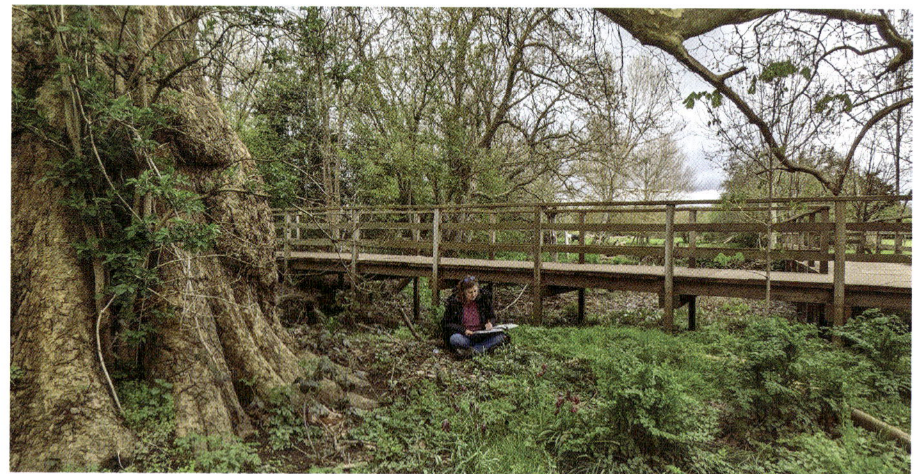

Sketching in the field can be both the most challenging but also the most rewarding practice. Sometimes, you may find yourself sitting on muddy ground drawing snake's head fritillaries!

DRAWING METHODS

Drawing Styles

I am a passionate believer that good drawing is the basis of all successful botanical art and cannot emphasise enough the importance of good skills in this discipline. I also believe that drawing from life is the best way to capture plants. Drawings in a botanical sketchbook can differ significantly in their level of detail, from loose, quick sketches to very tight scientific drawings. One thing they should all possess, however, is botanical accuracy. The artist should be aiming not only to capture the essence and spirit of their plant subjects, but also to communicate the fact that they have understood how the plant is put together.

Your botanical sketchbook is unique to you, so really you can employ any style that you like. Most of my drawings are pencil-line observational drawings, with or without tonal values added. When observing and recording colour, I add watercolour to my line drawings. Sometimes, I add pen and ink to my line drawings in order to clarify certain features. When I want to draw more loosely, I use pen and ink directly. The type or style of drawing usually reflects the purpose of the sketch.

Every one of my drawings begins with observation, and this is best done using measured drawing techniques on live specimens.

Measured Drawing

Measured drawing is one method of creating an accurate line drawing of a subject, either life-sized, enlarged or reduced. When making a measured drawing, you assess the distance between two points of reference, and transfer that dimension to the drawing surface as a line connecting those points. The distance between the two points is measured using the non-drawing hand, leaving the drawing hand to maintain contact with the drawing surface. The measuring can be done in several ways: using a stick such as a pencil; using a ruler; or using dividers. If using a pencil, the dimension is eyed up and noted by placing the thumb the correct distance away from the end of the

pencil. If using a clear ruler, the distance is recorded in millimetres or inches. When using dividers, the distance is measured by moving the points of the dividers to the required length. Once the distance has been measured, the piece of equipment (pencil, ruler or dividers) is placed on to the paper and the measurement transcribed with a pencil line by the drawing hand. It is also possible to observe angles and use multiple reference points of measurement.

Measured drawing is a very good way of blocking in and building up the main elements of a plant drawing before adding detail. I use a combination of measured drawing and drawing by eye.

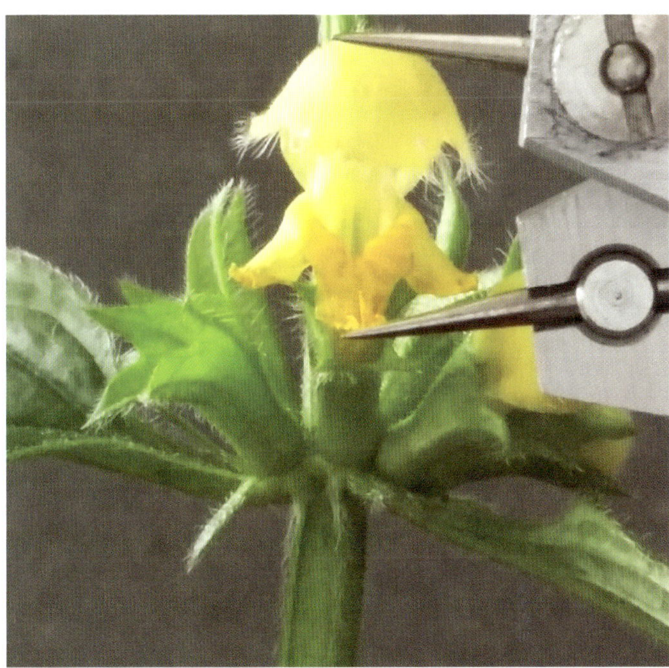

Measuring the flower of *Lamium galeobdolon* using dividers. The tips of the dividers are pulled apart until they match the desired length of the part being measured. In this case it is the distance between the top of the flower's hood, and the tip of the lower petal lip. The measurement must be taken against an imaginary flat plane in the air, which begins at the point of the flower closest to the eye. That length is then transferred to the sketchbook page as a linear mark before being converted to the appropriate drawn line.

The Perspectival Plane

When drawing three-dimensional objects, you need to
be aware of the perspectival plane. This is an imagined
flat plane, like a piece of glass, which exists between the
person doing the drawing and their subject. All measurements should be made from this plane of observation. The
plane should always be situated at the foremost point of
the subject. If you are drawing a life-sized representation
of your subject, you can simply transfer each measurement
directly on to your page. If you wish to enlarge or reduce
the drawing, you can do so by, for example, doubling or
halving the measurement taken. Proportional dividers
allow for instant enlargement and reduction by adjusting a
sliding scale that joins the divider points.

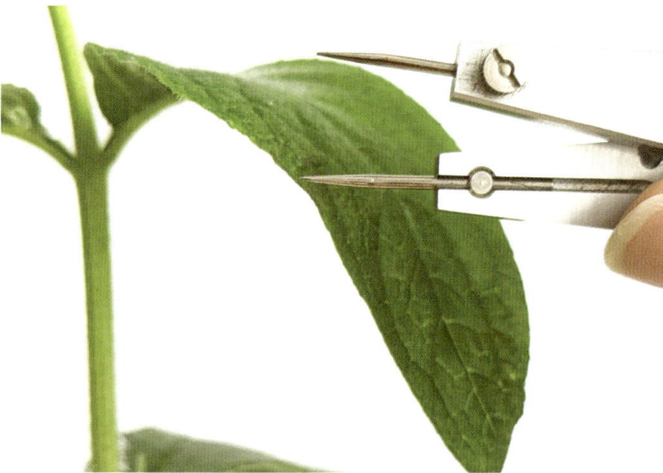

Measuring the vertical height of part of a foreshortened leaf of green
alkanet, *Pentaglottis sempervirens*, using dividers. It is important to hold
dividers perpendicular to the plant (or on a slight angle if that is your
decided measuring plane), as angling them back will give an inaccurate
measurement.

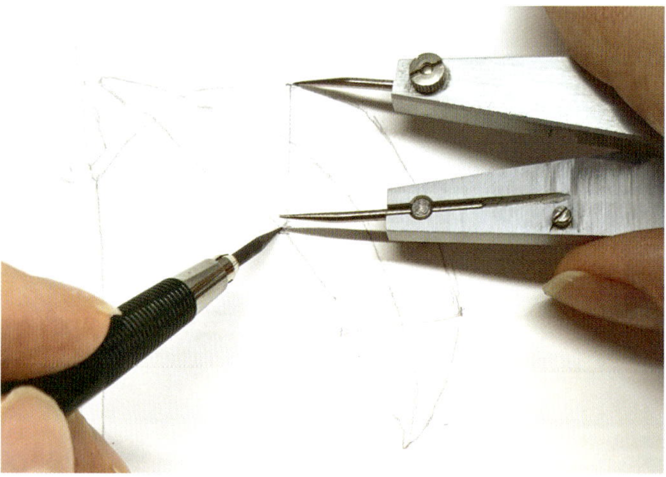

Transferring a measurement from the dividers to the drawing. The two points
are marked, and a line drawn between them. This line will later be erased.

Working from General to Detail

Keep your first pencil marks light and relatively loose,
as they will eventually be erased and replaced with more
complex and detailed marks. They are the backbone of
your drawing, allowing you to build up an accurate picture
of your plant. The first marks I make are simple lines,
which are then built up into to two- and three-dimensional
forms. Once you have the main parts of the plant in place,
you can start to add detail.

The process may seem tedious at the start, but it is
worth investing this time at the beginning of your drawing.
If you do not take enough care in the initial stages, you
could spend a lot of time drawing detail, only to find that
the proportions are incorrect, and you have to erase all
your work.

Erasing, Editing, Correcting

The pencil eraser is an editing tool, not just something
for correcting 'mistakes' – which is what you may have
been taught at school! I employ it vigorously at all stages
of my drawing, adjusting and correcting marks until I am
satisfied. When erasing a line, do not erase it completely
but leave it faintly visible; enough to see and work over.
Several tentative lines become one confident line. It is
rarely possible to create a perfect representation of a plant
on the first attempt.

So that early marks can be easily erased or drawn
over, it is important not to press too hard with the pencil
against the paper surface. Try to keep your hand relaxed
by holding the pencil loosely, at a lower angle to the paper,
and position the hand closer to the end of the pencil. The
pencil point does not need to be too sharp at this stage.
As the drawing progresses and detail is added, the hand is
positioned closer to the tip of the pencil and the point can
be much sharper. The size of detail in your drawing is only
limited by the sharpness of your pencil point. I use a lead
pointer to sharpen my 2mm lead holder clutch pencils,
and a scalpel or knife to sharpen my wooden pencils.

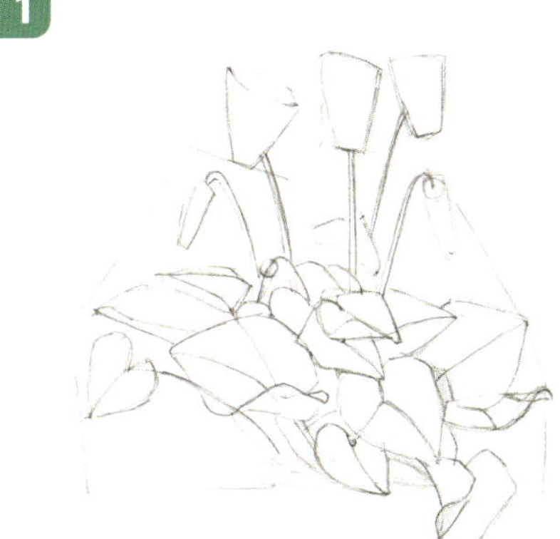

The first steps in drawing this cyclamen and its complex tangle of leaves are to place it in the optimum position, then measure and map out the basic shapes and their relative sizes and positions. It is worth taking the time to get this step right before adding detail. It is easier to edit and erase at this stage than after spending a lot of time on detail.

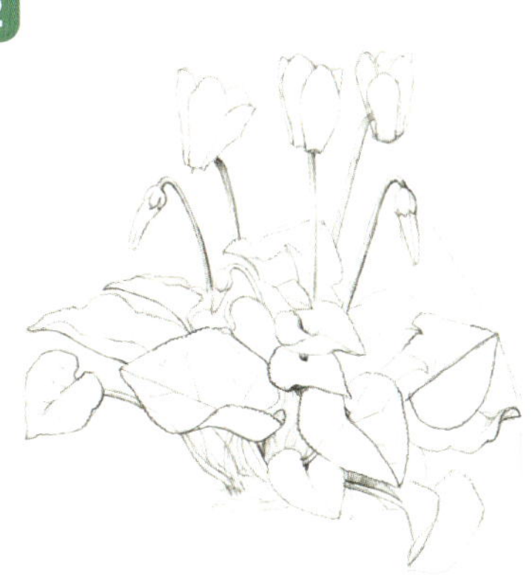

Mid-way through the cyclamen drawing, the positions, shapes and sizes of the plant's parts have been established. Now it's time to start looking more closely at each part, adding nuances of form and detail.

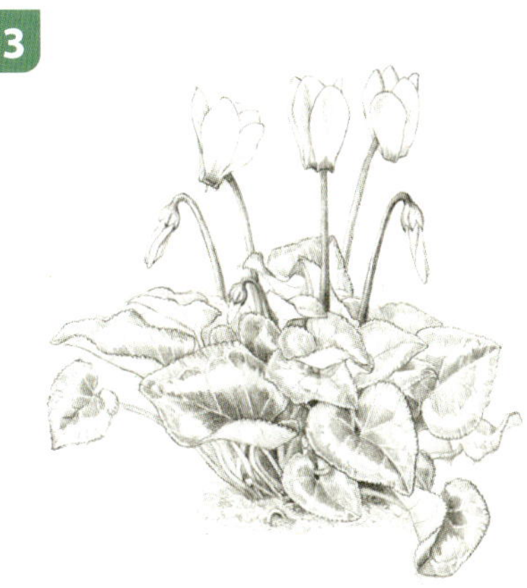

The finished cyclamen drawing. Towards the end of the project, the speed of drawing decreases dramatically. It is a pleasure to slow down and enjoy the final part of the process, where details, pattern and tone are all added with constant reference to the living specimen in front of you.

Adding Tone

Once my line drawings have been completed, I either leave them that way, or add tonal values to part or all of them. My choices depend on the purpose of the drawing. When drawing as a foundation to make colour studies, I may keep the line drawings clear for the addition of water-colour paint. In drawings for scientific pen and ink work, I add just enough tone to describe the volume and form of an object. Other, more general drawings may be taken further by adding a lot of tone.

Understanding tonal values is essential for showing three-dimensional form, and this is where I focus my application of tone. Occasionally, I attempt to replicate the tonal values of colour and, of course, surface pattern.

When applying tone, I begin with a light and gentle application of 2H pencil. Tone is increased by layering with the same hardness of pencil, applying more pressure, and/or adding subsequent layers of a softer (and therefore darker) pencil such as HB or 2B. Working slowly and carefully with miniature elliptical marks produces a softer and more nuanced effect. This method is best if you are looking for a more gentle, fine finish. However, if I am working quickly on, for example, preparatory drawings for a scientific illustration, my tonal marks become more linear and hatch-like.

Tonal drawing (left) and line drawing (right) of *Echeveria elegans*.

The graphite pencil is one of the most versatile drawing tools. Holding the pencil close to the tip gives maximum control. When sharpened to a fine point, its tip can be used to add sharp lines and fine details. When held closer to the end of the barrel and laid at a more acute angle to the paper, it can be used on its side to build up gentle, smooth tones. The tip of a sharp 2H pencil can be used to add detail to flowers.

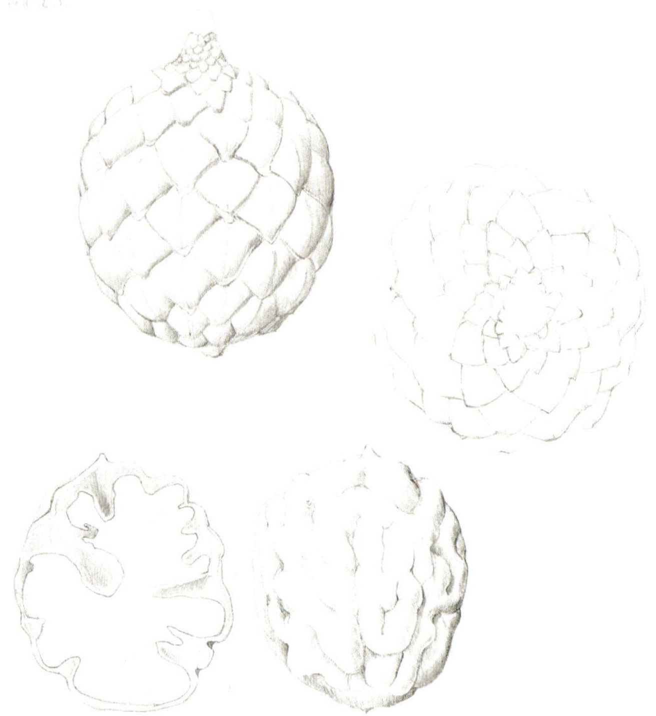

Sketch of *Calamus* fruit and seed in my scientific sketchbook. The upper view of the fruit on the right has had no tonal rendering added but has been left as a line drawing. It has enough information for its purpose.

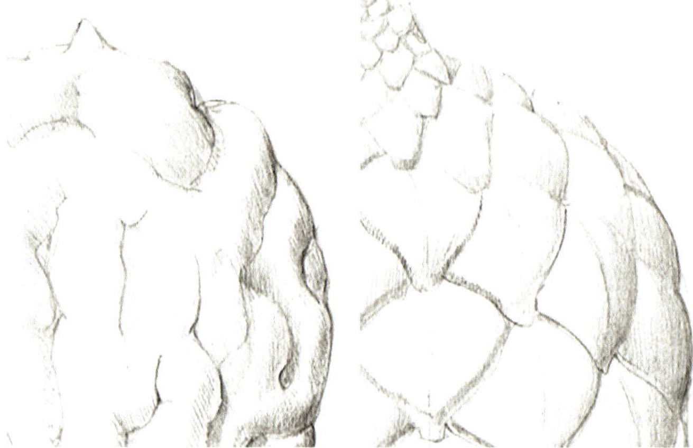

Detail of hatch-like pencil marks on the fruit and seed of the *Calamus* sketch. Tone has been added quickly. There is enough description of form to interpret this in the pen and ink illustration that it will inform.

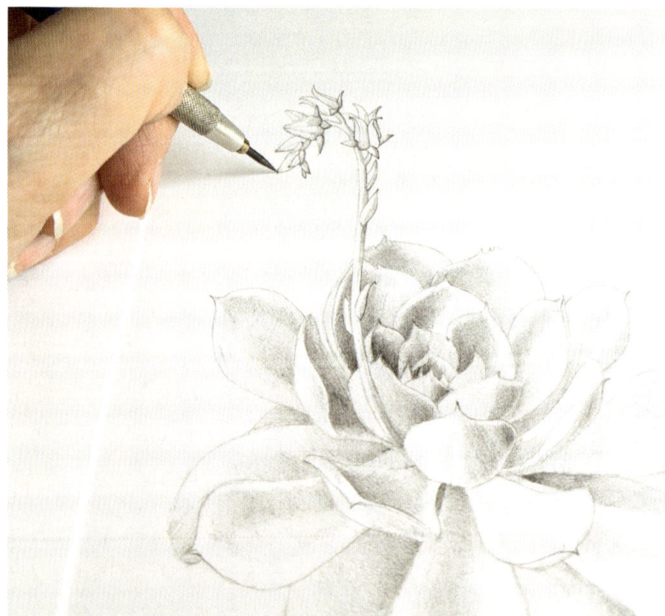

The pencil is held close to the tip for more control, and fine detail applied with its sharpened point. A piece of paper is placed under the hand to avoid smudging other work or depositing oil or dirt on the drawing surface.

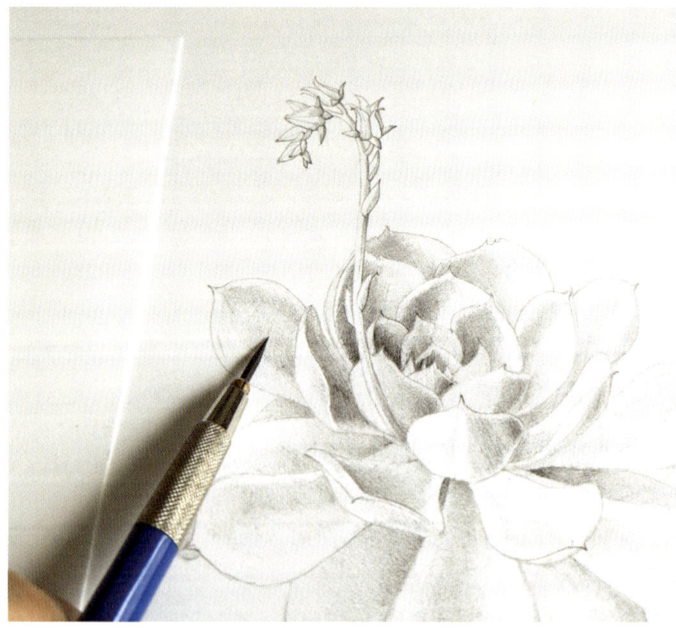

The pencil is held away from the tip and angled lower to the paper, using it on its side and applied in gentle elliptical marks to create smoothly rendered tone.

CAPTURING COLOUR

There are many ways to capture colour in a botanical sketchbook, including the application of wet media such as paint or dry media such as pencil, pen and ink, or coloured pencils. My focus is on the use of watercolour paint. Watercolour is very well suited to botanical subjects as it replicates the vibrant and translucent colours, textures and patterns of plants so well. It is portable in either tube or pan form and dries quickly. Large areas of colour can be applied in one brush stroke when washes are used, and detail can be built up by using less paint and the tip of the brush. Remember that watercolour is a transparent medium, so it should be mixed and applied in a dilution that allows either the paper, or previous layers of colour, to show through.

Colour Studies

Often, one of the goals of a sketchbook study is to create an accurate record of the colour of a plant. Working directly from a plant specimen is the best way to observe its colour. I like to work in a small sketchbook containing watercolour paper to make direct colour studies from plants. Starting with the pigments that I think will accurately represent the plant's colour, I usually have to test several different colours and mix combinations before I am happy with the result. Writing notes helps me to remember the colours I have used and how I have mixed and applied them. Colour mixes are also included in some of my sketchbook pages where watercolour has been applied over or alongside sketches.

Applying Watercolour to Sketchbook Paper

The amount of watercolour that can be applied to sketchbook pages is limited by the type and weight of the paper. Pages made from watercolour paper can take more wet paint than those comprised of cartridge paper.

The technique I most frequently use is adding watercolour to my drawings, although occasionally I apply the paint first and draw over the top of it. This means either including many of the details in the drawing before adding colour to it or focusing on colour first and adding details afterwards. When adding colour to pencil drawings, my intention may be to add colour to either a part or all of the drawing. The half-monochrome, half-colour look of a sketchbook study can be visually very appealing.

If there is a lot of graphite on the area of the drawing where I am going to add colour, I may erase it first and aim to replicate the tonal values with the watercolour. At other

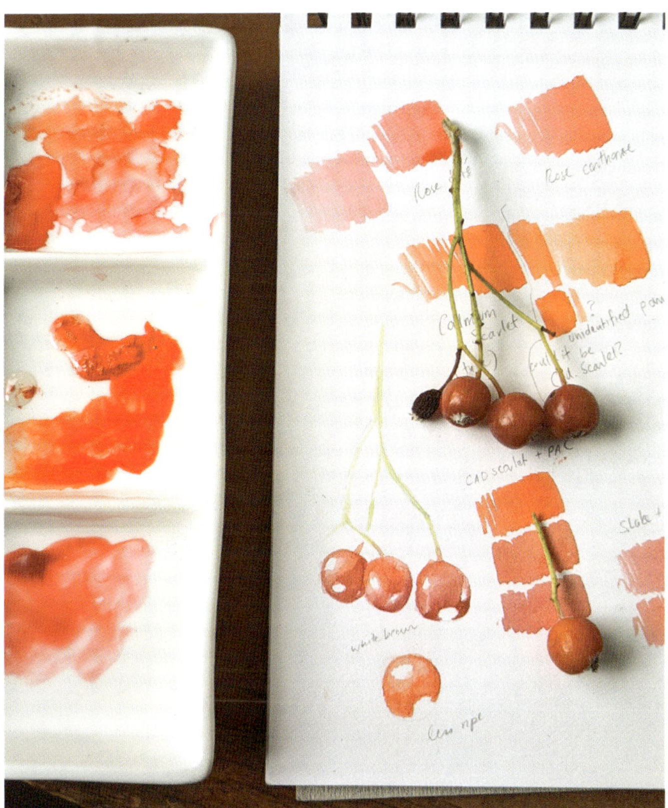

Colour studies for the berries of the whitebeam, *Sorbus alba*, trying out different reds and combinations of mixes to match the colour observed directly from the specimen. There is trial and error involved in this enjoyable process.

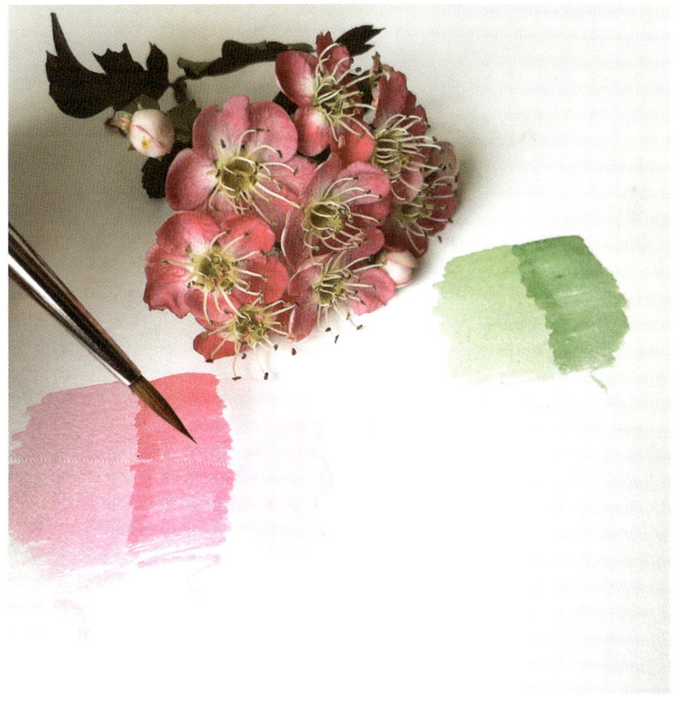

Colour studies of an unusual pink hawthorn, *Crataegus monogyna*.

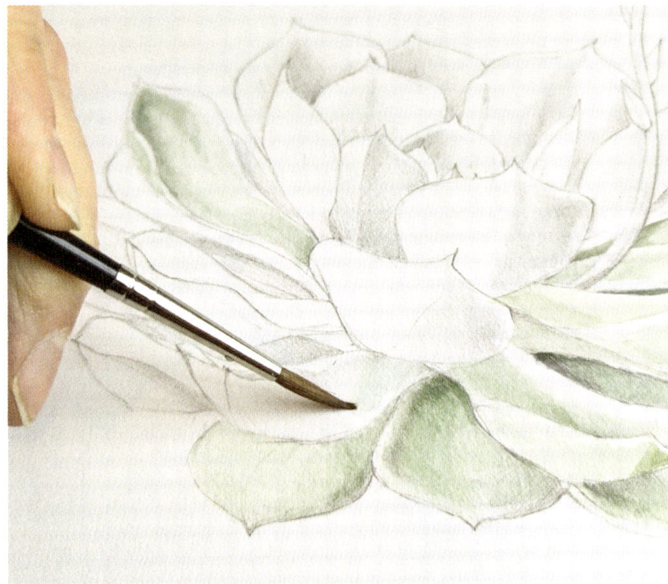

A brushful of watercolour applied to the leaf of *Echeveria*. Paint is dragged across the paper, filling a shape with colour. The aim is to load the brush with just the right amount of paint, so that it is empty at the end of the application. The larger the area to be covered, the larger the brush size needed.

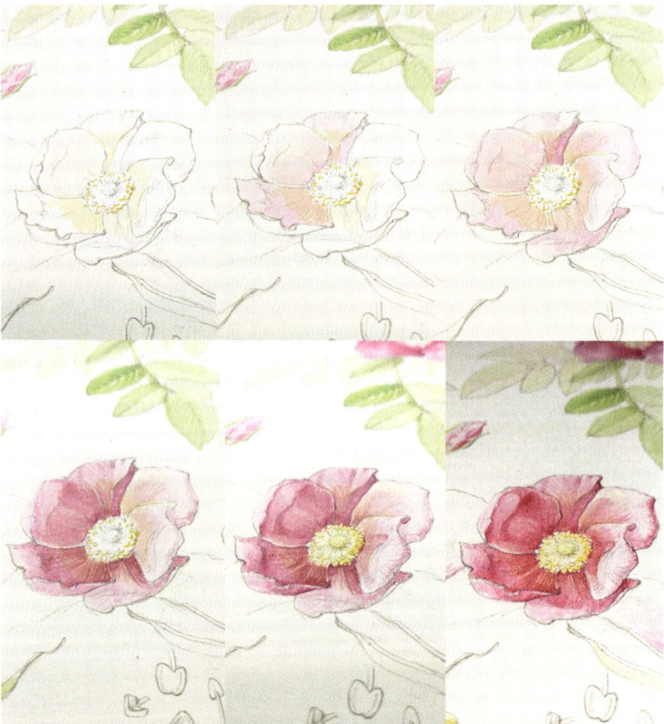

In this study of a *Rosa rugosa* flower, watercolour was applied quite loosely to the pencil outline drawing. Light washes were followed by linear marks made with the tip of the brush to build up colour, tone and form.

times I will apply watercolour to the pencil, using it to provide tone. The colour of the graphite will influence the watercolour laid over it. I may also leave the sketch outline and apply watercolour within it. Remember that pencil cannot be erased once watercolour has been painted on top of it. This can be used to your advantage in a pencil drawing with watercolour, as the detail of the pencil line will be maintained.

BASIC WATERCOLOUR TECHNIQUES

Wash: the application of a body of wet paint. Paint is dragged across the surface of the paper, then allowed to soak into its fibres. The brush is held at an angle of 45 degrees or less to the paper, allowing for the quick but controlled release of the wet paint held in its bristles. The brush should be loaded with exactly enough paint to fill the intended area. Successive layers should be applied once the previous one/s are dry, in order not to disturb them.

Dry brush: perhaps this might be more appropriately called 'drier brush', as there are degrees of 'dryness'. Wet paint is put on to the palette, then allowed to dry slightly or completely, before being picked up on the tips of a damp brush. The paint is applied to the paper using small strokes with the tip of the brush either intact or slightly furred out. Marks can be placed side by side or layered.

Drawing with the brush: the brush is loaded with just enough paint of the right consistency to allow it to be applied to the paper in a thin line. The bristles of the brush should be bent only slightly – just enough to release a controlled amount of paint. The point of the brush is kept intact to achieve a sharp line.

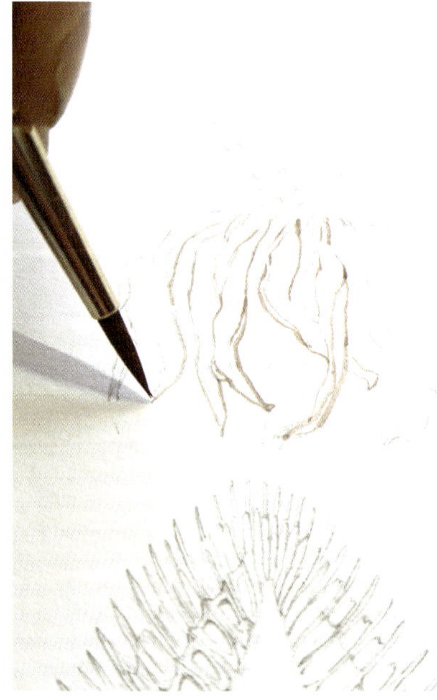

Drawing directly with the tip of the paintbrush over existing pencil guidelines. This may also be done without initial pencil work. Lines drawn with the paintbrush can be expressive and lively, while still maintaining accuracy.

Pen and Ink

I am more accustomed to using pen and ink techniques in my finished work, usually for scientific botanical illustration. Ink pens can be used in the same tight way over pencil under-drawing to sharpen and highlight lines and detail, as well as in a number of other ways.

Pen and ink can be used to draw directly in the sketchbook, with or without pencil underdrawing Drawing free hand in ink may sound challenging as it cannot be erased or corrected as pencil can be. This can produce drawings that are more carefully observed or a style that is looser and sketchier, as several more tentative lines are used instead of one sharp line. There is a sense of immediacy and life to ink drawings that are produced in this way.

Some fineliner pens are available in colours and tones other than black, including various shades of grey. The grey pens are very useful for making direct ink sketches, as they can be used like a pencil for the under-drawing of an ink study. The subsequent layers of darker grey or black ink cover up the working marks. Dip pens (nib pens) make a varied range of beautiful marks and can be used with inks of different colours.

Watercolour paint can also be added to pen drawings in the sketchbook. If you are using this technique, make sure your fineliner or dip-pen ink is waterproof. Once the ink is dry, washes of watercolour can be laid over the ink. More work can be done with the ink pen over the watercolour, and the two may be alternated until the desired depth of tone and colour is achieved.

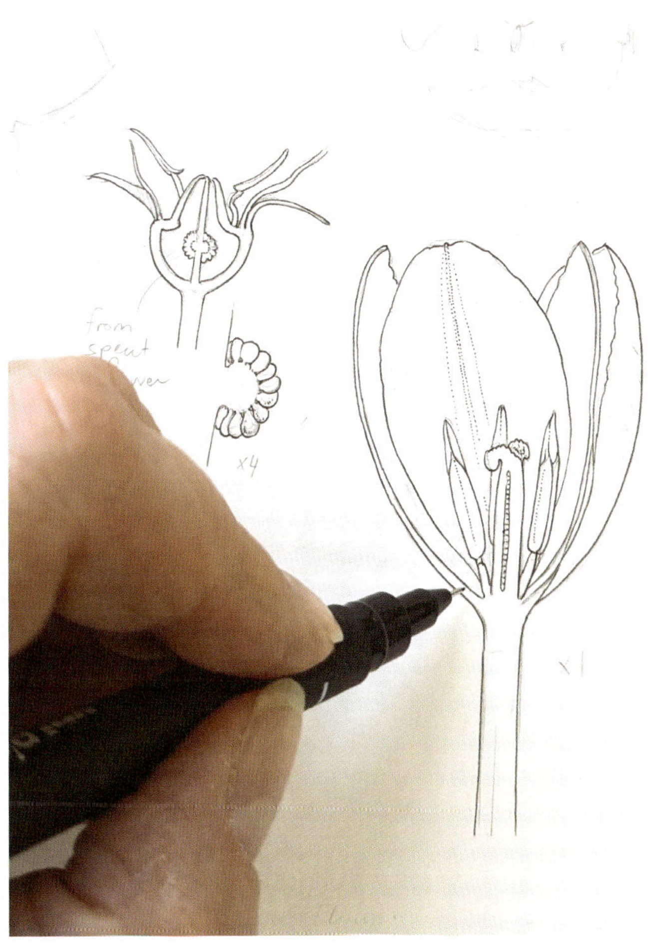

An ink fineliner is used to sharpen and clarify a pencil drawing of a tulip dissection and ovules of another flower on a demonstration piece.

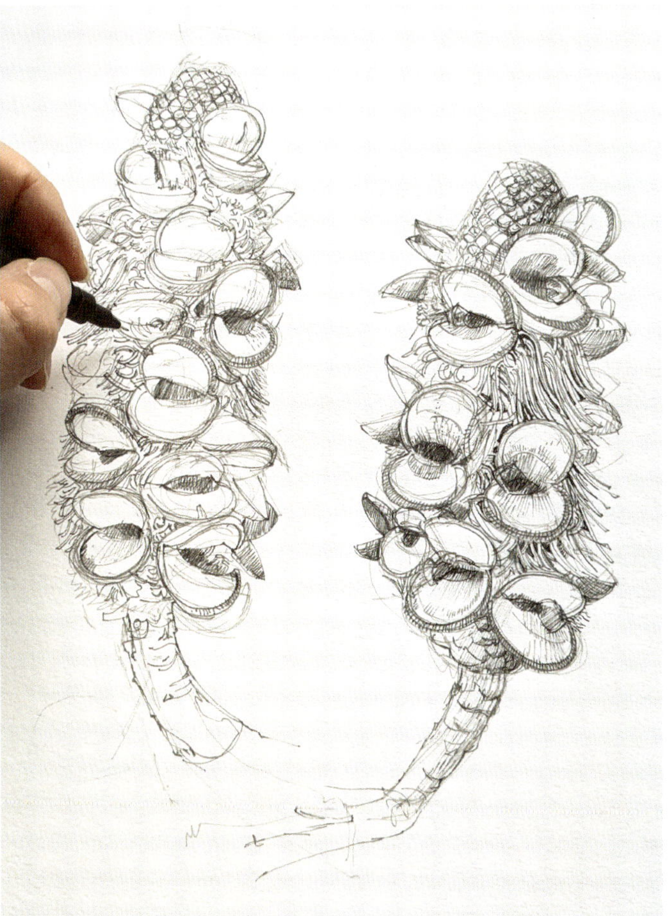

A sketchy, more loose interpretation of a *Banksia* cone created using a selection of fineliner pens from grey to black. Lighter grey pens were used much like a pencil to start the drawing.

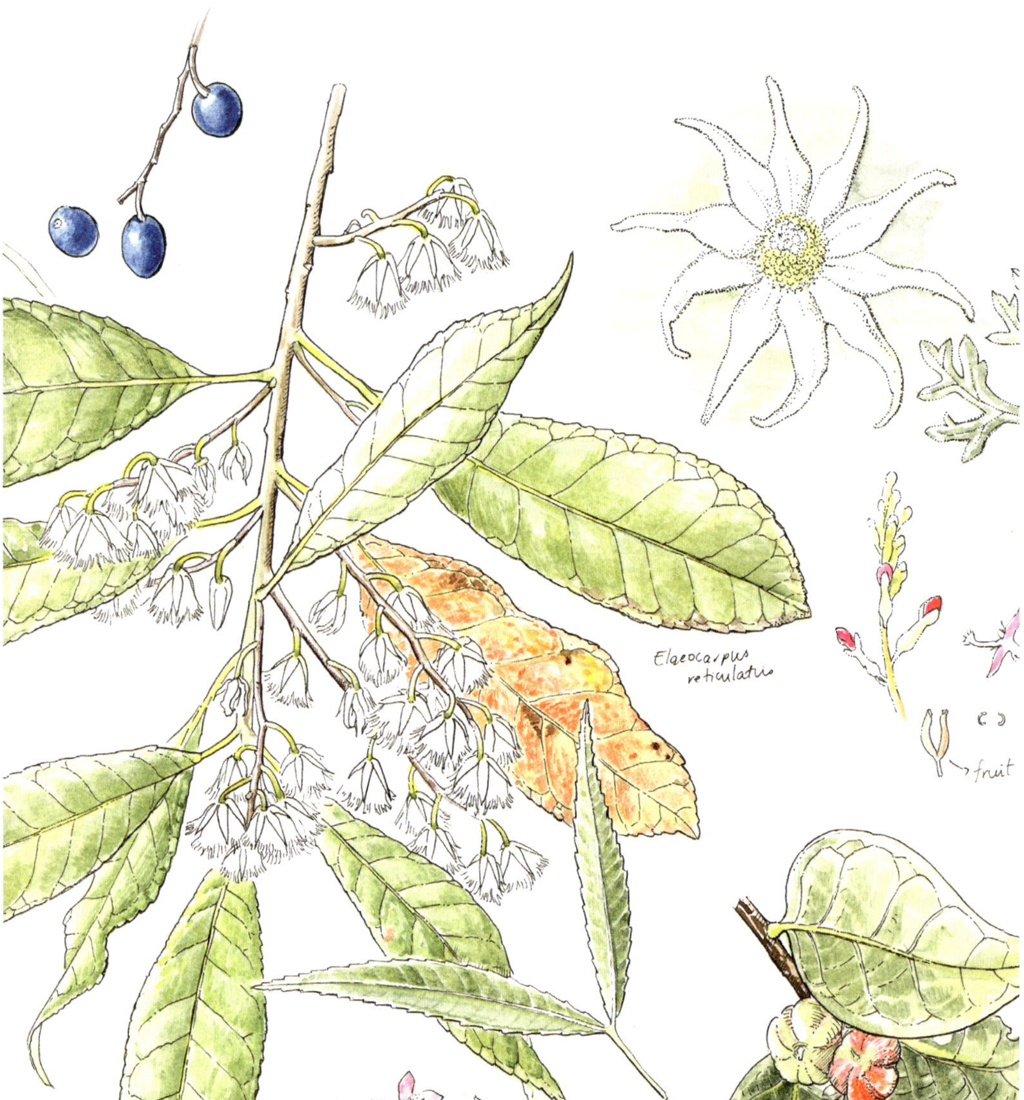

Pen and ink with watercolour. The plants were drawn in pencil, which was then drawn over in black fineliner ink. Several layers of watercolour were then laid down, and two or three alternating layers of ink and watercolour were added after that.

UNDERSTANDING PLANT STRUCTURE

Any artist drawing plants needs to understand at least the basics of plant anatomy – that is to say, the plants' structures and the way they are put together. It is not necessary to have a botany degree, but it does no harm to have at least a general knowledge of the subject and a plant glossary for reference. Information about specific plants is very easy to access via books and online. By drawing plants, you may well find that your knowledge of them grows quickly, especially if you decide to investigate and record a particular family or group. One of the benefits of drawing a plant from life is that you can touch, hold, bend, rotate the specimen, and pull apart stems, leaves, flowers and fruits. In this way, you can really get to know and understand them.

When drawing plants, try building up the structure from the branch or stem outwards. Think of branches and stems as supporting structures or backbones from which leaves and flowers grow as limbs. These limbs support leaf blades and flowers. The distances between these parts, and their relative sizes, occur in naturally pleasing and beautiful proportions, which the artist's eye can learn to instinctively recognise, appreciate and capture.

It is not possible here to describe all the types, shapes and arrangements of plant parts, but there are plenty of comprehensive botanical glossaries available that document them. However, there are some basic key points to be aware of when drawing plant parts. They will be demonstrated in detail in later chapters as they relate to specific projects.

Leaves

Leaf Basics

When drawing leaves, it is vital to consider both the structure and shape of each individual leaf, as well as the way in which they are arranged on the branch. A leaf is easily drawn when viewed flat or front on, but they become more challenging when being represented in three dimensions. The simplest way to approach a leaf and learn about its parts is to draw both sides of it: the lower, or abaxial surface (the surface facing the stem when attached) and the upper, or adaxial surface (the surface facing away from the stem when attached).

Leaves in Three Dimensions

When drawing a leaf in three dimensions, you need to observe how it moves through space, and how the movement changes its shape. There are many different leaf arrangements to be found in plants. For example, when attached to their stem, the leaves of *Lamium galeobdolon* are arranged in opposite pairs, and each pair is held at an angle of 90 degrees' difference to the previous pair. This arrangement is called 'opposite and decussate'. Drawing leaves as they move around a stem will give you an opportunity to see how leaf forms change in perspective. *Camellia* is another useful subject for studying the way that the shape of leaves changes as they move around a stem.

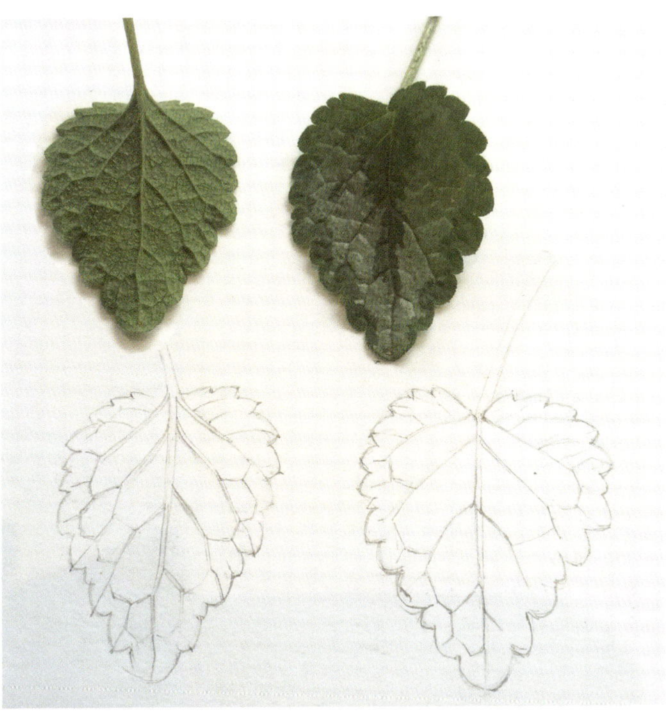

The same *Lamium galeobdolon* leaf has been photographed and copied on to this image, but it was drawn one side at a time: abaxial surface (left) and adaxial surface (right). The petiole becomes the mid-vein and smaller secondary veins branch out from the mid-vein, followed by tertiary veins.

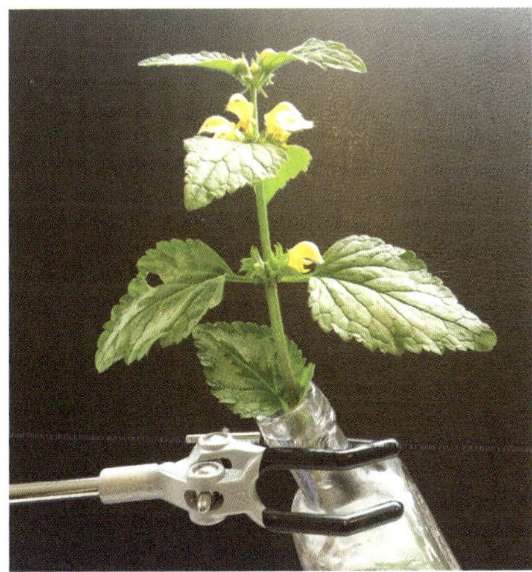

The leaves of *Lamium galeobdolon* are arranged in pairs, each of which is held at 90 degrees to the previous pair. The leaf in a pair coming towards the artist will be foreshortened, as will its partner leaf as it moves away from the perspectival plane. This arrangement is called 'opposite and decussate' – just one of the many botanical terms that you will learn as you need them.

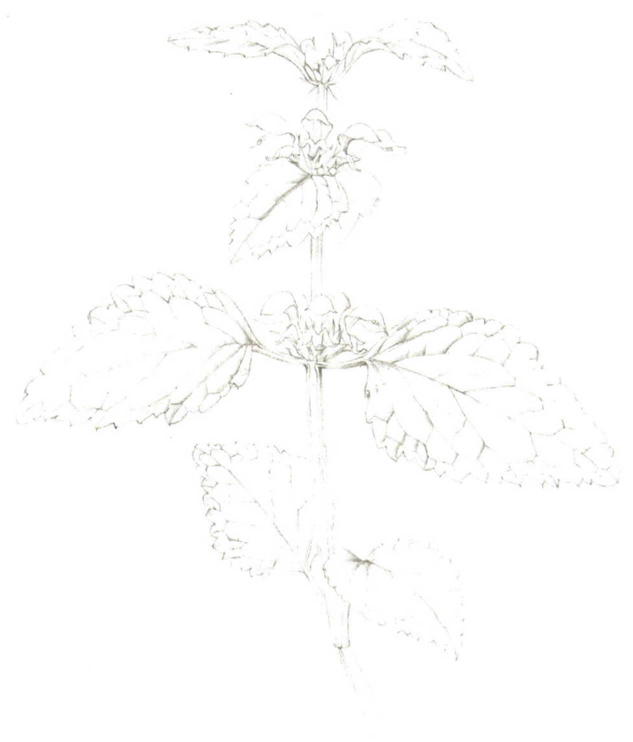

Lamium galeobdolon drawing, showing foreshortened opposite leaves.

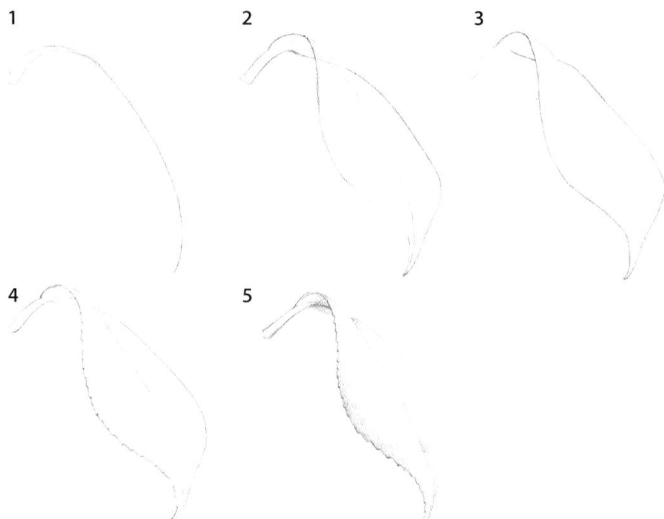

The correct way to draw a leaf, ensuring that hidden edges emerge in the correct place. 1: Draw in the petiole and mid vein. 2: Add in the edges of the leaf blade, including the parts of the far edge that cannot be seen. 3: Erase the hidden lines, paying attention to the leaf blade at the cross-over point. The mid vein will disappear at that point. 4: Refine details such as leaf margin serrations, and secondary veins. 5: add tonal values.

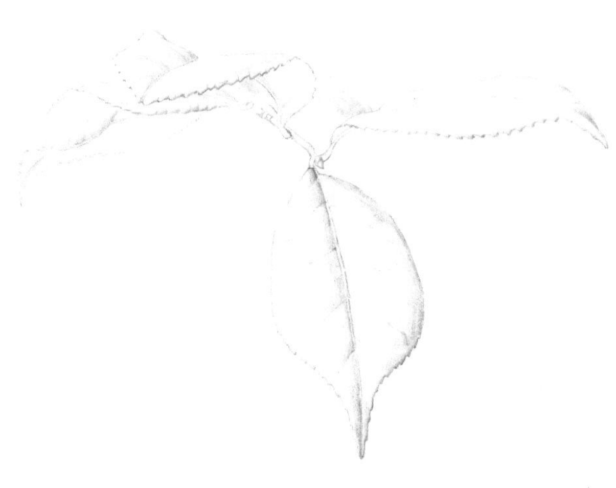

A branchlet of camellia arranged for drawing so that the leaves face in several different directions. Draw from the perspectival plane, observing the effect of foreshortening on leaves coming towards and away from your viewpoint.

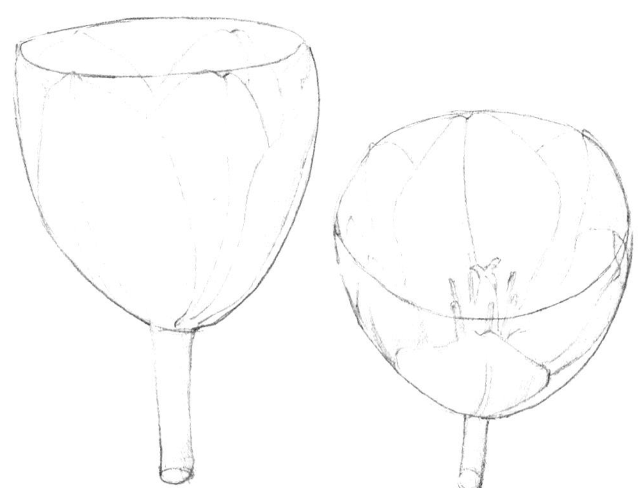

The basic geometric volume of a tulip flower is a bowl, or rounded cone. Imagining a super-imposed form over a flower can help with capturing the perspective of the collective petals (or, in this case, tepals).

When you are drawing from life in three dimensions, the leaves coming towards you will appear to be fore-shortened and this foreshortening will change all their elements. One way to ensure that the section of petiole through to the mid-vein looks accurate, and that both sides of the leaf blade appear to follow through, is to draw these parts all the way through, imagining where they go when they disappear behind the centre of the leaf blade before popping out again.

Flowers

There is much to know when drawing flowers, so they will be covered in detail in Chapter 5. One useful concept to keep in mind is that flowers come in some general three-dimensional forms. Because of this, you can start to draw them as simple voluminous shapes before adding in the petals and other parts that make up those particular forms.

Branches, Stems and Attachments

Many pieces of botanical art are let down by a failure to observe the character of the way in which the plant parts are joined to each other. This includes the attachment of leaves to stems, and the way stems move subtly or obviously between these attachments. For example, instead of being straight, stems are sometimes angled between

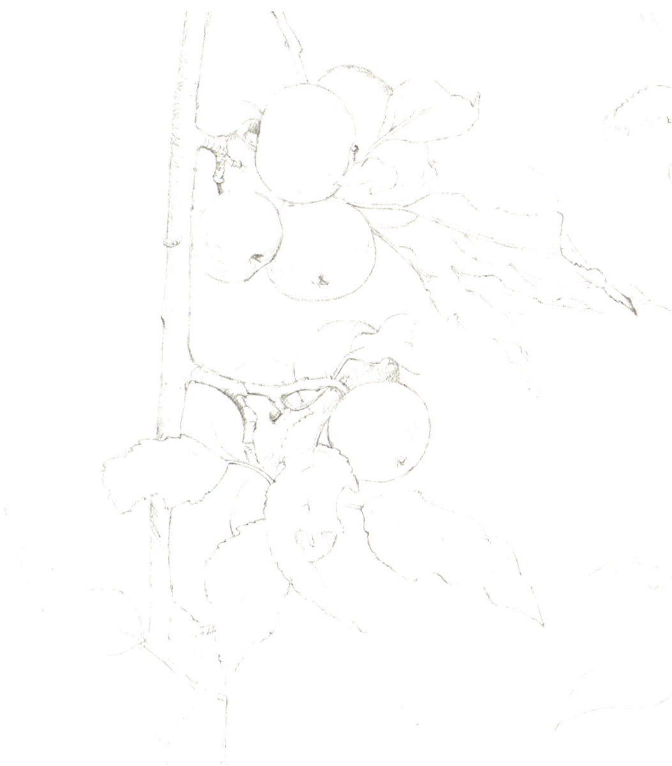

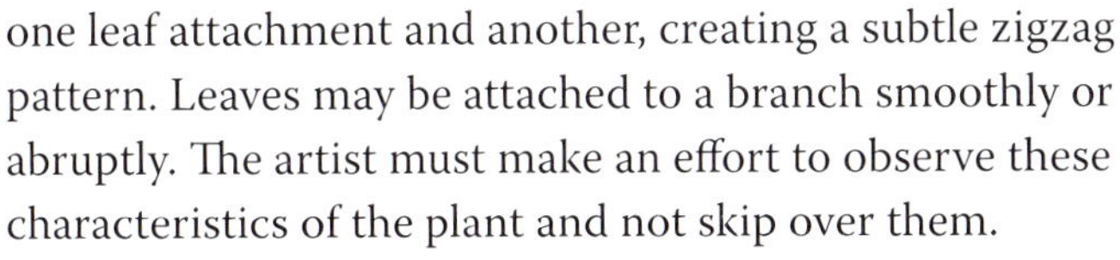

Pay attention to the structure of branches and attachment points of leaves, flowers and fruits. When drawing this apple branch, I had to consider where the parts joined, and look at the way in which pencil marks can describe the form of the branches.

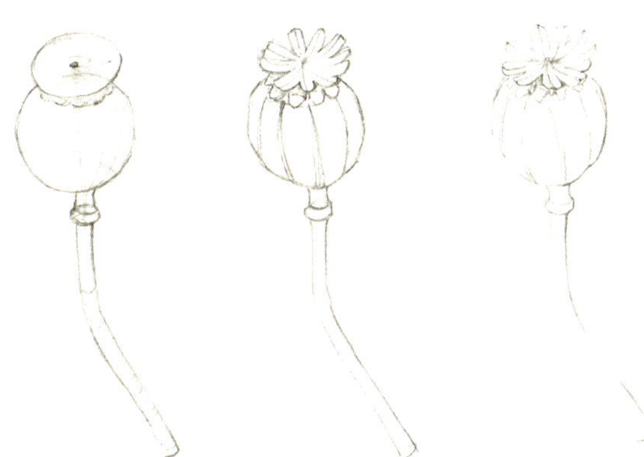

A poppy capsule is a complex structure. Breaking it down into a sphere, with cylinders beneath it and a flared cone on top, helps the artist to visualise how its basic geometric form rotates through space.

Anyone drawing and painting botanical subjects should refer frequently to one of the many excellent glossaries available in books and online. These explain some of the ways in which plants are put together and how these arrangements can help to identify the differences between species. It is impossible to learn about the huge variety of plant forms and structures all at once. Rather, it is a lifelong learning opportunity to study the botany of each plant that you draw. Before long, you will start to build up a repertoire of knowledge and botanical language.

one leaf attachment and another, creating a subtle zigzag pattern. Leaves may be attached to a branch smoothly or abruptly. The artist must make an effort to observe these characteristics of the plant and not skip over them.

Fruit and Seeds

Like flowers, fruit and seed structures can be sub-divided into a range of simpler forms. Once again, learning some of the terms and forms from a botanical glossary will be useful when finding out about the relevant structures. When reproducing fruit and seed structures, you will need to apply some of the methods for drawing three-dimensional forms. Observing the basic three-dimensional volumes of the forms and seeing how the light falls on them will explain them. Think about how to light your subject in a way that will show the form most clearly. For example, a rounded fruit is best described when lit from the side and slightly above.

PHOTOGRAPHIC REFERENCE

Although the best way to observe and draw a plant is always from life, there are times when you have to work from photographs. Ideally, any reference photos you use will be those that you have taken yourself. Even if you have good living material in front of you and are confident of completing the work with your specimen in view, it is still advisable to take photographs, in case something changes dramatically while the drawing or painting is in progress. The photographs will not be the primary source material for the drawing, but they can be consulted later if necessary.

Taking Useful Photographs

When taking photos of plant subject matter for drawing, there are a number of ways to ensure that they will be useful to you:

- **Set-up**: take as much care when setting up a plant specimen for a reference photo shot as you would when setting up for drawing.
- **Viewpoint**: think about your eye level. What is the best angle at which to view the subject?
- **Directional light source**: if possible, light the subject as you would wish it to be lit for drawing, whether from the left or right.
- **Type of light**: natural light is best. If using artificial light, consider how this will affect colour.
- **Capturing scale (size)**: try to include something for scale – a tape measure, ruler, graph paper – to indicate

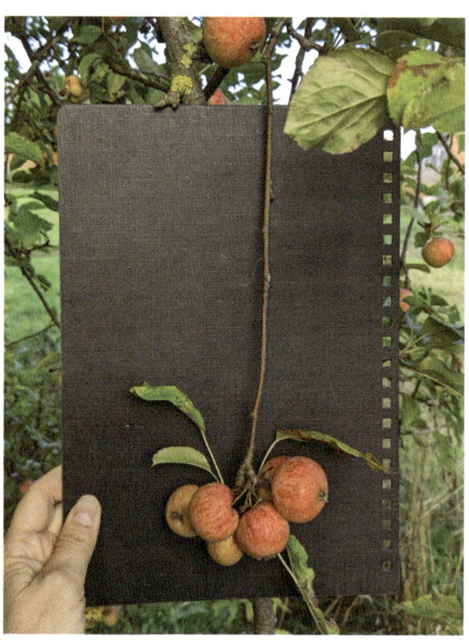

Holding up a piece of black card behind this small branch of wild apples while photographing it isolated it and made a more useful reference photo than one containing distracting background information.

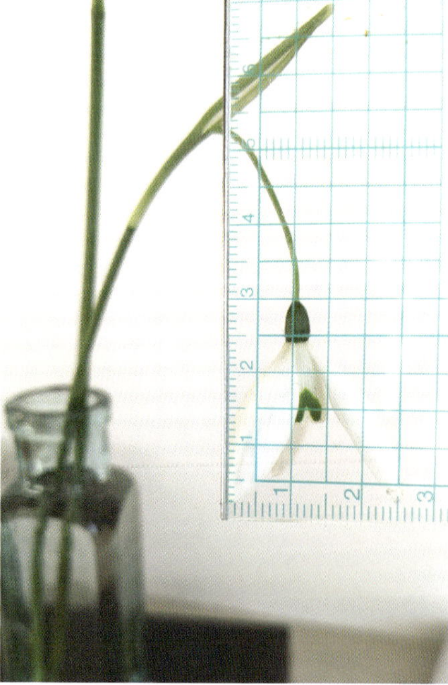

Scale: photographing this snowdrop flower with a clear ruler held against it provides scale in the reference photo. Measurements can also be taken from the parts of the flower touching the ruler.

the size of the subject. A transparent ruler held up against the subject is useful for parts of the subject on the plane of the ruler. Flatter parts can be laid on graph paper and the measurements read off. Callipers can also be held up to or around a subject.
- **Camera lens**: a wide-angle lens such as that used for the widest shots on a phone camera will create the most distortion of the subject. If possible, set the lens to the size that is closest to the human eye. In digital camera lenses this is 35mm.
- **Use a tripod**: when using a heavier camera, a tripod will help you to achieve sharper images by reducing camera shake.
- **Background**: remove distracting material from the background of the subject. You can do this by photographing it against a piece of board, fabric or paper.
- **Colour correct at point of photography**: review digital images on the screen immediately after taking them, so that you can compare the colours with real life and adjust the settings accordingly. Every camera lens will read and interpret colour differently. In addition, every screen and printer will reproduce colours differently. Therefore, true colour can only really be observed from life.

Drawing from Photos

It may seem easy and convenient simply to trace directly from a photo on to the sketchbook page to begin a drawing but there are drawbacks to using this method. First, you will not have a full understanding of what you are drawing, as there will be no interpretation or clarification taking place. When using photographic reference, I prefer to use minimal tracing and sketch from the photo, as this feels more like sketching from the living material. Ideally, you should only use your own reference photographs or, if using photographs from another source, make sure you truly understand the subject you are drawing rather than drawing blindly.

Colour from Photos

Painting true colour from photographic material can be a tricky task, unless you can be sure that the image you are seeing on screen or in print has been adjusted or calibrated to be as close to the real-life colours as possible. This is because colour is interpreted differently by every camera lens and every form of printing. It is possible to adjust the colour as it appears on your screen whilst holding it up to the live plant – changing the settings to make it warmer or cooler, and increasing or decreasing brightness and contrast.

GETTING STARTED

What to Include on the Page

What to include on your sketchbook pages depends a lot on the purpose of your drawing. For example, when I am drawing in my scientific sketchbook, there are very specific parts of the plant that I need to include in my drawing. I may be following the helpful instructions of a botanist, but even then I will take the lead and use my instincts to decide what parts of a plant to explore and investigate.

On the other hand, when I am drawing just to explore a plant, I will use knowledge from various sources to inform my work. It may be necessary to do some research on the plant, such as finding out which plant family it belongs to and observe how that is reflected in its structure. Whatever the purpose, I always find that, as I start to draw, the plant reveals more and more of itself to me. Curiosity and delight take over and the discovery and documentation process start to feel very natural.

Setting off on Your Adventure

Now that you have some understanding of the methods and technique you will need to make botanical sketchbook studies, you can see how I put them all into practice through the examples in the following chapters. Many of the sketchbook pages have been created during my 30-year career as a professional botanical artist and illustrator. Others were made especially for this book. Coming up with some fresh approaches to inspire you has taught me that there are always new and exciting plants to look at, and unfamiliar techniques to learn. It is time to begin your own botanical sketchbook adventure!

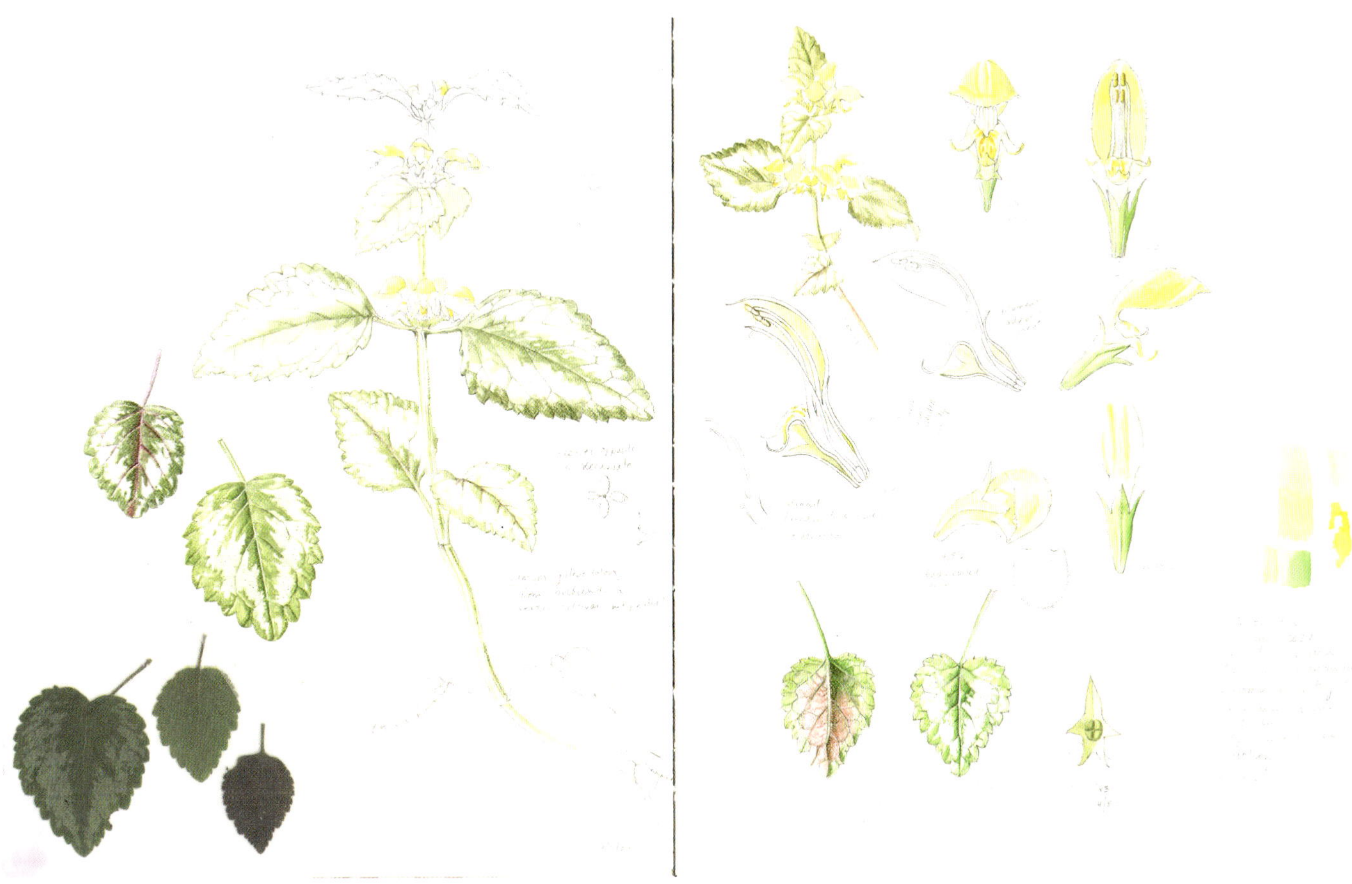

When I started drawing this unassuming yellow archangel (*Lamium galeobdolon*) plant – a weed that planted itself in a rough patch of my garden – I could not have predicted it would inspire me to illustrate over two pages of my sketchbook. It provided so much material for drawing, including flower dissection, leaf studies and colour work. Curiosity will elevate even the most common of plants to the most interesting of specimens!

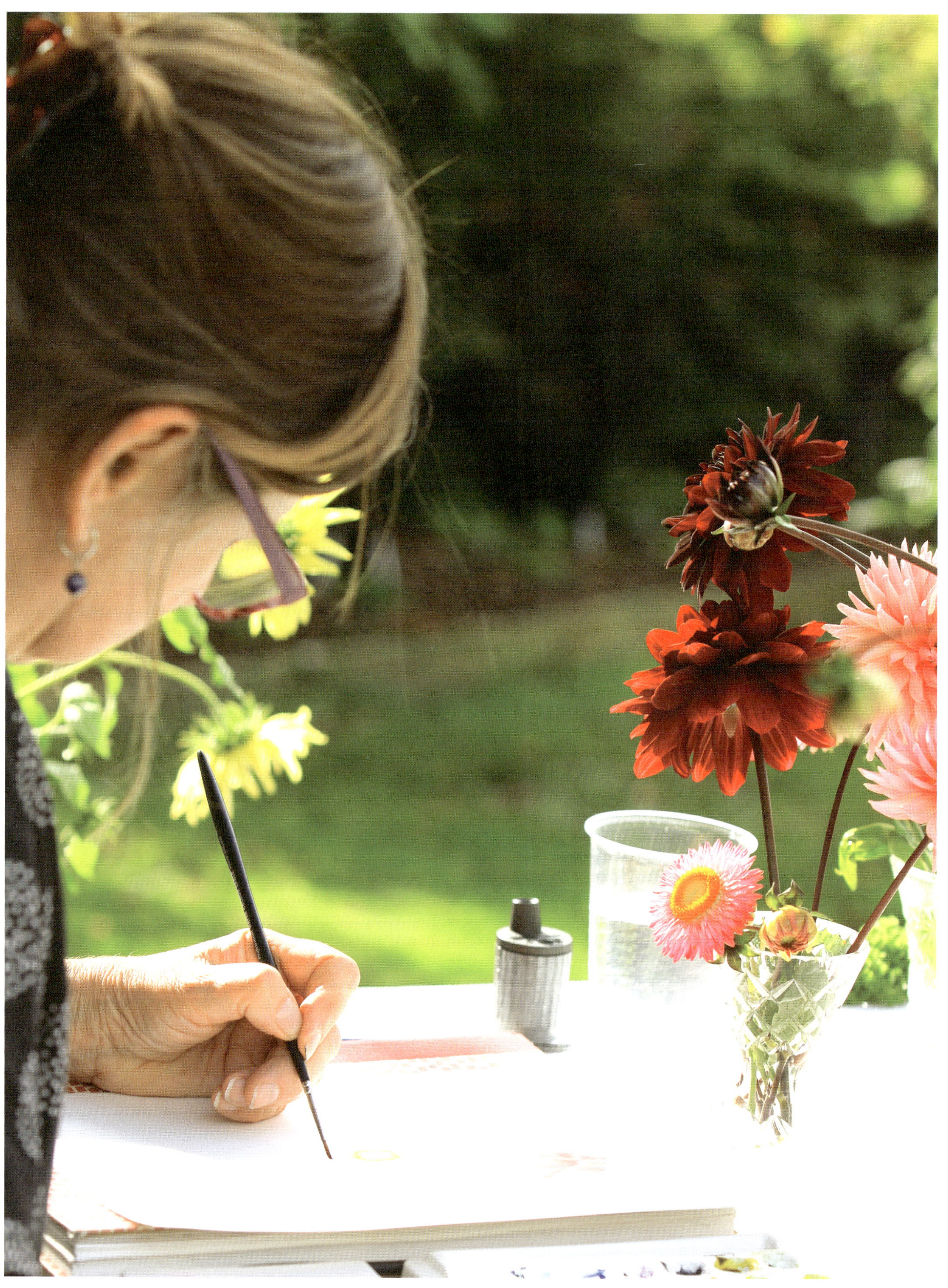

CHAPTER 3

FLOWERS

I t will come as no surprise to learn that flowers are the focus of many pieces of botanical art and illustration. Seasonal and ephemeral, beautiful and sometimes weird, they need to be captured with skill and speed by the artist. Whether the reason for capturing them is aesthetic or scientific, it is important to get them right. This chapter will show how the botanical sketchbook plays a vital role in learning to observe and draw flowers with accuracy, and to capture colour successfully. It will outline some approaches to flower drawing, using examples from my own sketchbook projects around the topic.

DRAWING FLOWERS ACCURATELY

By drawing in an informed way, you should be able to produce flower drawings that are both scientifically accurate and aesthetically pleasing. In its simplest form, the science of the flower lies in its parts and how they are put together. For a botanical artist to portray flowers accurately, they should recognise for example the number of its parts, the types of male and female parts within it, and how they are arranged in relation to each other.

The way a botanical artist defines the art of a flower depends very much on their response to it, and how they wish to portray it. As an illustrator I take an analytical approach, and to me the beauty of a flower lies not only in its outward forms and colour, but also in all the beautiful shapes and forms within it. Whatever your approach, it is important to draw and paint flowers with accuracy and understanding.

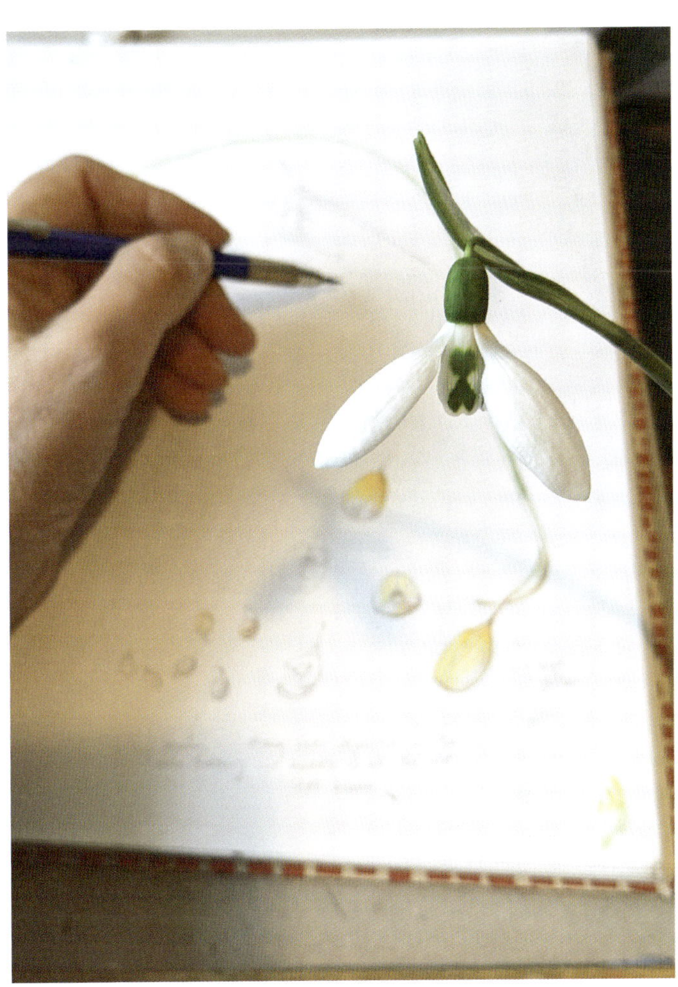

Drawing a *Galanthus elwesii* flower. These simple flowers have such elegant forms. As well as being pleasing to look at, the green markings on the inner tepals are unique for each species.

It is incredible to think that, despite the huge diversity of form and colour in flowers, they are all essentially made from the same basic elements.

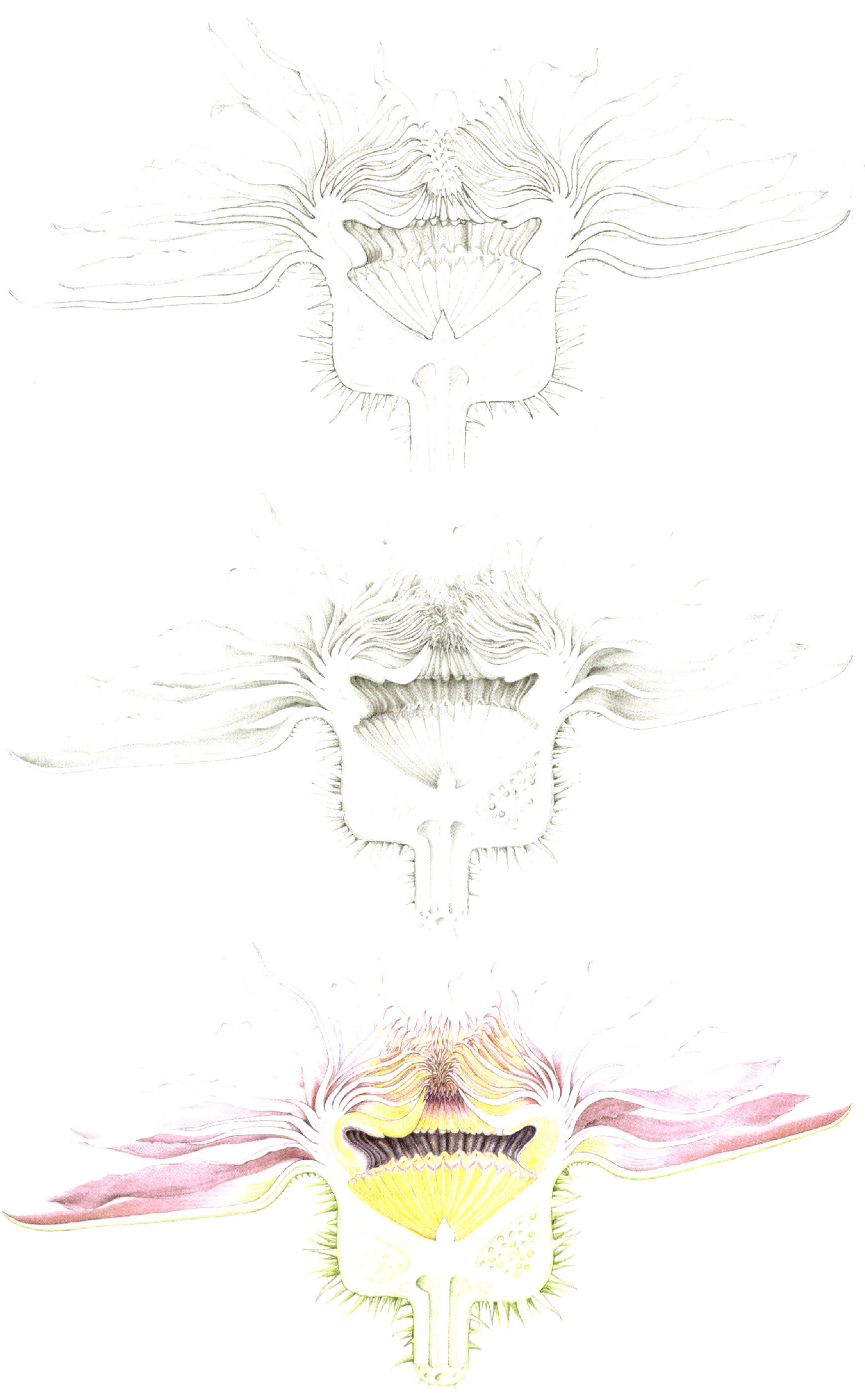

Science and art: a longitudinal section of the flower of the giant water lily *Victoria cruziana* reveals important scientific information about its internal parts and how they are arranged. It is also interesting and beautiful to look at. My initial detailed sketch (top) was used to make a detailed graphite rendering and a watercolour illustration.

Observational Drawing

The best way to understand and draw a flower is to observe and work from it from life. With the flower in front of you, it is possible to observe and sketch it from all angles. Every botanical artist will have their own approach to sketching flowers. Mine is an analytical one and I enjoy moving from the general aspects of a flower to its specifics. My first drawings attempt to capture the shape, form and feel of the flower. The drawings then become more specific as I delve into the flower's structures, which I find endlessly fascinating. Multiple sketches allow me to really get to 'know' a flower, until I reach the point at which I feel confident to draw or paint it for whatever purpose.

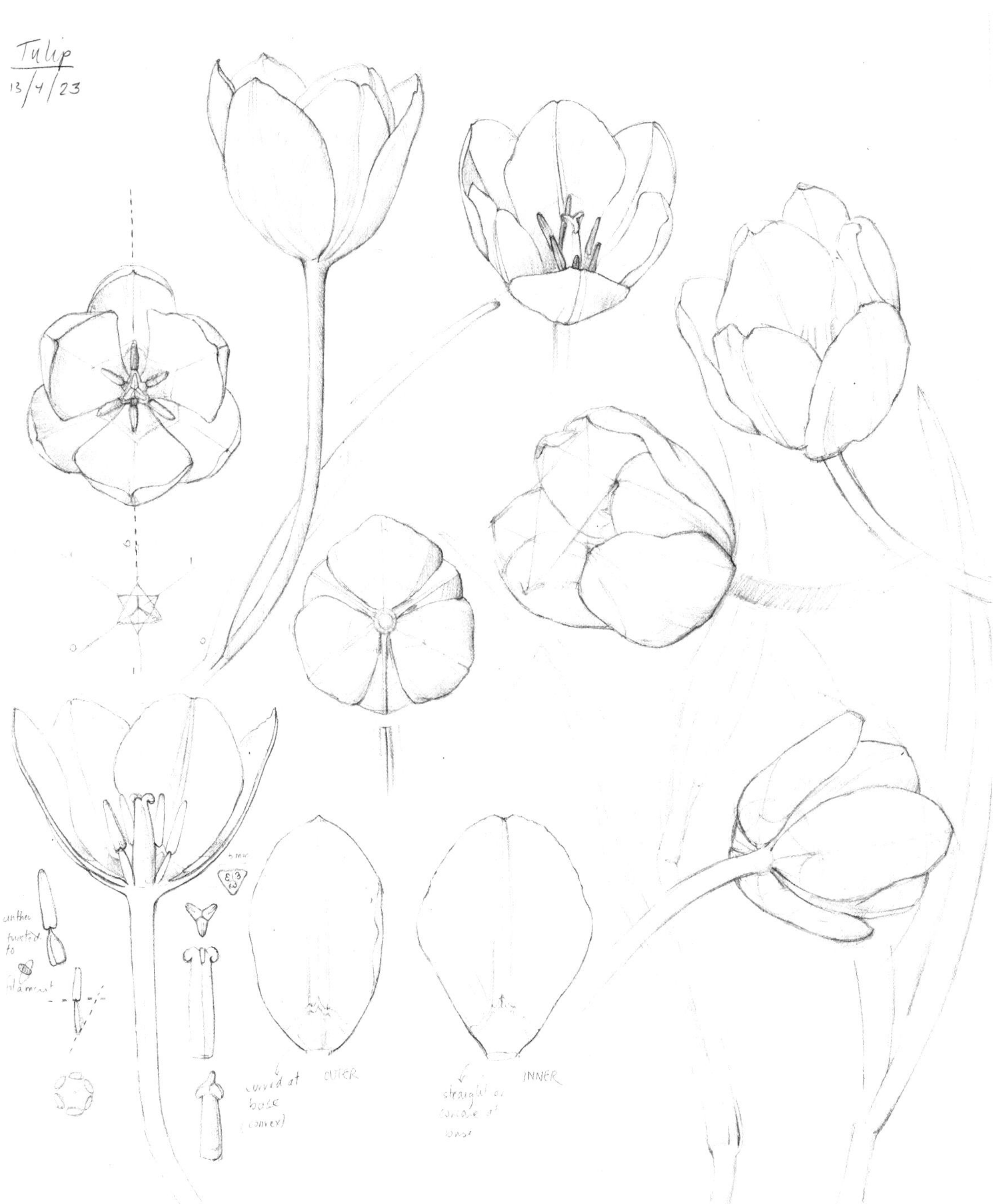

Sketchbook studies of a tulip, drawn from life. My drawings move from the right of the page to the left, becoming more specific and detailed as my observations become increasingly focused. Drawing the flower from different viewpoints helps me to understand how it is put together. For the final drawings on the page, I took it apart to look at the parts inside.

Breaking Down the Drawing Process

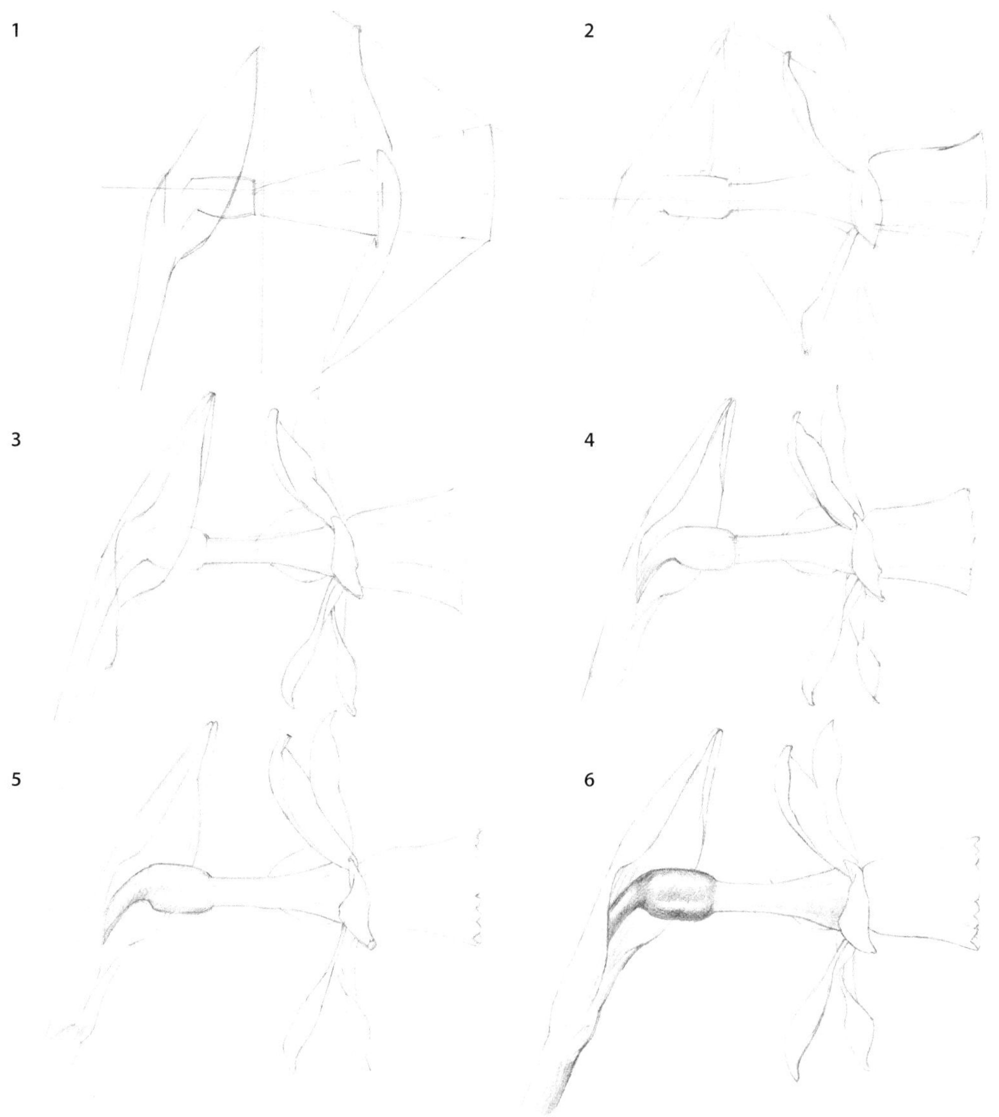

Flowers can be broken down into simpler geometric forms, both two-dimensionally and three-dimensionally. This *Narcissus* 'Tete-à-Tete' flower was positioned in a simple lateral view and captured in a sequence of steps.

1: Measure the height and width of the flower.

2: Start sketching in the forms of the flower, measuring the distances between tepals, corona, ovary and spathe to help place them and accurately record the relevant proportions.

3: Refine forms and begin to remove measuring lines.

4: Refine forms further, adding details such as the parallel lines in the spathe, and add tonal values to show volume.

5: The drawing is nearly complete, although the ovary is a strange shape.

6: The drawing is now complete, with the shape of the ovary adjusted, detail sharpened and more tonal values added.

Botanical Analysis

The botanical sketchbook will play a very important role in your personal investigation and understanding of flowers and their structures. My professional work as a botanical illustrator has trained me to see flowers from a very analytical viewpoint, and that is the way I enjoy drawing and painting them. A large part of plant identification relies on a close study of its flowers' characteristics – for example, a plant's flowers can reveal a lot about its pollination methods – and the process of drawing can help the botanist too to have a better understanding. Drawing, rather than simply looking, aids observation in a unique way, as it requires the artist to make decisions. They must commit to the shape of a petal's edge or be definitive about where exactly a stamen's filament becomes fused to a corolla lobe.

Botany has its own special language, which is translated into visual form by the botanical artist. There are many hundreds of botanical terms – and many excellent illustrated glossaries that are very helpful. In simple terms, you can start by counting a flower's parts, understanding what they are and what they are called, and communicate that understanding through your artwork. One way of getting to know a flower in detail is through dissection.

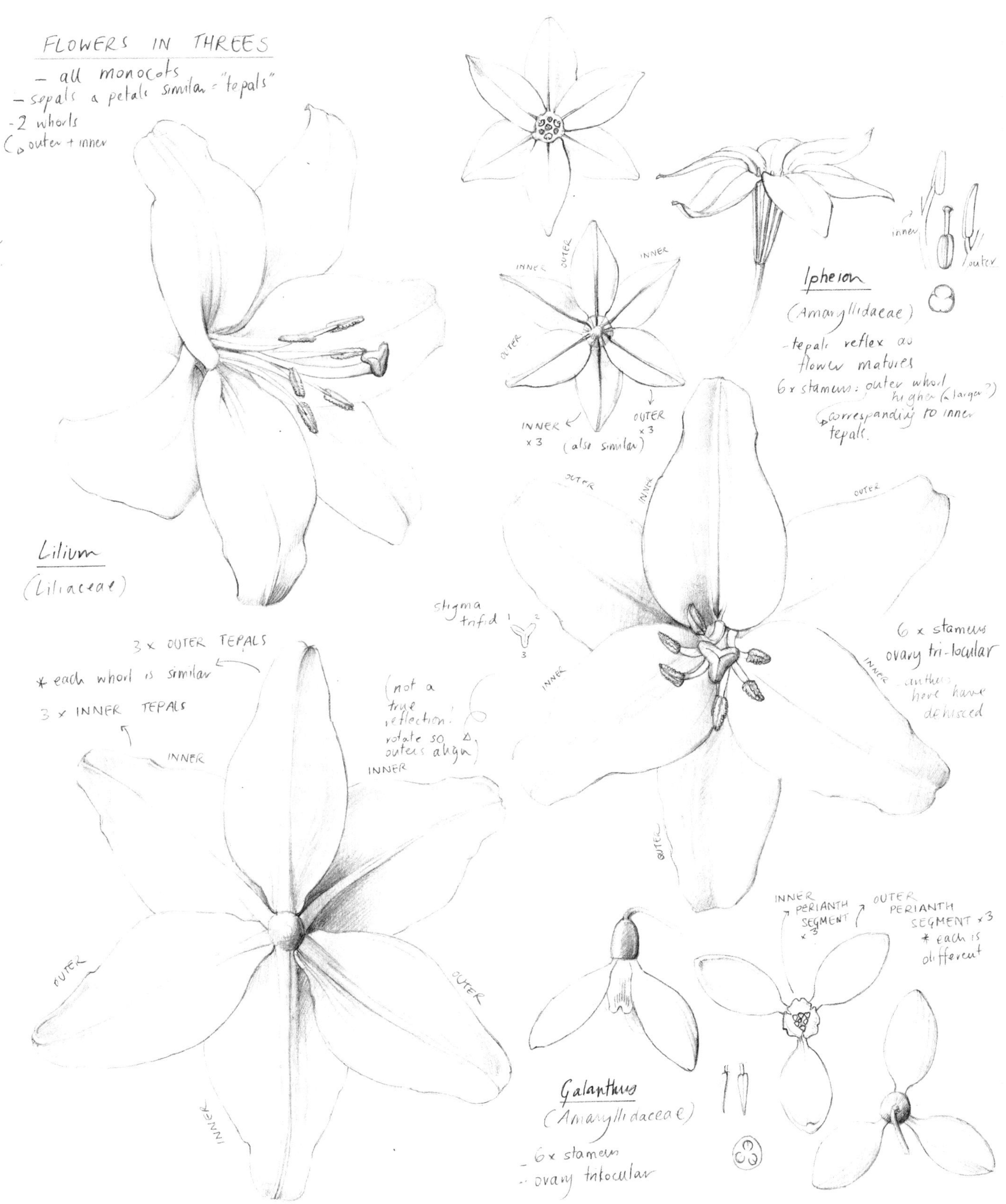

A sketchbook page showing examples of some monocot flowers. These share a common feature of flower parts in threes, which includes their tepals (sepals and petals, which look very similar to each other), their stamens, and ovary locules. Each flower also has tepals in two whorls (rings): an inner one and an outer one. Identifying numbers of flower parts is an easy starting point for a botanical artist to develop their knowledge of concepts in botany.

DRAWING FLOWER DISSECTIONS

Dissection is the science of taking a subject apart in order to understand it. Botanical artists and illustrators may draw flower dissections either to get to know a flower for their own benefit, or because they need to illustrate it for specific projects.

Whatever the reason for including flower dissections, there are conventions that the artist should understand. The most common form of flower dissection is a longitudinal section, also known as a 'half flower'. This is a very specific way of cutting a flower in half, which shows exactly how it and all its parts are put together. Ideally, you should have plenty of flowers to hand when cutting sections. It is almost impossible to cut a perfect half flower, so you may need to cut more than one. Each half will contain exactly half the number of parts contained in the whole flower. Often, a flower section will be a composite diagrammatic drawing made from several cuts; provided each flower is from the same plant and at the same developmental stage.

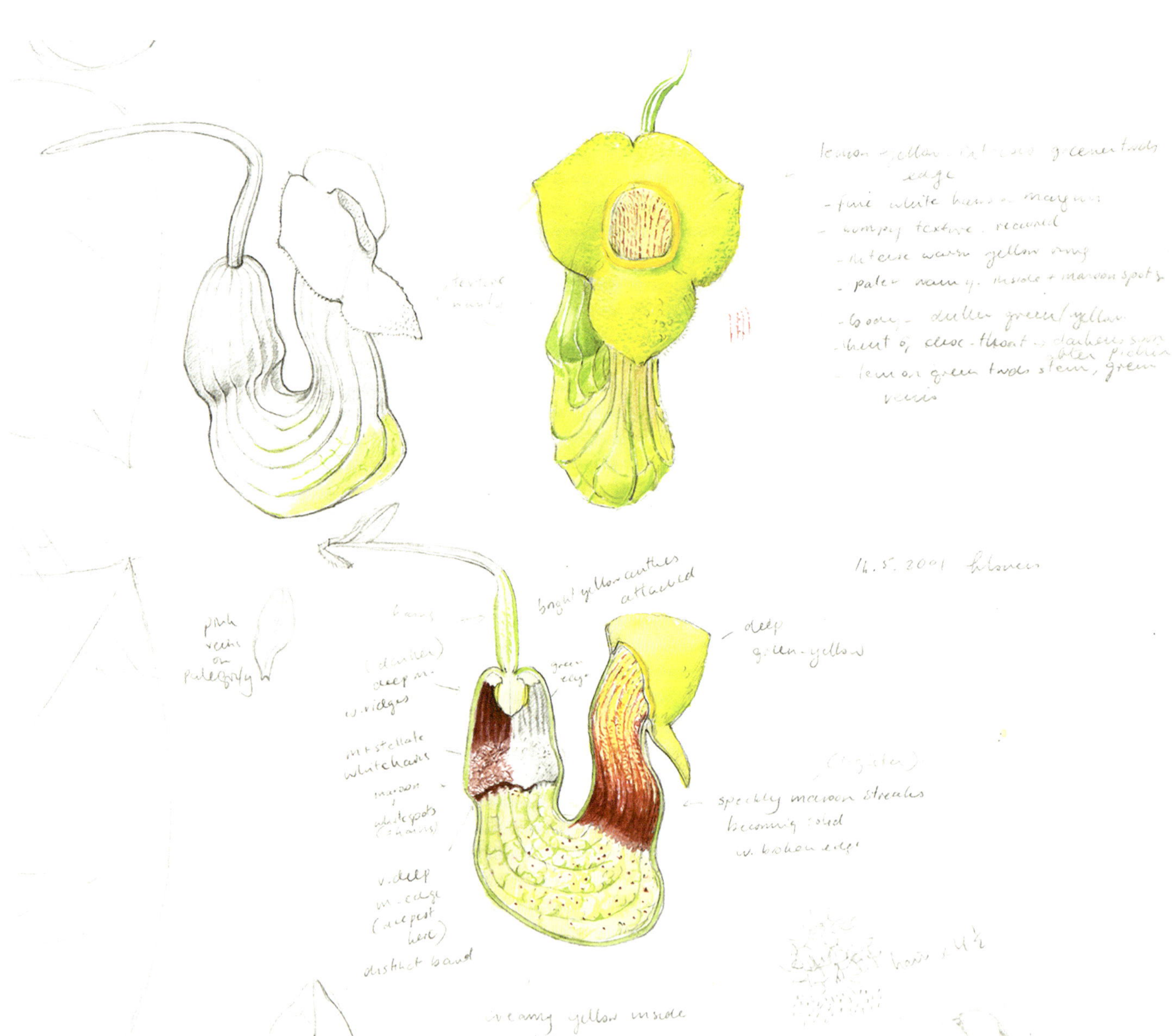

Even weird-looking flowers can be attractive! I loved cutting this *Isotrema manshuriensis* flower open. Looking at its insides, I began to understand how it attracts and traps insects to aid its pollination.

Cutting a Longitudinal Flower Section

Before dissecting a flower, you can get to know it by first drawing it whole in preparation for cutting. The best way to get started with an exploratory drawing of a flower is to draw it from several different angles: from the side (lateral); from the front (ventral); and from the back (dorsal).

1. Observe your flower and determine its axis of symmetry. An actinomorphic flower has more than one line of symmetry; a zygomorphic flower has only one.
2. Prepare by drawing the flower from different angles, marking out the line of symmetry on at least one. Sketch out a floral diagram, noting how many parts there are in the flower, and any they will be arranged in the half flower.
3. Prepare a receptacle for your flower, such as a petri dish lined with wet paper towel to keep the cut parts fresh.
4. Using a scalpel with a fresh blade, carefully make the cut, moving through all parts of the flower. This may take more than one cut so pause and change the angle if necessary.
5. Separate the two halves.

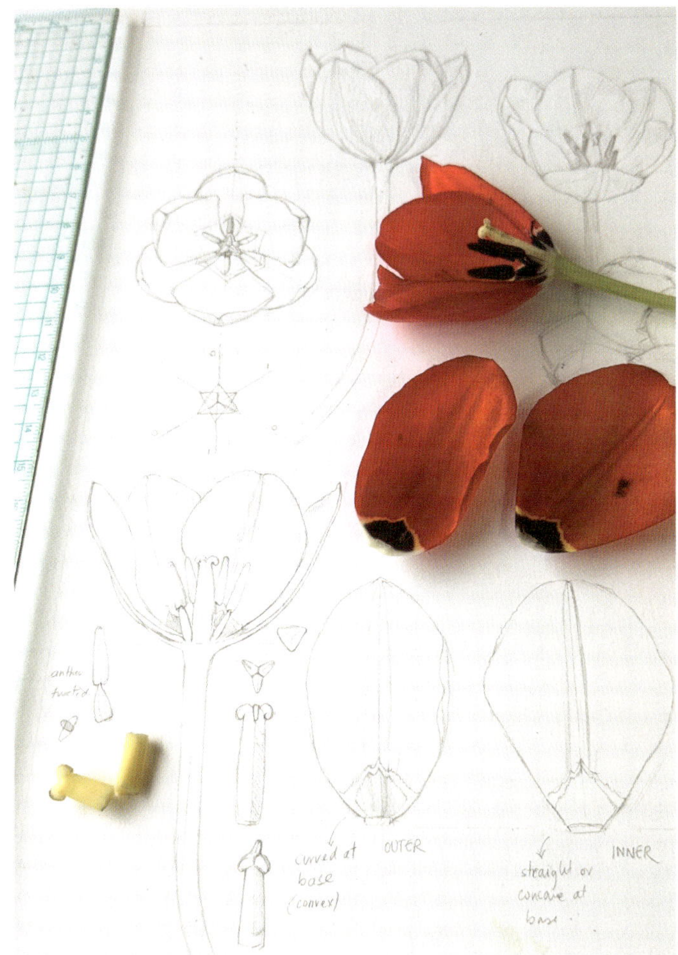

Before carrying out any dissection, get to know the flower well when it is intact by drawing it from different angles. This will also help you to understand where to make the cuts.

Cutting a longitudinal section of the jade vine flower

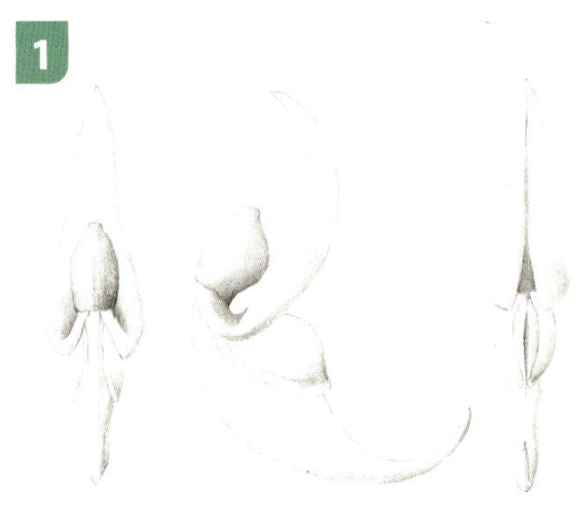

Before cutting and drawing a longitudinal section of this jade vine flower, I first drew it from three standard views: dorsal, lateral and ventral. Drawings such as these will help to clarify the position of a flower's axis of symmetry, preparing the artist for making the cut.

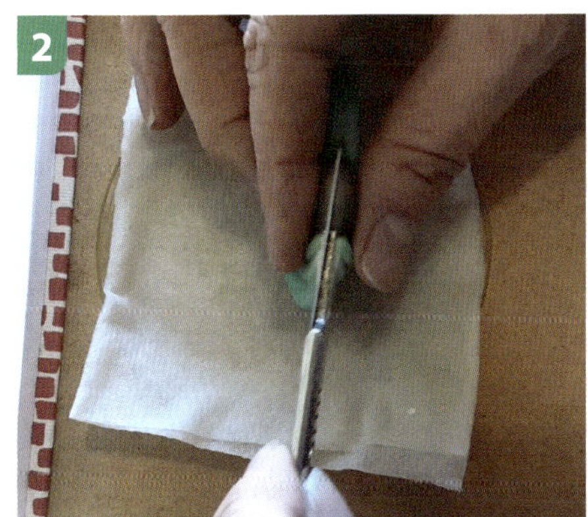

Cutting the jade vine flower along its axis of symmetry using a sharp new scalpel blade. On this flower it is most easily observed and cut from behind. The rest of the cut was made with the flower lying on its side.

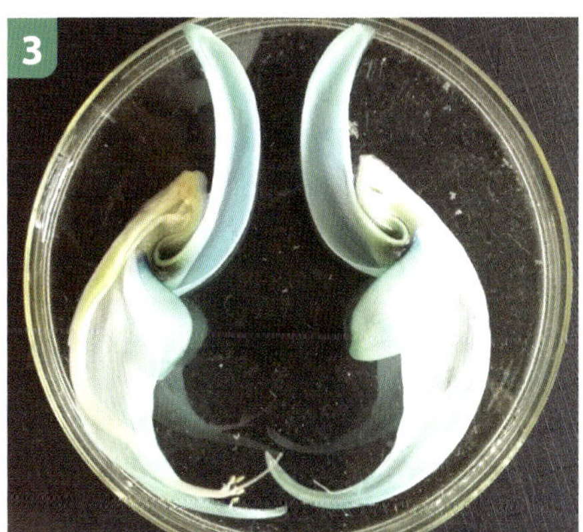

The two halves of the longitudinally dissected jade vine flower in a petri dish.

Drawing a Longitudinal Flower Section

1. Measure the parts of the flower dissection with a ruler or dividers, focusing on the flat cut surface.
2. Transfer the measurements to your paper and draw, enlarging if necessary.
3. Clarify any parts of the cut flower that are broken. You are drawing a perfect example of your cut flower so may need to move parts from one of the cut halves to the other (it is rare to have a perfect cut each time).

4. If you have cut through thin tissue such as a petal, demonstrate that this cut surface has a thickness by drawing it with a double line. Uncut edges have a single line as usual.
5. Leave cut surfaces clear of shading, but lightly shade parts moving away from the cut surface.

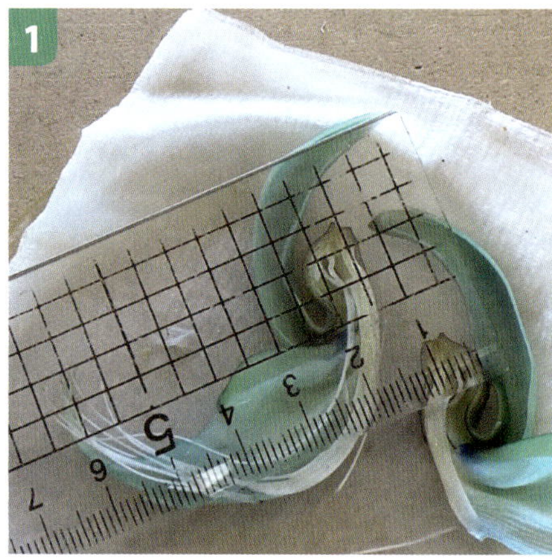

Measuring the parts of the longitudinal flower section using a clear ruler.

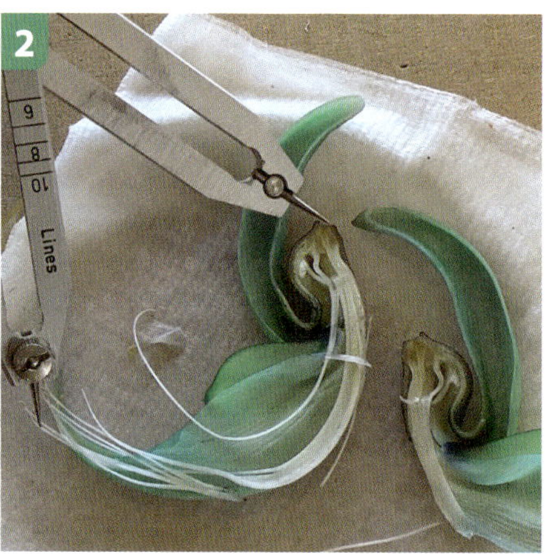

Measuring the part of the longitudinal flower section using proportional dividers. Using dividers is the easiest way to enlarge a drawing directly from the specimen.

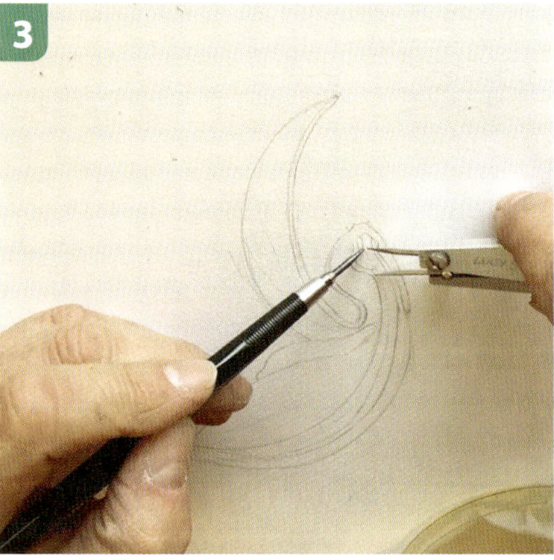

Transferring measurements from the specimen to the drawing using proportional dividers.

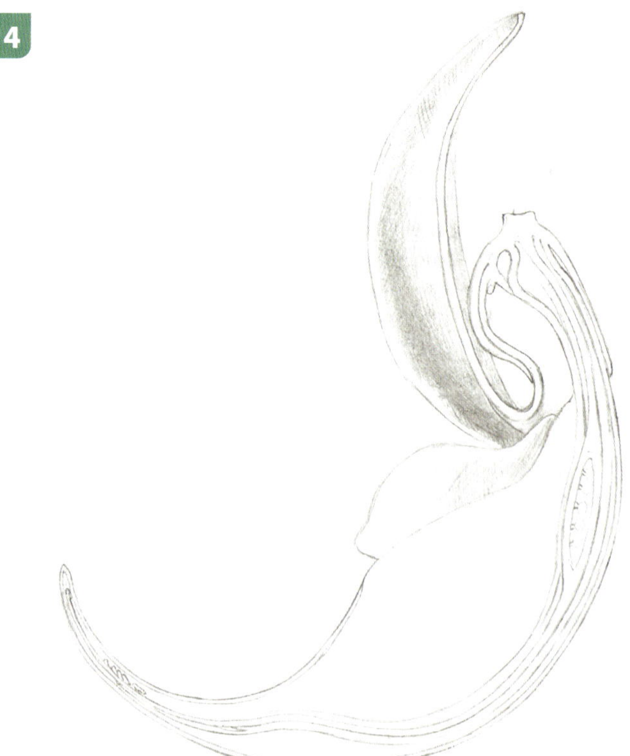

The finished longitudinal section drawing of the jade vine flower. Note that the stamens are drawn in place as they would normally be before being disturbed by cutting. Pollen from these stamens is extruded through the tip of the flower when it is squeezed by the visiting bats that pollinate the flower in the wild.

CAPTURING FLOWER COLOUR

The subject of colour can be a daunting one for botanical artists who are just starting out. However, it is simply a matter of learning to see and analyse colour in flowers and determining through experience and experimentation which of your watercolour pigments to use and how. Every time you paint a new subject you need to think through this process.

Experimenting with Colour in the Sketchbook

I like to investigate flower colour in my sketchbooks before tackling finished pieces. One of my favourite ways to do this is to devote a page in my small watercolour sketchbook to the flower that I am working on. There is no pressure to draw the flower or get its colour right the first time. Instead, the page reflects a process of experimentation, trying various colours and their mixes laid on paper alongside the subject.

I also like to apply colour directly to my sketchbook drawings of flowers. Sometimes I record the colours formally on these pages, but at other times they are noted informally with just a quick squiggle of paint. When trying out different colours and mixes, remember to record what worked best so that you can replicate it at a later stage. After a lot of practice, you will find the process becoming easier, quicker, and more enjoyable.

Observing Colour

The ideal situation for observing colour is in natural light and from life. Be aware that artificial light creates colour biases. Daylight bulbs are useful in reducing this bias to a degree. Cameras will struggle to capture some colours accurately, and computer screens and printed material will also interpret the same colour in different ways. It is possible to adjust your photographic images against your live specimen to make them more accurate.

Adding Colour to Pencil Work

In a finished piece of work, I will completely erase all the pencil under-drawing before replacing it with watercolour. In my sketchbook, however, I may erase it completely, partially, or not at all! There are no rules. Watercolour in my sketchbook may be laid on to the drawing either as a loose or tight wash, or with a dry brush. The type of application depends on what I am colouring. In a flower dissection, for example, I may wish to keep some of the sharp pencil lines so that the delineation of flower parts is not obscured.

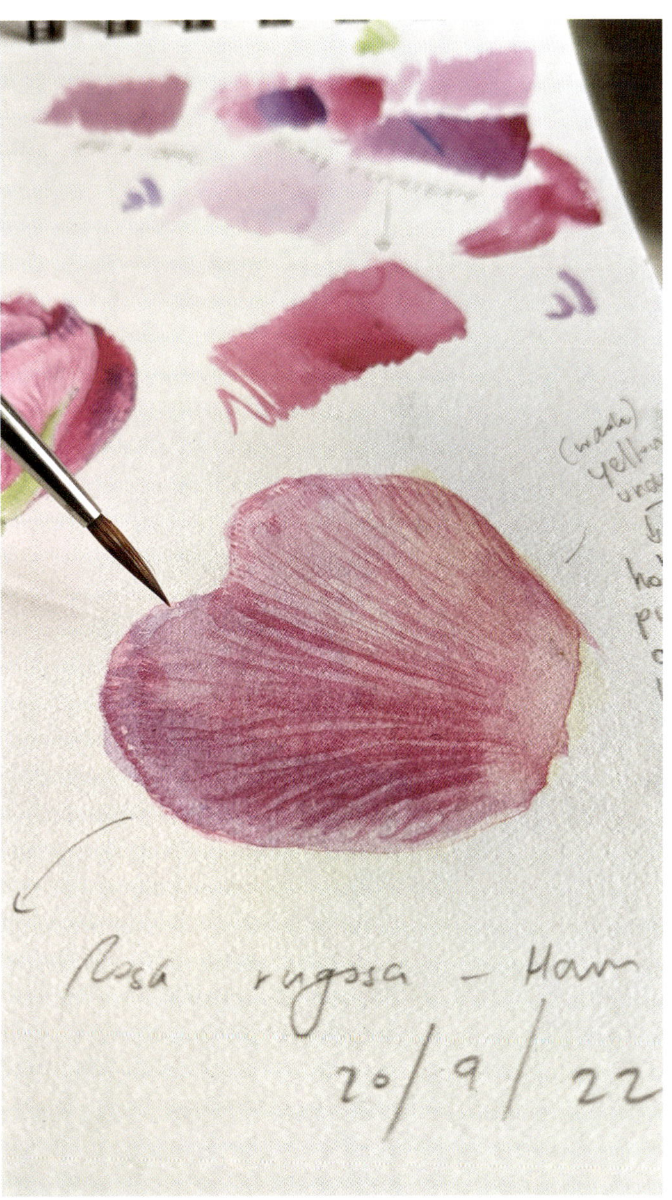

Experimenting with the colour of a *Rosa rugosa* petal. One of the challenges was making the pink vibrant and warm in some parts, and cooler in others. I tried placing a warm yellow wash at the base of the petal where the pink was warmer (more yellow), and a pale blue wash at the edge of the petal where it was cooler (more blue).

Working from the Potted Plant

This cultivated variety of the foxglove *Digitalis purpurea* was growing beautifully in a pot that I was able to bring into the studio for drawing. It possessed several attractive inflorescences, so it was perfect for drawing the plant's flowers. In the wild species *Digitalis purpurea*, the flowers, although arranged spirally along the inflorescence, hang more to one side. In this cultivated variety, the flowers were arranged more evenly along the inflorescence.

An inflorescence is a structure on which flowers are borne. The *Digitalis* inflorescence provided a great drawing opportunity, allowing the capture of many flowers arranged along the inflorescence, all held at different angles and at different stages of opening.

On the first day I drew the *Digitalis* inflorescence, it had a slight double bend at its tip. The following day, I noticed that the inflorescence had straightened and several of the flowers were more opened, so I drew it again. I preferred the second drawing and did not want to put anything else on the page, so I went back to the first drawing to add detail to the flowers.

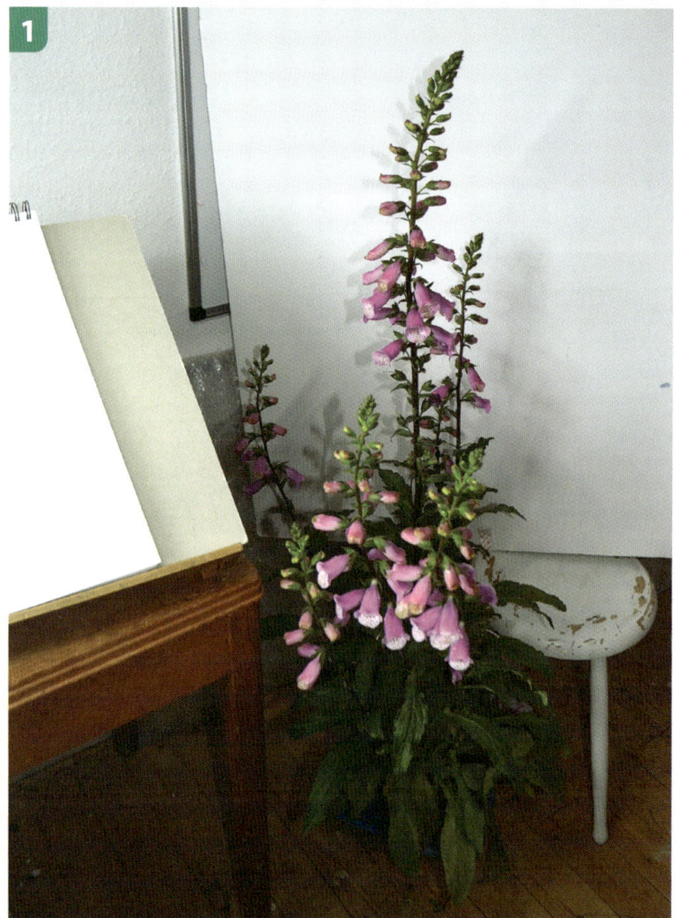

My drawing set-up for the *Digitalis purpurea*. When placed on the floor, this potted plant's inflorescence was at just the right eye height for me to draw, with my drawing chair at its lowest setting.

Two drawings of the *Digitalis* inflorescence, made a day apart. On the second day the inflorescence had straightened up, and some of the flowers had opened further. I wanted to draw it in its new position, partly because I preferred it but also because I felt I could draw it better a second time.

Individual Flowers

Next it was time to remove some flowers from the inflorescence and look at them more closely, drawing them from different angles before cutting and drawing a longitudinal section. I selected a couple of flowers, both of which appeared to be the most open. After drawing the first flower, I cut the longitudinal section following the usual steps (*see* above). I discovered that this flower's anthers had already opened, so it was not possible to draw them accurately. In flower dissection, it is conventional to draw anthers before dehiscence (the botanical term for opening), so that the important characteristics of their shape, size and structure can be viewed.

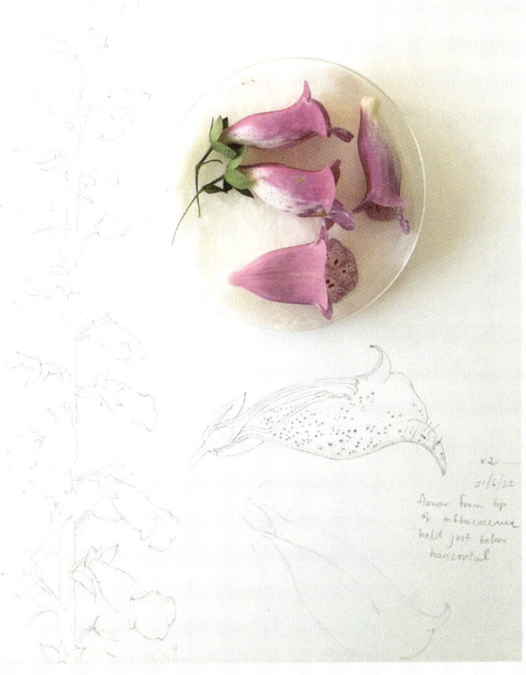

A selection of flowers removed from the *Digitalis* inflorescence and placed in a petri dish, ready to draw alongside the inflorescence drawing.

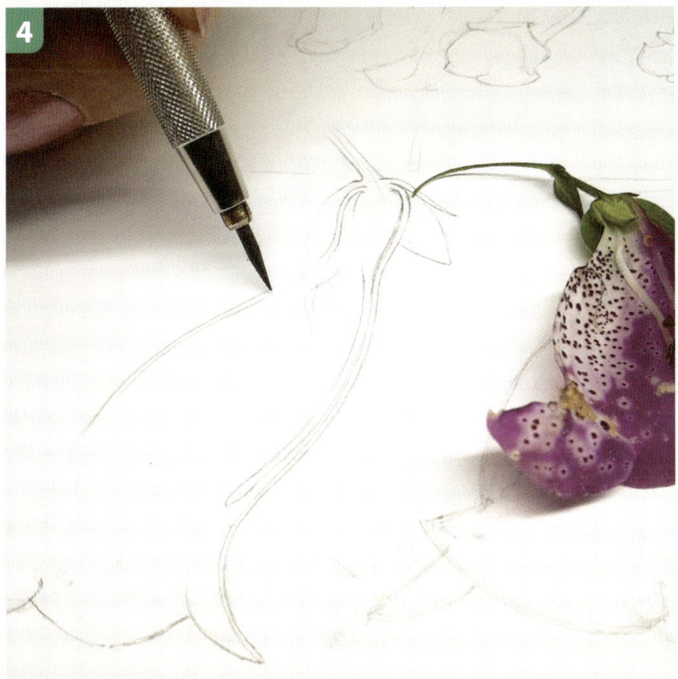

Drawing a half flower of *Digitalis* at a magnification of ×2. Care is taken to draw a double line to show that the cut surface of the corolla (the joined petals) has a thickness.

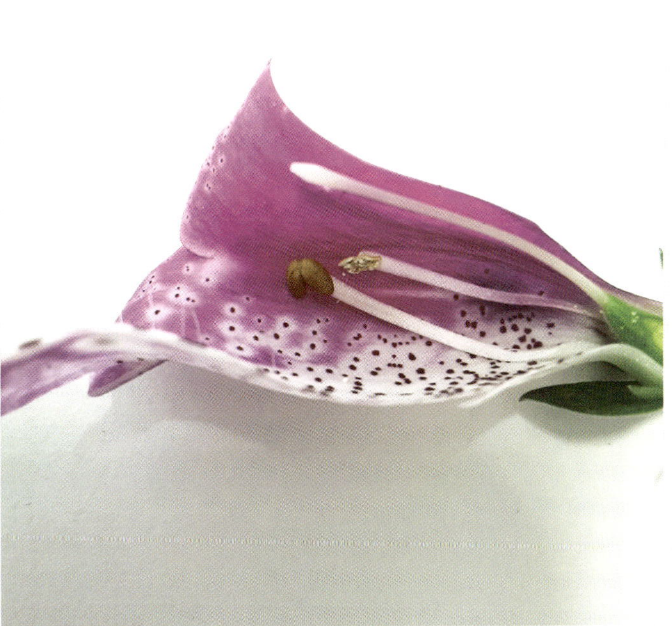

A *Digitalis* half flower with one anther dehisced, the other still intact. Note that the flower's style has not yet opened, as this species' flowers are protandrous. This means that they release their own pollen before becoming ready to receive pollen from another plant.

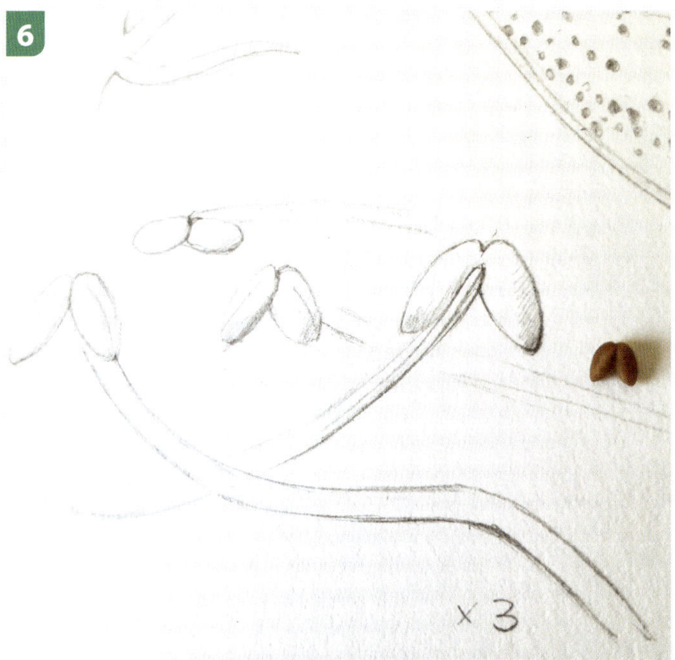
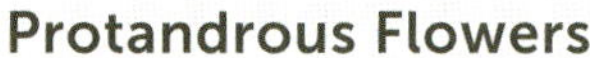

Drawing the anthers of the *Digitalis* flower at a magnification of ×3. The anthers in the first dissected flower had already opened. Dehiscence deforms their shape, so it is important to find some that are intact; these are more informative.

Protandrous Flowers

The second flower I chose to dissect was one whose anthers had not yet opened. I took the opportunity to enlarge them alongside the flower drawings, showing clearly where and how the filament was attached to the anther as well as the anther's shape. Observation of flower maturity is very important when drawing a flower dissection. *Digitalis* flowers are protandrous. This means that the male parts of the flower (anthers) develop before the female parts (style and stigma), in a strategy that limits self-pollination. You can observe that in the flower whose anthers have opened, thus finishing the male stage, the style is now fully developed as it has split into two, exposing its surface ready to receive pollen. This contrasts with the flower with intact anthers; its style is still intact. If this flower were to be drawn with, for example, closed anthers and an open style, it would be clear that it had not been observed properly, and that the artist did not have the correct botanical understanding.

Adding Watercolour

Finally, it was time to observe and add colour to both the inflorescence and the flowers. When adding colour to the drawings I used a combination of wet-in-wet washes for the larger areas, and dry brushes to paint in the dark purple spots.

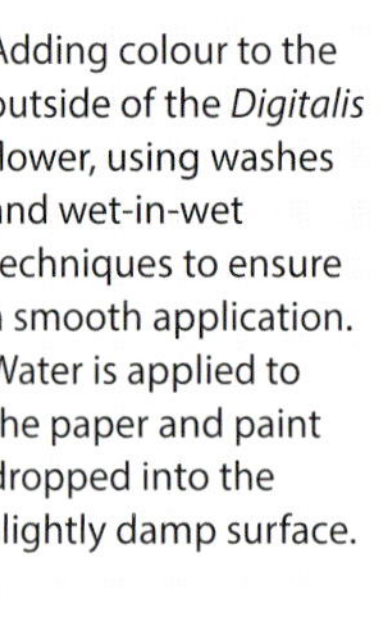

Adding colour to the outside of the *Digitalis* flower, using washes and wet-in-wet techniques to ensure a smooth application. Water is applied to the paper and paint dropped into the slightly damp surface.

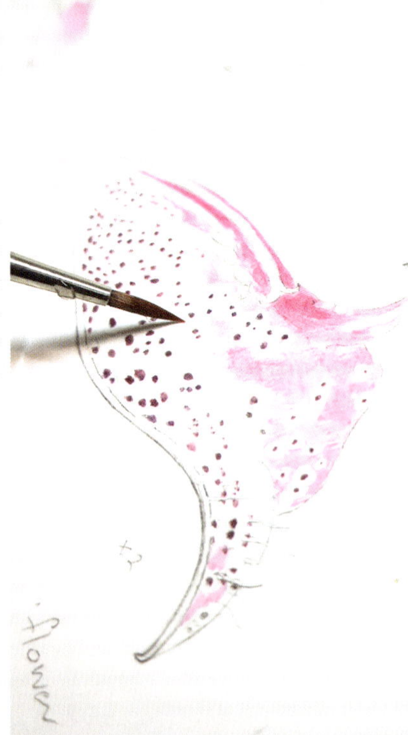

Adding colour to the half flower of *Digitalis*, using a very small brush to paint around the stamens and style, and carefully painting around the white patches, which have fuzzy edges. I was careful to keep the cut surfaces free of paint to show that they are a featureless, diagrammatic detail.

The dark spots were surrounded by white areas, with edges that were not sharp, but slightly fuzzy. These parts needed to be painted carefully with a dry brush, working around the white areas. Using the white of the paper in this way is best practice for watercolour painting. It was also important to keep the cut surfaces of the half flower unpainted, to emphasise that they represent a cut surface rather than tissue with form.

The finished sketchbook page of *Digitalis* is a good investigation of a foxglove inflorescence and the details of its flowers. There is still space on this page, which means that, while I am happy to leave it free, I will be able to add even more detail at a later date.

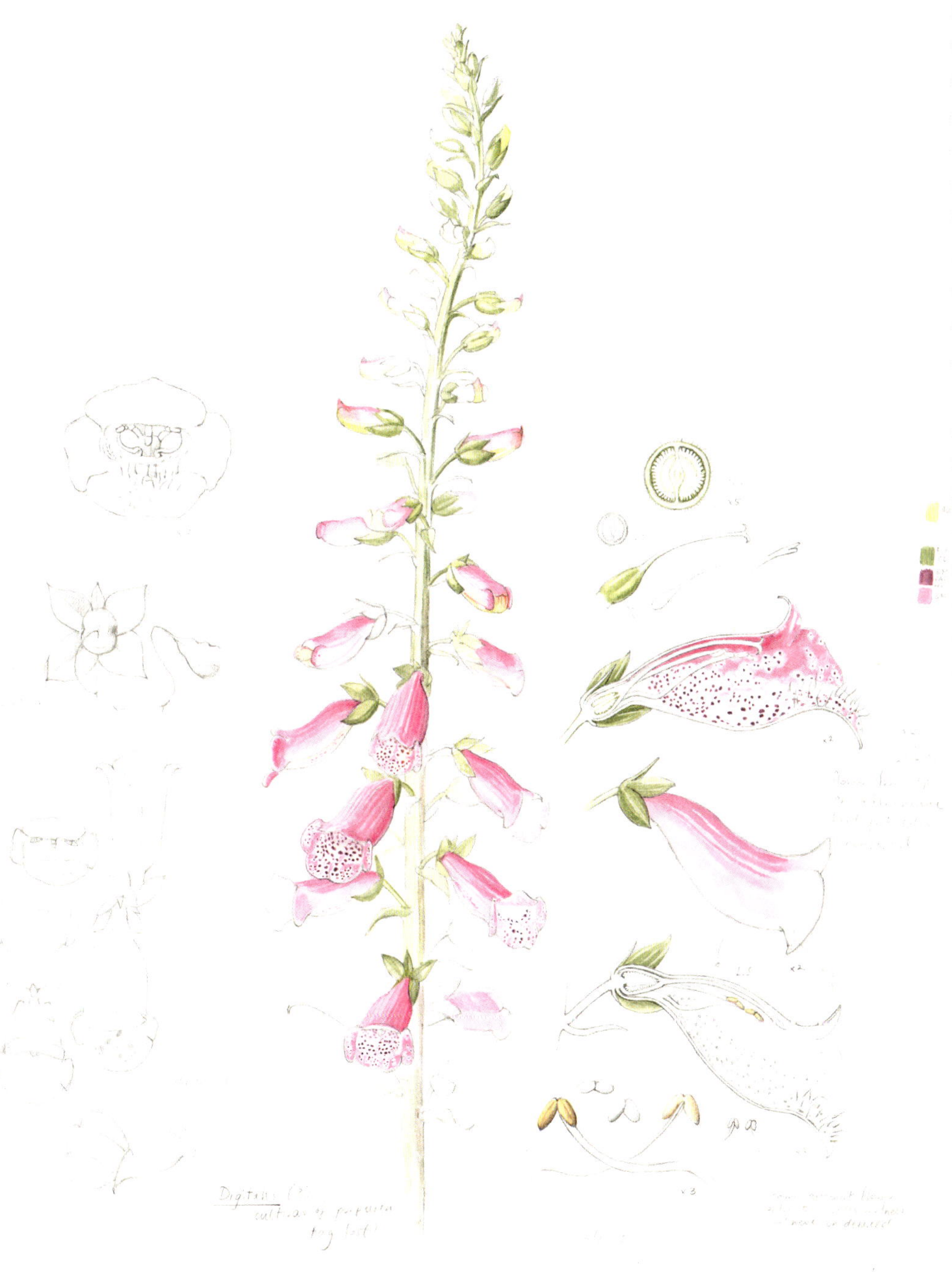

The finished study of the *Digitalis* inflorescence and flower details made in the A3 watercolour sketchbook, in pencil with watercolour added to some parts of the drawing.

Exploring Inflorescences

Having drawn and dissected a single flower of the jade vine, I wanted to explore the flowers further, focusing on their development. Just one inflorescence shows all its stages. The flowers develop from bud to maturity from the part of the inflorescence closest to the plant's stem, with the least mature flowers at its tip. As the inflorescence is pendulous, this is the part hanging closest to the ground when viewed on the vine.

I was particularly interested in investigating and drawing the way in which the size and shape of a jade vine flower changes as it grows from bud to mature flower. As I was drawing it, I also started thinking about how the position of the flower changes in relation to the inflorescence axis as it develops. Finally, I wanted to try to capture the amazing colour of the flowers at all stages.

With permission from the plant's curators at London's Kew Gardens, I selected a series of flowers from one inflorescence, choosing each flower at a stage when it looked noticeably different in shape and size from the last, until I had a good range from bud to open flower. As I had to take the flowers off to draw them, I very carefully observed the angle at which they were held to the stem and placed them in a prepared container at the same angle.

One at a time, I took each flower and placed it on the sketchbook page at the correct angle. I started the flower drawings on the top left-hand corner of a double-page spread of my sewn-bound sketchbook. I had planned to carry on across the double-page spread. However, as I laid each flower down with the pedicel (stem) bases aligned, an unexpected but beautiful curve started to appear naturally. I decided to follow the curve that the flowers were giving me.

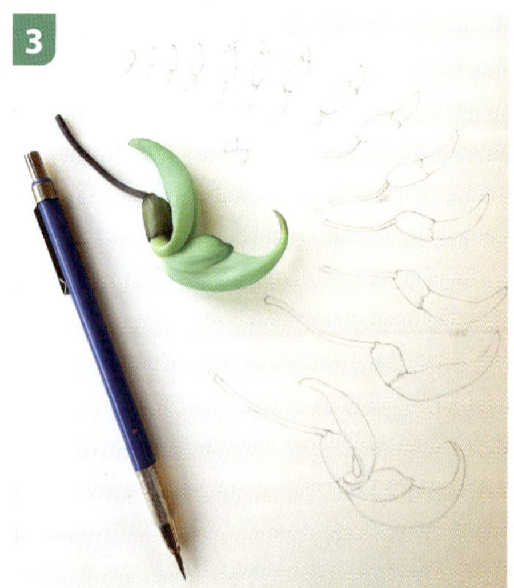

The jade vine flowers at fourteen stages of development were placed carefully on damp paper towel in a plastic container. I wanted to capture the exact angle at which each flower was growing in relation to the axis of the inflorescence. They were photographed with a ruler for scale reference, then lifted out carefully on the container's lid, ready to be sketched from life.

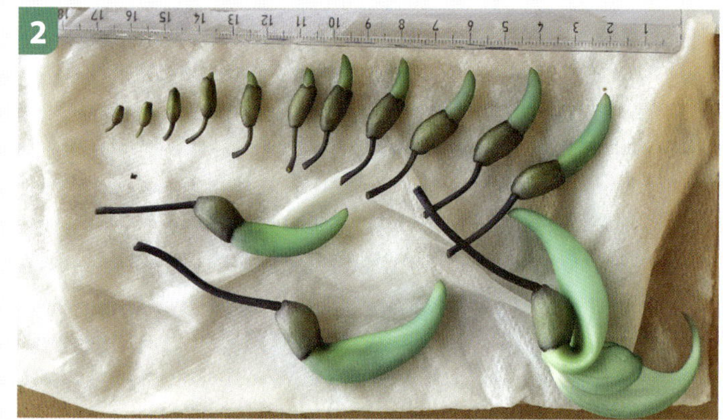

The jade vine *Strongylodon macrobotrys*, a member of the bean family *Leguminaceae* from the Philippines, produces stunning blue-green flowers borne on hanging inflorescences. The flowers make a fascinating subject of study, both for their unusual form and incredible colour.

Getting ready to draw the open jade vine flower, the final specimen in the sequence of developing flowers. A beautiful curve accidentally emerged as I was drawing the various stages.

Dissections Showing Flower Development

For the second part of this study, I wanted to dissect the flowers at different stages, to see how the internal parts were developing. I made dissections of four of the stages and, using a microscope, drew them at the same enlarged scale. I had to reduce that scale to fit the more mature flower on the same page as it was so much bigger than the smaller ones. This is part of the study that I would like to pursue further.

Capturing Colour

Now I wanted to add colour to the page. The unique and rather elusive colour of the jade vine flower is difficult to capture on screen or paper. Once I had drawn the stages of flower development, I prepared to return to the plant with my watercolour pigments and my small colour sketchbook in hand. I chose what I thought might be the right pigments, picked an open flower straight from the vine and attempted to match its colour as quickly as possible with my watercolours. I was surprised at how green the flower was; I had prepared many blues but not enough greens. My concept of the flower's colour had been influenced by the fact that I had usually looked at flowers that had already fallen off the vine. These were much more blue – indeed, I could see the picked flower turning bluer even as I painted it.

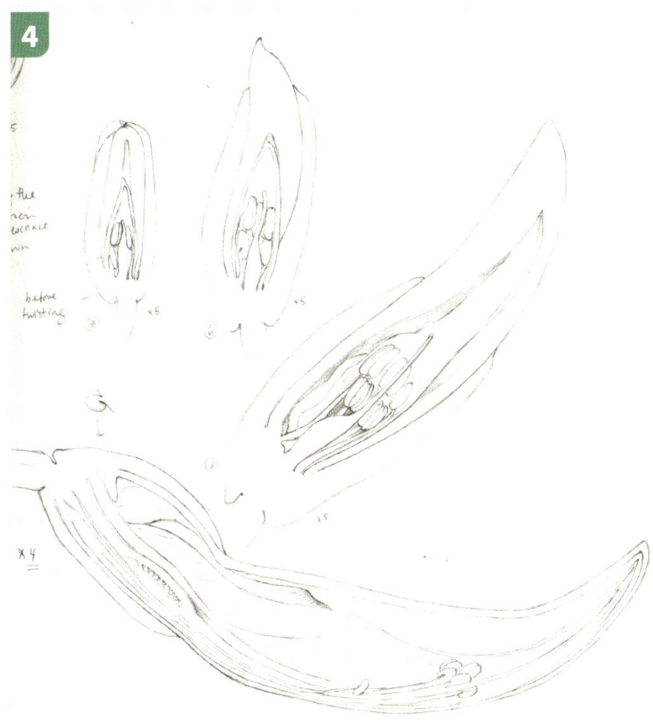

Longitudinal dissections of five stages of the jade vine flowers on the facing page (one not seen). The first four buds were easy to draw at the same scale, but a later-stage flower was so much bigger that I had to reduce the scale from ×5 to ×4. Continuing this study and drawing all the developmental stages at the same scale will require a very large sheet of paper.

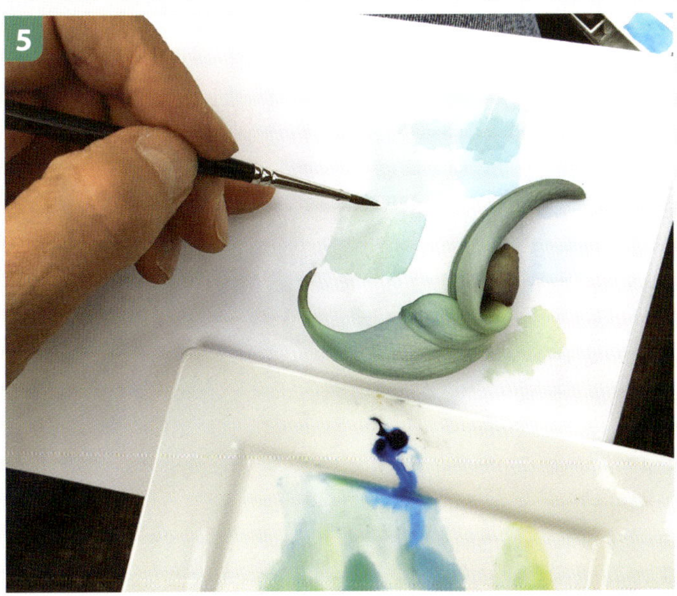

Jade vine colour study. In order to capture the colour as soon as possible once the flower was off the vine, I had my paints all ready to go. The colour was a lot greener than I had anticipated. I sat on the floor of the glasshouse and used a fresh ceramic palette, as I was concerned that my usual watercolour tin palette would muddy the brightness and freshness that I needed. I chose Winsor Blue (green shade) and Aureolin, as both are very bright, transparent colours, and used very dilute mixes to capture the bright intensity of the colours.

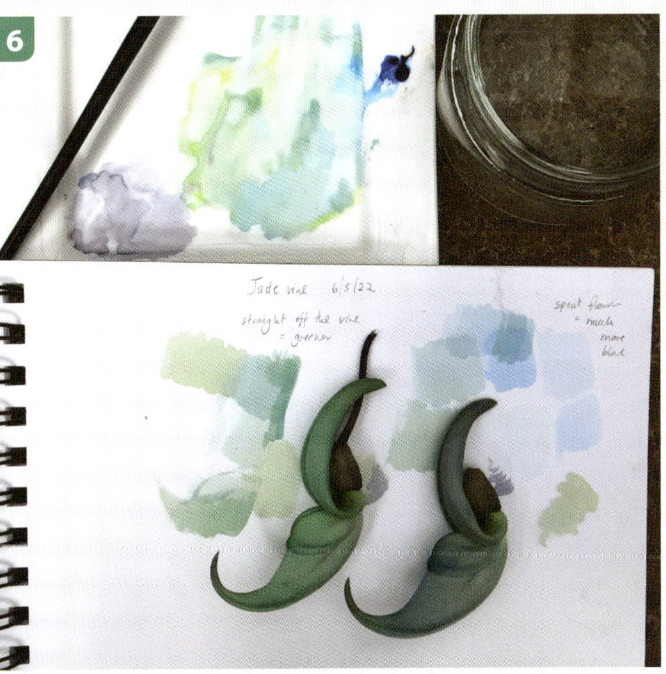

Recording the colour difference between a fresh and an old, fallen flower. The older flower is much bluer.

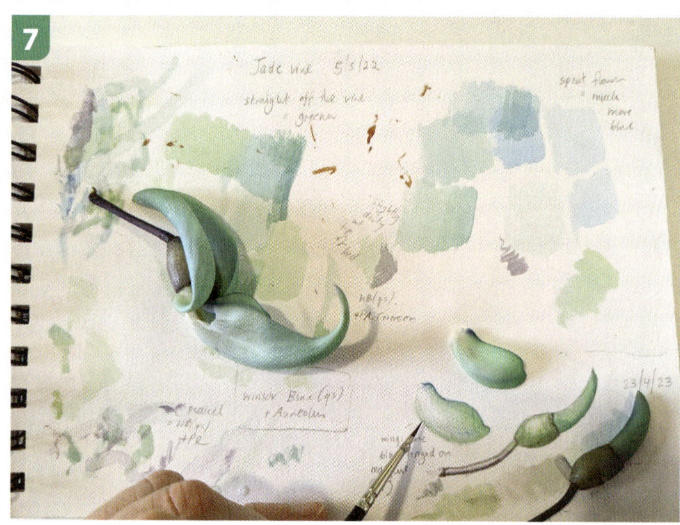

A year after the first colour study was made in my small watercolour sketchbook, I was able to add some more observations about the colour of the jade vine flowers.

Successive Growing Seasons

All that was left to do now was to add colour to the page showing the flower stages. Unfortunately, I only had time to colour two of the open flowers before the vine finished flowering. Thanks to my sketchbook notes, however, I knew the dates when I might be able to return for the following season's flowering. Revisiting the same plant with the previous year's drawings and finding matching flowers to paint was extremely satisfying.

Along with filling in the flower dissection gaps, the next parts of the jade vine plant I would like to draw include a whole inflorescence. I would like to start looking at the plant's leaves as well. I have already drawn the fruits throughout its developing stages; *see* Chapter 4.

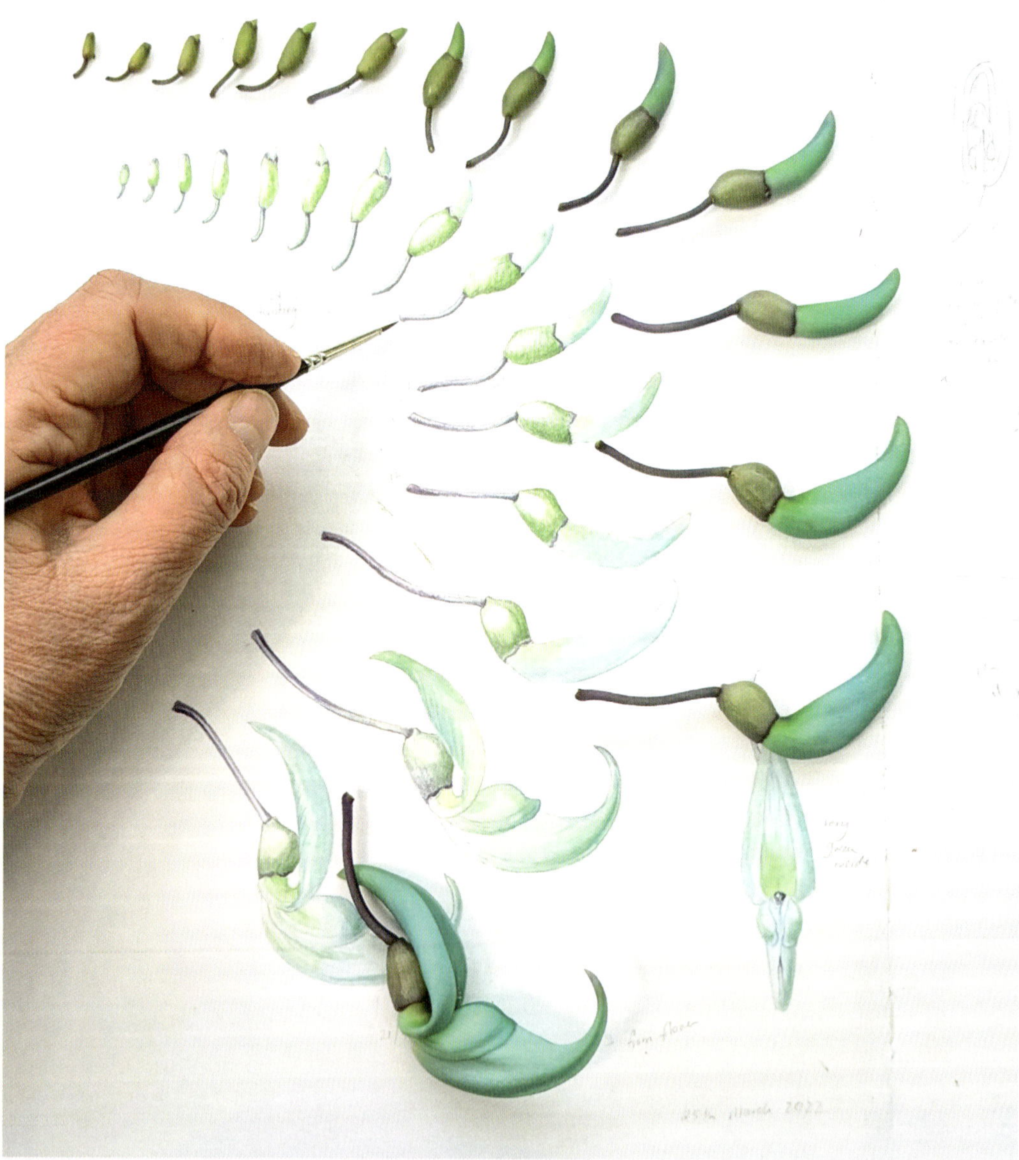

After waiting an entire year for new flowers to emerge, it was extremely satisfying to pick fresh flowers to match my drawing and complete the colour study. This should only ever be done from the same plant.

The Developmental Stages of a Daisy Capitulum

Having illustrated a few flowers from the daisy family before, I wanted to find out more about *Echinacea purpurea* as it is such an attractive and popular plant. In this study I wanted to understand how the shape of the whole capitulum (the flower head) changes as it matures. There are always flower heads at different stages to be found on a group of plants and it is fascinating how the flower heads with their pink petal-like ligules can be seen in such a variety of forms and colours as they develop.

Capitulum is the botanical term for a flower head in the daisy family. The tissue on which the disk florets sit is called the receptacle and on the outer edge of the receptacle are ray florets, which encircle the disk florets that cover the rest of the receptacle. The common name for *Echinacea purpurea* is cone flower, which derives from the conical shape of the receptacle as it develops.

Specimens at Different Growth Stages

By picking and drawing several flower heads, from very young to very mature stages, I was able to observe and illustrate all the stages of the capitulum at once. This plant conveniently flowers over a long period of time, so you can usually observe all the stages in the same clump of plants.

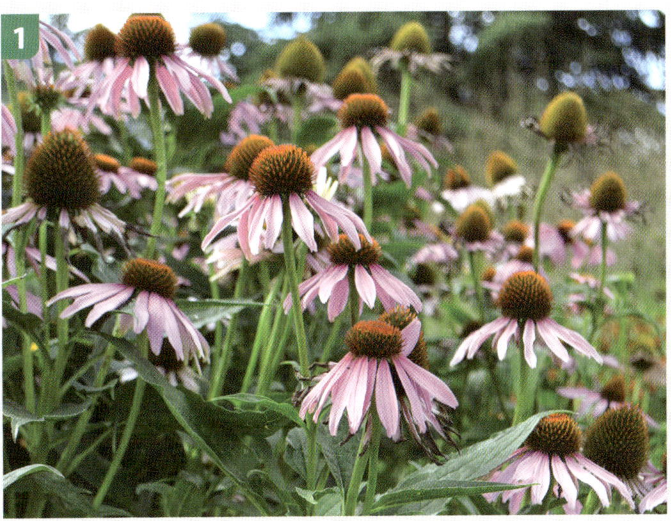

Flowering *Echinacea purpurea*. It is from the daisy family now known as *Asteraceae*, but formerly *Compositae*, alluding to the fact that its flowering bodies are in fact a composite inflorescence. Each of these flower heads contains hundreds of tiny florets. Those on the inside are called 'disk florets'. It is only those on the edge, called 'ray florets', that have petal-like structures, called 'ligules'.

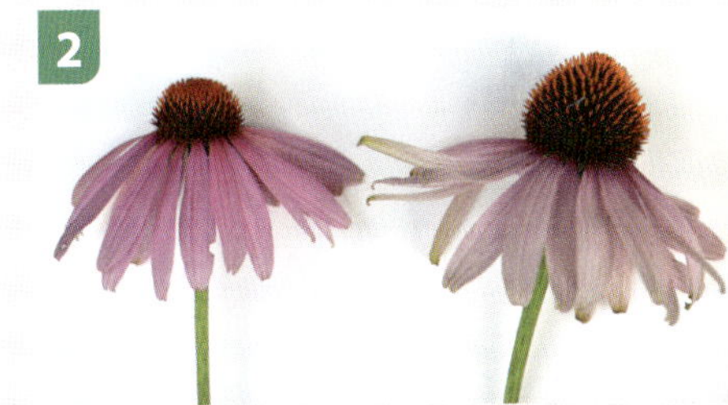

Two of the *Echinacea* flower heads, laid against my sketchbook page. The colour of the ligules is already fading as the flower head matures.

As always, I made colour studies from the specimens as soon as possible. As these would be very detailed drawings, I knew I may have to rely on some of my photographic reference by the time I came to painting them.

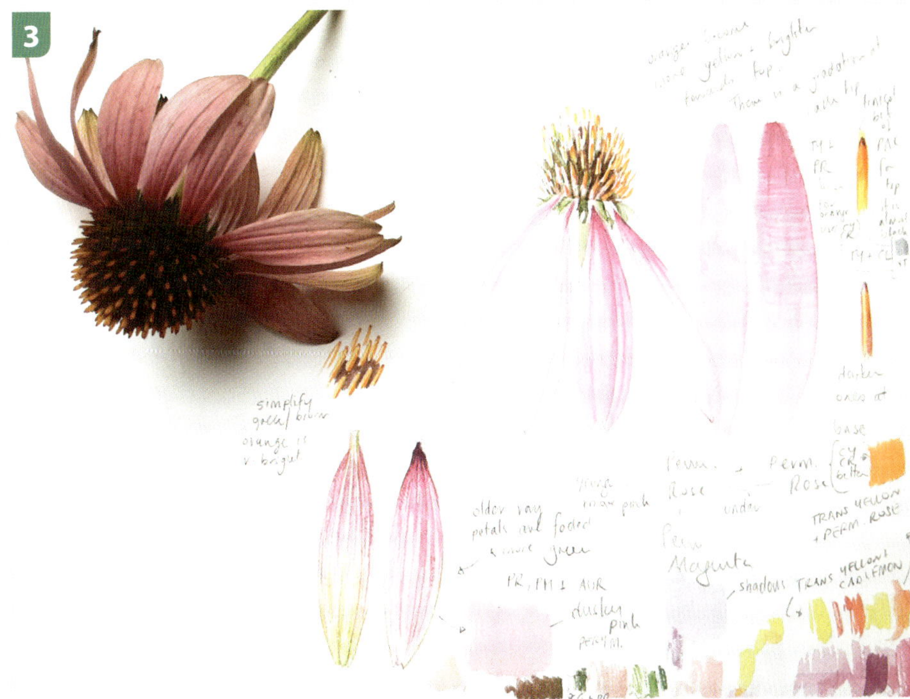

I originally hoped to draw six developmental stages of the capitulum across a double-page spread of my Venezia scrapbook, but unfortunately only had time to draw three: two flower heads at the stage when the petal-like ligules were still colourful, and a third head with faded ligules developing achenes. Achenes are the fruits of an *Asteraceae* flower and consist of one seed per disk floret. The ligules on the final head were shrivelled up and brown – a natural state, but exaggerated by very hot weather. I drew them all life-sized, or ×1.

I ruled a horizontal line across the page so that the heads could be lined up at the same level. For each flower head I also ruled a vertical line, so that the whole flower head and its section could also be lined up.

Adding Colour to Detailed Sections

One of the most obvious changes in the flower heads is the fading of the ligules as they mature. (These are the 'petals' of a daisy flower.) I wanted to capture the rich pink of the youngest heads and show how the colour starts to fade in the second stage. The other change in colour can be observed in the disk florets.

As well as changes in colour, I could see the receptacle growing upwards so that its cone shape became elongated and stronger. By looking very closely I could see the orange receptacular scales detaching from the disk florets and spreading out as the cone-shaped receptacle grew upwards and outwards. Adding colour to the tiny florets required my very small 00-sized brush. I painted very carefully in order to maintain the sharp pencil lines showing the difference between parts. On the bract of each orange receptacular scale there is a dark spot of red.

Next Steps

I really enjoyed drawing the shapes and colours of these *Echinacea purpurea* capitula, especially in longitudinal dissection. As with any flowering material that I dissect, it was fascinating to see the way in which flower parts are squeezed in, and how they form lines and patterns.

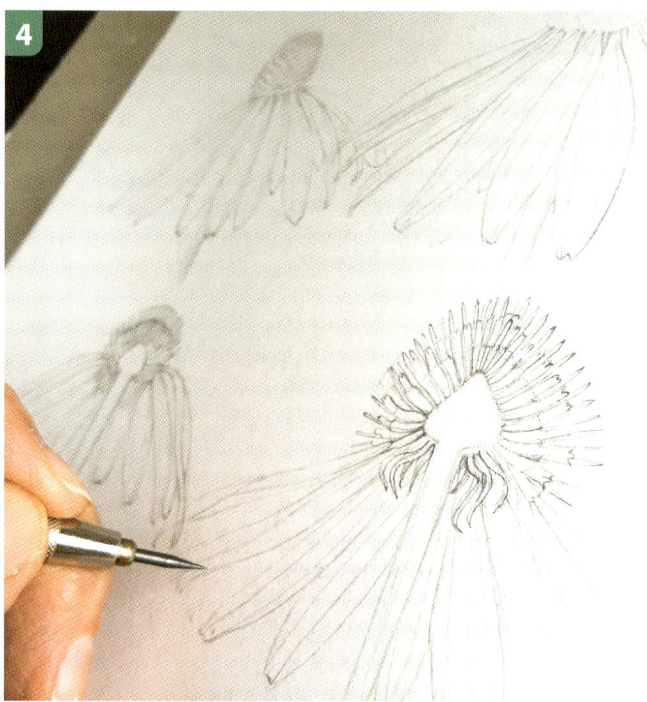

Stretching across a double-page spread of the Fabriano 'Venezia' sketchbook, I drew three of the developmental stages of the capitulum. Each flower head was drawn first whole then in longitudinal section and they were carefully lined up for better comparison of inside and outside.

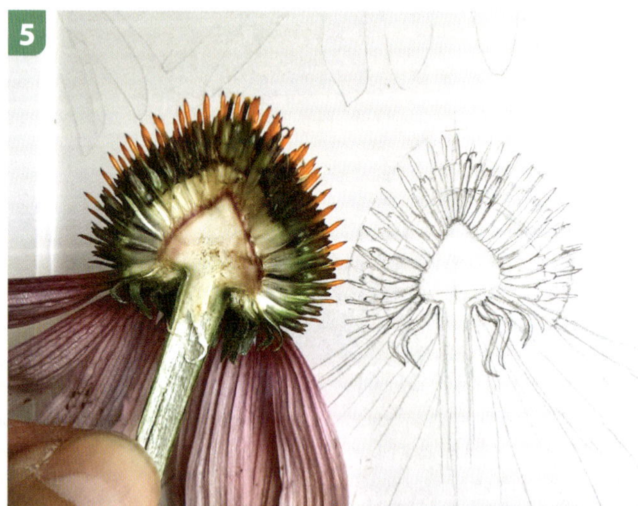

While drawing the longitudinal section of the capitula, I was checking the specimen the whole time to see how the florets were attached, and how the 'receptacular bracts,' or 'paleas', fitted in between the disk florets. These orange bracts give the *Echinacea* flower heads their distinctive spikiness.

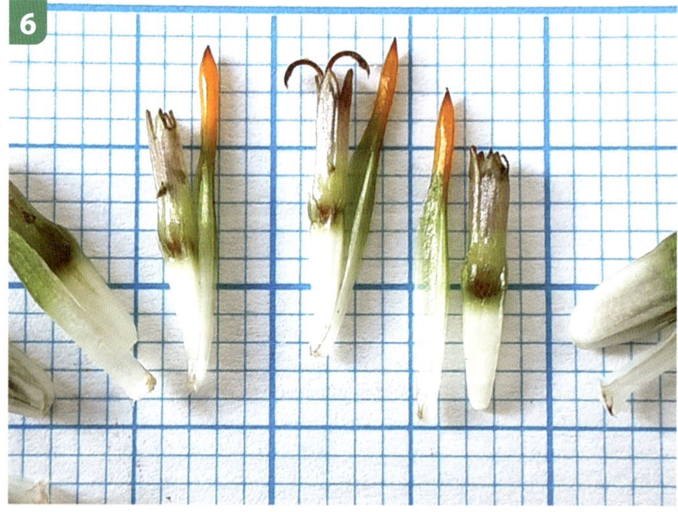

Photographing disk florets on 1mm graph paper allows the tiny flowers to be measured accurately and helps with seeing the detail in them.

Having originally hoped to draw at least six stages of the *Echinacea* capitulum's delopment but only drawn and coloured three, I would like to return to this study and fill in some of the gaps during a later growing season. I have learnt a great deal about these flower heads, especially in observing the spiky orange receptacular bracts, which I had always wanted to understand. The next step will be to do more focused studies of the ray and disk florets at a much higher magnification, so that I can dissect and draw the florets in more detail.

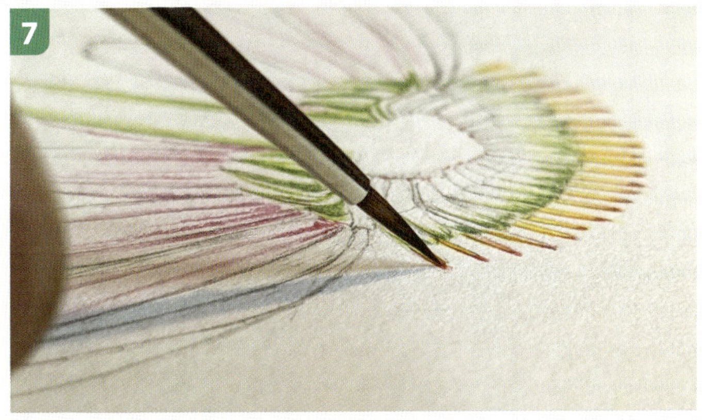

Using a very small 00 brush to paint the smallest details on the tiny ray florets. In hindsight, enlarging the drawings would have allowed me to show the detail more thoroughly.

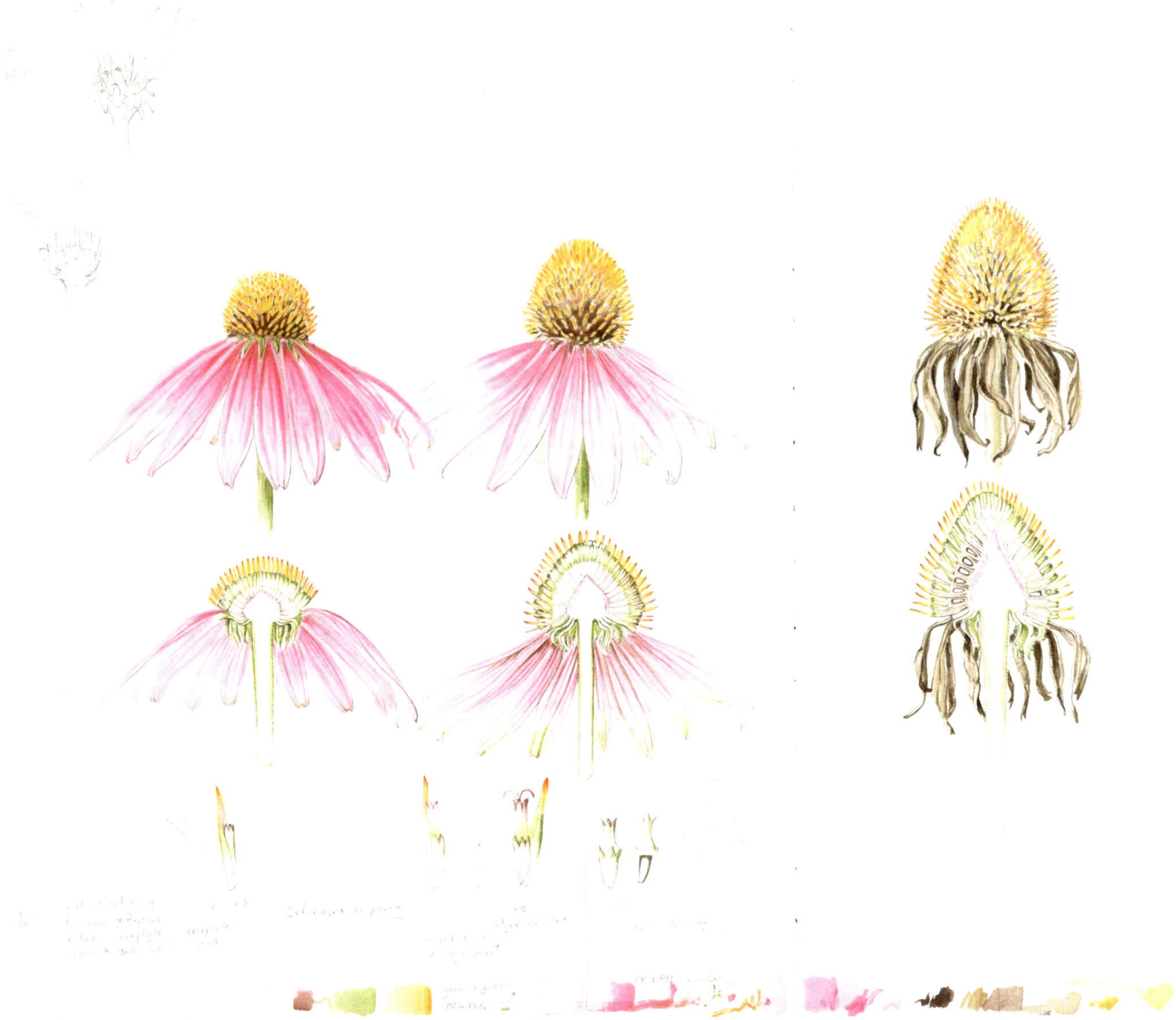

The final sketchbook study of the development of *Echinacea purpurea*. It was most enjoyable working these drawings up to a high level of sharp detail throughout both the drawing and the colouring stage.

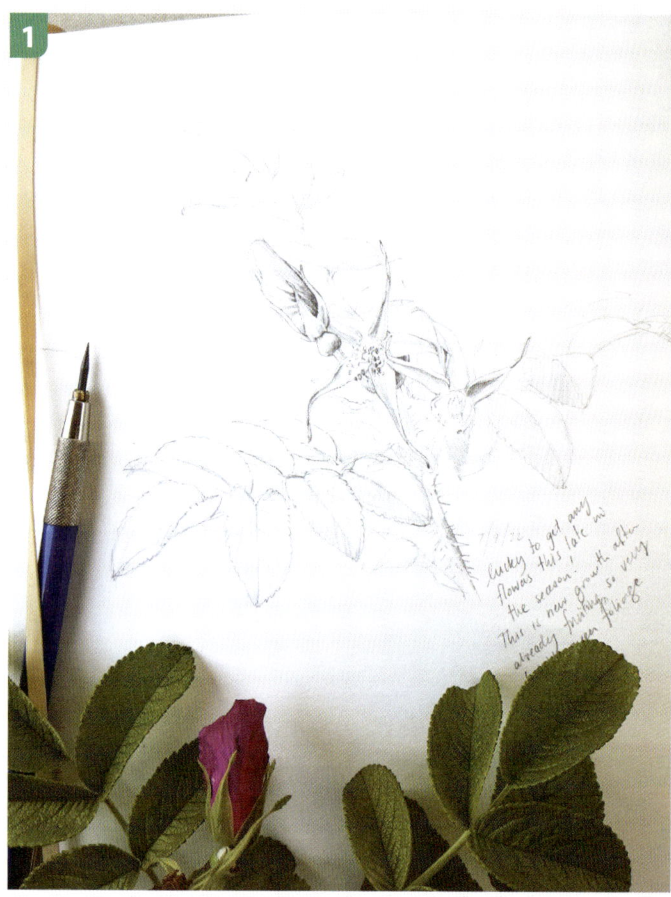

Loose, relaxed sketches helped me to warm up and get to know the *Rosa rugosa* flower before moving on to the next page. This plant made very sturdy specimens and it probably helped that I did not have to carry them far to my studio. One of the buds that I had cut and drawn then opened, giving me something new to draw. The smell was divine.

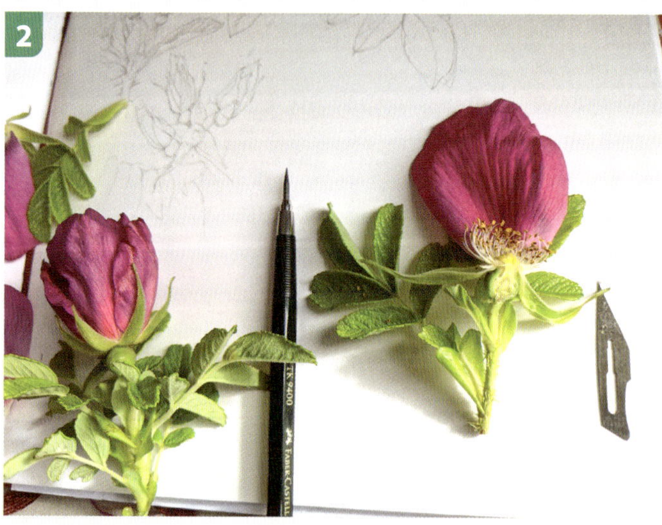

The rose flowers were not only beautiful to look at, but also featured some very pleasing forms. I drew the dissected flowers immediately after cutting them. Inevitably, some petals will drop off – when drawing a longitudinal section of the flower you will need to imagine them back on again.

My First Rose

These are the flowers of the same *Rosa rugosa* bushes whose rosehips I drew (*see* Chapter 4). I wanted to get to know these flowers better on an artistic level, as I had never drawn or painted a rose before! On a scientific level, I wanted to observe and draw the way in which a rose's carpels work, as I had never looked at one or fully understood the concept before.

To study these flowers, I cut material from bushes growing in a nearby car park. As I started the work in late summer, many of the flowers had already developed into fruit, so I kept a watchful eye on how many buds were left to open as autumn approached. Having the roses at home not only made for an enjoyable drawing and painting study, but also filled the studio with a beautiful scent. The specimens I cut from this plant were very good to draw from, as they were extremely sturdy and long-lasting.

Different Types of Sketches

The first drawings on the left-hand side of the two-page spread are loose and sketchy. This approach was good for relaxing the hand and getting to know the feel of the rose flowers and leaves. On the second page I began a more controlled approach, drawing flowers as they opened. After drawing the flowers whole, I made two longitudinal flower sections. One was from a just-opened flower, whose anthers had not yet opened. The second was made from a flower in a more advanced stage of development, with anthers that had finished releasing their pollen.

Rose Flower Morphology

I paid special attention to the carpels within the receptacle wall, seeking to clarify how each individual carpel (consisting of a locule, a style and a stigma) is anchored in the receptable wall. Its style is drawn into a bunch with the other styles so that their stigmas project into the flower chamber. Drawing these helped me to understand how the rosehips formed later. The dissections were informative, but not in the strict style that I would use for a scientific illustration.

I would like to return to this subject to look in more detail at such features as the hairs and glands that can be found on *Rosa rugosa*'s flowers, and to dissect and draw a carpel.

With the rose specimens lying on my sketchbook, I was able to look constantly from the specimen to my drawing, and back again. Rather than pick up a dissection tool, I prodded and poked the specimens with my sharp pencil tip.

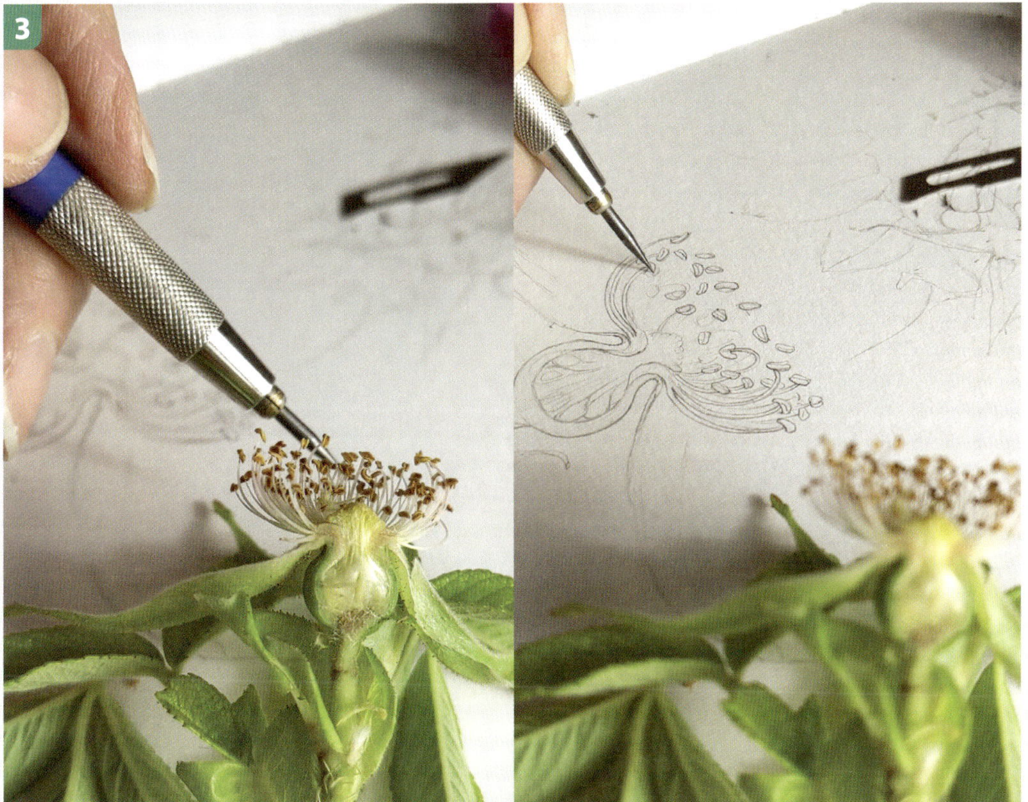

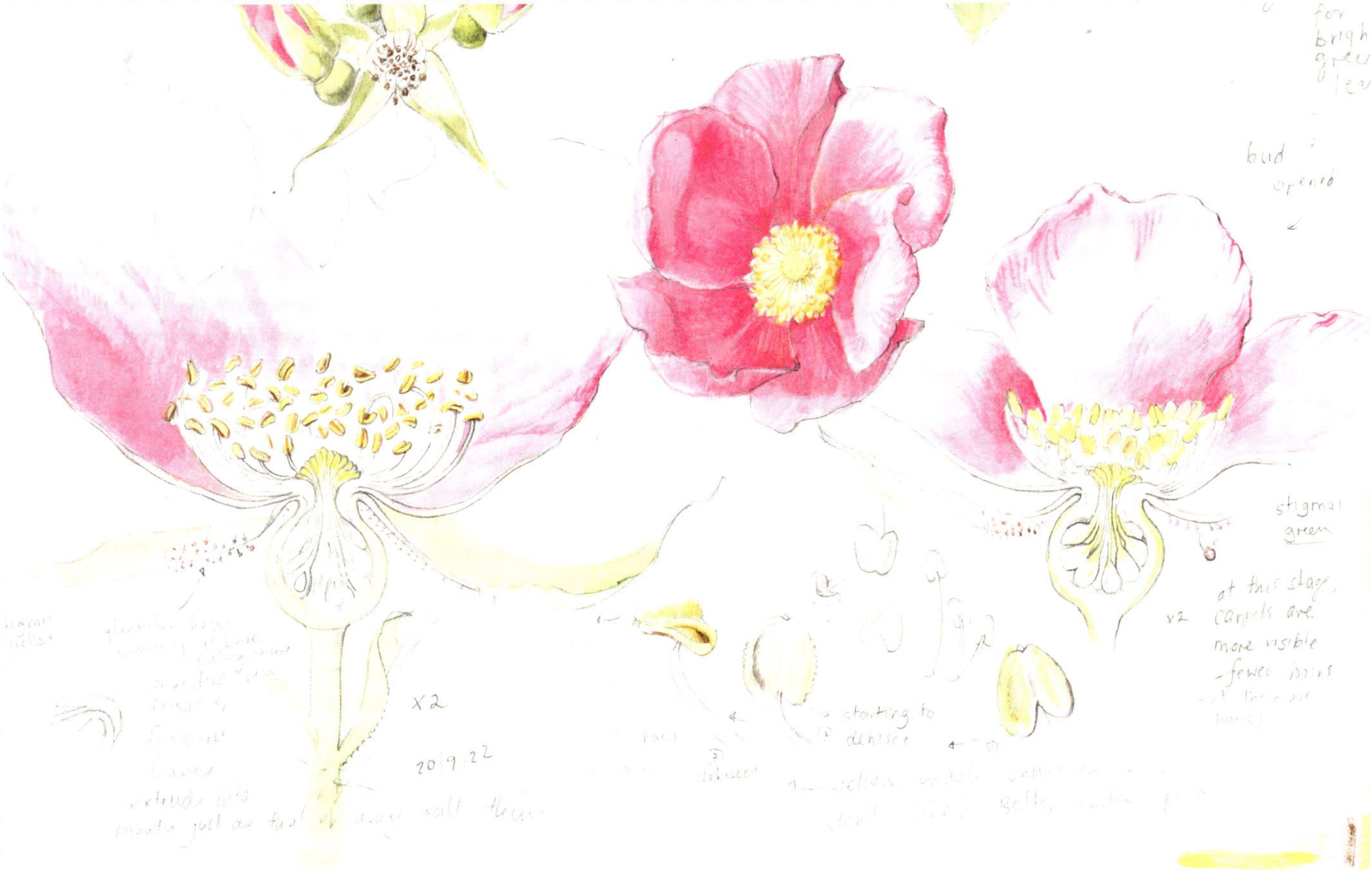

Detail of sketchbook study showing dissected flowers of *Rosa rugosa* and their anthers before they have dehisced or opened (right), and after (left). The colour and shape of the anthers change dramatically.

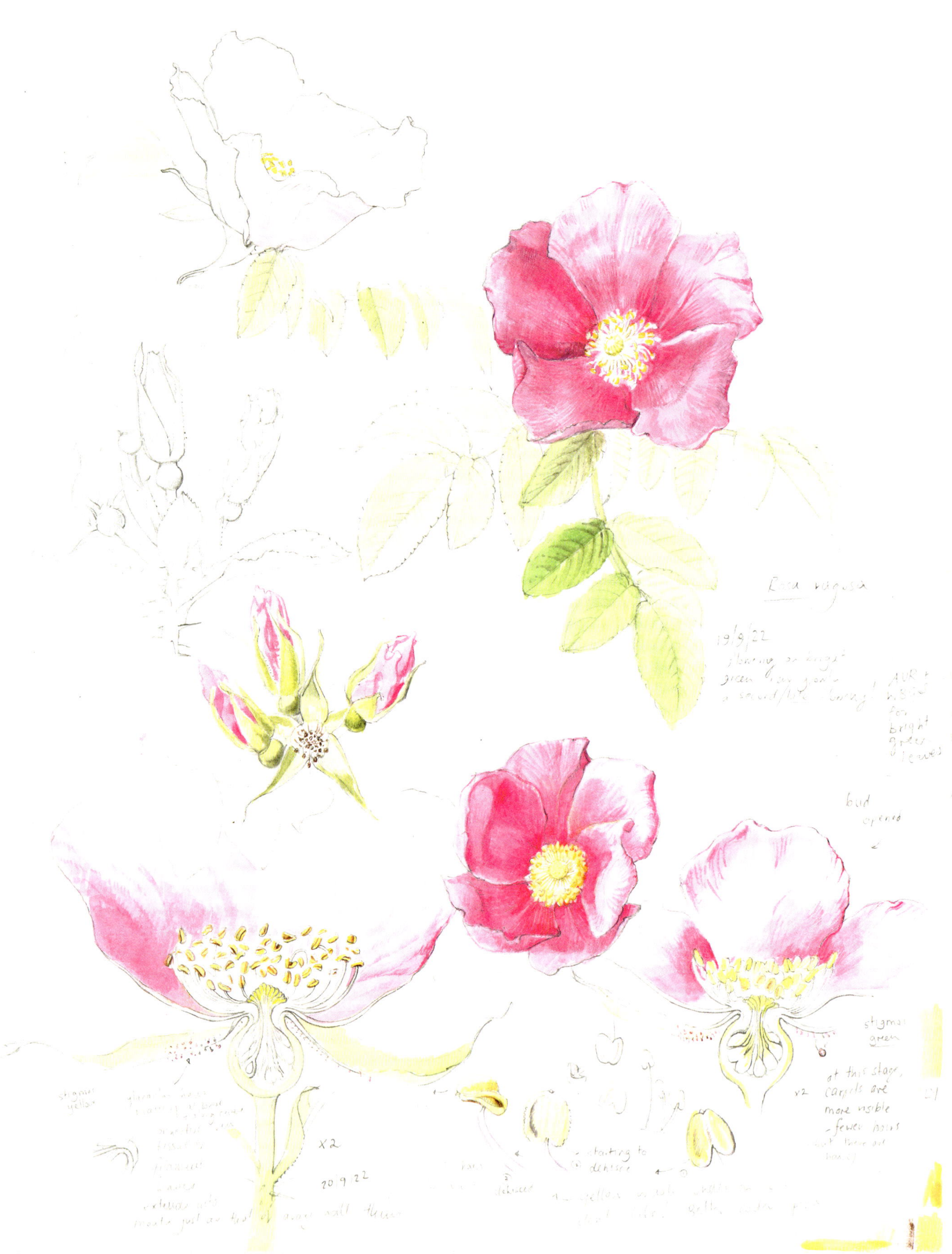

The final sketchbook study of the flowers of *Rosa rugosa*.

STARTING YOUR FLOWER SKETCHBOOK

There is so much enjoyment to be gained from drawing and painting flowers. Their beauty engages the heart, whilst their forms can engage the mind. Because I love exploring and illustrating the seemingly infinite ways in which flowers are put together, my studies tend towards a scientific approach. Both my head and my heart are definitely involved in my work.

What will your sketchbook flower studies look like? Will they take a more artistic or scientific approach? There is only one way to find out: start looking and learning, open your sketchbook, gather your materials and start drawing some flowers.

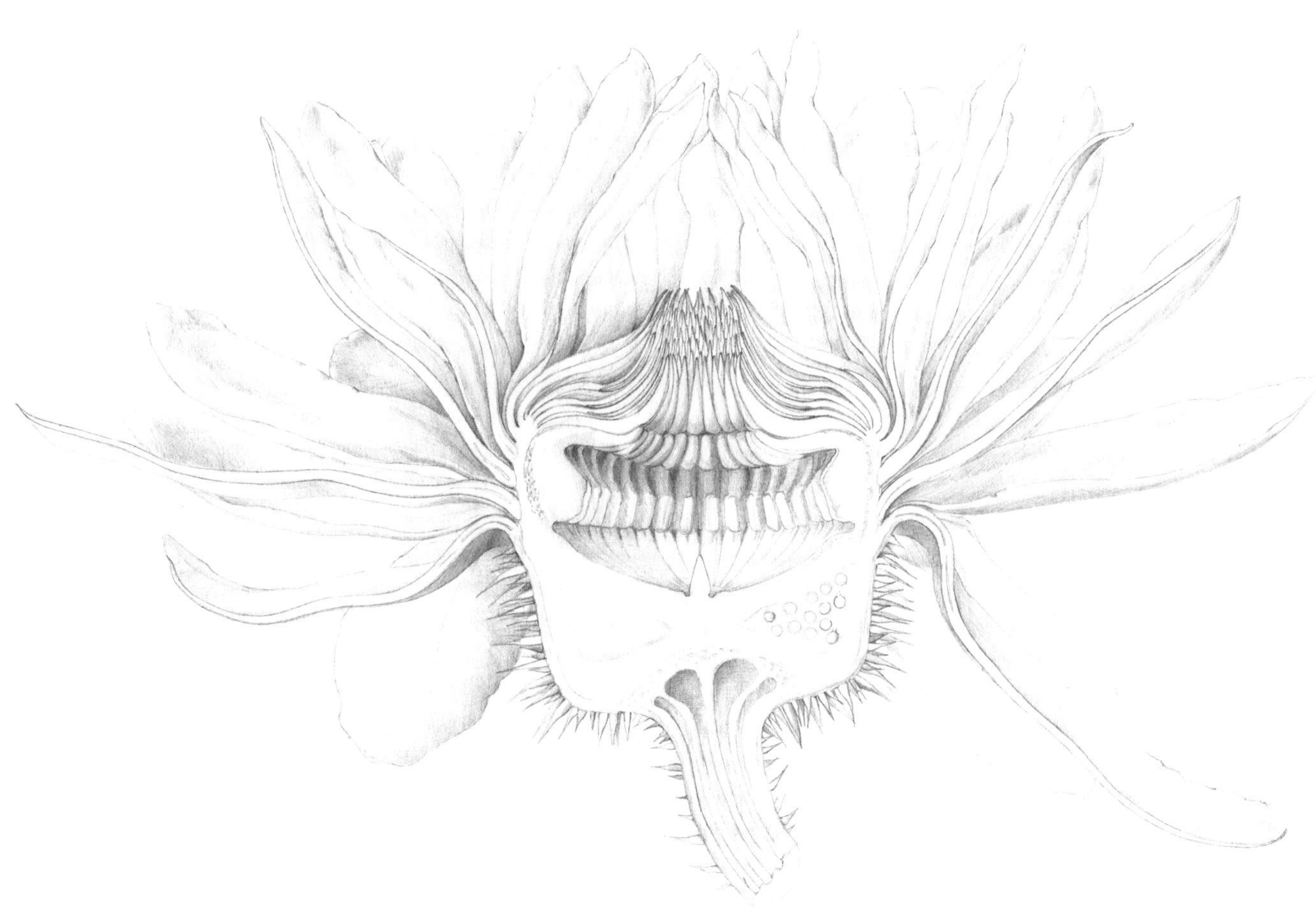

The ultimate flower dissection? There was no need for microscopes or magnifiers when drawing the large flowers of the giant water lily *Victoria boliviana*, which measured 32cm in diameter. This is the first-night flower of the species, which opens over two nights, changing dramatically in form and colour between each night before sinking below the water. The drawing was made in preparation for describing and illustrating the plant as a species new to science.

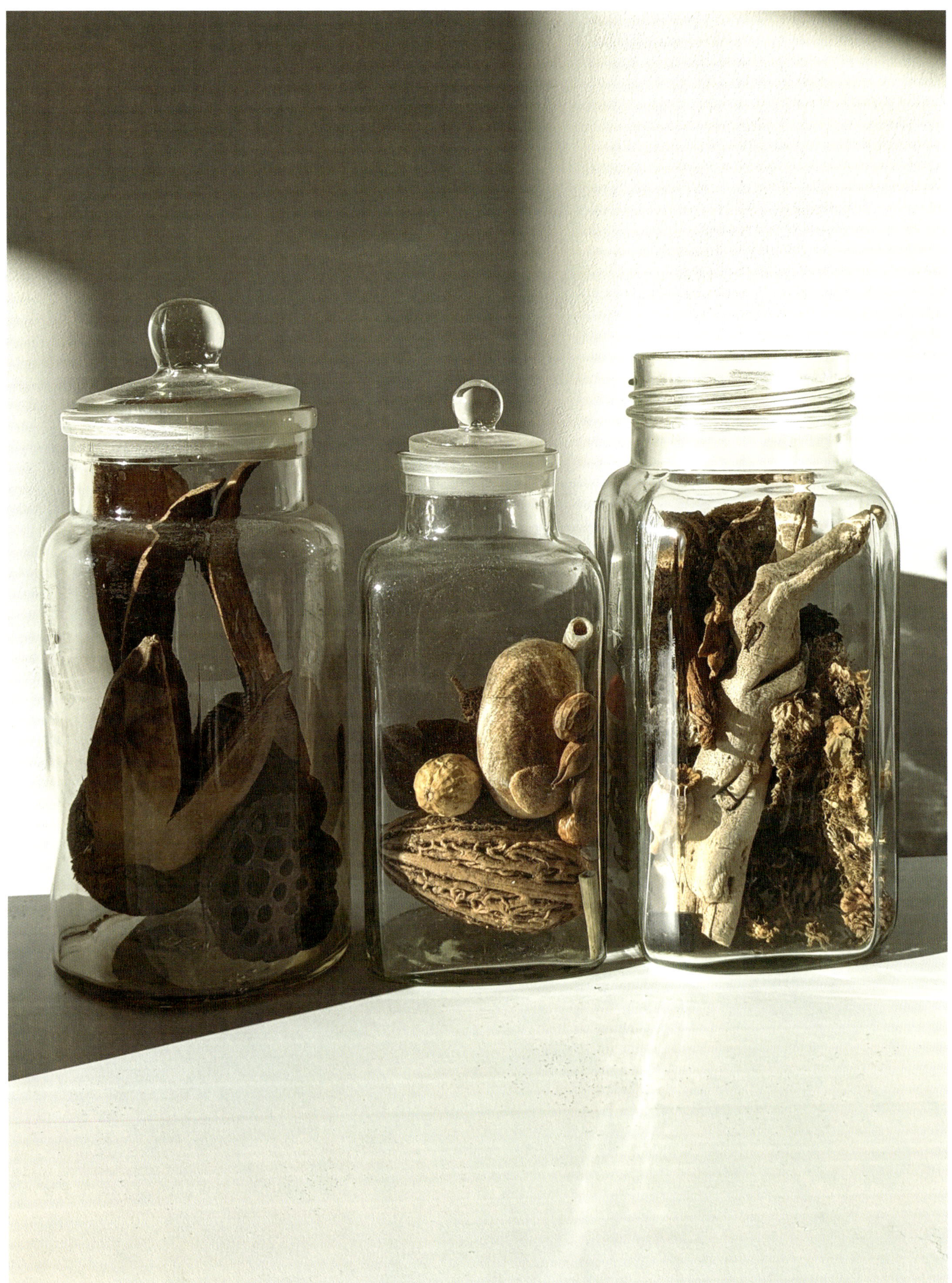

CHAPTER 4

FRUITS, PODS, CONES AND SEEDS

The fruiting bodies of plants come in every shape and size imaginable. They produce the miraculous packets of new life that are known as seeds. Their forms may reflect their origins as flowers and demonstrate a variety of ingenious methods of ripening and dispersing a plant's seeds. Whether they are drawn fresh or dried, their wonderful range of forms, textures and colours make them perfect subjects for botanical sketchbook studies.

There are so many reasons why I enjoy drawing fruits and seeds. Their voluminous forms are very pleasing to the eye and to the hand. They make great practice subjects for observing and depicting tonal values. I also like to understand how and why they develop the shapes they do, especially when I have followed their growth from their beginnings as an ovary in a flower. It is the satisfying conclusion to a flowering and pollination story. Each of those stories is unique – gymnosperms, for example, reproduce without flowers, producing a wonderful variety of cones in the process. Whatever your reason for drawing this kind of material, four different projects are described here to inspire you.

'Fruit' does not necessarily mean the produce on display at the local supermarket or grocer, although those places can be excellent for sourcing plant material. I have drawn many a shop-bought berry or other piece of fruit for my botanical illustration classes. In this context, 'fruit' also refers to the fruiting bodies growing on plants in my and other people's gardens or in the wild. Just as I watch with interest as the first flower buds appear on the plants that I observe and study around me, I also give attention to the fruits that eventually come from them.

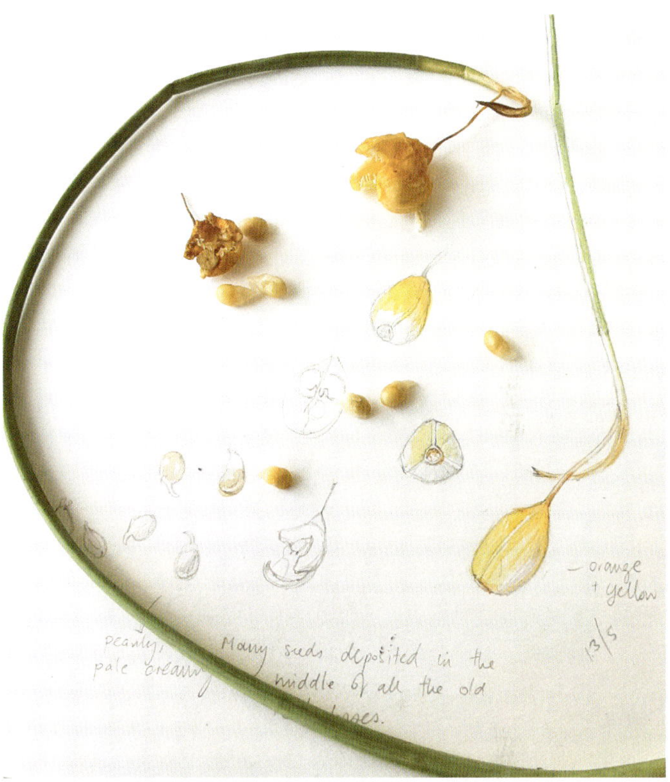

Looking closely at a clump of *Galanthus elwesii* snowdrops, I was intrigued to find ripe orange fruits weighed down with seeds, deposited amongst the dying leaf bases when the fruit splits open.

Like treats in a sweet shop, this collection of fruits, pod and seeds waits patiently for their turn on the sketchbook page.

Fruit Development

I love watching the rosehips of *Rosa rugosa* on my neighbourhood bushes as they develop through the year. I had drawn and painted ripe rosehips from these plants before, but not in as much detail as I would have liked, so I determined to capture them more fully in the autumn. I

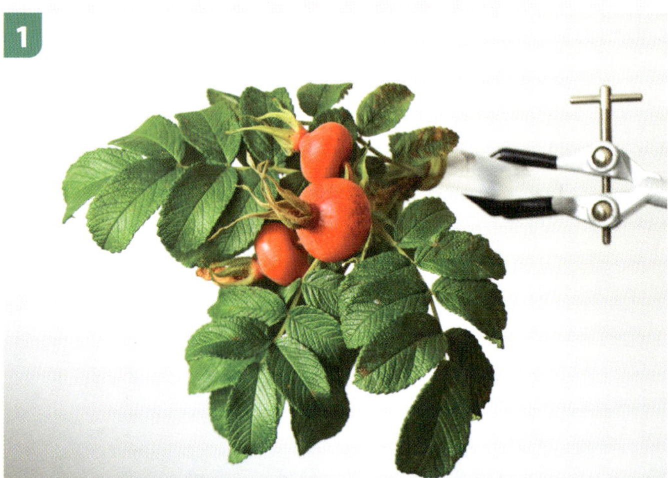

I kept my first specimen of ripe rosehips fresh by putting it into a water-filled florist's tube, which was then fixed in the clamp of the retort stand, and angled to reflect the position of the branchlet when on the rose bush.

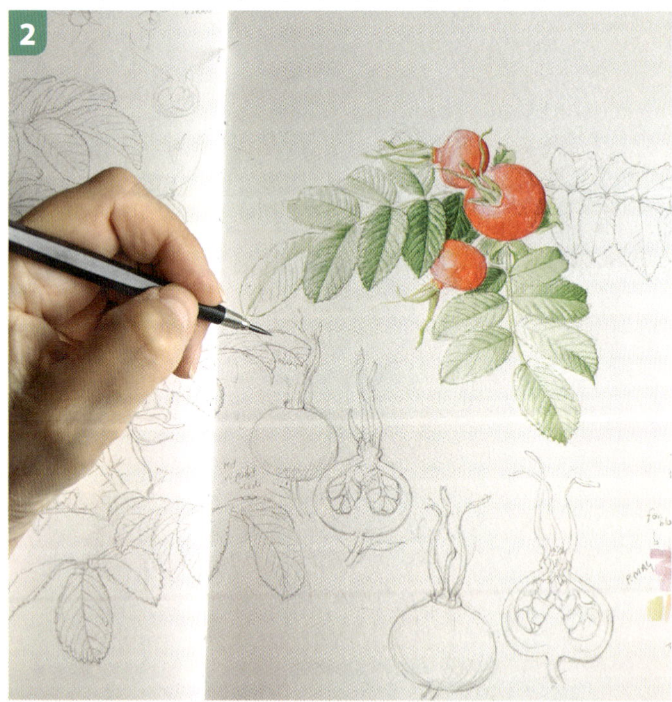

The first specimen with the ripest rosehips, which I drew and painted in one sitting. Rather than finishing the entire drawing and adding colour to the whole piece, I left some of the leaflets at the sketchy drawing stage, only painting some of them and the rosehips.

also wanted to have a better understanding of the process of their development. This project started with my examination of the flowers of *Rosa rugosa* (*see* Chapter 3).

The 'hips' of roses are not single fruits, but swollen receptacles that contain numerous seeds, each one of which has developed from a single carpel held inside the flower's base. I kept an eye on my local *rugosa* plants, from the time the first green hips began to develop. As the ripening stage progressed, I collected hips, with leaves still attached. I was delighted to record the changes in shape and colour of the hips through these stages. By dissecting the hips, I could also show the development of the seeds inside.

Telling the Story

A double-page spread was the instinctive choice for this project. This is often the case for the illustrator wishing to tell a story with a beginning and an end, with the open pages being reminiscent of a storybook. In this case, the story was to be that of the growth of a fruit. The idea was to present the story so that the reader would follow it like a book, from left to right. The story would begin with the small green rosehips at the earliest stage of development, and end with the ripest hips opening to reveal mature seeds. Fortunately, I could see that there were many flowers and hips at all stages of development, promising abundant drawing material to come.

However, I started telling this story at its ending, because the first rosehip specimen I cut and drew was one with very ripe, red fruits. I positioned the branch containing a cluster of rich red rosehips on the right-hand side of the spread.

Collecting and Setting up Specimens

My priority was to draw branchlets with their hips in place. As there was abundant material, I was confident about cutting enough to bring home for drawing. Each branchlet was hydrated not long after cutting, in a florist's tube filled with water. They made excellent specimens, with little or no wilting. The florist's tube was then placed in the clamp of the retort stand and angled in such a way as to reflect the hips' natural growing position on the branch.

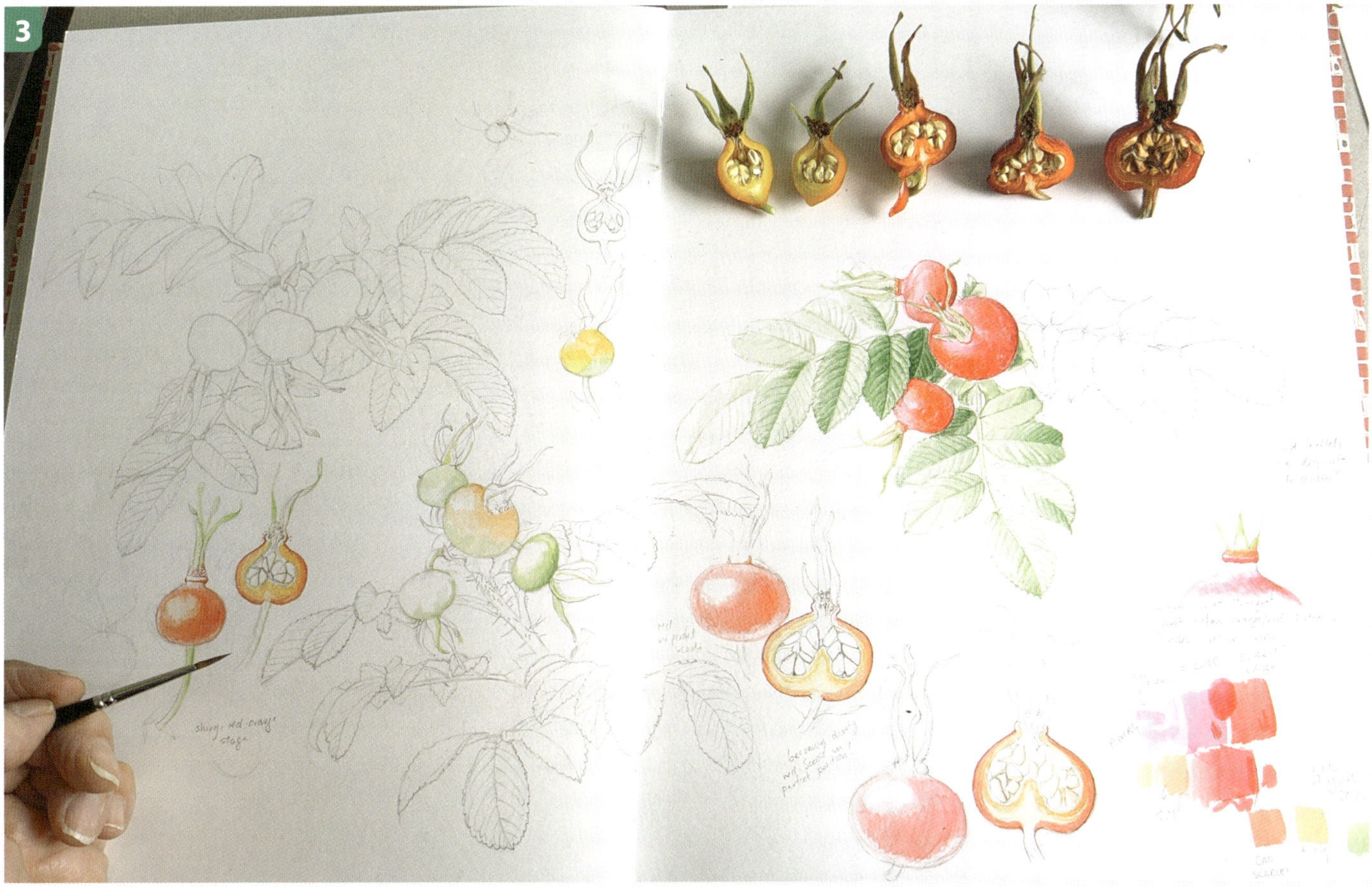

Over several days, more branchlets of rosehips at different stages of development were added to the pages. Fortunately, there was a lot of plant material to choose from so I was able to select the best specimens available.

Making a Close Study of the Hips' Development

Alongside depicting the rosehips held on their leafy branchlets, I was eager to study them more closely, both inside and out, from both a scientific and an artistic point of view. From the outside, I was interested in their shapes and colours. On the inside, I wanted to see how they were constructed and how their seeds developed. For each branchlet I would add a single rosehip and depict it both whole and in longitudinal section.

The first questions I wanted to answer for myself came from a scientific angle. How does the shape of the hip change as it swells, and what happens to the calyx and the stamens as it does? How are the carpels attached to the receptacle? Do they hang freely or are they attached somewhere? Through the process of answering these scientific questions, I discovered all the elements of these hips that appealed to my artistic side. As I drew the hips to explore their structure and colour, I became aware of their beautiful curves, and appreciated the rounded nature of the pinched-in part at the top of the hip through which each carpel's stigma once squeezed.

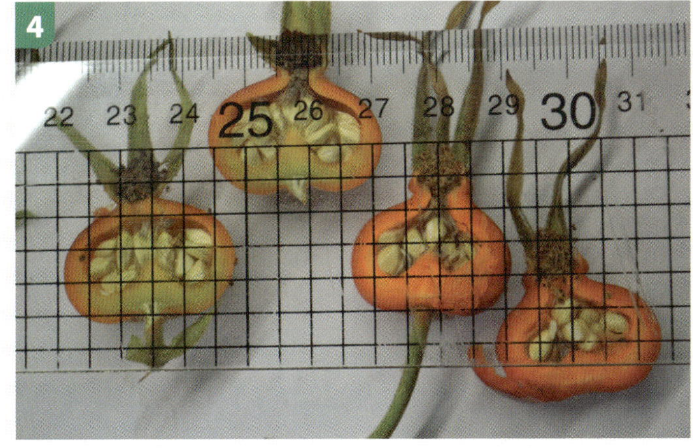

As I was unsure how long the dissected hips would last, I photographed them. With a clear plastic ruler directly on top of them, the reference photos would be of more use, as they would show the scale and size of the hips and their internal parts.

As they grow larger, the developing seeds become more and more squashed into the space inside the hip. As a result of this, the mature seeds possess a pleasing angularity and an attractive pattern is produced in the longitudinally sectioned hip.

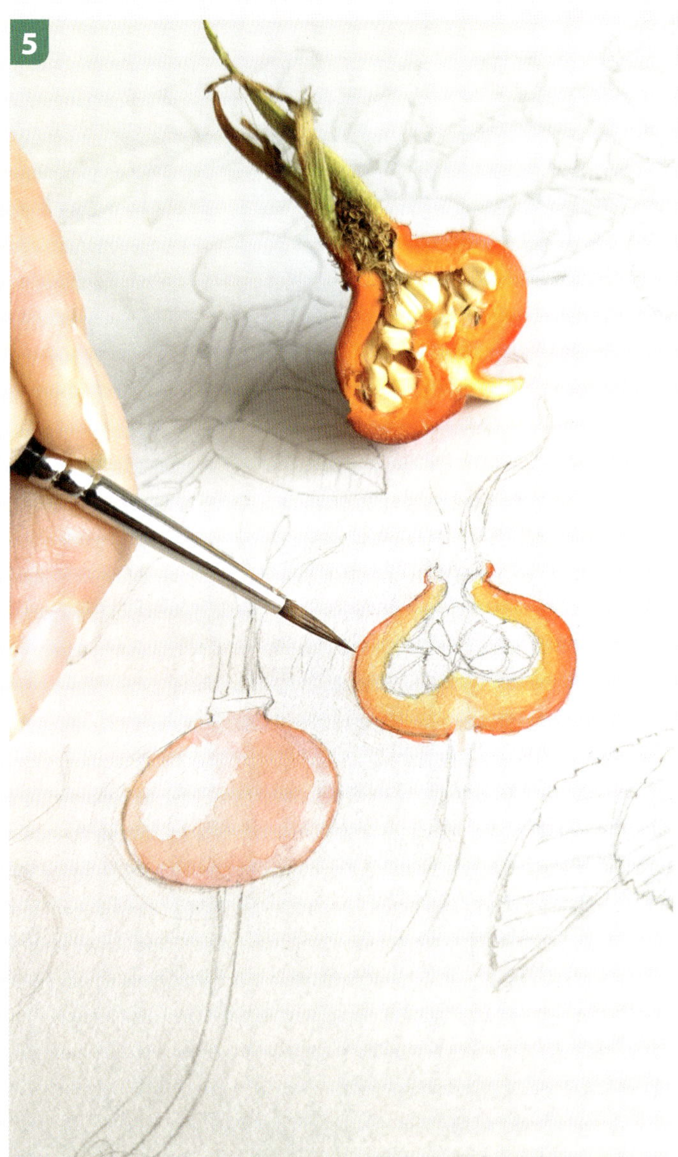

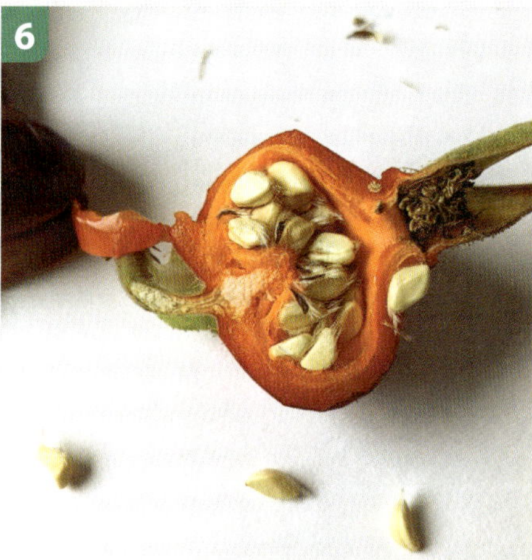

Observing how the seeds of *Rosa rugosa* are packed tightly into the maturing rosehip.

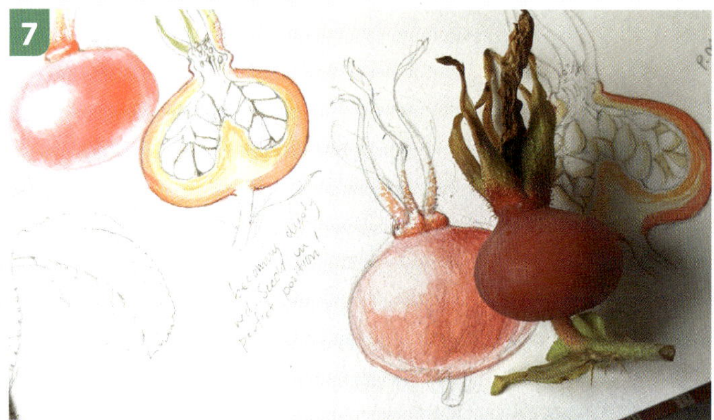

Capturing the colours of rosehips using live material. There is an infinite variety of colour and texture in rosehips: shiny, matt, warm and cool reds, bloom, smoothness, wrinkled texture. Both colour *and* texture change throughout the ripening process.

Art informs science, and science art: by prodding and poking the tissue of the hips' inner wall, I observed how the seeds were attached to it. I might not have thought about the different types of tissue here (inner and outer wall) had it not been for the change in colour between the two, which I enjoyed painting.

I wondered how the carpels and developing seeds attach to the hip. I had observed a difference in texture in the inner wall of the hip. By poking and prodding the seeds I discovered they are in fact anchored to the inner wall, deriving the energy they need to develop from there.

Working from Life

It is much easier and more rewarding for the botanical artist to make all the observations when working from actual specimens rather than photographs. This is true not only in terms of the pleasing shapes and structures of the hips, but also their colours. The colours of rosehips are so

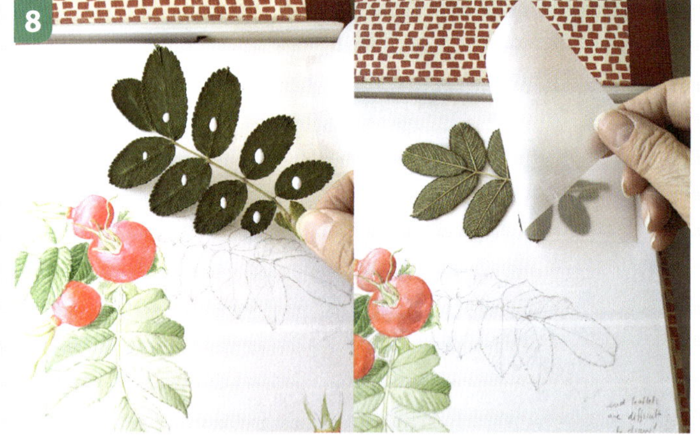

Adding a pressed leaf to the page. I pressed this leaf from the drawing beneath it and decided to glue it to the page to add information and serve as reference for further studies. I placed it abaxial (lower) side up as the venation is clearer on that surface.

beautiful and are best appreciated and painted from life.
I may not have come close to capturing everything, but I
made a start.

While I was drawing the first fruiting specimen of the
Rosa rugosa, I also pressed one of its leaves and decided to
add it to the page. I applied PVA glue to the upper surface
of the leave and glued it down so that the lower surface of
the leaf would be visible. To protect the facing page
from the leaf, I folded a piece of tracing paper over the leaf
and taped that down with magic tape.

Keeping an Eye on My Plant

This winter I saw that the *Rosa rugosa* bushes had been
given a dramatic pruning. The bushes that had reached
over my head were now trimmed to below waist level.
After they had been cut back, I watched them every day
and was very relieved to see fresh buds emerging from the
stems in the early spring. There is now vigorous growth on
the bushes in spring, and even a few early flowers. As often
happens with a plant that I have worked on, I have become
quite attached to these *Rosa rugosa* bushes.

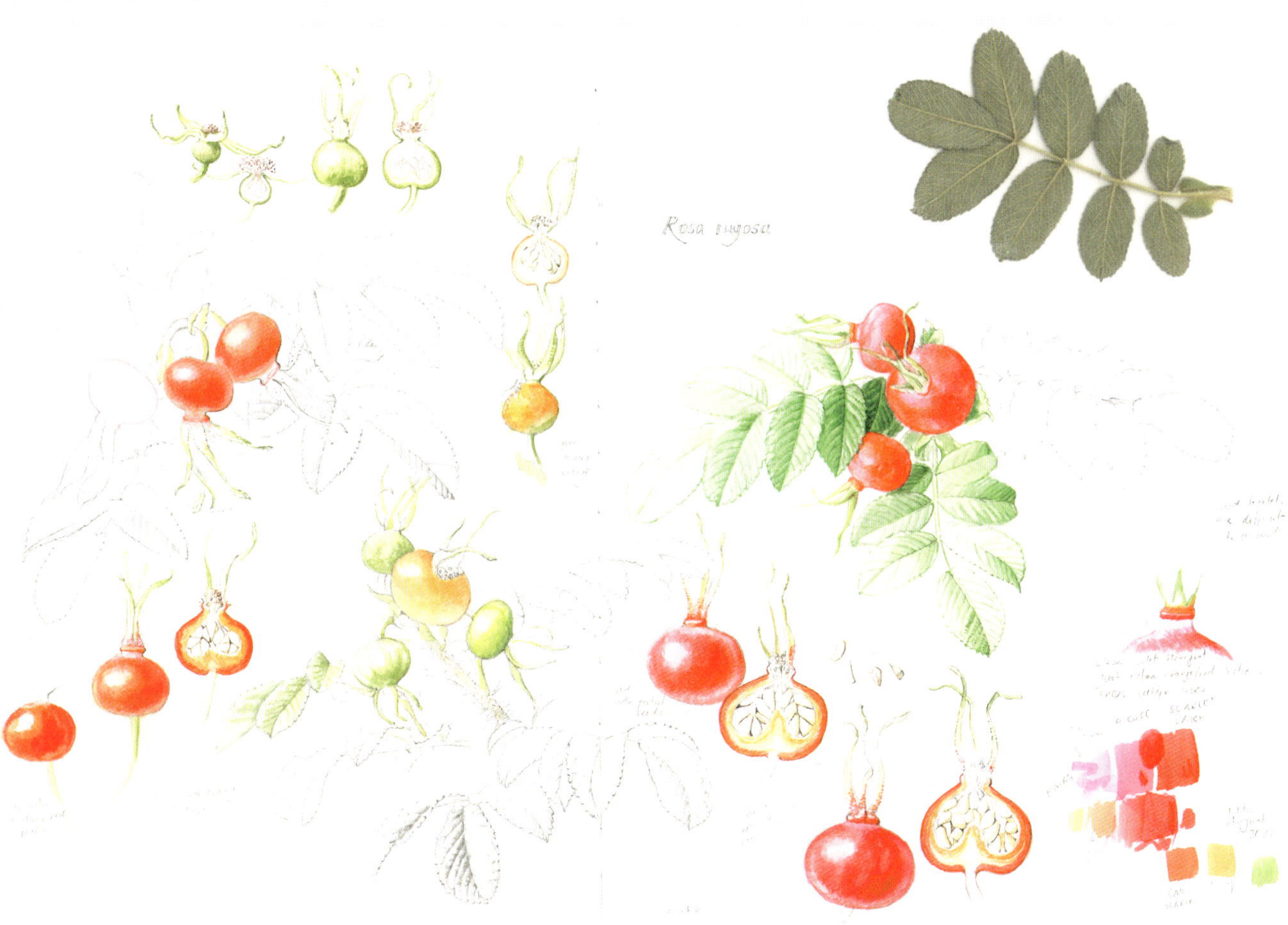

The completed double-page spread of *Rosa rugosa* fruit, with many of the stages of the hips' development captured. I deliberately
kept parts of the study uncoloured, working up the colours of the hips alongside pencil line and shading work. This not only
highlights the hips' colours, but I also like the effect of colour alongside monochrome work and the interesting variety of drawing
marks and textures this creates.

1

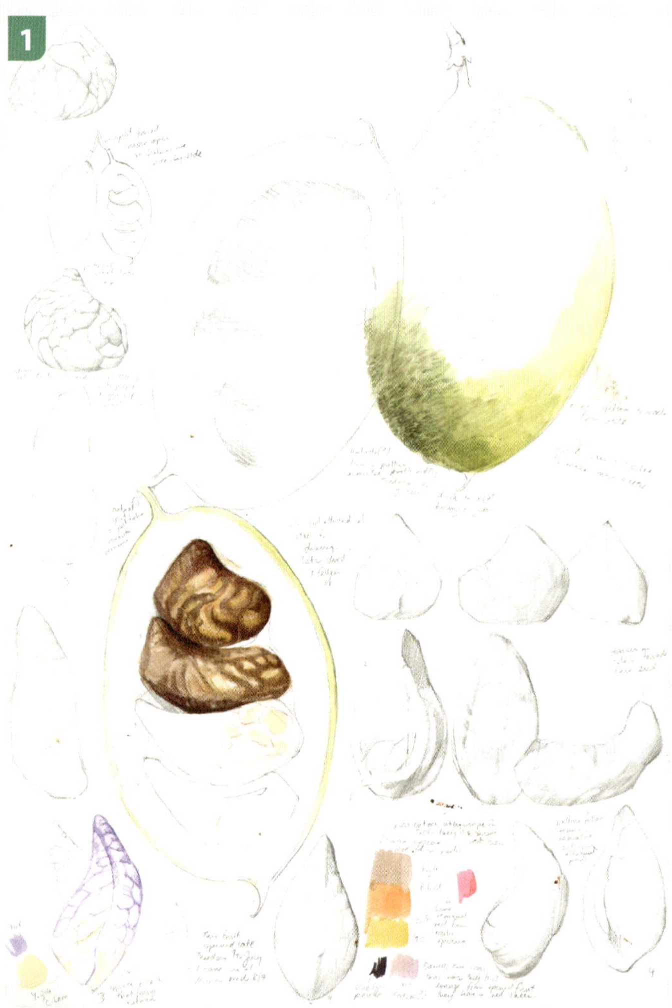

The first jade vine fruit I drew – a very ripe specimen that had just split. The large seeds are covered in a red-brown outer skin. Underneath this, the creamy seed surface is covered in pale violet veins. As I had only one page of my A3 sketchbook left, I crammed a day's work on to this single piece of paper.

2

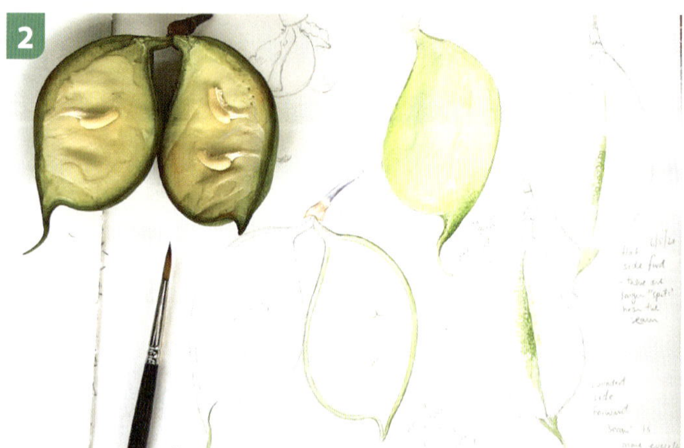

The first two stages of the jade vine fruit: the first (partly obscured) is a fertilised flower with persistent petals; in the second, the seeds are beginning to develop, with their obvious placental attachments.

Starting from the End

My interest in illustrating the jade vine *Strongylodon macrobotrys* began when I first saw its amazing fruits. It seemed incredible to think that such a huge fruit could develop from the tiny ovary of the jade vine's beautiful flowers.

The staff of the Princess of Wales Conservatory at Kew Gardens had given me permission to come and draw one of the plant's ripe fruits as soon as it opened. As happens all too often, I left it until the last minute and when I raced to the site to draw the plant's very last fruit, it had opened overnight and had almost rolled into the pond. Luckily, it was rescued, and I was able to use it as a subject.

When I got to Kew, I discovered that I had only one page left in my sketchbook. This made for a very crowded page, full of overlapping detail. I started by drawing the large fruit opened up, which is how it naturally split. On this one page I drew the opened fruit with its seeds sitting in the cavity of one of its halves. I added paint to these sketches in situ. Back in the studio, I examined each seed in more detail, peeling away the red-brown coatings to discover a creamy white interior with curious veiny indentations that were violet in colour.

Filling in the Back Story

I was allowed to collect specimens of the jade vine fruit from Kew at several different stages. The very first stage of the fruit is a fertilised flower, which still has some of its petals attached. I did not cut this developing fruit, as it was more important to wait until the glasshouse staff knew that they had enough fruit to spare later. I drew the first stage from photos and from observation from life in the glasshouse. At the same time, I was given a very young fruit, which I drew and painted in the glasshouse.

After the first fruit, I drew two more stages, from two to three months old. I had to cut these fruits open along the seam that runs around its periphery – this is the line along which it will naturally split when ripe. Cutting the unripe fruit in this way revealed the placental attachments that echo the attachment of the ovules to the ovary wall, which I illustrated in the dissected jade vine flower. (*See* Chapter 3).

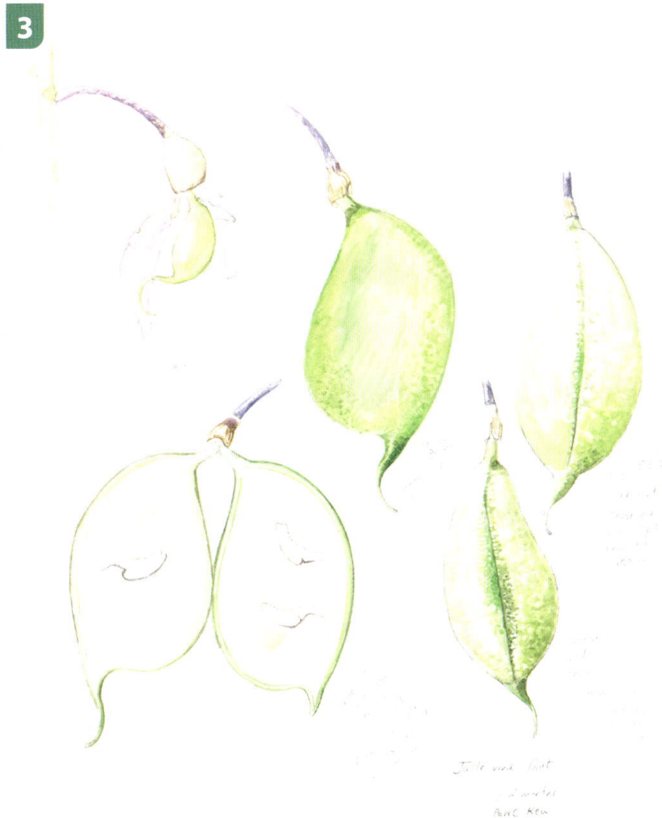

The jade vine fruit at around two months old. For both this and the later study, I added watercolour to some of the pencil work.

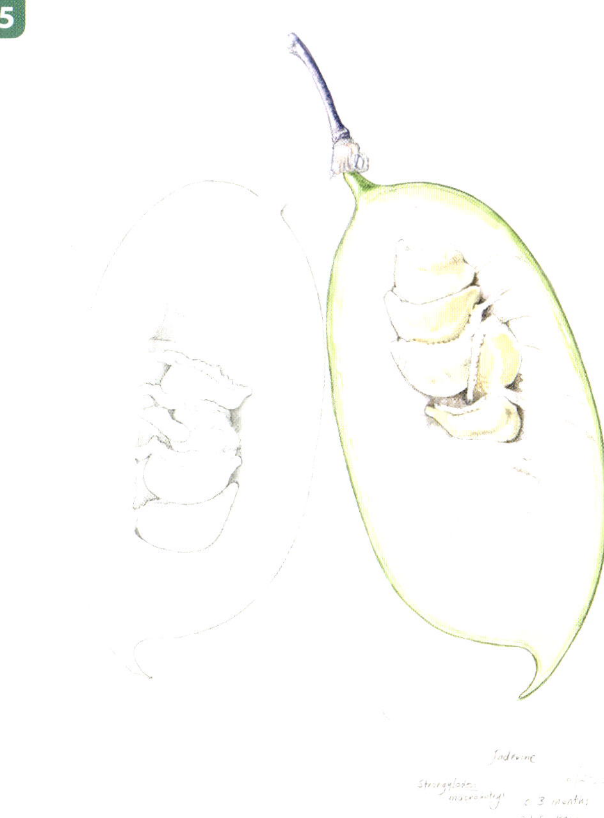

At around three months old, the seeds are starting to look like those in the mature fruit, perhaps showing the beginnings of the brown seed coat.

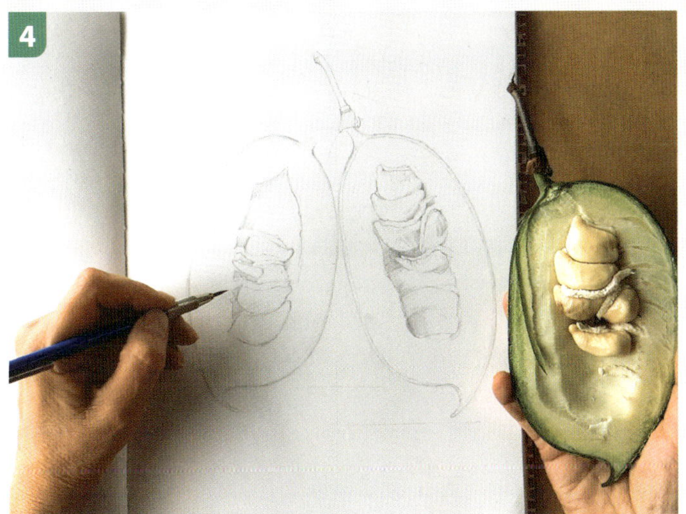

Cutting the unripe fruit and pulling the halves apart when they were not fully developed or ready to be exposed.

More Questions to Answer

The jade vine fruit and seed development drawings will probably continue for some time. There are still a few questions to answer. For example, when does the thin red-brown seed coating appear? I have yet to collect a fruit that shows this stage.

It is not unusual to work backwards, as I have done in this case. It can be a good way to answer one of the questions that botanical artists most often seek to examine in their sketchbook work: 'How did this plant material develop into its final shape?'

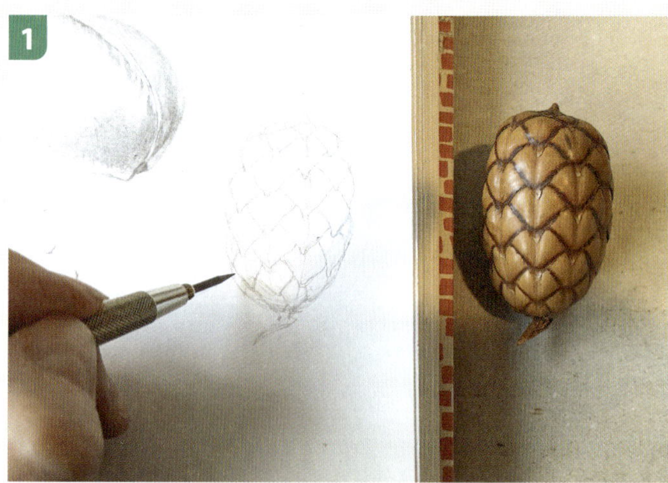

I love drawing and painting the fruits of calamoid palms. Palms from this group have scaly fruits that remind me of the skin of the lizards I played with as a child. I found this *Raphia* fruit at a plant stall many years ago.

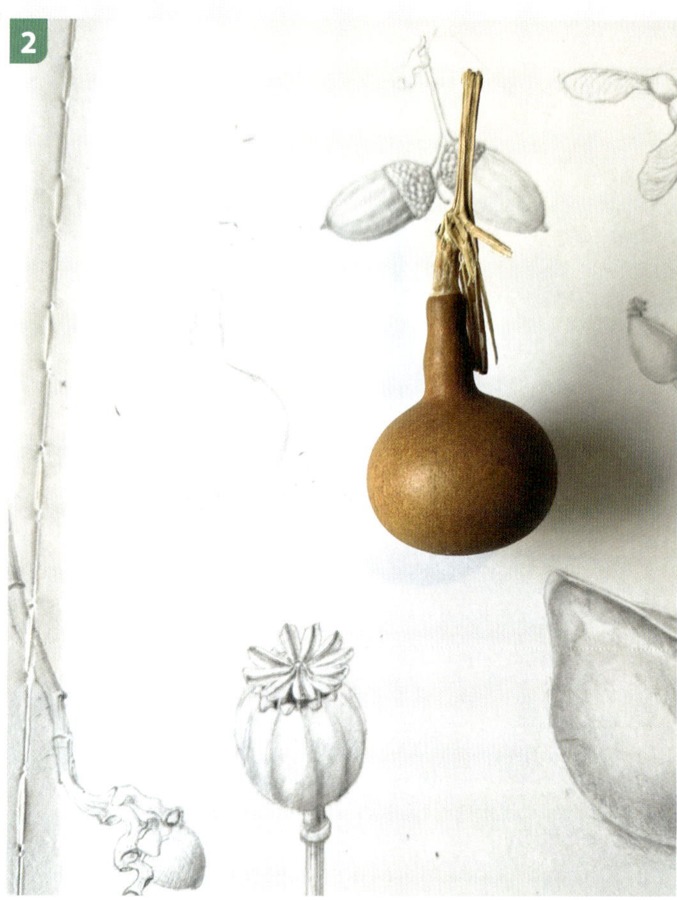

The simple but beautiful rounded form of this miniature gourd, gifted to me by a student, makes a useful study in rendering three-dimensional form. Although I am left-handed, I like to light my subjects from the left.

These studies in graphite began as little demonstration pieces for my botanical art students. Made from both fresh and dried material, each new study was added to the same sketchbook page as this seemed a good opportunity to create an attractive piece of art. The first item on the right-hand side of this double-page spread was a drawing of the poppy seed capsule. The large, winged drift fruit followed. Soon, these two items were joined by other fruits and seeds.

Guidelines for Unplanned Compositions

Bringing together an unrelated collection of objects such as this presents several challenges. The first is to balance the composition with items of different sizes, shapes and volumes. In this particular project, as each piece was added at a different time, I did not always know what was coming next. I could only hope that a balanced composition would evolve organically with the placement of each form in turn.

There are a few basic rules to follow here: heavier objects are placed closer to the bottom of the page; hanging objects are placed as they would occur naturally; those on long stems growing from the ground (such as the poppy seed head) emerge from the bottom of the page.

Maintaining Consistency

The light source under which you observe the objects should be kept consistent for each one. Multiple light sources can cause confusion when reading the three-dimensional volumes in a piece. (Lighting was just one of the aspects of drawing being demonstrated in this project. It was also good practice for techniques such measured drawing, pencil use, observation of form, and the interpretation of tonal values.)

Consistency across the piece was also achieved through technique, with each piece being drawn using line only first, and then tonal values being added. Each drawing was made from life and shown life-sized. As a left-hander I worked from the right-hand side of the page to the left, to avoid smudging the previous pencil work.

As the pieces began to spread across the fold of the page, I started to realise that it was quite an unlikely combination of items. However, as I continue to add each new object in a pleasing way, I hope that some kind of harmonious composition can be achieved in an unplanned, organic fashion.

These dried palm fruits (species unknown) were being discarded from a herbarium collection. Like any botanical artist would, I could not bear to see it being thrown away and took it for my collection. Such collections are ideal for drawing during the winter months, or at any time when you do not have easy access to fresh plant material.

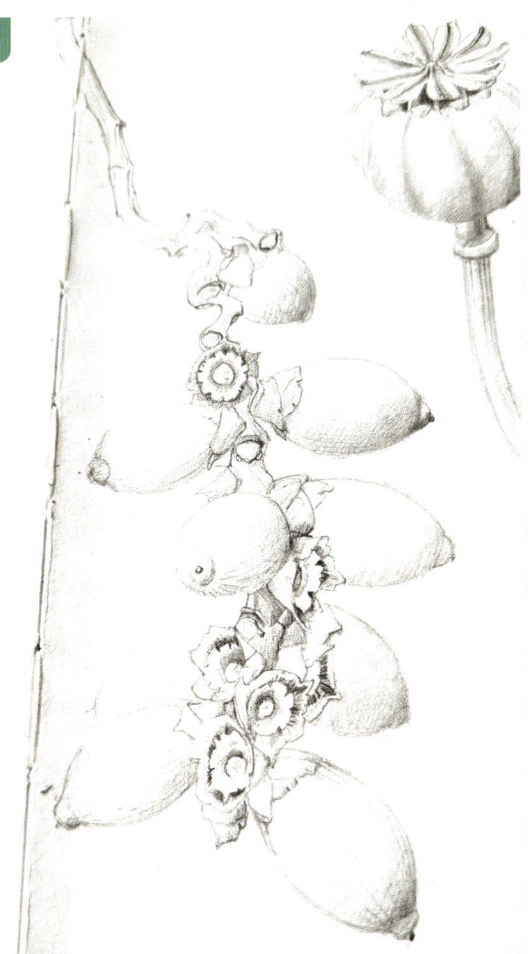

The ongoing double-page spread of dried fruits from my collection. The next fruit, a specimen I bought at a botanic garden in Berlin, is sketched out in place and ready to render in pencil. Thanks to the preserved nature of the dried fruit pods, the drawing can be picked up at any time. Perhaps during next winter, when there are not many living plants to draw, this page will be completed.

Unlikely companions on the page reflect an eclectic collection: dried tropical palm fruits alongside a European poppy seed head. Working into the sewn crease of the double-page spread looks attractive in the book but can be quite difficult to photograph without capturing a cast shadow.

DRAWING DRIED FRUITING MATERIAL

Many botanical artists have a collection of dried cones, pods and seeds. Mine has been amassed over time – some were gifts, while others were salvaged from my garden plants, or just found. They all sit on my shelves in containers and jars, just waiting to be drawn some day.

One of the advantages of drawing dried material is that it has been preserved. It is long-lasting and not liable to the quick changes that challenge the artist when drawing living, growing material. Collections of dried material are particularly useful to draw and paint during the times of the year when there is not much growth around. It can be drawn either in a planned set-up, or in a composition that unfolds organically as items are added.

Many years ago, I was presented with the gift of a box of seeds and pods from Western Australia. They sat on my bookshelf in their plastic container for a long time while I wondered what to do with them. At one time, I constructed a small, concertina-style sketchbook just for them, with the intention of drawing an individual piece on each page; but that idea did not take off. It was only when I decided to try a sketchbook with toned paper that they finally found their home.

Experimenting with Media

I decided to use this collection to experiment with two new methods/media: drawing directly with ink pens, and working on toned paper. So much of my pen and ink work is drawn tightly and precisely for the purposes of scientific illustration, with very careful under-drawing in pencil. In this case, I wanted to loosen up and enjoy pen and ink in a different style. My fear of 'making mistakes' in ink was overcome when I discovered that grey pens can be used in the same way as pencil. The lightest grey pen is pale enough to use for under-drawing. In this case, rather than erasing lines, as you would for pencil, it is easy to cover up the grey marks with subsequent layers of darker-toned pens. As I would be using a toned paper, I chose to use a white ink pen for highlights.

My goal in this project was to draw every single piece of material in the container, capturing the variety of unusual shapes and forms. I chose to draw over a double-page spread of the tan-toned sketchbook, working from right to left so that my hand would not smudge any recently added ink. As I wanted to be loose and quick, I completed the two pages over just two days of drawing.

Setting Up and Preliminary Sketches

I laid the pieces directly on to the sketchbook pages, looking for a pleasing and balanced composition and taking care to distribute the larger items evenly over the two pages. As the seeds and pods were all relatively small, there was plenty of space to lay them out in this way. Being dried, they would not deposit anything unwanted on the paper, as fresh specimens might do. Once I was happy with the arrangement, I took a photograph for reference, so that I could replace any pods that had to be moved, or fell off while I was drawing.

Using the lightest grey pen as if it was a pencil, I sketched every pod in place in order to capture the arrangement. I wanted to fix the position of each specimen before carrying on with the drawing. It was fun to lift each item one at a time and replace it with a sketch, while trying not to disturb the other pods around it; however, it was usually necessary to move neighbouring pods out of the way.

Once these preliminary drawings had been completed, it was possible to move the pods off the page and out of the way of my drawing hand. I felt confident using an ink pen without first under-drawing in pencil, as the light grey pen was only slightly darker in colour than the paper.

Working up Detail and Tone and Adding Highlights

After the initial pen sketches had been made, I went back over each seed or pod one at a time adding in detail, using the darker grey and black pens. Any corrections that I felt were necessary could be done simply by adjusting the drawing using the darker pens. Care was taken to keep the light source consistent while drawing and observing tones.

For parts of the pods that were lighter than the paper, and to accentuate highlights, I used a white Sakura 'Gelly Roll' pen with opaque ink. I learned to take care not to use too much of this pen. It looks exciting when it is first applied, but its ink tends to dry a lot brighter than it first appears, so it is easy to overdo it!

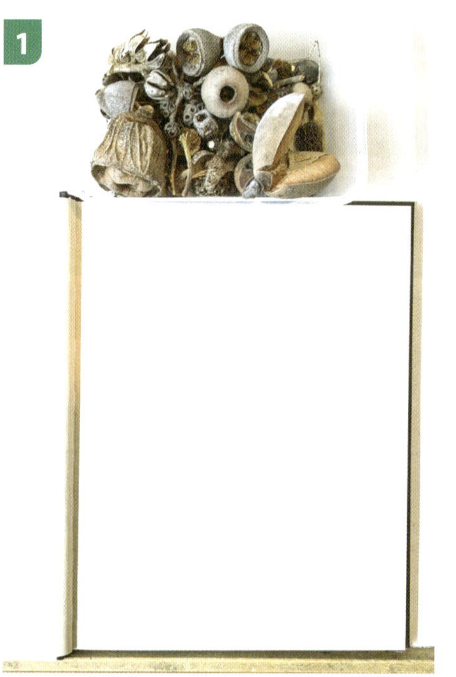

1 The exciting moment before this pod and seed collection was released from its plastic container of captivity. The pods and seeds had waited many years to be drawn, perhaps because I needed to identify the perfect medium and paper.

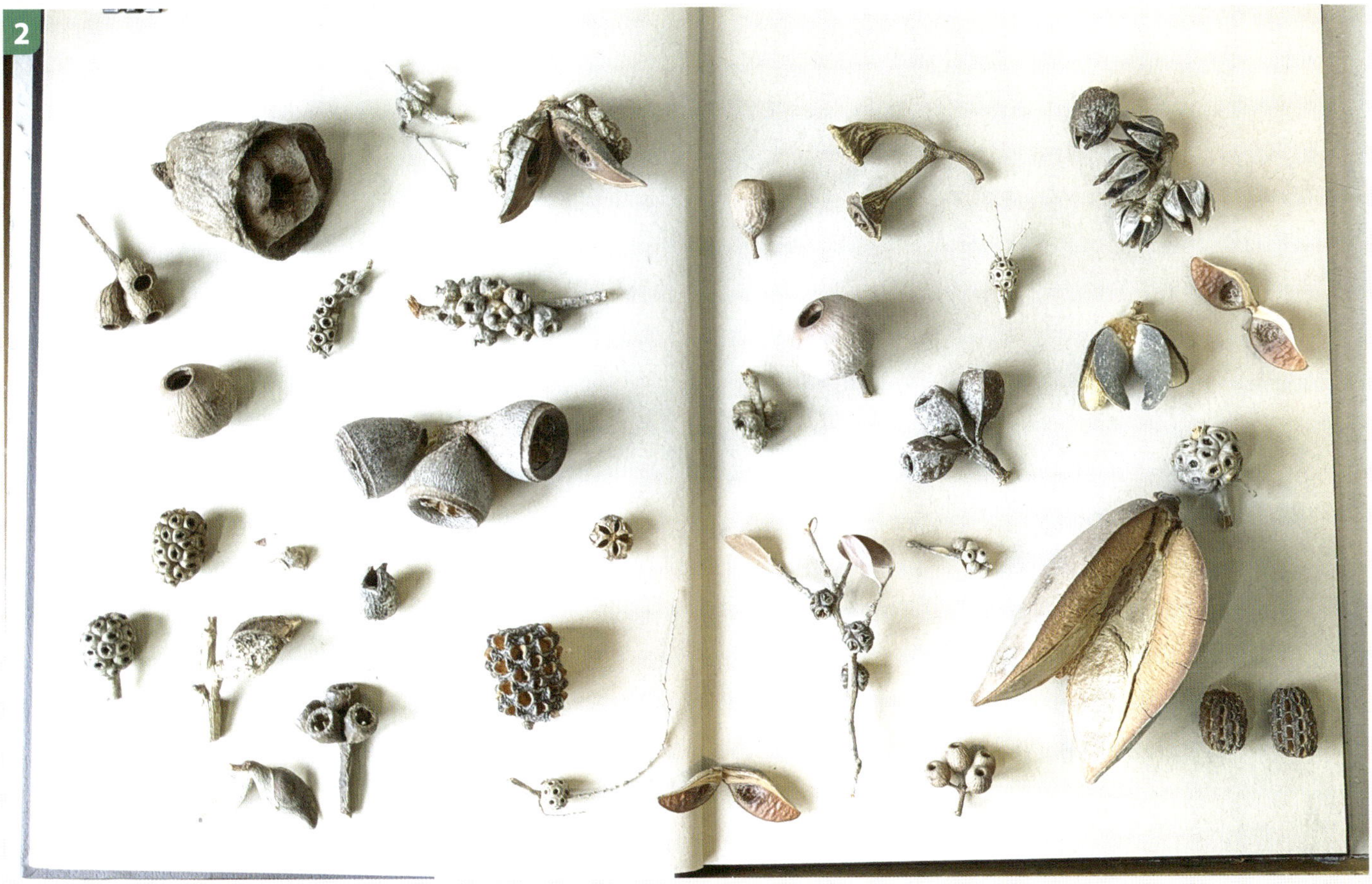

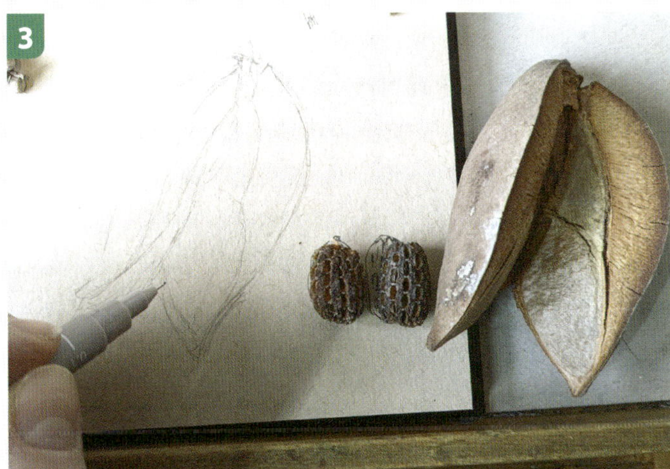

There is no simper or more satisfying way of designing a composition than this. You can instantly see the effect of the placement of the pods.

Drawing each pod in place, starting at the bottom right-hand corner of the double-page spread. The light grey pen feels like drawing with a pencil, except that it cannot be erased.

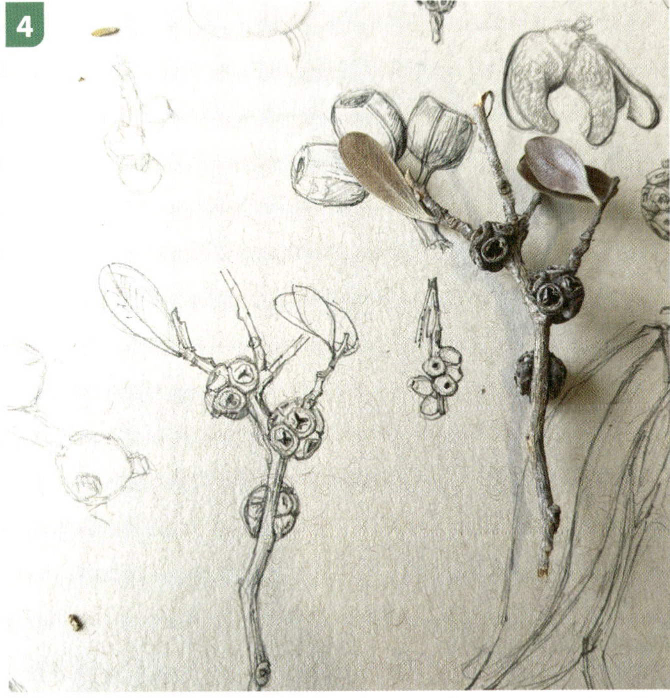

Building up more detail and tone, using darker pens in accurate but loose, quick marks that suit the subject matter.

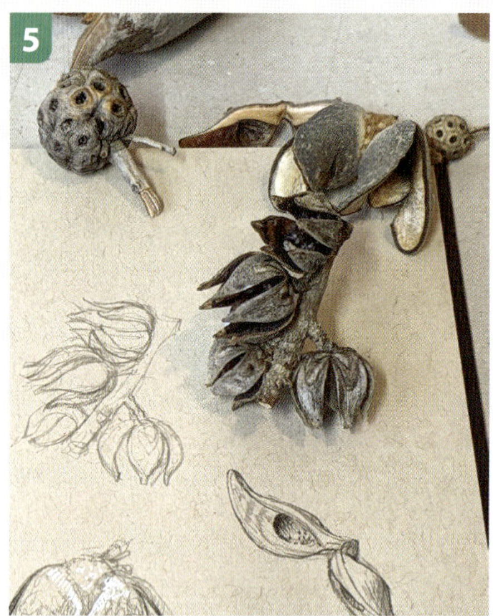

Drawing in this way with pen, circling around forms with multiple lines, allows you to really feel the three-dimensional shape of the pods.

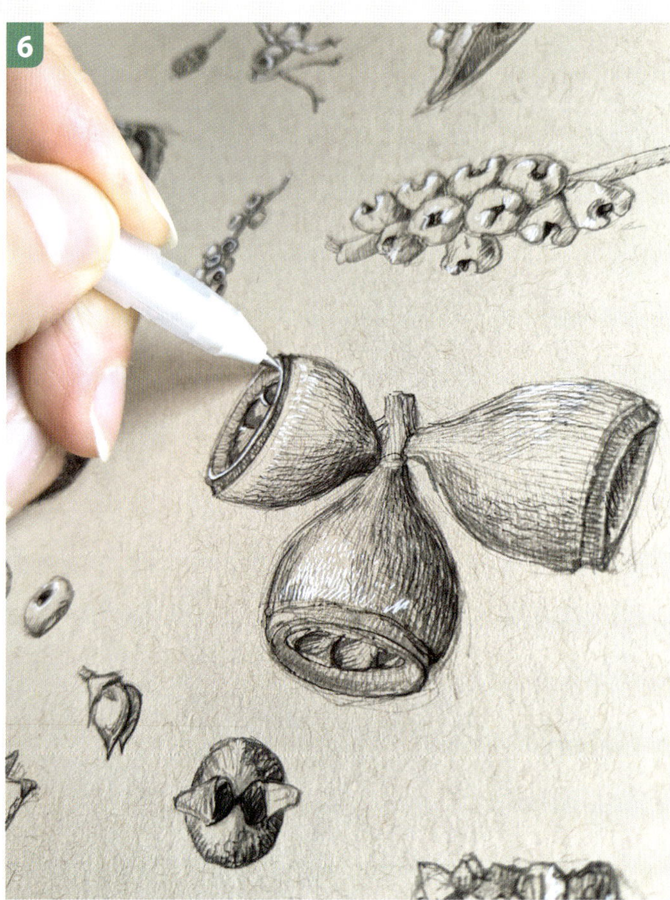

Adding highlights with the opaque ink of a white Sakura 'Gelly Roll' pen. Care must be taken when using this type of pen. White represents a big tonal leap compared with the grey pens, so it can stand out if applied too heavily.

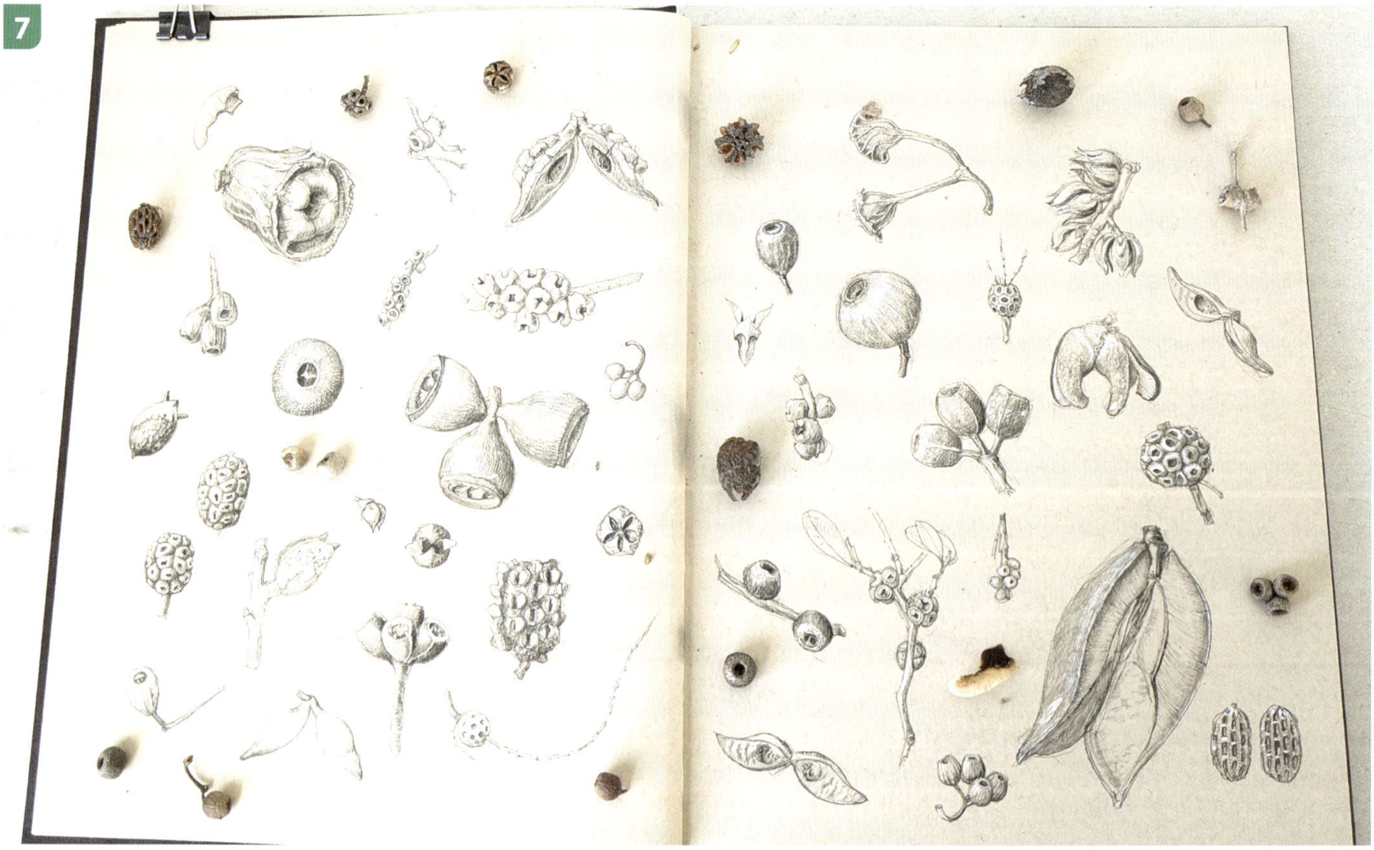

It was very satisfying to see all the gaps filled in with the final handful of tiny, detailed pieces.

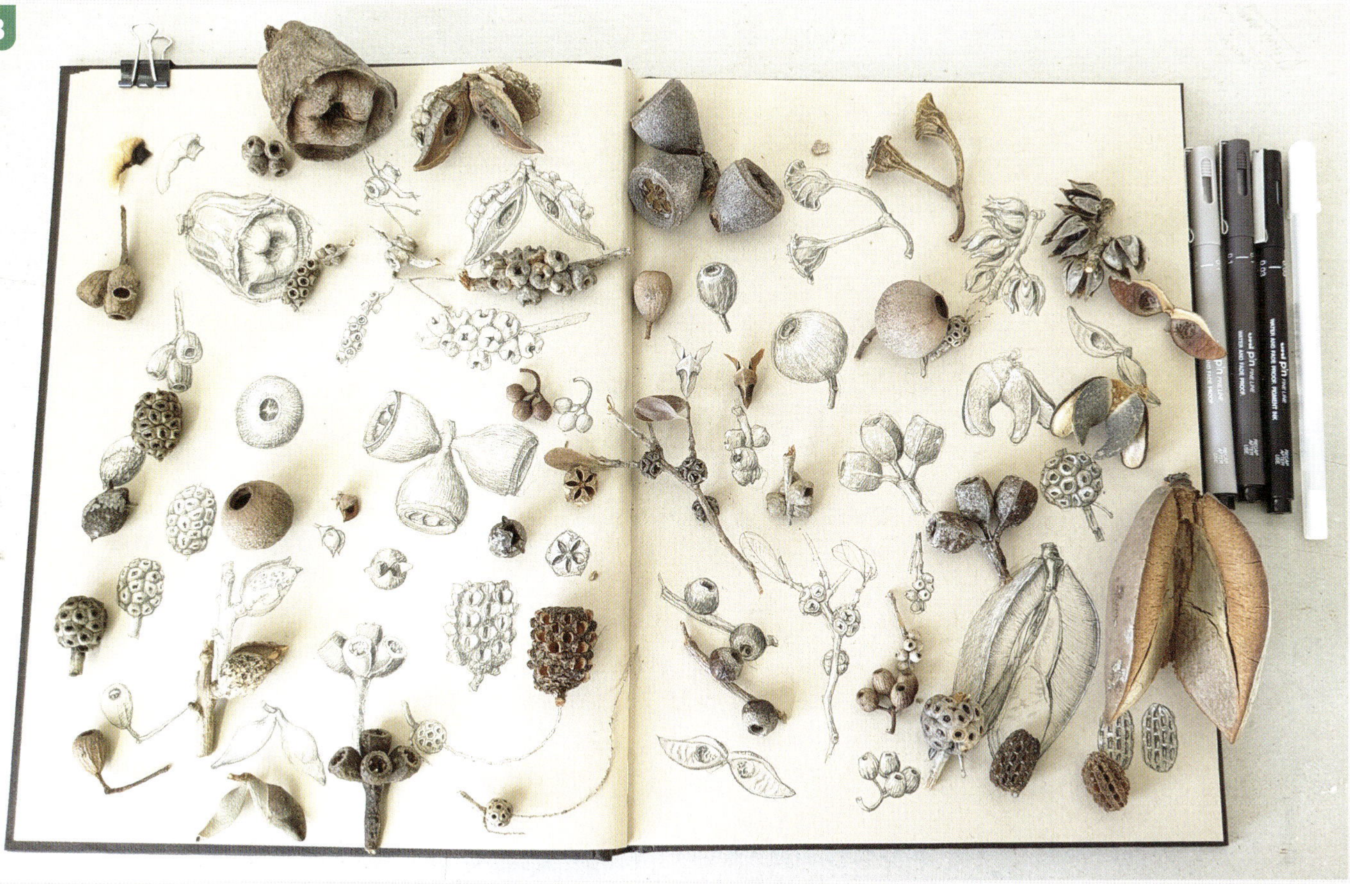

The final pages look very appealing, with the seed pods placed alongside the drawings. The sketchbook used was Strathmore's '400 Series Toned Tan Mixed Media Paper' (A4 size), Uni Pin 'Fine and Delicate' pens in light grey, dark grey and black, and a Sakura 'Gelly Roll' white ink pen.

Filling in Compositional Gaps

Once I had drawn in the bulk of the collection from the original layout, I could see that there were some gaps. Fortunately, there were still some small items left over, many of which I had overlooked in my first selection. I enjoyed placing them on the nearly finished pages to see where they would best fit, before drawing them in.

Once this drawing had been completed, I contacted the botanist who had gifted the seeds and pods to me, in the hope of receiving some identifications. To my delight, he was able to give me a name for every item. There is space on the double-page spread to include the names, but at the moment I am not sure whether I want to do this or leave the pages as they are. What would you do?

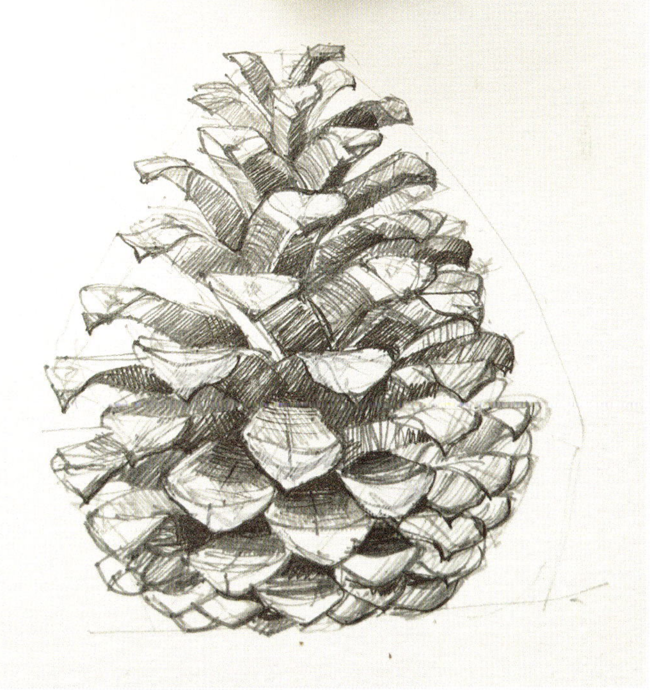

Every botanical artist has at least one pine cone in their collection. This one has been sketched using grey and black ink pens.

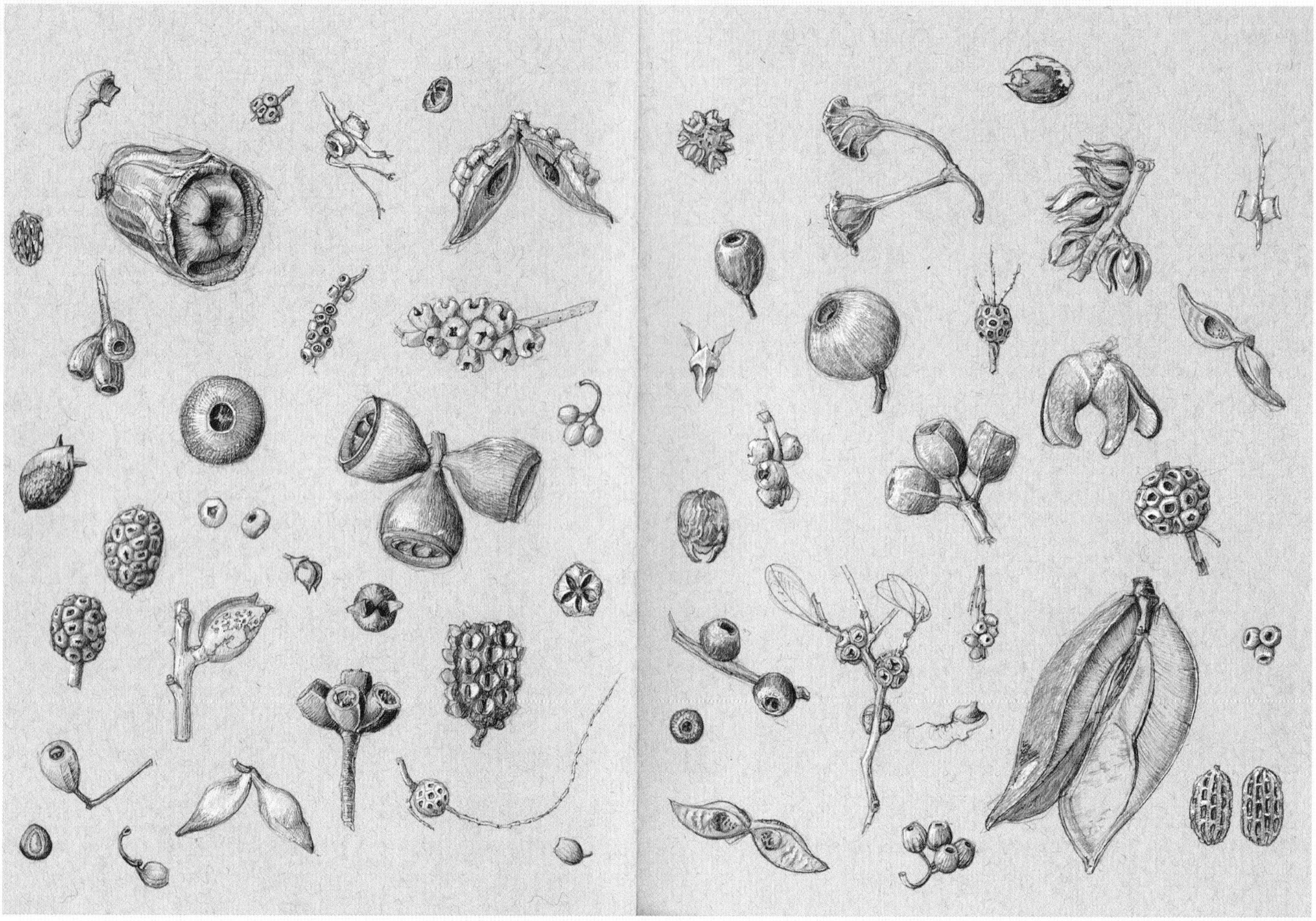

A scan of the final artwork. After all these years, the botanist has been able to identify most of the species from my drawings. I am still deciding whether to add the names of each piece.

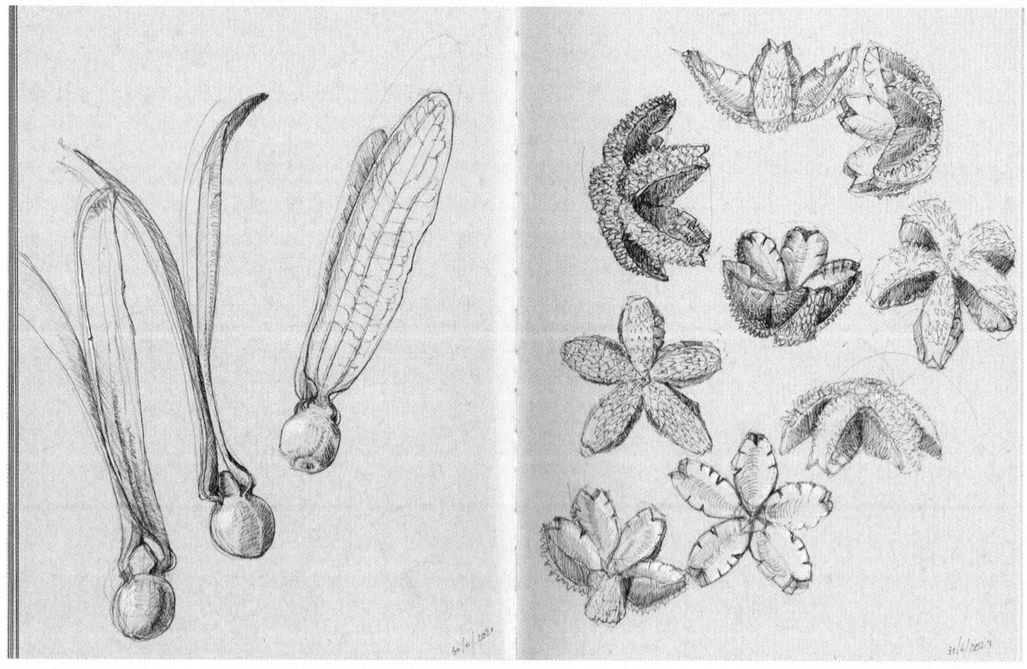

More seeds and pods from my collection sketched in ink. Note how on each side of this double page spread, a single specimen drawn from different angles quickly fills the sketchbook page.

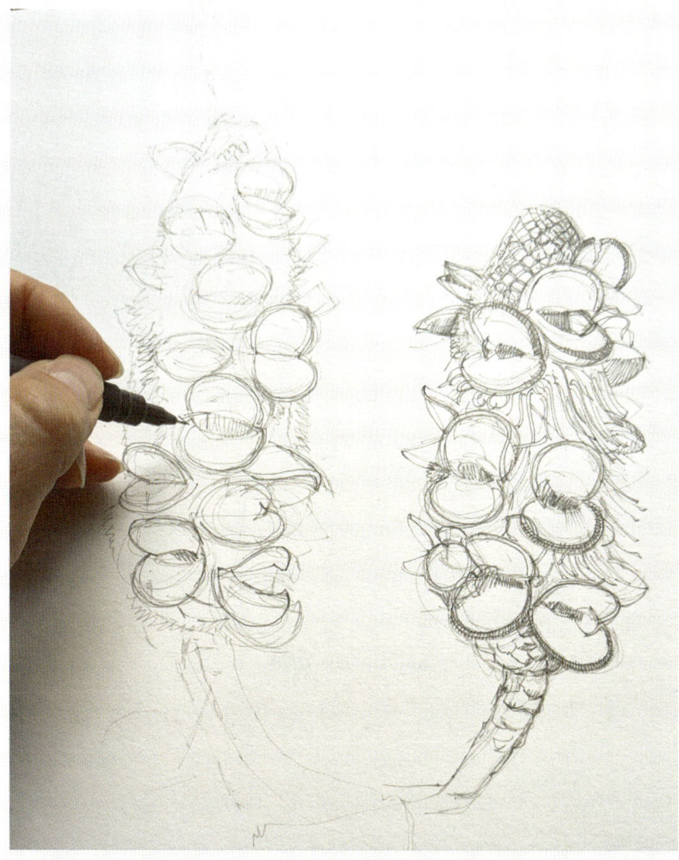

A wonderful *Banksia* pod given the loose pen and ink treatment. These are from my cousin's house by the ocean north of Sydney, where I was able to do a lot of drawing. Lighter grey pens were used to start off the drawings.

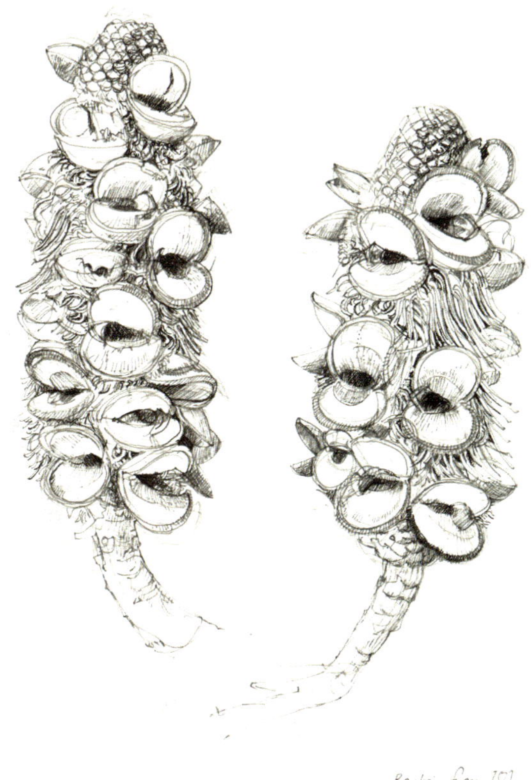

The completed *Banksia* pod sketch made in layers of grey and black fineliner pens

Fruits, seeds and pods in their multitude of different forms offer exciting and conveniently portable subjects for drawing in a botanical sketchbook. I still have many jars full of interesting items to draw and will continue to keep a watchful eye on and collect from all the living plants fruiting around me. Nature offers such a cornucopia of artistic delights to explore and illustrate, maybe it is worth dedicating a separate sketchbook just to its fruits and seeds.

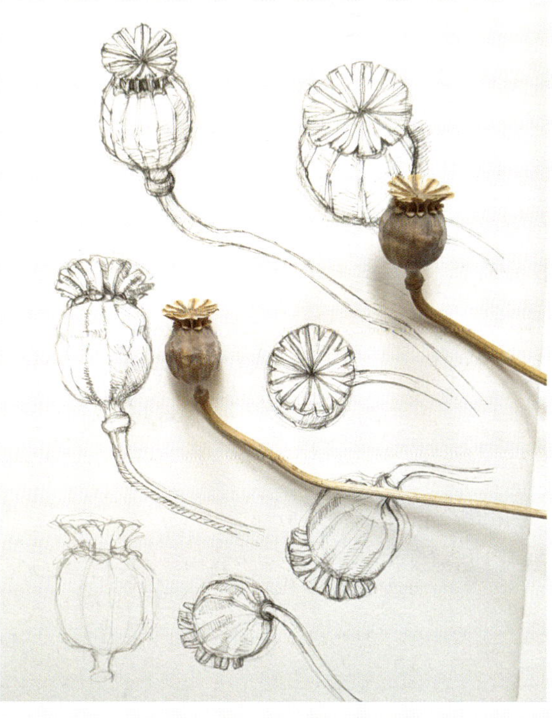

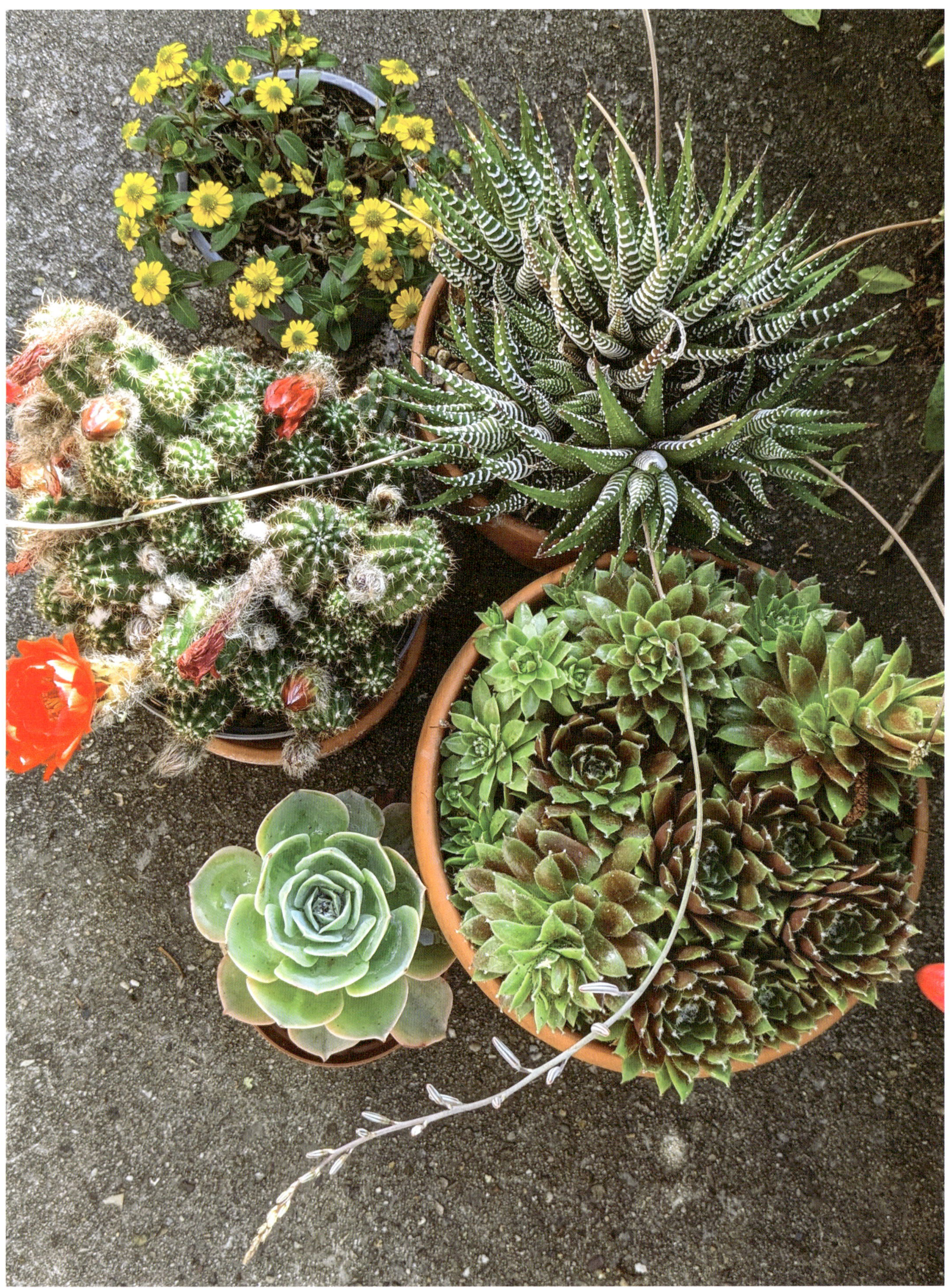

CHAPTER 5

SUCCULENTS, CACTI AND OTHER POT PLANTS

I f you do not have a garden or a wild area in which to find plants to draw, you can still find inspiration in pot plants, of both the indoor and outdoor variety. Seeing a plant every day builds a useful familiarity and getting to know it well will help when you begin drawing and painting it.

SUCCULENT PLANTS

Succulent plants are defined as plants that have swollen stems or leaves, which have evolved this way to store water. The term can be applied to many plants across a range of families, genera and species. They are very popular to grow in pots as they are relatively easy to keep alive, and grow and change quite slowly. Their fleshy leaves and stems come in a variety of interesting shapes and colours and their elegant inflorescences can be surprisingly colourful.

Many succulent genera such as *Echeveria* also possess leaves that are arranged in pleasing spiral-patterned rosettes. The spines of cactus plants present a drawing and painting challenge, but they are worth it when their flowers arrive. Their beauty is enhanced by the contrast between their ephemeral, brightly coloured blooms and their spiky stems.

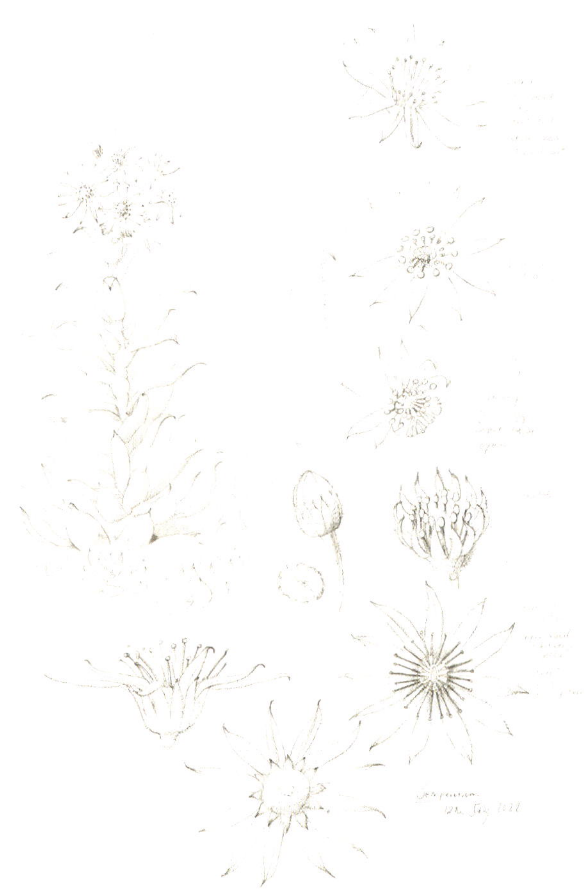

Although succulent plants may sit around not doing very much most of the time, once they flower, there can be a dramatic and rapid change in their appearance. This *Sempervivum* 'Blue Boy' was a cluster of small, dark green, maroon-tipped rosettes until one of the plants produced a huge inflorescence. Drawing its fascinating flowers from bud to opening was a great pleasure, and I look forward to capturing the colour of the inflorescence when the plant flowers again.

A pot plant collection provides ample material for botanical sketchbook studies. Succulent plants with their stiff leaves and spirally growth forms are particularly fun to draw.

Two graphite drawings of a flowering *Echeveria elegans* plant. The first one (right) has been left as a line drawing, while the second (left) has had tonal values added to reflect the form and colour of the leaves. The second drawing shows the centre of the plant more clearly; the inflorescence makes a pleasing S-shape as it curves into the leaf rosette.

After a large pot overflowing with *Echeveria elegans* had been split into three smaller pots, they all began to grow very happily and soon started flowering. Each plant possessed a very similar form to the others, but in three different sizes. I wanted to try drawing them and capturing their beautiful colours.

Drawing a Small Plant

I thought that the smallest plant, measuring 15cm in diameter, would make a good warm-up piece before attempting to draw the largest plant. With its inflorescence just starting to emerge, the rosette shape of the leaves at the base was perfect. I drew this plant twice because, although I liked the leaves on my first attempt, the centre of the leaf rosette was not visible. I changed the angle of the pot so that the viewpoint would look more directly into the centre. This new angle also showed a more pleasing arching shape of the inflorescence, and there was more depth to the drawing.

Leaving the first drawing in outline only, I worked up the second drawing more completely by adding tones to show the three-dimensional form of the leaf rosette. It was interesting to see what a difference the tonal layer made to depicting the thickness and texture of the leaves.

Drawing the Large Plant

After drawing the smaller plant, I was ready to focus on the larger version. As I was planning on adding watercolour to this study, I chose the A3 spiral-bound watercolour sketchbook, with a vertical orientation.

When drawing a plant as seemingly complex as this from life, it is very helpful to find and use the spiral patterns that can be found within its leaf arrangement. The spiral arrangement of a rosetted succulent such as this one is most clearly visible from above. When looking at this arrangement from the side the spirals are slightly flattened but form arching lines.

The process of using this spiralling arrangement to help you draw the leaves of the *Echeveria elegans* plant can be broken down into four steps:

Step 1: Finding the Spiral Lines

Use the leaf tips to plot out the spiral formation or arrangement of the leaves. Measure the distances between the points where they fall on the perspectival plane and draw lines to join those points, to indicate whether they are in the correct place. At this stage you also need to observe the general dimensions and proportions up the whole plant, including width and height, to make sure among other things that the drawing will fit on the page. You may also wish to leave enough space around this drawing for flower details to be added.

Step 2: Sketching in Basic Leaf Shapes

Working backwards from the leaf tips, start sketching in the leaf shapes. Succulent leaves are often very simple in shape, each one a slightly smaller or larger version of the previous one. In this case they become smaller towards the centre of the plant; those on the outer edge of the plant are older. The repeated shapes are presented in different viewpoints and angles, which allows you to see and draw the leaf shape changing gradually as it turns through 360 degrees. A different aspect of the leaf's form is revealed in each new view. Observe the silhouettes made by those leaves on the edge of the plant. The negative shapes created between them will also help you to refine those shapes.

Step 3: Erasing Working Marks and Refining Shapes

At this point, the plant is really beginning to take shape. Most of the working lines (for example, those joining the

The process of drawing the *Echeveria elegans*. 1: Find the spiral line patterns and plot in the position of the tips of leaves. 2: Block in basic leaf shapes and the position of the inflorescence. 3: Look at leaves more closely and draw their forms in more detail. 4: Finalise detail of leaves and flowers on inflorescence and add tonal values.

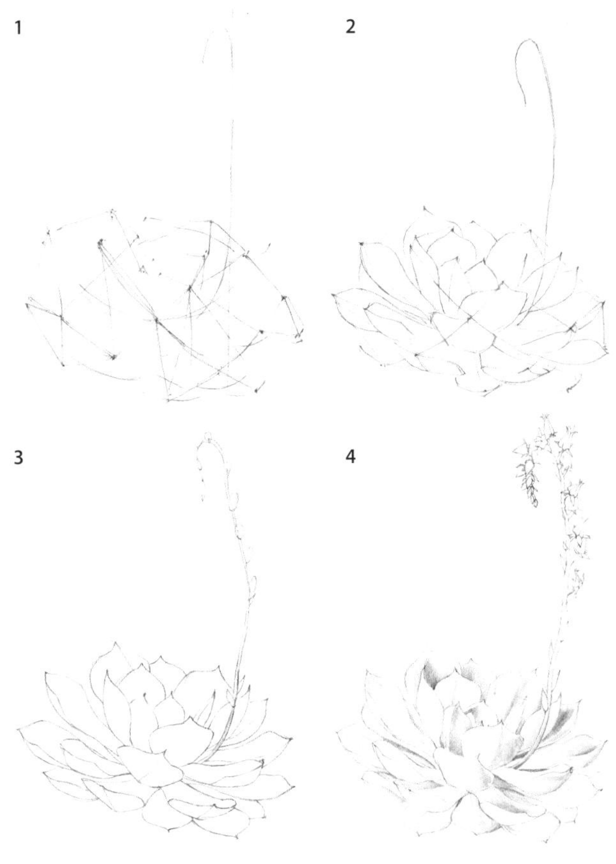

plotted leaf-tip points) have now been erased as it is time to focus on each individual leaf. The shape of the flower spike can be refined and the way in which the flowers are arranged along it can be marked in. The flowers lower down on the spike are more spaced out, while those towards the tip are more tightly clustered. As this inflorescence is still developing, the lower flowers are more developed than those at the tip; the flowers at the tip are still in bud and will be the last to open. Apart from helping the artist to capture the growth pattern, this is also an assurance that there will be plenty of flowers to remove for drawing and dissection.

Step 4: Adding Detail and Tone

This is the last stage of drawing, when all the shapes, forms and structures are finalised. At this point, my drawing slows down as I take care to study and draw each individual leaf, while at the same time ensuring that the form of the entire plant is correct. Finally, I observe the way light falls on the leaves and add some tonal shading.

This view of the inflorescence was pleasing as there was a beautiful and logical arrangement of flowers on it. It was possible to show the flowers from nearly all possible angles and at every stage of development – from tiny bud to spent flower head – and the arrangement complemented the beautiful arching curve of the whole spike. The spike could also be seen clearly emerging from between the leaf bases of the plants. Drawn outdoors, the plant was positioned in such a way as to have the light coming from the left-hand side, as that best illuminated the forms.

Adding Flower Details to the Study

Now it was time to focus on one of the *Echeveria*'s flowers and add detail to the study. The inflorescence had been drawn from an angle that would show off as many flowers as possible, in a variety of poses. However, I also wanted to draw a single open flower in more detail. I chose one that was open, with anthers that were fully developed but not yet dehisced (opened). As the flower was a little too small to draw in detail life-sized and still be able to see its inner parts clearly, I drew it at a scale of times three, using my proportional dividers to measure and create the enlarged version.

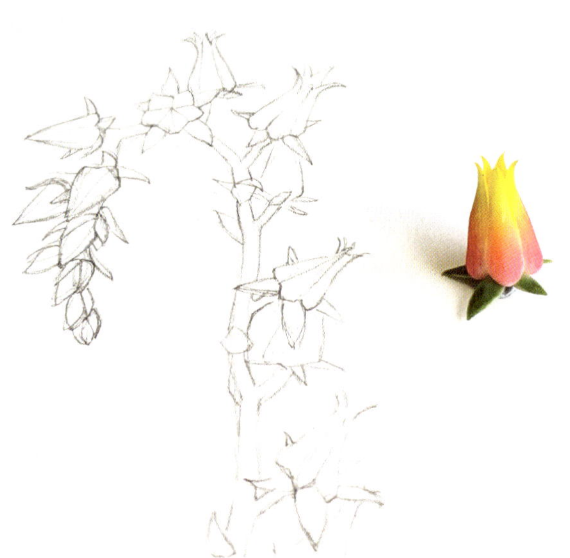

Focusing in on one flower gives more information than can already be seen on the drawing of the inflorescence on the main plant in this study.

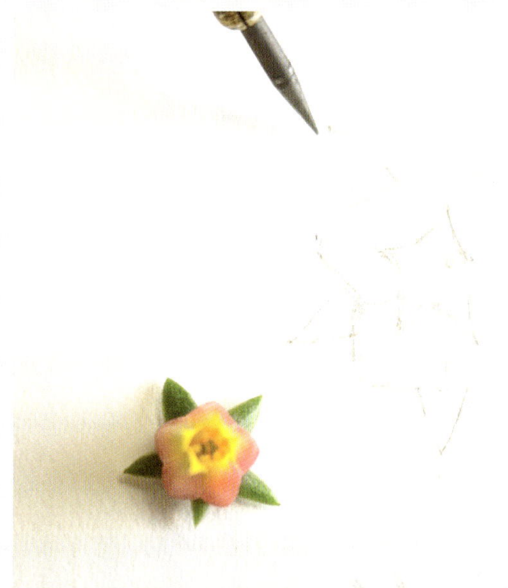

Looking directly down on the flower is a slightly unnatural aspect, but it gives a clear view of the alternating arrangement of its five petals and five sepals. Here, the flower is being drawn at a magnification factor of three, or '×3'.

When drawing flowers in this way I like to begin by drawing them whole from three different angles: from the back, from above and from the side. I also drew this one tilting slightly forwards, as it is most commonly seen on the inflorescence. Once these were drawn, I was ready to make a longitudinal section of the flower. Cutting it along one of its axes of symmetry provided two exact halves of the flower and allowed me to observe and draw its inner parts.

Adding Colour to the Pencil Study

With everything in place with the drawing of the *Echeveria elegans* and its flower, it was time to add some colour. I worked on the flower colour first. I knew the flowers would not last as long as the leaves and wanted to capture it before they died. The overall colour palette of this plant is pastel. Avoiding the use of opaque white in watercolour, these colours need to be combined and applied in quite dilute mixes, which use the white of the paper to create the pale effect.

Rather than add paint to the whole study, I decided to leave this piece as a combination of graphite pencil and watercolour. This gave me the option to return to it and add more paint in the future, or use it as a reference piece if I wanted to make a more polished and finished artwork of the plant. Making this study has given me more confidence to tackle this type of subject in the future.

Before cutting, I drew a quick diagram to make sense of the flower's arrangement and determined that there were five each of sepals and petals, five stamens, and five ovules, all arranged alternately. This diagram helped me to know where to make the cut.

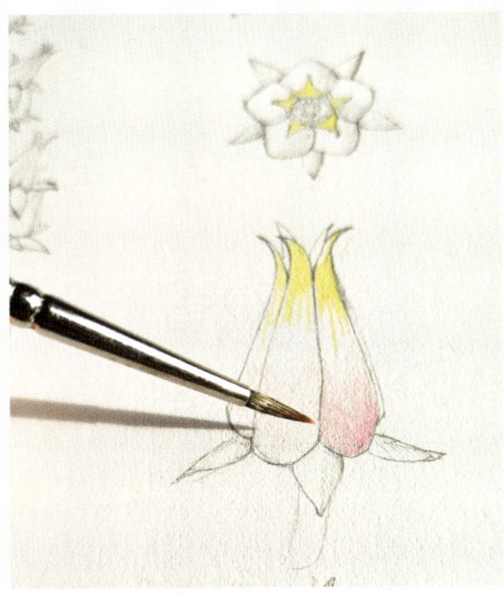

The pale blue-green of the *Echeveria* leaves called for light washes of very dilute paint, mixed using Prussian Blue and Cadmium Lemon. There were two options here: I could erase the graphite that had been applied to describe the darker tonal areas before adding paint, or I could leave it to paint over. When mixed with the green, Paynes Grey worked well as a shadow.

Adding watercolour to the *Echeveria* flower drawings. After experimenting with mixes of warm yellows and magenta, I applied the same colour to each flower in turn.

Before and after: adding watercolour to the pencil study really makes the details pop. I experimented with painting over some of the graphite instead of erasing all of it first.

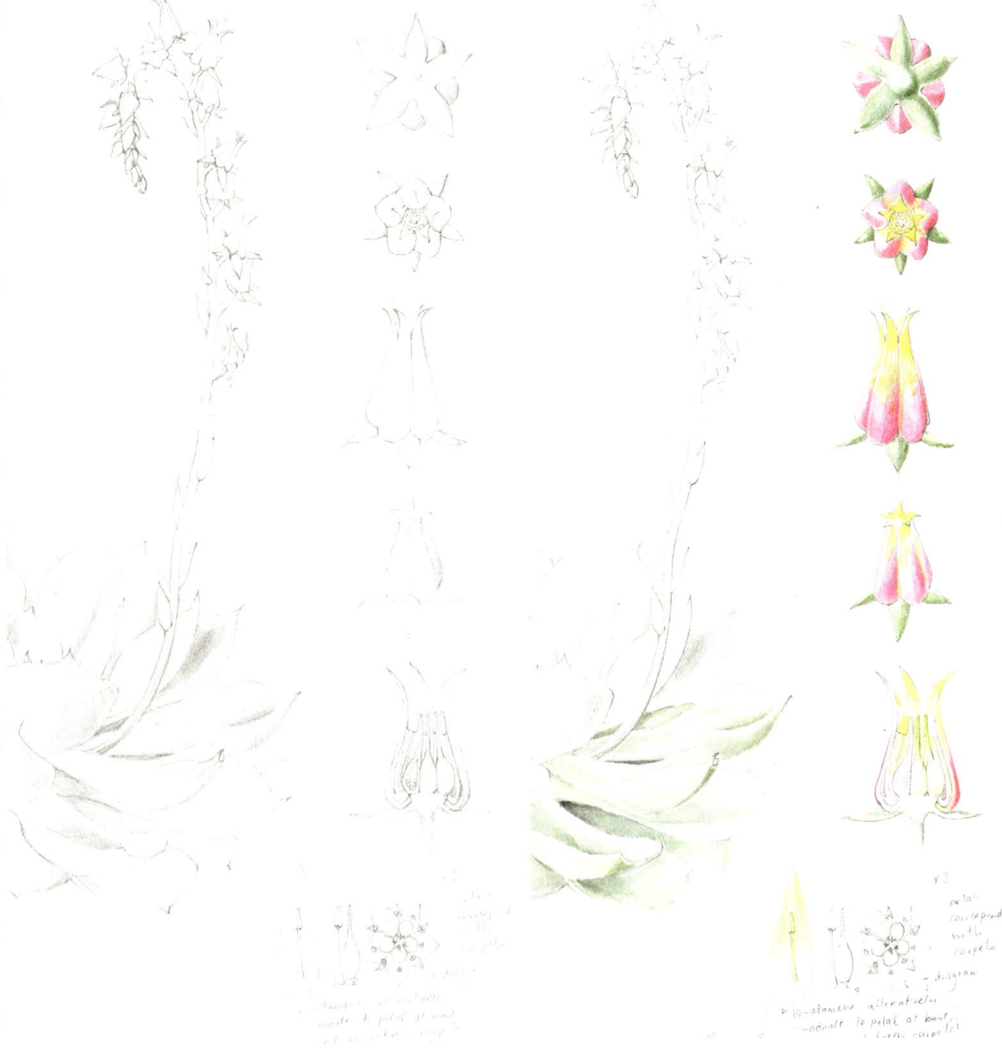

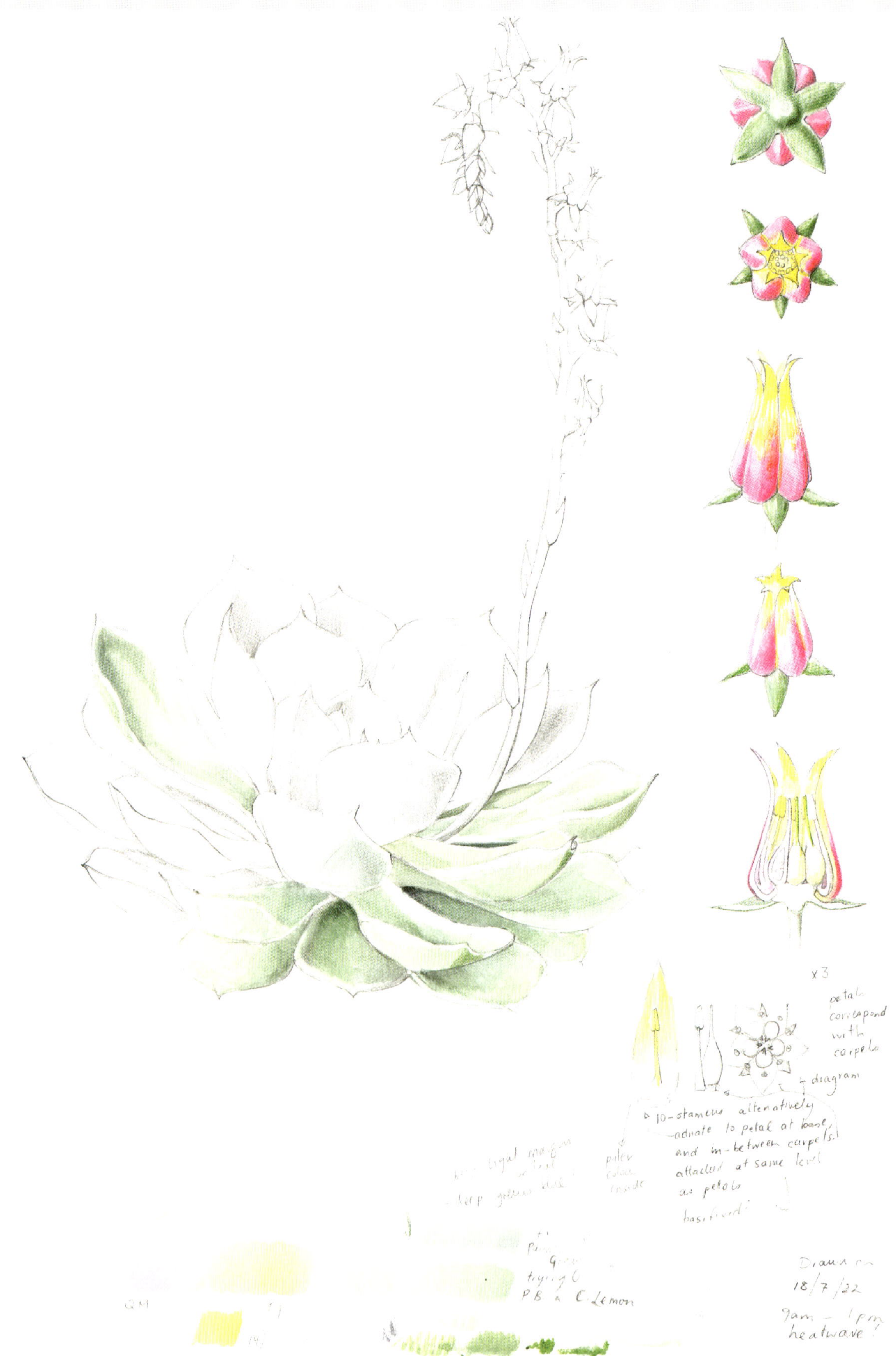

The flowering *Echeveria elegans* sketchbook page with a half-coloured drawing of the flowering plant, enlarged flower details and notes on the plant's structure and colour.

Another plant from my family's succulent collection, this unassuming little green cactus in the genus *Echinopsis* bursts into life annually with surprising bright orange-red flowers. Having watched it flower for several years in a row, I vowed to capture it on paper one day. Fortunately, I was around when its first buds began to emerge from the spiny stems in May. When several flowers bloomed from the top of the central plant, I decided now was the time to draw this beautiful subject.

Prioritising Ephemeral Flowers

Cactus stems may be slow-growing and easy to capture, but the flowers are short-lived. For this study I drew the body of the cactus quickly and simply without adding in any of its spines, knowing that there would be plenty of time to study them later. Focusing instead on the ephemeral flowers, I positioned the plant in such a way as to best show off the two main blooms. I started with simple shapes before progressing to individual petals. There were two types of petal: more rectangular outer petals and more rounded inner petals. At the centre of the flower there were whorls of stamens surrounding a ten-pronged style.

This flower was challenging because its form changed quite dramatically throughout the day. For this reason, after drawing the flowers that were attached to the cactus on the first day, I drew it again, choosing three more flowers that opened over successive days. My aim was to show the variety of flower forms observable at different times of the day. The flower also preferred to be fully open when in direct sunlight. Simply taking the plant from the front doorstep where it had been growing (which was in full sunlight) to the studio table (which was not) caused it to start closing.

Recording Colour from Life

This flower's petals were so bright and iridescent that it was impossible to capture the colour properly on a photograph. The petals tended to look dark red when photographed but were in fact much more orange. What appeared at first glance to be red was in fact a combination of bright red-oranges and, towards the centre of the flower, yellow. It was even possible to see shades of magenta and crimson, all in one petal. Painting these colours on to the bright white watercolour paper required the careful use of a tiny dry brush to maintain the intensity of the

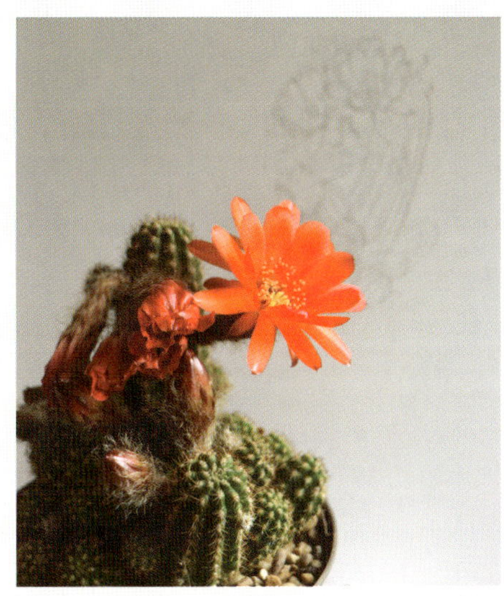

The flowering *Echinopsis* with my drawing in the background. The flowers are very sensitive to light and start to close without it, which made it challenging to draw them indoors.

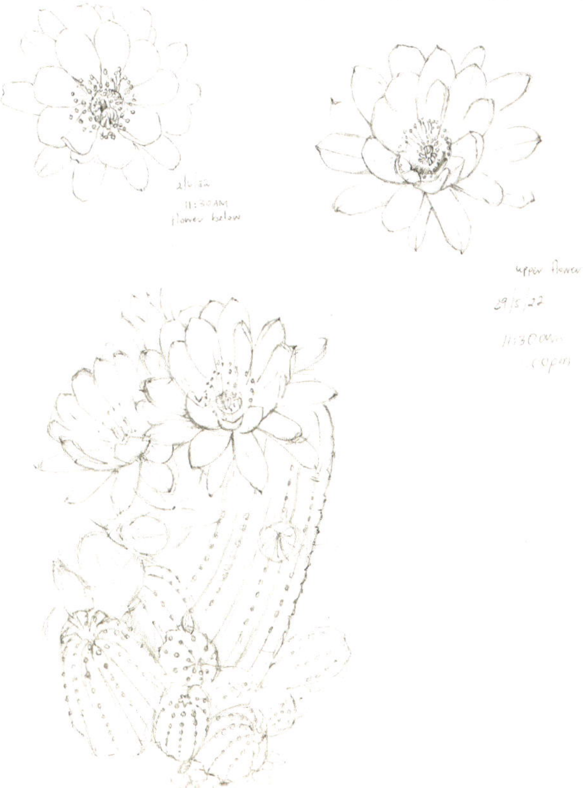

The first sketch of *Echinopsis* drawn in the A3 watercolour sketchbook. It shows the placement and forms of the flowers but leave details such as spines to be added at a later date. I prioritised drawing the flowers, as they are the most ephemeral elements of the plant. Sensitive to light and time of day, I drew these from different angles and at different stages of opening, in an effort to get to know and understand them.

iridescent hue.

When making this kind of colour study, I am trying not only to capture the correct colour, but also to discover how to apply the paint. In this case, I applied washes first, before layering up yellow and red side by side with very small brush strokes. I observed that the outer petals were not as bright as the inner ones.

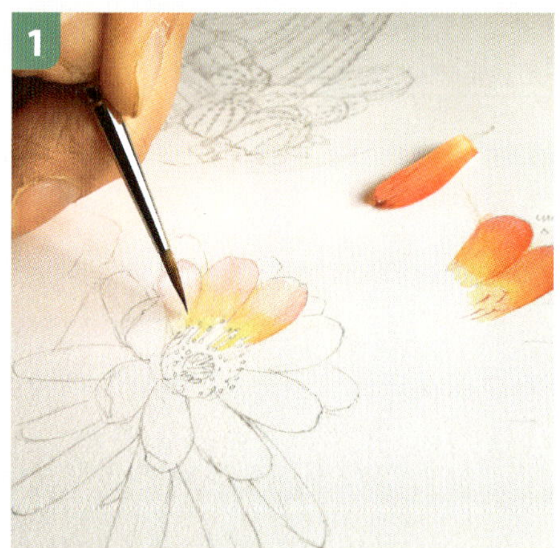

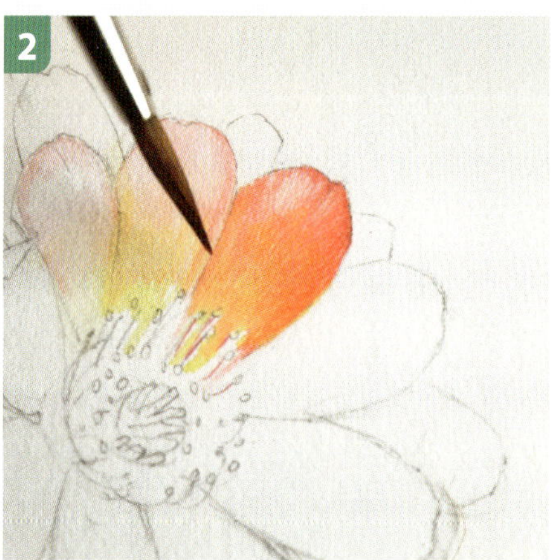

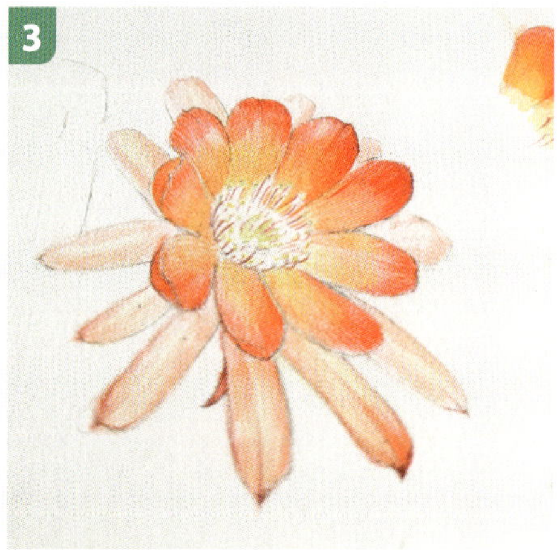

Adding colour to the *Echinopsis* flowers. 1. Testing colours and paint application to build up petal colour, with petals alongside. Warm yellow and rose were first put down as washes.

Adding tiny brush strokes of intense colour to try to capture the iridescence of the petals.

The completed flower. The outer petals were duller in colour than those on the inner part of the flower.

Flower Dissection

As the final buds of the *Echinopsis* cactus grew and opened, it was time to make and draw a dissection of one of the final flowers of the season. I drew a very sharp scalpel carefully through the centre of the flower, taking care to cut from the ovary outwards without crushing and deforming the delicate petals. As soon as the flower was cut in half, I propped it up and took some photographs, alongside a ruler to indicate its size. I also made a spirit specimen of it by placing it in a jar containing clear alcohol. If necessary, I would be able to use these references at some time in the future to complete the drawing.

While I am happy with the way this sketchbook page is developing, more attention needs to be given to the colours, especially the greens. Thankfully, the slow-growing nature of the cactus means that I have plenty of time to observe it, provided I keep it alive. There are already new flower buds emerging; these, along with the flowers preserved in alcohol, will provide me with more than enough material to draw.

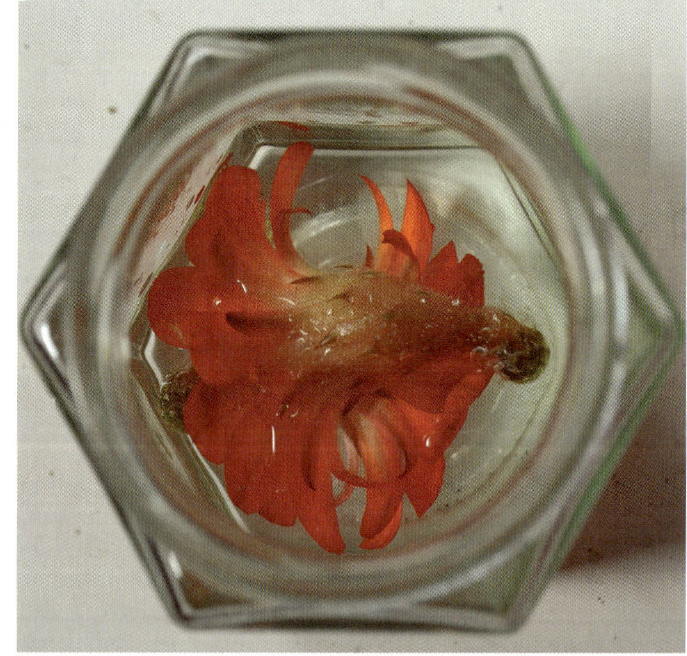

Two halves of the longitudinally dissected flower of *Echinopsis* placed into a small jar of clear alcohol. While the flower's colour would soon disappear, its forms remain intact, allowing me to study it at leisure in the future.

When drawing a dissected flower, I like to make the cut parts of the section extra crisp by outlining them with a very sharp HB pencil. There is no need to draw both halves of the flower. Often the style and stigma remain on one cut half anyway, and that is what has happened here. I could have cut them in half but chose to leave that part of the female parts intact, while still showing a dissected ovary.

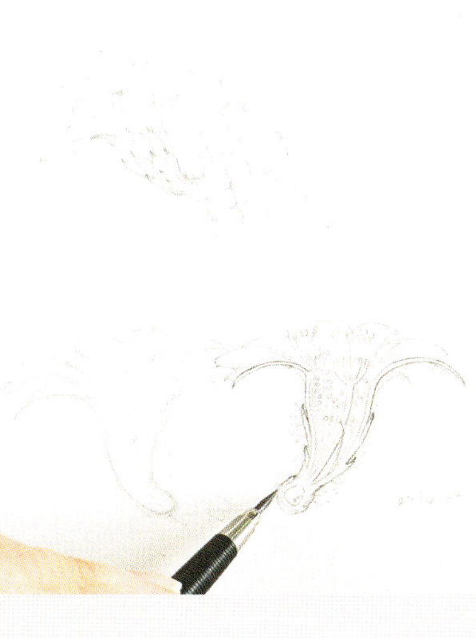

The final study page of *Echinopsis*. The main drawing of its flowering habit remains quite loose and sketchy. There is still a lot of work to do on this page, but thankfully there is plenty of time to return to the plant.

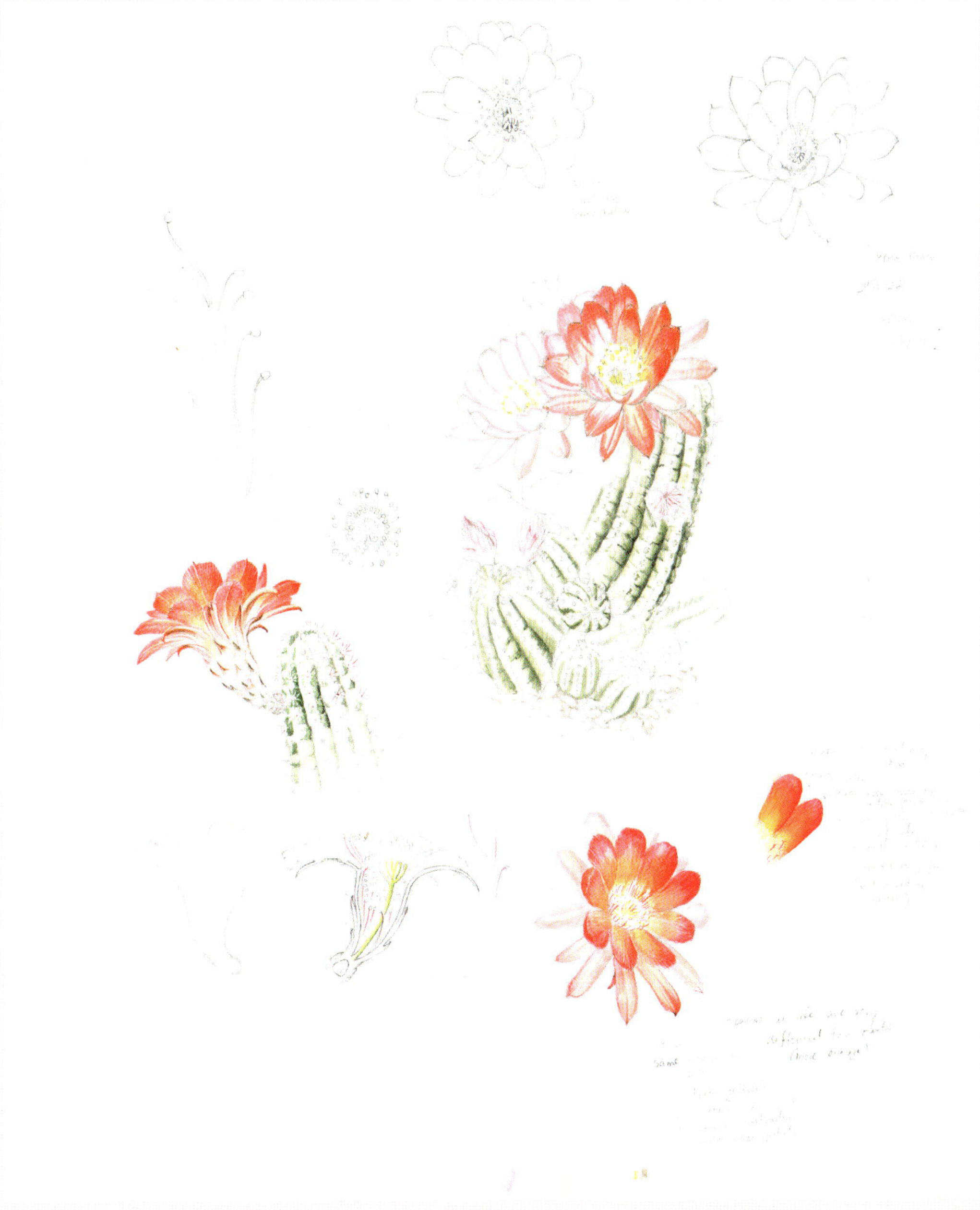

Detail from the study page of *Echinopsis*, showing the outside of the flower as it emerges from the stem.

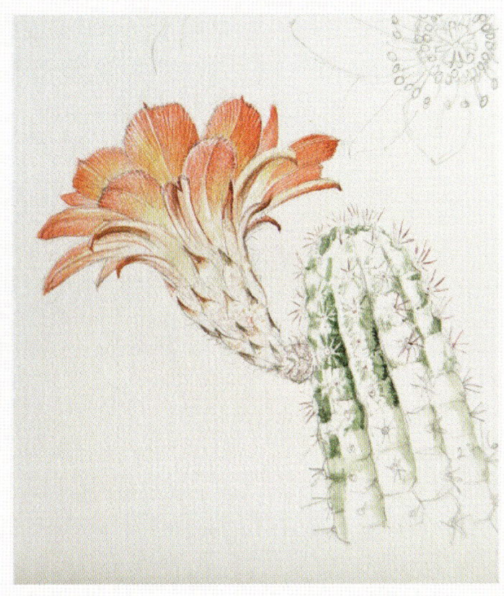

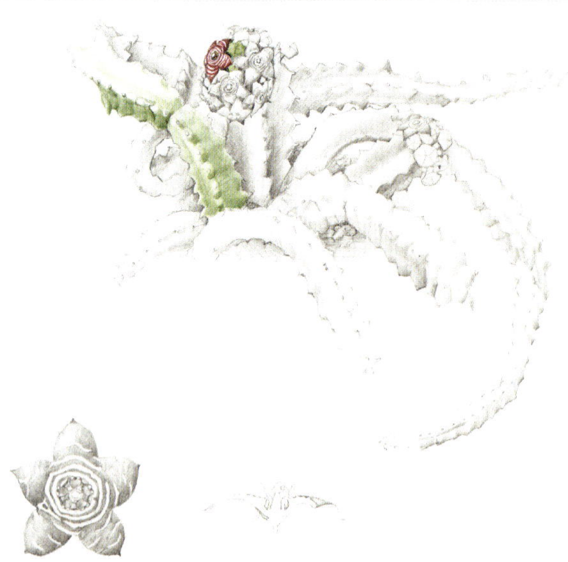

My second attempt at drawing the *Caralluma europaea* pot plant. With its new growth hanging down from the rest, it was difficult to find a pleasing position for it. I added tones to the whole plant, before erasing some parts and replacing them with watercolour. Here, I was already thinking about looking at the flowers in more detail, adding a flower from above and one longitudinal section. As soon as this drawing was complete, I devoted the next sketchbook page to drawing the dissected flower.

Loaned to me by a friend, this plant was one of the first succulents I ever drew. *Caralluma* comes from the plant family formerly referred to as *Asclepiadaceae*, which is known for having flowers with extremely complex and interesting internal parts. This plant, which was growing in a pot, had fascinating tiny flowers that were most unusual – and very smelly.

To begin with I drew the whole plant, positioning it in the best way possible to capture the flowers growing from the top of its stems, but also trying to place its stems into a pleasing arrangement. The plant had a mixture of old and new growth, which I found quite challenging, and for this reason I drew it twice before I was happy with the composition. Eventually I used the curving new growth at the base of the plant to bring the eye into the foreground. I worked the drawing up with tonal rendering before tackling the flower itself.

Drawing the Flowers

Measuring around 20mm in diameter, it was clear that the tiny flowers could not be investigated without the aid of a microscope. I knew very little about the flowers before drawing them, so decided to work on the internal details as best I could and look for explanations afterwards. Generally, it is advisable to do your research beforehand, but sometimes it is difficult to wait.

I was fortunate to have a botanist to consult about the flowers after I had drawn them. With his help I was able to identify and label the various special flower parts, including the pollinia, or packets of pollen held in pairs. The shape and structure of the various parts are key in identifying differences between species.

Fresh Specimens for Colour Reference

The flowers from which I made the first drawings and dissections were not suitable for observing colour once I had finished drawing them; instead, I made spirit specimens by placing them into a small jar of alcohol. Because I was able to take freshly opened flowers from the plant at the same developmental stage as the original versions, it was straightforward to add colour to some of the line drawings. The addition of colour helped to distinguish the flower parts from each other even more. In particular, the yellow pollinia with the red-tipped connective tissue suddenly jumped off the page. Before adding watercolour with a very small brush, I erased most of the graphite from each section so as not to dull the effect of applying the paint.

Creating a Finished Piece

To create the final artwork, all the elements of this composition were traced from the sketchbook pages on to watercolour paper and re-drawn carefully with a 2H pencil. I then slowly worked up the painting using watercolour techniques, starting with washes before moving on to many layers of finely detailed dry-brush work. The finished piece is now in a private collection.

Drawings of *Caralluma* flowers made with and without a microscope, at magnifications ranging from ×3 to ×18. It is amazing how much complexity can be squeezed into such a tiny flower. Here they are shown with colour added, but they began as simple line drawings. Adding colour helped define the structures such as the pollina (left) even more clearly.

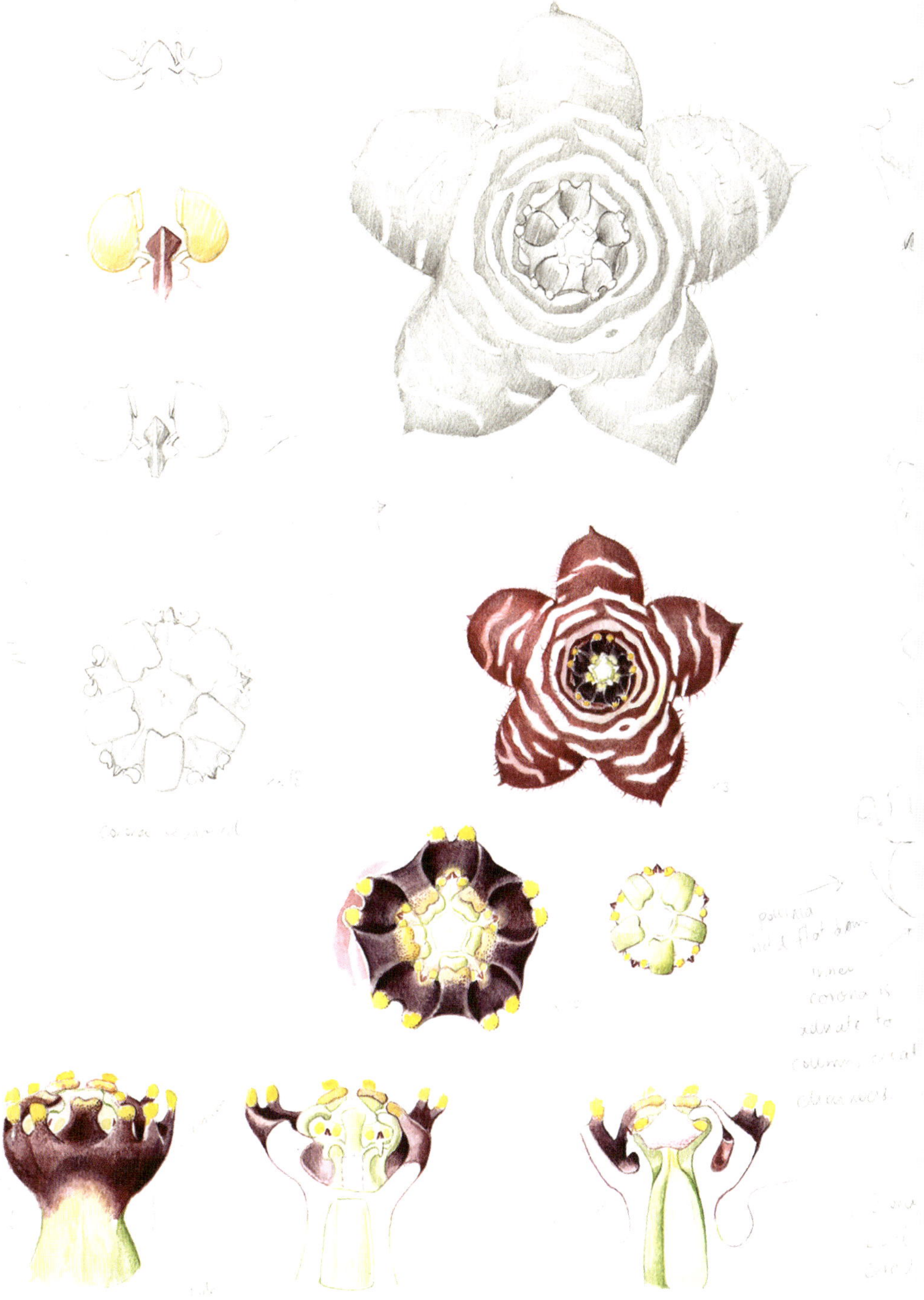

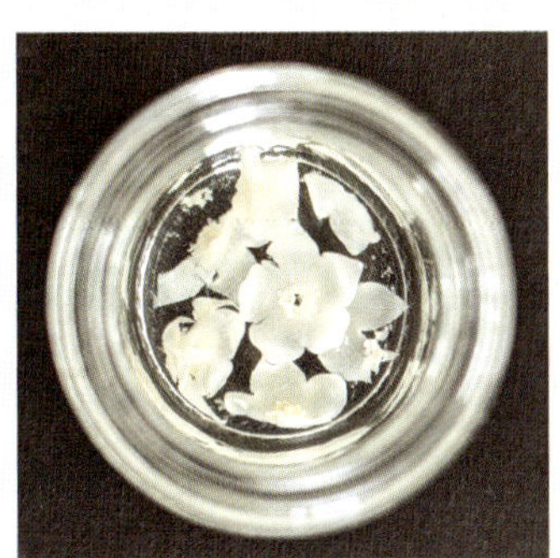

My spirit specimens of the *Caralluma europaea* flowers. While plant material placed in alcohol loses all its colour and takes on a ghostly appearance, the term 'spirit' refers not to this but to the alcohol itself. Spirit specimens are so useful. Although these were preserved ten years ago, their structures remain intact and I can still examine and draw them today.

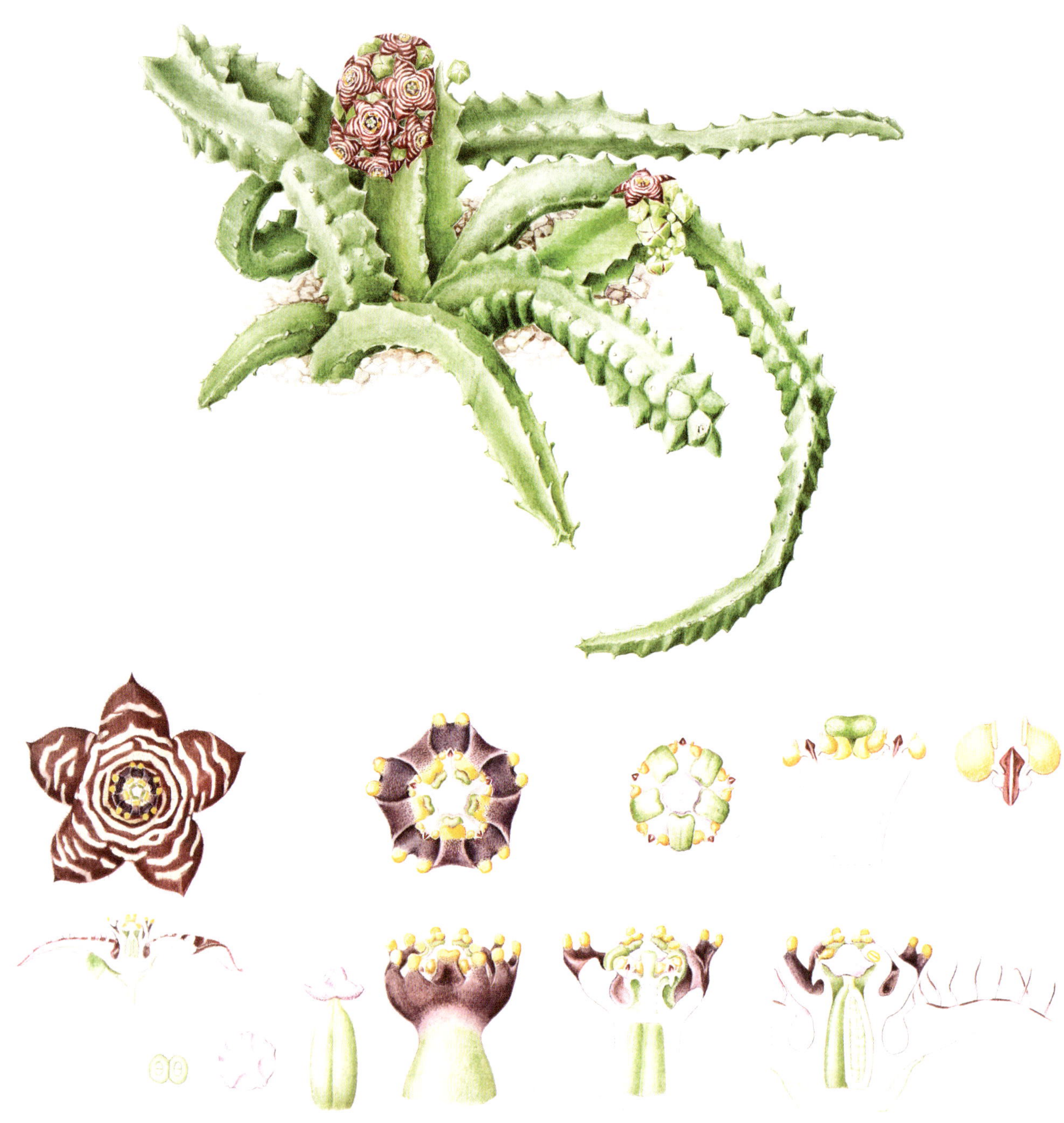

The finished *Caralluma europaea* piece in watercolour, with all the elements that I had drawn in the sketchbook worked up on watercolour paper at a high level of detail.

The subject of this study was an indoor pot plant that is not a succulent. I had admired *Stephanotis floribunda* from afar for some time, spotting it for sale quite often in the indoor plant displays in the garden centres. I loved its tubular white flowers, and the way in which they are held in inflorescences, which show the flowers off from all angles. *Stephanotis floribunda* is related to the *Caralluma europaea* of the previous project. They are in the same family (*Apocynaceae*) and subfamily (*Asclepiadoideae*) but, apart from some similarity in flower structure, there is little resemblance between them.

My original plan was to look closely at this plant's flowers but, in a familiar turn of events, I did not capture them in time. Instead, I had to redirect my focus – very happily – to drawing its beautiful paired leaves.

Just at the right time, I was lucky enough to find a potted *Stephanotis* for sale in full flower. Setting the plant up in a position that best showed off the flowers, I sketched in the position of the leaves as they climbed up the pot's wire support. At first, I drew the support lines in, but I later erased them. Originally, I had been most interested in the flowers. However, as I began to sketch the whole plant, I came to appreciate the leaves more and more.

Drawing Short-Lived Inflorescences

There were two main inflorescences to draw, each of which held both buds and open flowers at different stages and in a variety of positions. The flowers were the first parts to which I added details, as I knew they would not last. Indeed, over the two sessions it took me to draw in all the flowers and leaves, several flowers finished and fell off.

Once the flowers had gone, I had plenty of time to work on the leaves. The white flowers had called for very little shading, but I enjoyed layering up graphite on the leaves to show their deep colour and descriptive tones. The edges of the dark green leaves captured the light, so I paid attention to reproducing this aspect. The line drawing was made in 2H pencil, HB was added later to sharpen some of the lines. Both were layered repeatedly on the leaves to build up tone.

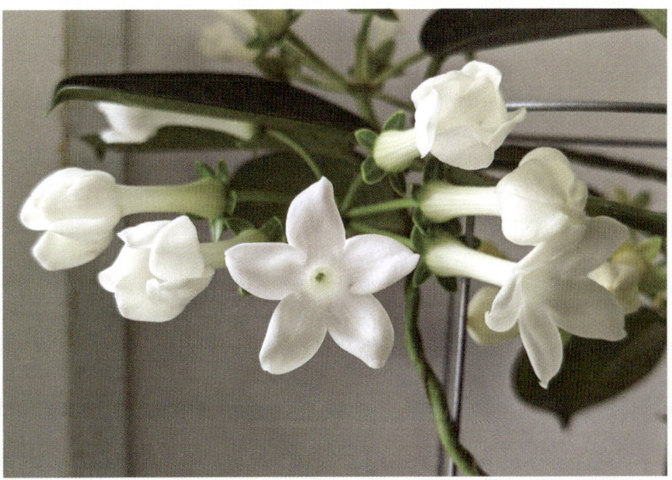

The white flowers of *Stephanotis floribunda* are borne on inflorescences that emerge from the axils of paired leaves. This plant is in the same family and subfamily as *Caralluma europaea*.

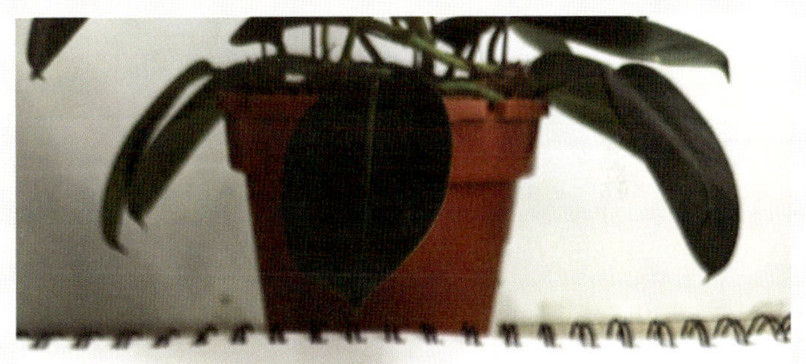

A *Stephanotis floribunda* in a small pot was the perfect size to draw in my A3 spiral-bound watercolour sketchbook. The slow growth of its leaves allowed me to take my time and revisit the drawing over months, as they did not change much.

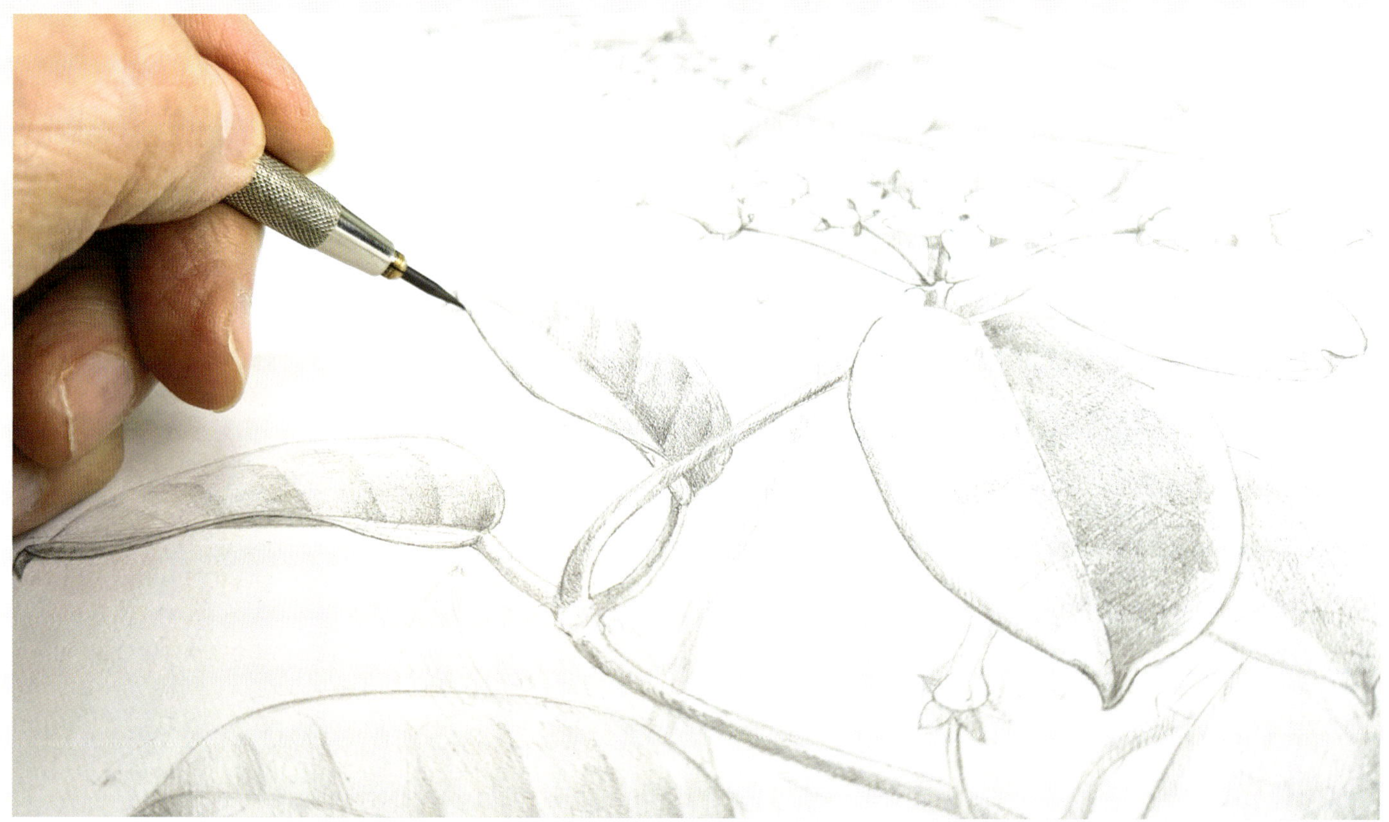

Beginning with a line drawing, layers of tone were gradually built up, minimally on the white flowers but darkening the plant's leaves. The darker and slightly shiny upper surface of the leaves required several layers of graphite, beginning with 2H pencil and adding HB and B. While it is best to layer softer pencil grades over harder ones, I like to repeat the 2H pencil over the softer layers occasionally. If applied gently, it can have a subtle blending effect on the layers beneath.

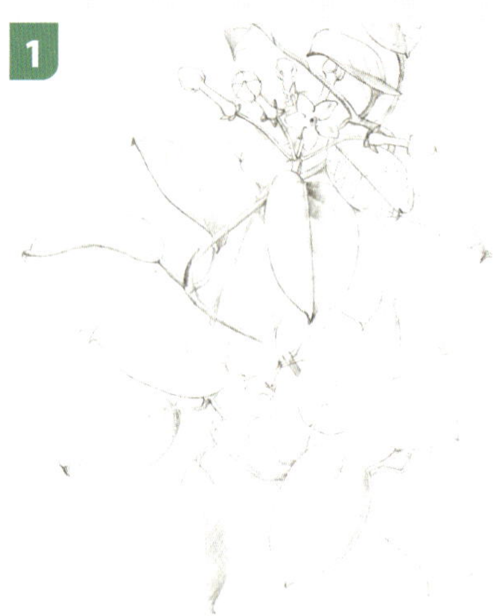

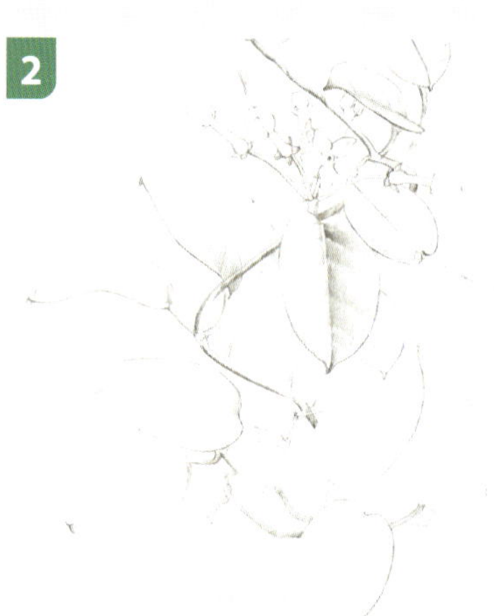

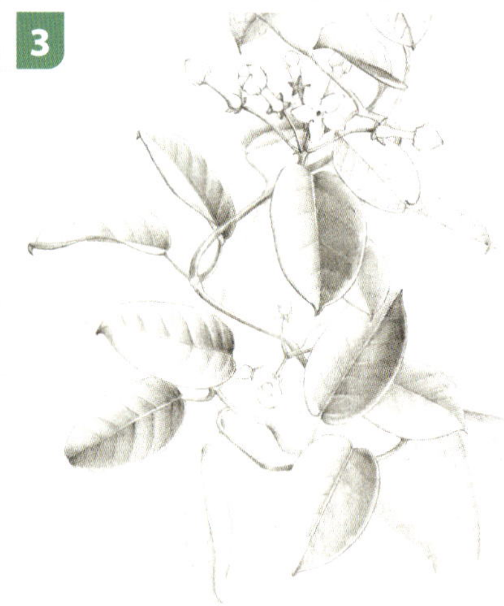

Blocking in complete, the line drawing is still quite sketchy in places. I am still deciding where I want to take this drawing.

I am thinking about making this drawing a more finished, tonal piece. Some details are now receiving more attention and becoming more refined. Tonal values are now being observed and built up gradually with layers of 2H and HB pencil.

Details such as leaf veins are more subtle, and a full range of tonal values has been added. The white flowers have been cleaned up. The drawing has the level of refinement that I want, retaining some of its sketchiness.

A Fun Study

This sketchbook study was one that changed tack along the way. I may have been attracted to the plant originally for its flowers but, partly because of the circumstances, I stayed for the leaves. Drawing the *Stephanotis* was a fun study in leaf shape and position, as the paired leaves twist and turn in every direction. It called for a depiction of the contrasting textures and colours of the upper and lower leaf surfaces, as well as some satisfying foreshortening.

This was never intended as a study for a final piece of artwork, so I enjoyed working on it with no time pressure and with no particular result in mind.

My *Stephanotis floribunda* pot plant continues to grow quite happily. Its leading growing shoot has been cut off, so I am relying on side shoots to appear if this plant is to get any larger and produce more flowers. I am hopeful that the tiny buds that have appeared in one of the leaf axils may produce some more flowers for me soon, and I will be able to do some more detailed work on them.

Many plant lovers and artists have a collection of pot plants. Perhaps you take yours for granted and have never thought to draw or paint them. Perhaps it is time to look at them with fresh eyes and appreciate them from an artistic point of view.

Why not choose your next pot plant based on how pleasurable it might be to draw and paint it? Enjoy getting to know your potted friends a little better by immortalising them in your botanical sketchbook.

This page was carefully removed from the sketchbook so that a good scan of it could be made without the spiral binding casting a shadow. When removing a page from a spiral-bound sketchbook, cut the paper rather than pulling it, as that can deform and damage the binding. Removing it also allowed this sketch to be stored in a more protected environment, where the graphite would not be smudged.

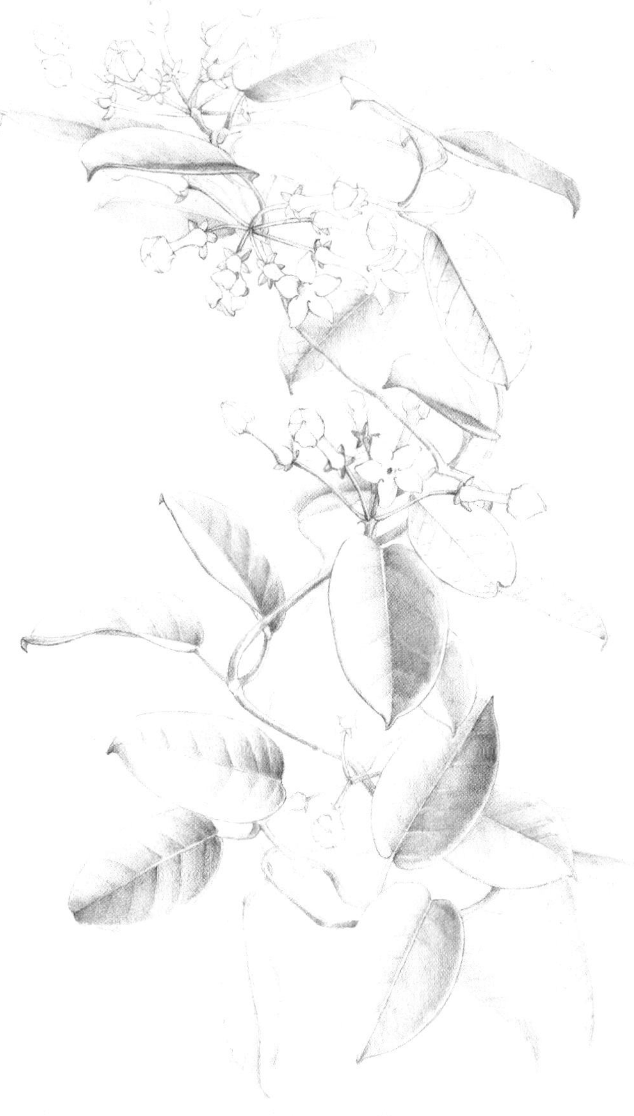

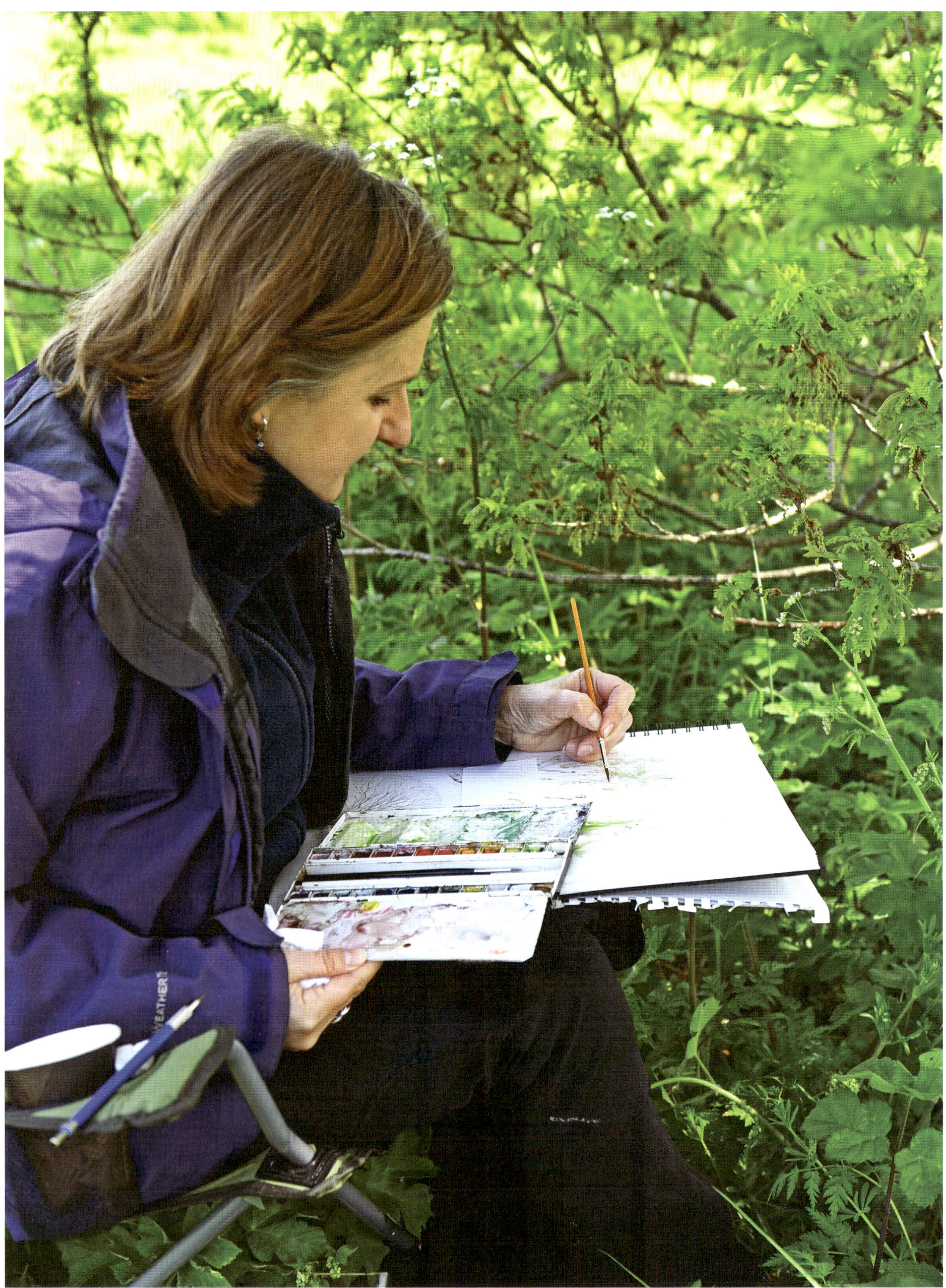

CHAPTER 6

WORKING IN THE FIELD

Drawing in nature is the perfect way to immerse yourself fully into your environment. An hour spent with nature is never wasted; neither is an hour spent drawing! Using your botanical sketchbooks to capture plants growing in situ creates an indelible impression of time and place.

Of course, it is a pleasure to work in a studio, where everything is under your control. But for many botanical artists, their love of plants originates in their experiences of them growing in the wild. When a plant is observed in the place where it grows – a botanical garden, a public park, a managed forest, a protected reserve or out in the bush – it is seen at its most natural.

CHALLENGES AND REWARDS OF WORKING OUTDOORS

Whether the subject is found in a cultivated or wild place, working from life in situ presents unique challenges. When sketching a plant where it grows, you have less control over both your subject and your surroundings. The subject is in a fixed position, so the first thing you need to do is find a place to sit or stand that will give you the right viewpoint or angle on the part of the plant that you wish to draw. When working outdoors you will need to deal with all sorts of weather, issues of accessibility, insects and other wildlife, and other people! Your equipment will need to be more portable than the set-up that you would use when working in the studio, and you may need to carry a stool or chair, and a drawing board or easel.

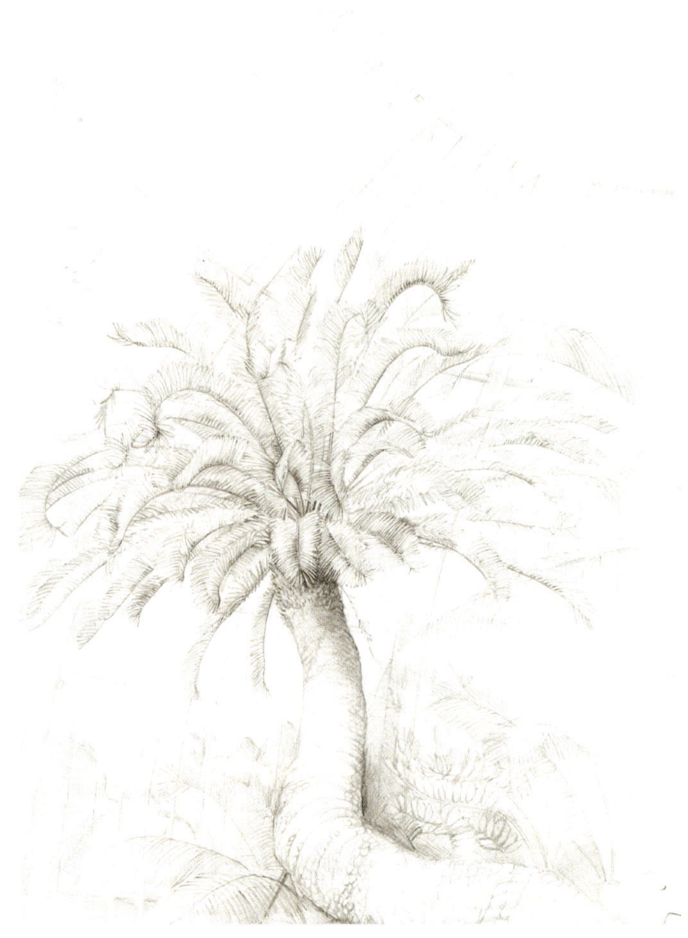

Sketchbook drawing of *Encephalartos altensteinii*, made completely in situ. There were a few challenges in capturing this potted cycad growing in the Palm House at Kew Gardens: the hot sun beating through the glasshouse walls, curious looks from visitors, and trying to isolate the subject from the many other pot plants. Whenever I look at this drawing, it takes me back to the heat of that setting.

Working in the field is both challenging and rewarding, providing full immersion in nature.

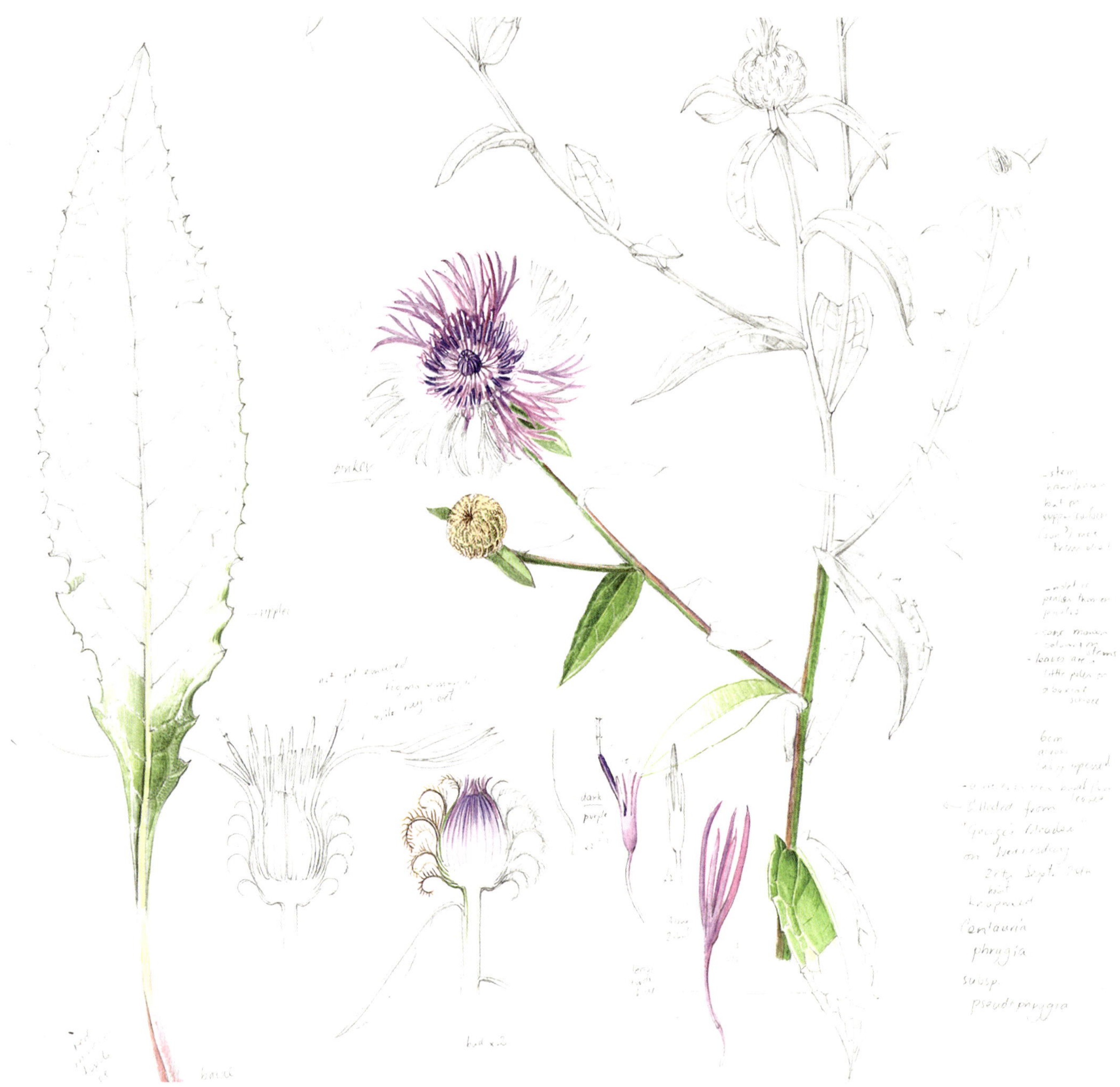

From the more gentle setting of Zalanpatak in Transylvania (Romania), the knapweed *Centauria phrygia* was sketched for a watercolour painting to be included in *The Transylvania Florilegium* (published in 2018 by AG Garrick and Addison Publications). Material was collected from a nearby meadow and taken indoors immediately, where it was sketched from life.

However, dealing with these challenges is well worth the effort. I have had some of my most memorable sketchbook experiences when sitting outside drawing a plant in its own environment. Once you have set yourself up in a comfortable position and started to draw and paint, you will find that your focus becomes highly attuned to your plant. You will experience a true immersion in nature.

EQUIPMENT FOR SKETCHING OUTDOORS

Apart from the usual equipment (*see* Chapter 1), there are extra considerations when choosing your equipment for working in the field. These include portability and protection. As well as art materials, you must also think about equipment for yourself, so that you can keep comfortable physically, whether standing, sitting or moving around:

- **Sketchbooks**: a hard-backed sketchbook offers good protection from whatever surface you are leaning on. If you are using a spiral-bound sketchbook, take an extra piece of cardboard of the same size, to protect the artwork on the exposed piece of paper that has been turned over. Take a plastic bag to wrap the sketchbook in during transportation and to protect it in case you need to lean it on a wet or damp surface. Consider the size of your sketchbook – both how portable it is, and how practical it will be when drawing in an outdoor situation.
- **Pencils**: all pencils are essentially portable. However, the lead in wooden pencils can be broken easily in transport, so carry them in a protected zippered pouch or pencil roll. Clutch pencils are the most portable, as you can draw the lead back inside the holder. Even the sharpest point on my 2mm lead holder is protected this way when not in use. If you will need to sharpen a wooden pencil, take a bag or something to dispose of the shavings, avoiding littering. If you like to sharpen your pencils with a scalpel or knife, and you are travelling by air, remember not to carry these in your cabin luggage. The lead pointers that are used to sharpen clutch pencils are easy to transport but should be emptied of graphite beforehand, as a full pointer tub can lead to messy spills.
- **Watercolour paints**: pans represent the most compact and portable way of taking watercolours outdoors, unless you are planning to draw substantial plants at a large scale, in which case you will need the greater volume provided by tubes. (If you are travelling by air, be aware that cabin pressure can cause watercolour tubes to try to expel some of their contents.) I use a folding enamelled metal Winsor & Newton pan box, which provides a flat surface for mixing and wells for washes. There are also special watercolour field kits available. They ingeniously pack everything you need into a small box, including pan paints, palette surfaces, a water bottle and water container (*see* Chapter 1).

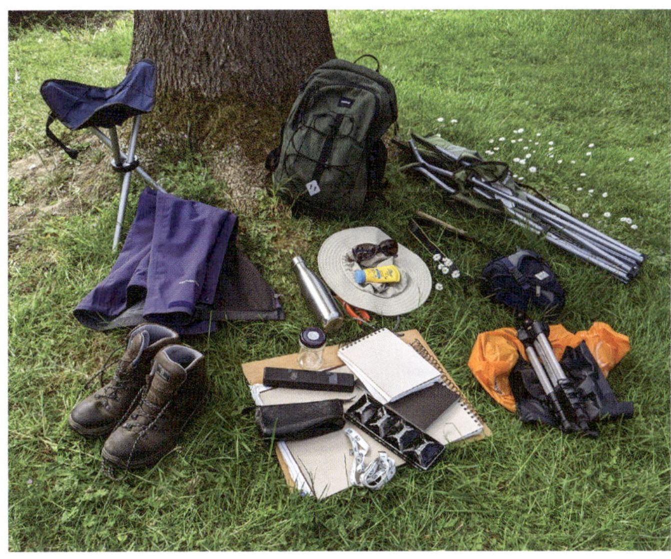

Equipment for sketching plants outdoors, including art materials and a drawing board, plastic bags, water and water jar, camera equipment, something to sit on and suitable clothing.

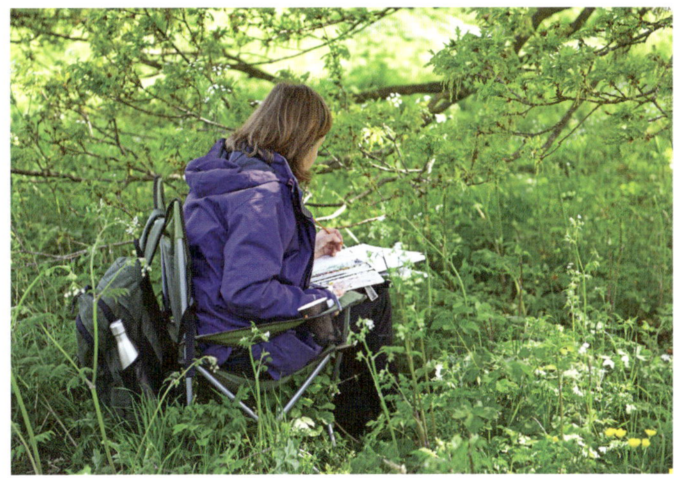

My luxurious set-up: a comfortable folding chair with a back, over which I can hang my backpack with equipment and water bottle. The pocket in the armrest of the chair is perfect for a water jar, and my clutch pencil clips handily on to the armrest as well.

- **Paintbrushes**: carry them carefully in order not to damage bristles; use with plastic cap sleeves and/or a brush roll or case.
- **Water**: carry it in a bottle and pour it into a small glass jar or plastic cup for use.
- **Ink pens**: ink pens are very portable, but be aware that technical pens such as Rotring can sometimes be affected by the cabin pressure in an aeroplane. Fineliner pens are probably the most practical types to carry around; dip pens and ink are the most challenging, as wet ink is more easily spilled.

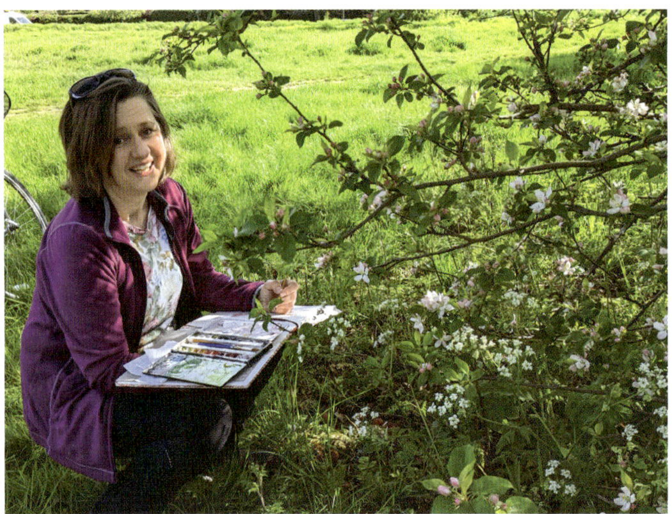

Drawing apple blossom. It may look as though I am levitating, but I am sitting low to the ground on a small folding stool. Its legs were sinking slowly into the soft soil!

- **Chair/stool**: if you need something to sit on, you could take a folding chair, but a small folding stool may be better if you need to carry your equipment over a long distance.
- **Weather-appropriate clothing**: in hot weather you will need a hat (as well as suncream), plus clothing to protect the rest of your body from heat and sun. In cold weather, you should layer up in warm clothes. Sitting still can make you feel the cold more intensely than if you were walking around. Whether dealing with heat or cold, be aware of how your body is coping. It is easy to become so absorbed in your sketching that you forget about these things.

PHOTOGRAPHY

Good reference photographs are very useful for backing up drawings. This is especially true if you are working somewhere where you are not permitted to take samples of plants. Unlike the process of photography in the studio, it is harder to control environmental conditions outdoors, especially the quality and source of the light. If using a larger camera, a tripod is recommended to reduce any shaking. Try to avoid photographing subjects in harsh sunlight, as some details will be bleached out and others made translucent or obscured by shadows.

Carry a piece of cloth or card with you to place behind subjects, to isolate them from an otherwise distracting background, or to cast shade. Sometimes, you can use your sketchbook for this. When taking photographs, include a ruler or some sort of object to indicate scale. If you have nothing with you, your hand may have to suffice.

Consider the direction of the light hitting your subject and choose a set-up that suits the way you usually work, if you can. If possible, find an angle on your subject with a suitable background colour to show it off, and avoid back-lighting, unless this is how you are used to painting.

GETTING SET UP

Viewpoint
Think carefully about where you can sit or stand to view the plant, as the options will be limited by its location. Access to the plant may be impeded by other plants and natural objects and it may be difficult to get close enough to observe and draw details.

As it may be impractical to stand for long periods of time you will be limited in your choice of viewpoint by the height at which you can sit – whether on something that is already there or on a seat that you have brought with you. As well as a folding stool or chair, you can take a cushion in a plastic bag for comfort and protection from wet surfaces, especially when sitting on the ground is the only option. A bin liner makes a good seat protector; with a few carefully ripped holes, it can also double as an emergency raincoat!

Weather
Outdoor environments present the greatest range of challenges to the sketching artist, with weather at the top of the list! In a hot climate, you must take care to find shade and wear a hat and sunscreen. Working in direct sunlight is difficult as it creates intense glare, particular if you are working on white paper. An umbrella can provide shade where none occurs naturally. Ideally, pick times when the weather and light are bearable, avoiding the hottest parts of the day.

Obviously, rain and wind will cause problems too. You may need to seek some sort of shelter, either temporary or permanent, and be aware that wind can flap both your plant subjects and your paper and equipment around. Elastic bands and clips can be used to hold pages down in these conditions.

This apple tree grows in my local nature reserve and I have no idea what variety it is. The soil in the reserve is unique, as it was brought from central and outer London to fill in the gravel extraction pits that once existed there. The apple tree could have germinated from a seed that came in with the soil, or perhaps someone threw an apple core away many years ago. The result is a beautiful small, bushy tree that produces an abundance of blossom and small fruits every year. It first caught my eye when I was looking for some small subjects for students to draw, and I picked a few of its ripening apples to show them. I drew sketches of the tree in situ in late autumn as its fruits were ripening and returned in spring when it was in bud and blossom.

Three Little Apples

As an example for my botanical art students, I made some quick sketches and colour studies of three tiny apples, each measuring no more than 4cm diameter. I had never painted an apple before. I experimented with layering various watercolour pigments, beginning with pale lem-on-yellow under-washes and layering over these washes with smaller brush strokes of reds and rose.

This study was not just about matching the colours, but also very much about discovering which types of layering and mark-making worked best. It was a joy to discover that the marks on the skin of the apples were very similar to the marks created by puddling small amounts of water from the brush, interspersed with small dry-brush strokes. It was almost as if the apple skins themselves had been painted with watercolour.

Under the Apple Tree: Finding the Perfect Spot

One afternoon, I went for a walk on the reserve and found the perfect spot to sit and draw the loaded branches of the apple tree, which were hanging almost down to the ground. I set myself up on my folding stool in a position tucked away in the long grass surrounding the tree. I was almost hidden by its branches, positioned so that one of them fell perfectly across my line of sight. Drawing for several hours until the sun was beginning to set, I had the added delight of listening to the tree's visitors, who came and went throughout the afternoon, talking about the tree, and picking and tasting its fruit.

I had brought my Fabriano 'Venezia' bound sketchbook, and realised I would have to work across a double-page spread with the book held vertically, in order to capture

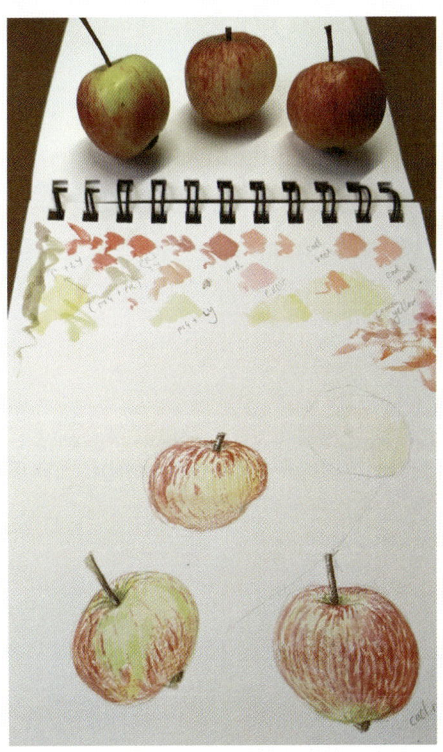

The almost-ripe wild apples were so small that the three of them fitted easily on a page of my small (A5) watercolour colour-study book.

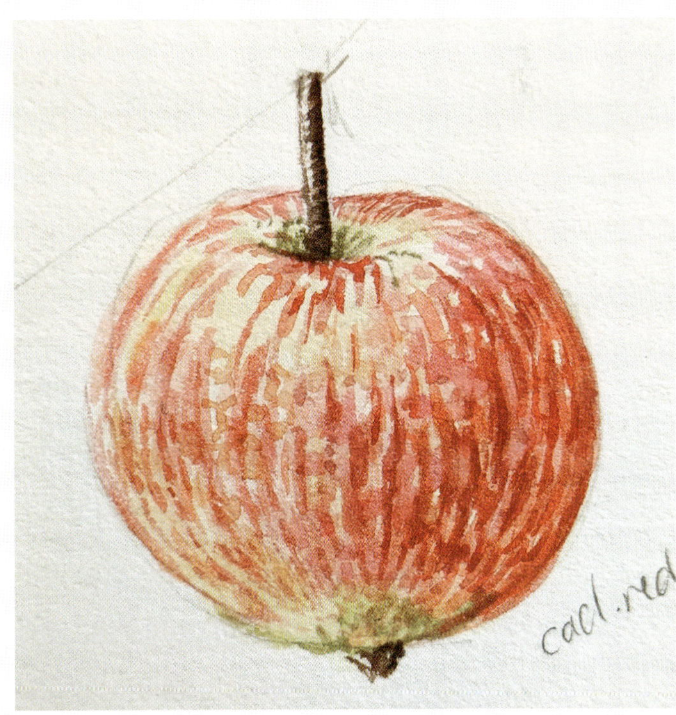

The marks on the apples were replicated very naturally by small, puddled brush marks of red and rose laid over light yellow washes.

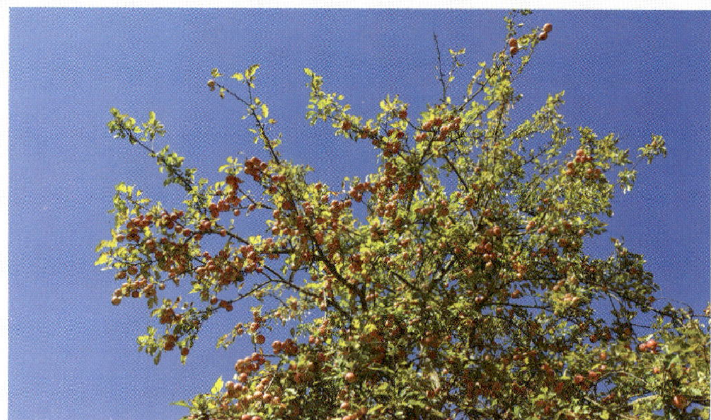

The wild apple tree, laden with hundreds of ripening fruits. I have just realised I never tried tasting one!

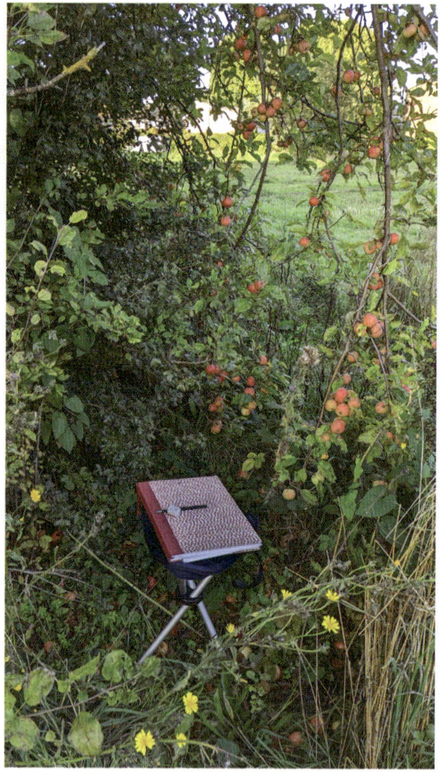

The perfect drawing spot. Tucked away in the long grass and hidden by the drooping branches of the wild apple, I spent a very enjoyable afternoon sketching the fruits that hung down directly in front of me.

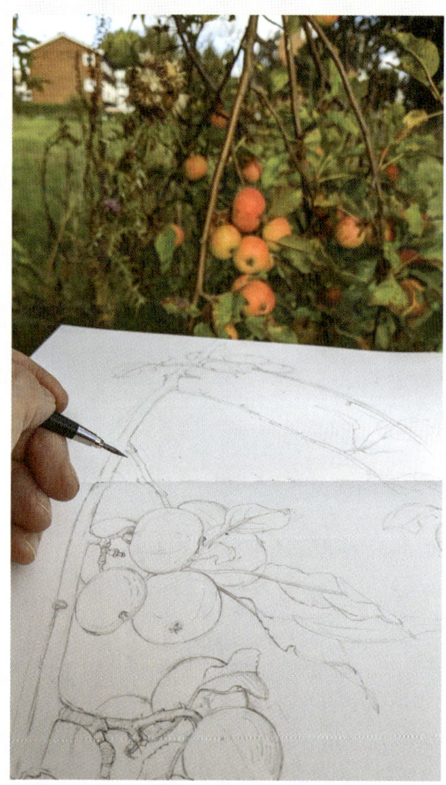

In this position I could draw a branch containing several clusters of apples, which, after careful planning, fitted perfectly on the double page of my sketchbook.

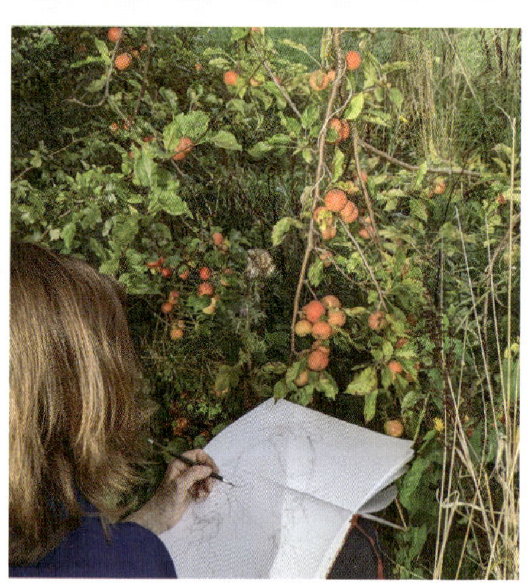

Enjoying adding more detail and capturing the essence of the apple tree branch.

the branches I had found. I began by sketching in the main forms of the branch, taking measurements to ensure I was drawing it life-sized. I also made sure to determine how it would fit on the page. It is always wise to avoid getting half-way through a lovely drawing, only to find out that there is not enough room to fit in the whole subject!

Once the basic shapes were sketched in, I went over each part of the drawing adding more accuracy and detail. As I was working with the book balanced on my lap, my style naturally became looser. I liked this feel of the drawing, as it suited the natural and imperfect nature of the subject matter. The leaves were dry and beginning to curl, in contrast to the solid spherical forms of the little apples.

Recording a Moment

I had planned to put some colour on this piece. However, I had enjoyed my afternoon of creating this particular drawing so much that I decided not to add anything to it. I felt that the drawing captured a moment in time, and I wanted to leave it as it was.

I love this drawing, not just for itself but because every time I look at it, I am reminded of that magical afternoon. I can smell the fallen apples fermenting underfoot and feel the warm setting sun on my back.

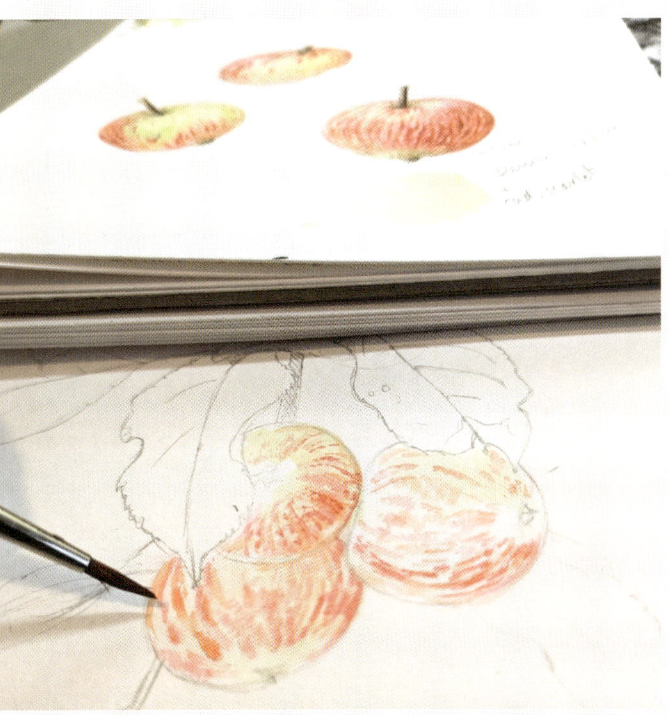

The original colour study of the apples was useful when it came to adding tonal values to this sketch and there was no fresh material available.

The final double-page spread of the apple drawing. I decided not to work up this study any further, but to leave it exactly as it had been produced on the day.

Photographic reference for the second sketchbook page capturing the apple branch. As I did not have a ruler to add to the photo to give scale, I used my secateurs instead.

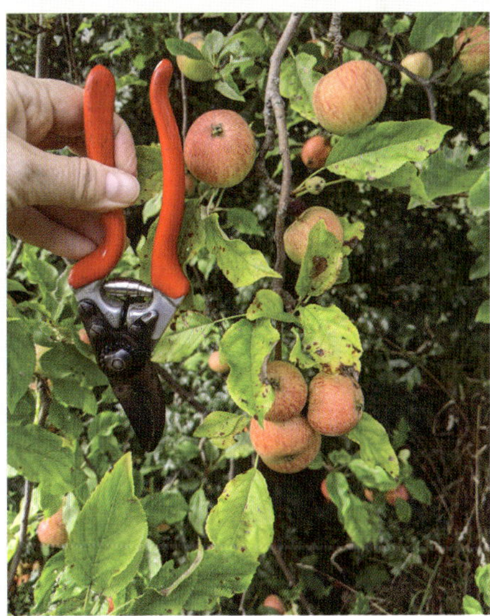

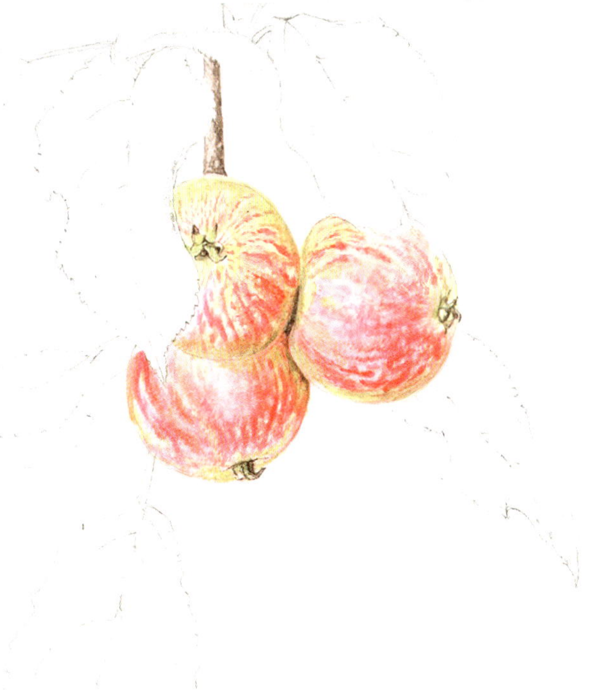

Part of the second apple page. I left the leaves uncoloured, originally because I had no fresh material to work from but also because I liked the resulting effect.

Working from Photographs

Later, I decided that I would like to include some colour alongside the original sketchbook study. I planned to do this by drawing another branch of the apple tree. As I was unable to find a suitable day to draw and paint in situ, I turned to some of the many reference photos I had taken.

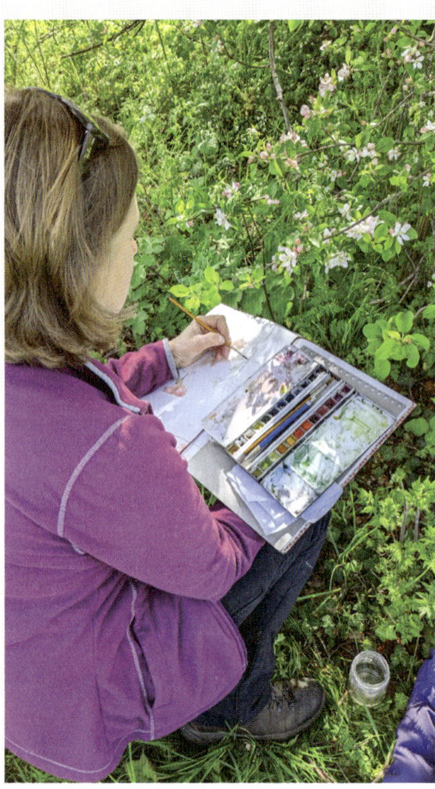

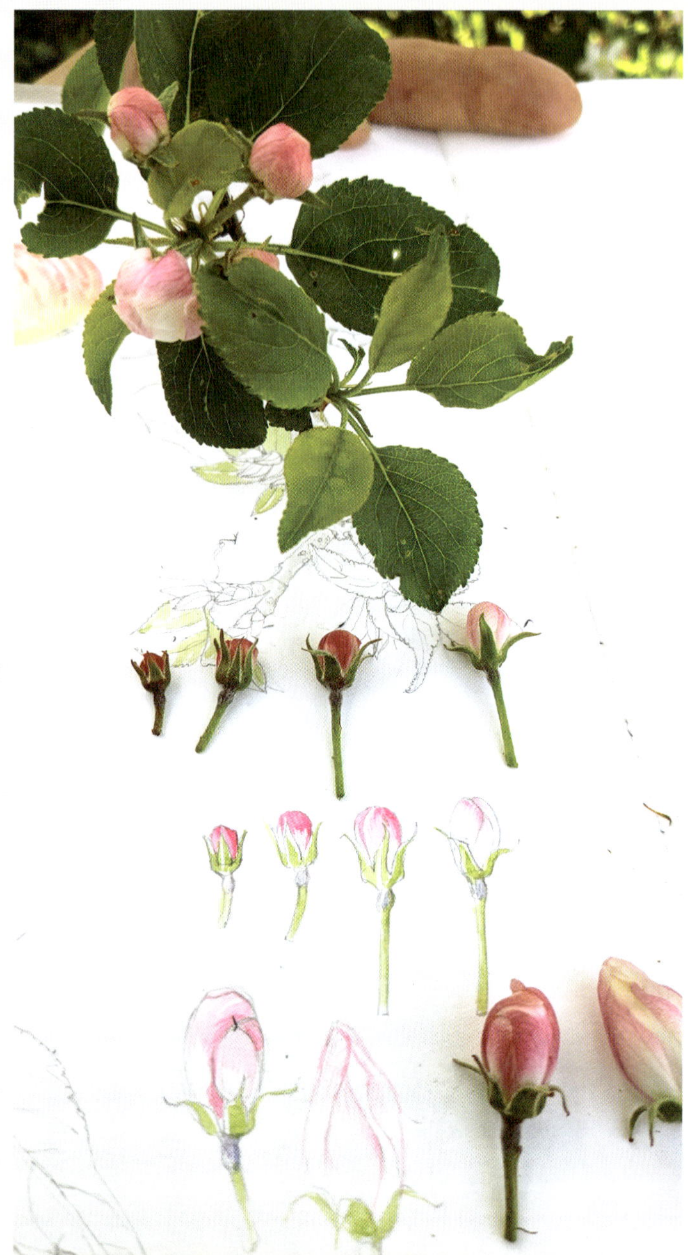

Drawings of the apple tree's blossom buds at different stages of development, with colour observed and added using watercolour.

Capturing Apple Blossom

I returned to the apple tree in spring for its beautiful blossom. By sitting on a low folding stool and balancing the watercolour tin on the open page of the hardcover sketchbook, I was able to sit directly beneath the flowers. Here I focused on drawing the flower buds at different stages. I chose a much small piece, which would fit on just one page of the Fabriano 'Venezia' sketchbook. The facing side of this double-page spread is waiting for drawings of open flowers.

As well as using the photographic reference, I looked at my original colour studies of the apples. I decided to leave the leaves unpainted for two reasons: I did not want to mix their green colour based only on photographic reference; I also liked the look of the coloured apples against the outlined pencil leaves. I may add colour to these leaves at some time in the future when fresh reference is available, or I may simply leave them as they are. The joy of keeping a botanical sketchbook is that it allows you to be flexible and enjoy making the most of whatever happens. In this case, I was quite pleased to discover a new style that I may incorporate into future artwork.

Drawings of the tiny *Nymphaea thermarum* water lily, made in situ in the Tropical Nursery at Kew Gardens. This plant was extremely rare and could not be moved from its growing place. It was an interesting experience sitting and drawing in the damp but controlled environment of the nursery, getting as close as possible to the specimen.

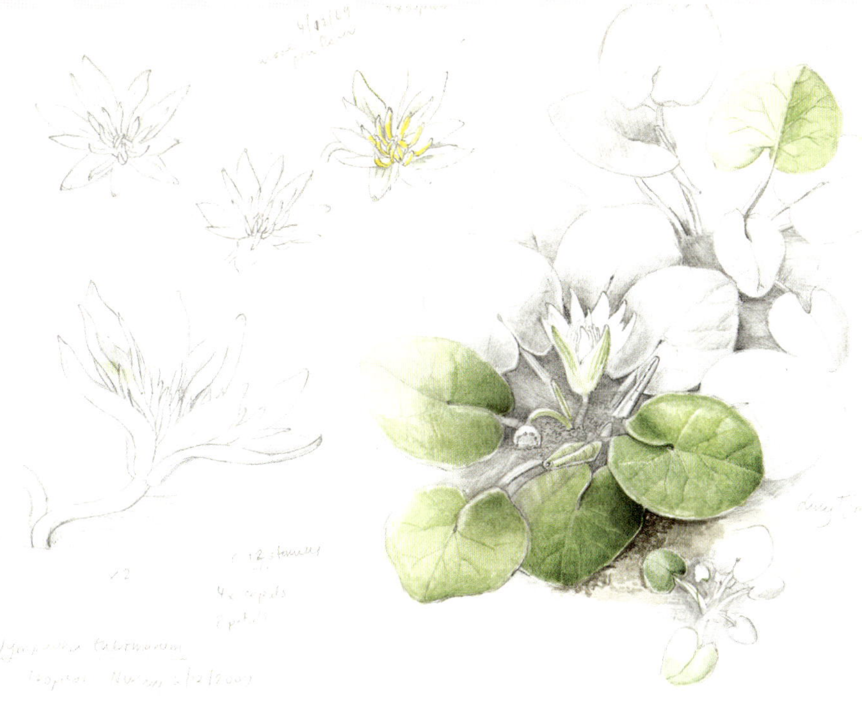

One from the archives, this was a commission to draw the world's smallest water lily, *Nymphaea thermarum*, which was growing in the Tropical Nursery at Kew Gardens. Unlike many water lilies, this species is the perfect size for a sketchbook page. At the time when I drew it, it was very rare. One of Kew's horticulturists (Carlos Magdalena) had only just managed to germinate the first seeds from a cultivated specimen for the first time. To keep it safe and healthy, it could not be moved from the nursery. However, it was slightly more portable than a typical water lily, as the plants sat in pots only partly submerged in water.

A Watery Environment

Over several visits to the plant with my spiral bound A4 cartridge paper sketchbook, I was able to capture the water lily as it grew, with buds and flowers and later fruit. The challenge in drawing this plant was avoiding the water that was all around me. Perched on a stool, I rested my sketchbook on the damp nursery bench, making sure it was protected by a plastic bag underneath.

I focused on two different views of the whole plant, then zoomed in on flowers at different stages. I had to enlarge the flower to two times, in order to fully draw some of the details inside, as it was only 1cm across. I drew the flower several times, looking for the best angle from which to draw it, capturing it from bud to fully open flower.

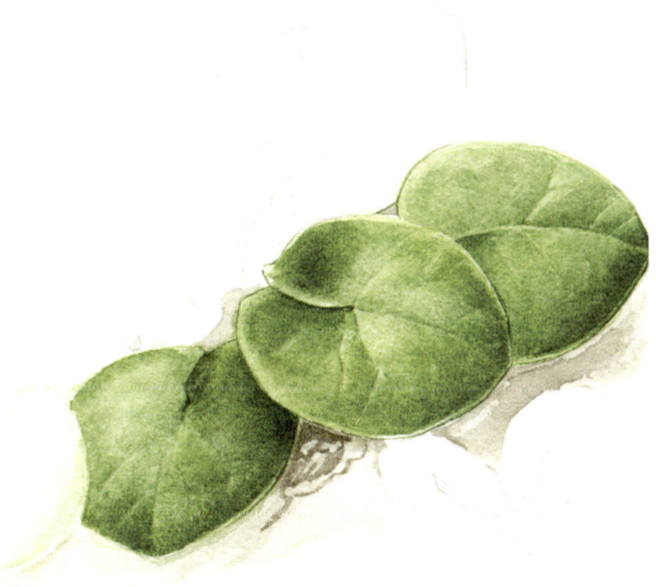

Testing the paint on a piece of watercolour paper gave me a better indication of how to work on the final *Nymphaea* piece, which would be published in *Curtis's Botanical Magazine*.

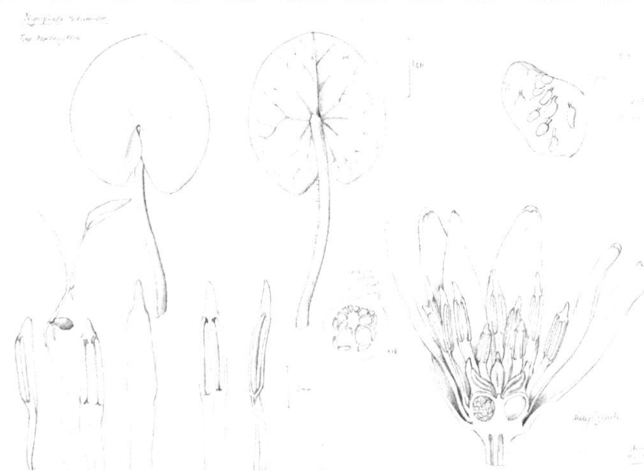

Sketchbook page of *Nymphaea thermarum*, showing details of a leaf, a seedling and parts of a flower. Each of these drawings was made from a specimen that had been preserved in alcohol.

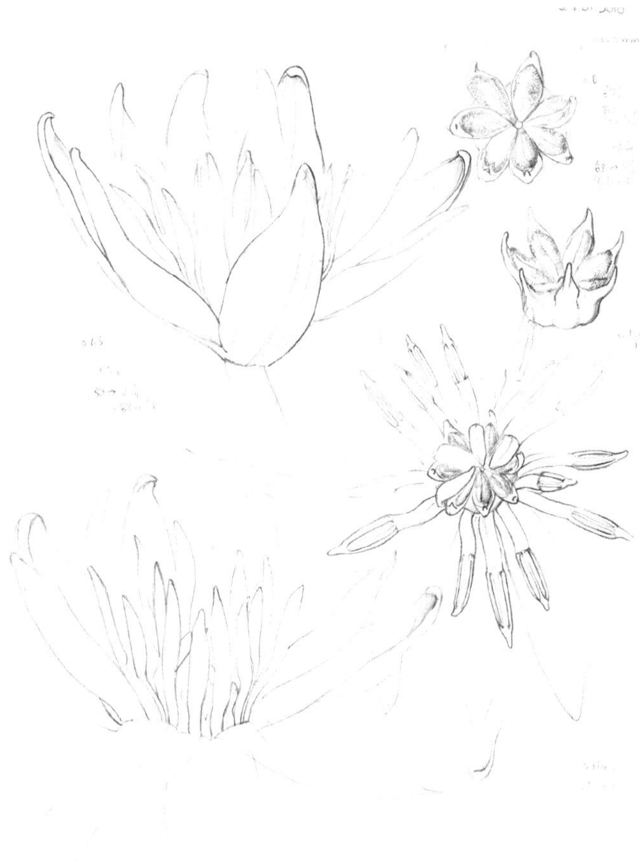

More details of the flower of *Nymphaea thermarum*, looking at the whole flower from different angles, drawn using the microscope.

Adding Colour

With the drawing complete, I was able to return to the specimen and focus solely on capturing its colour. Applying watercolour directly to the drawing, I erased most of the tonal rendering that I had added to the leaves beforehand. Still, the pencil on the paper darkened the colour considerably and I could not visualise how the colour would look on the final study. For this reason, I took a small offcut of the watercolour paper that I planned to use for the finished piece and made some more colour studies. As well as providing me with a nice clean white surface to work on, this also gave me a better idea of what the finished piece would look like. This was especially important, as the finished watercolour piece would be worked on away from the specimen.

Focusing on Detail

With permission from the horticulturists, I was able to take some plant material away, and placed a leaf, a flower, and later a seed into a small jar of alcohol mix. With these spirit specimens I was able to make more drawings away from the plant, using a microscope to focus on parts of the flower that were too tiny to describe life-sized.

The details include the ovules in the longitudinal section of the flower's ovary, and its stamens. I was also able to look at the venation of the leaf in more detail. I filled four A4 pages of my sketchbook with these drawings. Studying these details not only helped me to understand the plant, but also created work that could be used in the pen and ink illustration that would accompany the watercolour piece.

Final Pieces

From the preparatory sketchbook studies, I was able to produce two illustrations for publication. The first was a watercolour piece designed to show the whole plant in an artistic yet informative way. The second, a pen and ink illustration, showed more of the salient details of the plant, including views that could not be seen on the plant study, such as the underside of a leaf and parts of the flower.

Using my botanical sketchbook was essential here, as it would have been impossible to have worked on either of the final pieces directly from the living specimen.

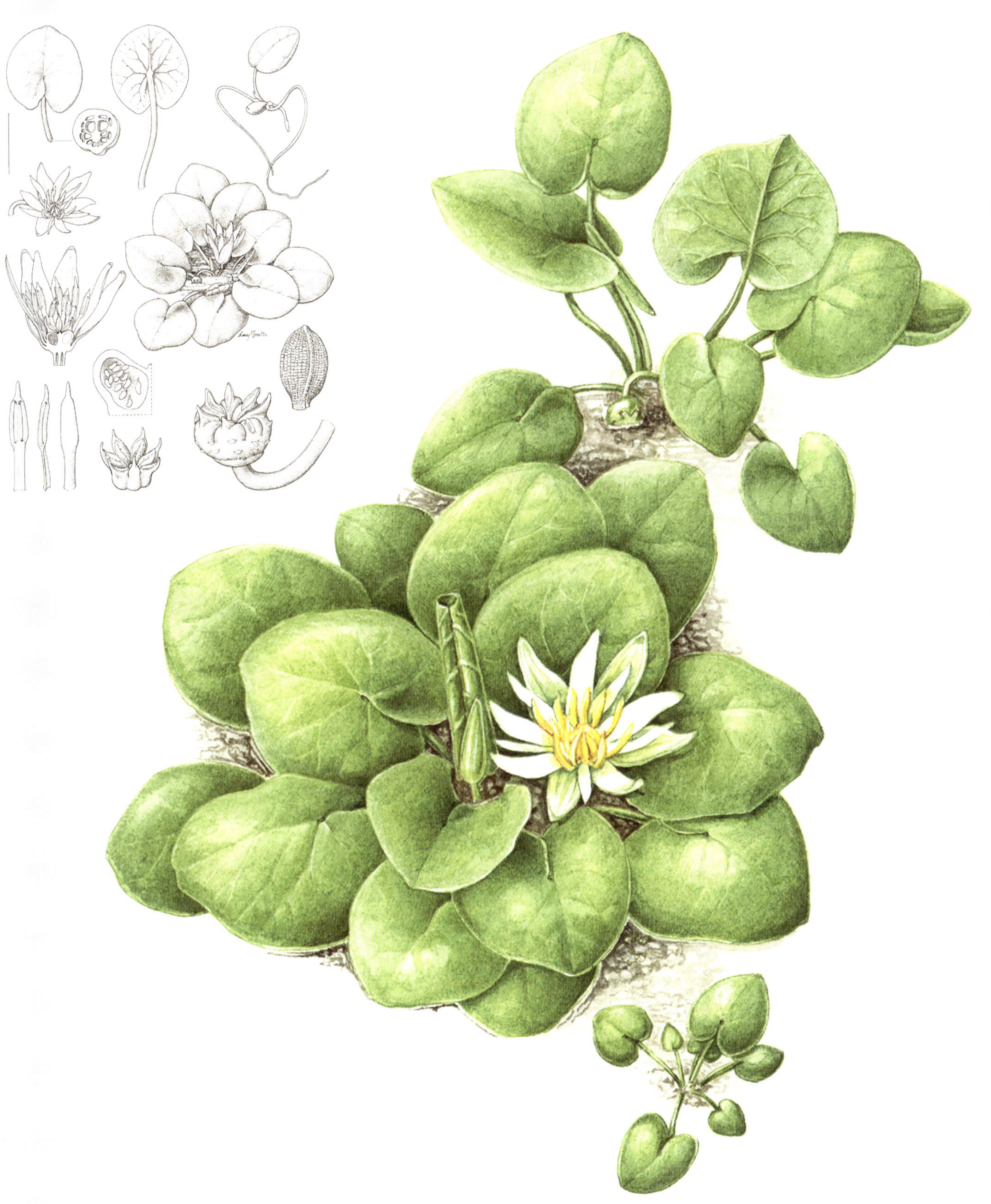

The finished pen and ink illustration, and watercolour painting, of *Nymphaea thermarum*. Both contain many of the details investigated and drawn in the sketchbook. Published in *Curtis's Botanical Magazine* Volume 7(4), 2010.

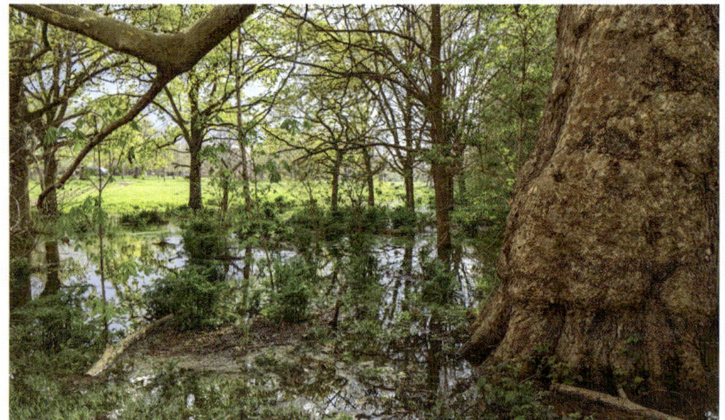

Looking down from a footbridge on an early spring afternoon at the area I have nicknamed 'The Island.' This patch of ground can be completely submerged in flood tides, and the snake's head fritillary *Fritillaria meleagris* loves to grow there at the base of a huge plane tree.

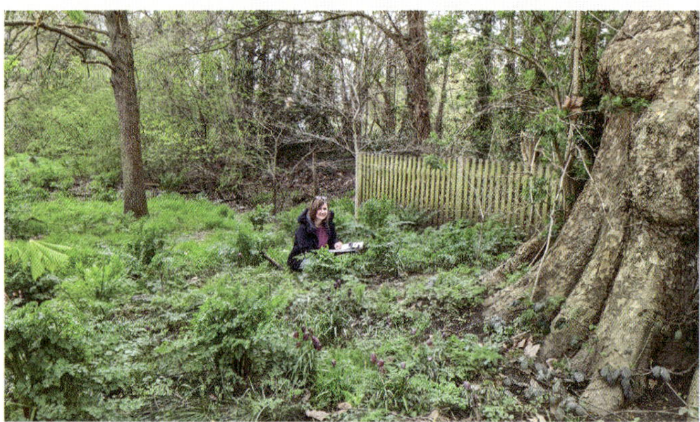

The same patch of ground, photographed a few weeks later, from a slightly different angle and on a less sunny day. In a flood tide, I would be sitting underwater. Other plants are starting to grow and will soon crowd the island with dense vegetation. Incidentally, the island has a large resident water rat that often runs up and down along the fence.

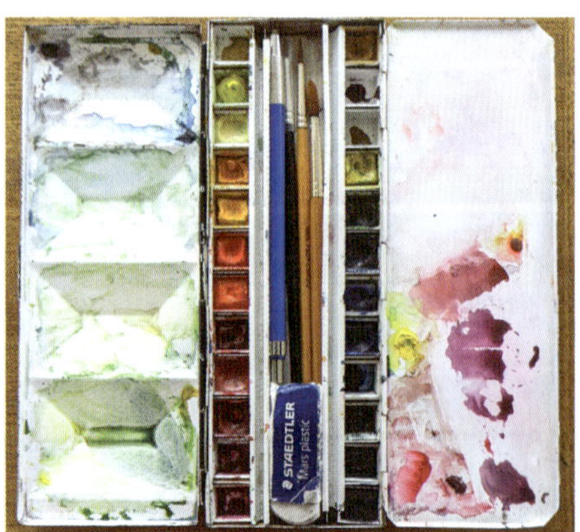

By doing preliminary work using a potted fritillary, I was able to mix up in advance some of the colour that I thought I might need. Here, the rest of my palette is clean and ready to be worked on. My pencils, paintbrushes and eraser are packed into the centre section of my portable watercolour pan tin.

Preparation

For many years I have regularly cycled past a patch of ground on the banks of the River Thames, where small streams run around an area with a huge plane tree in the centre. On flood tides, river pours into those streams, turning the ground into an island and sometime completely submerging it. Each year, around April, the island is home to several drifts of the snake's head fritillary spring-flowering bulb, *Fritillaria meleagris.* I had taken plenty of photographs of the delicate flowers over many seasons but, like so many of the seasonal plants I observe and think about, I always hoped to stop one day and draw them from life.

This year I was determined not to miss the flowers and kept looking every few days to see whether they had started to emerge, hoping I could fit a visit into my schedule. By preparing in advance, I would make sure that my time with the wildflowers would be focused. I had bought a pot of *Fritillaria meleagris* the previous year and it was coming into flower at the same time as the wild plants. As soon as my potted plant's flowers were ready, I made some colour studies at home to give a good indication of which pigments I would need on the day.

Working on 'The Island'

Finally, in early spring, the perfect day arrived. Checking the tides, I was happy that this was not a day of full submersion for the island. With my bicycle loaded with field equipment, including sketchbook, pencil case, watercolours and a small folding stool, I headed for 'The Island' to finally draw and paint the fritillaries. I had already realised that in order to observe them properly I would need to be down at ground level. I knew that the site would be muddy and damp, so I had packed a cushion and a plastic bag.

Accessibility was one factor in choosing which clump of plants to draw. I needed to find a place to sit where I would not damage any of the other plants. The second factor was finding a specimen with a pleasing and typical form – that is to say, one that represented the species well.

For such a small and apparently simple subject, it took a surprisingly long time to draw. This is not unusual with plants with quite sparse forms. Unlike big plants with lots of parts and details, there is 'nowhere to hide'. The leaves of fritillaries are simple and elegant, and arch out gracefully from their central stem, and over the terminal flowers.

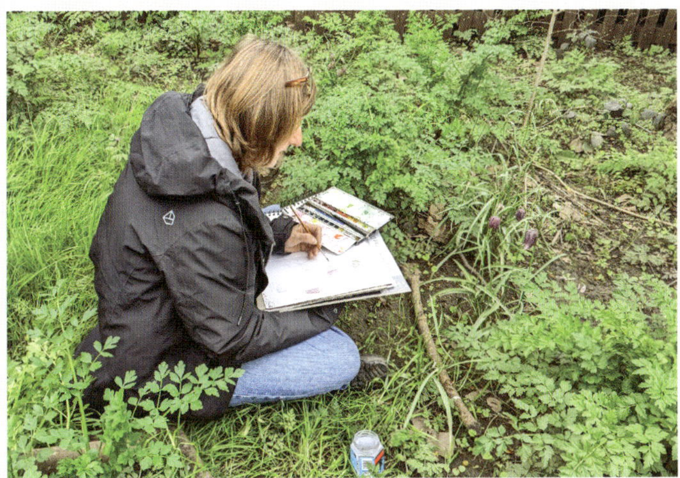

Taking care not to trample any other patches of flowering fritillaries, I set myself up on a convenient log covered in a plastic bag. People crossing the nearby footbridge often wonder out loud what I am doing. My presence seems to make them look a bit closer, and I enjoy hearing their astonishment as they notice the flowers for the first time.

Sketch of the fritillary with its flowers and gracefully arching leaves. In a clump such as this, they frequently overlap and interlock. This can be challenging to draw, as too many awkward star-like overlaps can be visually jarring.

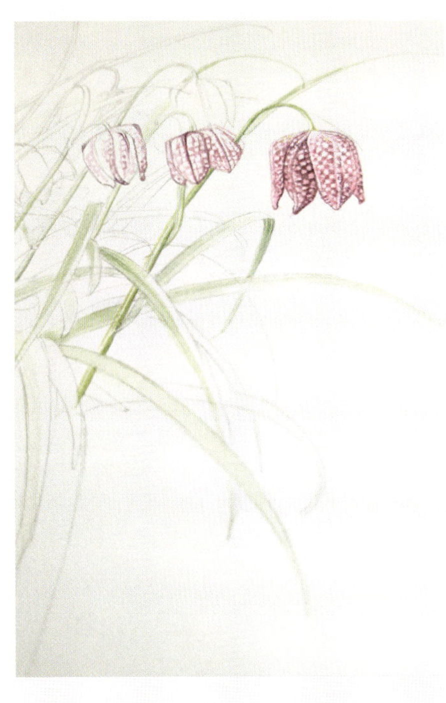

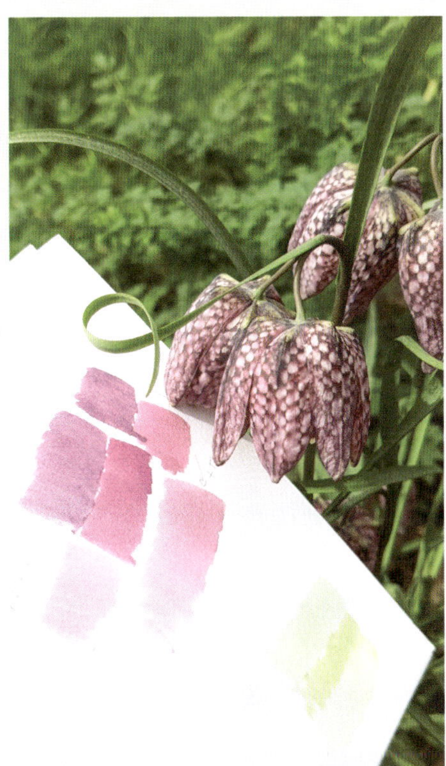

Testing my colour mixes against the living wildflowers. It is very satisfying when you feel you have captured the colour of a flower and can get on with painting it. Although the plants are abundant here, I had to study them on a do not disturb basis. Never assume that a plant or part of a plant can be picked.

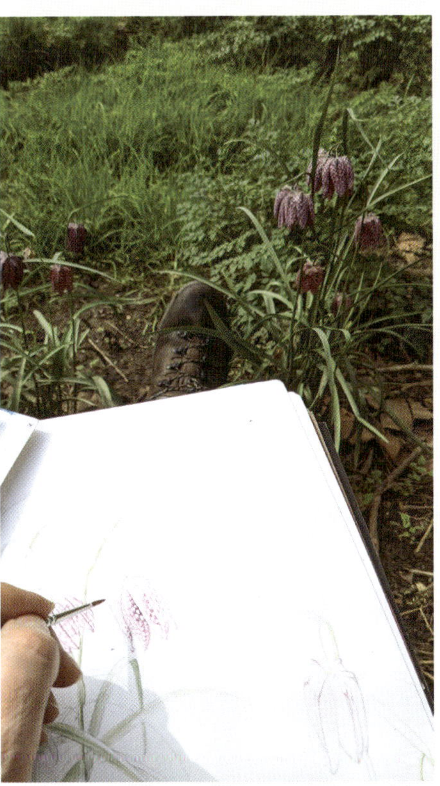

My view when I am sketching. I had hoped to sit comfortably on a stool but instead had to set myself up cross-legged on a piece of river driftwood. My leg is held out, probably because I had moved it to stop it going to sleep.

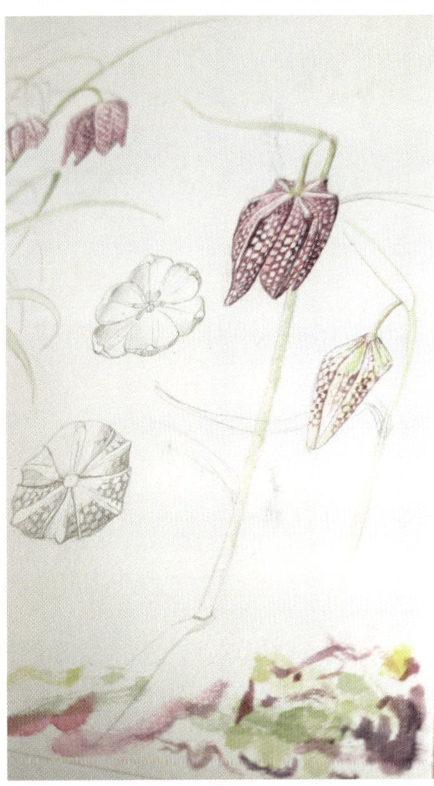

Another part of the sketchbook page showing a fully open flower and a bud in colour plus drawings of a flower looking directly down on it from above and from below.

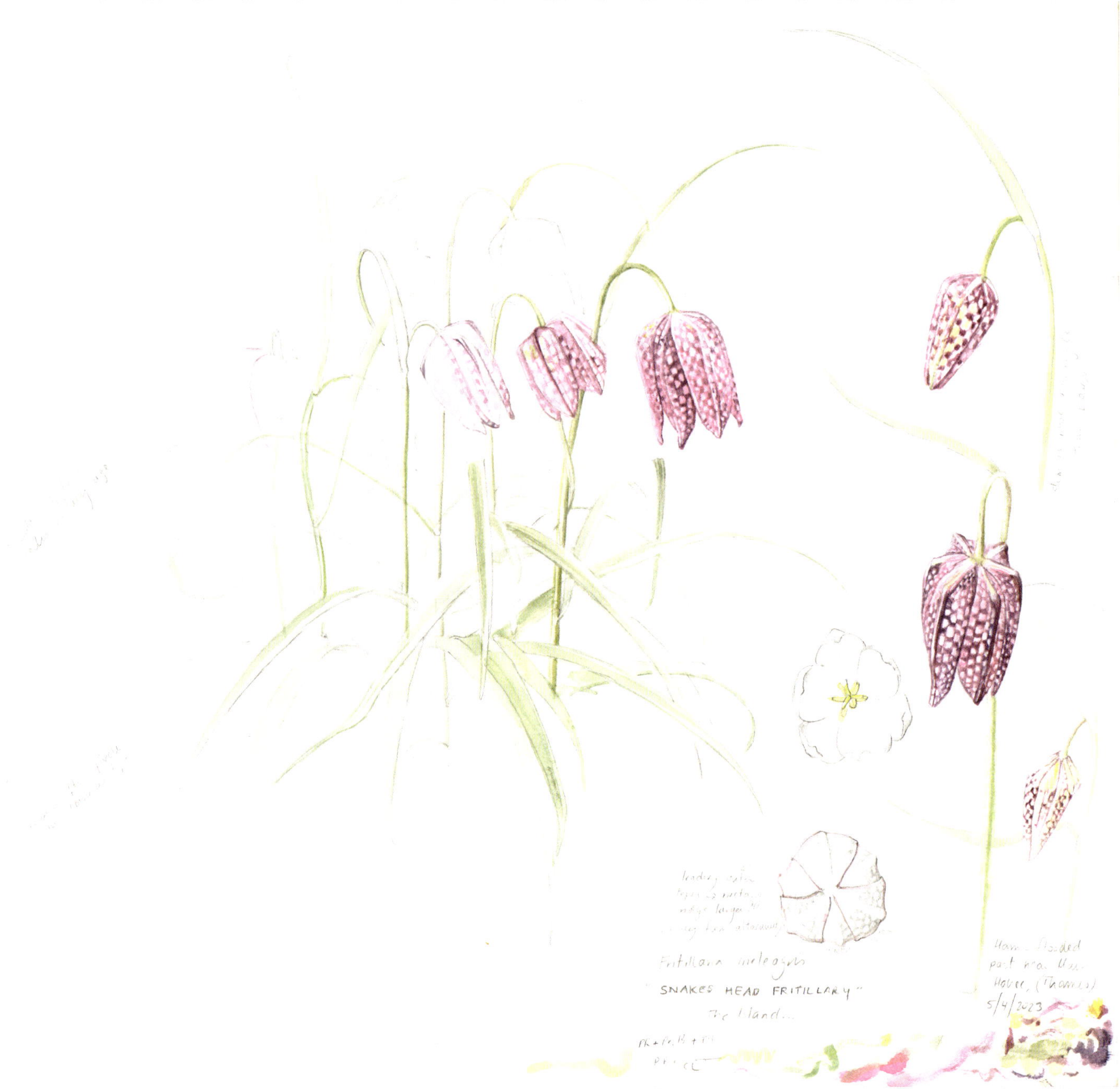

The sketchbook study of the snake's head fritillary, *Fritillaria meleagris*. There will have to be another visit to 'The Island' very soon to sketch details of the plant's fruit capsules.

I am very pleased that I have finally managed to sketch the *Fritillaria meleagris* plants from life. I would have liked to return several more times during the same growing season, as there is still so much more to capture, but it seems that there is never enough time. Now that I have done it once, however, I am sure it will be much easier to revisit next year – and perhaps for many years to come.

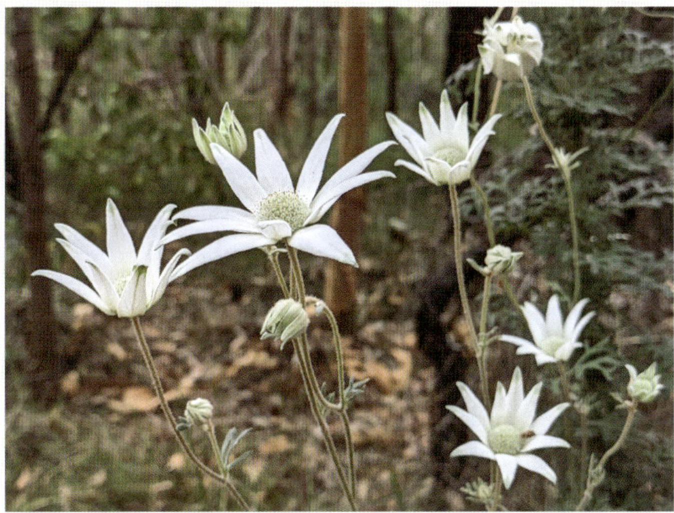

Flannel flowers (*Actinotus helianthi*) growing in the beautiful bush reserve of Oatley Park in southwest Sydney, Australia.

On a trip back to my birth city of Sydney, Australia, I took my sketchbook along in the hope of making some sketches of early summer wildflowers. I was very fortunate to stay in an area of southwest Sydney that has a unique nature reserve at Oatley Park, on a promontory that projects into the Georges River. During daily walks, I was treated to a huge variety of beautiful native Australian plants, which were bursting into flower in the warm late spring weather.

Capturing Diversity

For this project I relied largely on photos. All the plants in the nature reserve are protected, so it was not possible to take away any specimens. I did some sketching on site but did not have the time to sit and work for long periods. I decided to simply create sketchbook pages that captured as many as possible of the flowers that I had seen. Obviously, I was not able to study them to the same degree of detail as plant specimens in my studio, but they would be drawn as accurately as possible.

My aim was to capture an impression of the vast number of diverse and beautiful plants that could be found in this one small place. I started drawing a selection of plants in pencil across a double-page spread of my Fabriano 'Venezia' sketchbook without any plan, letting the composition unfold organically. Once these were in place, it became obvious that the sketches would benefit from the added impact of pen and ink. After that, I felt that their colours could not be ignored, so I decided to add watercolour to the ink drawings. In this way, both composition and

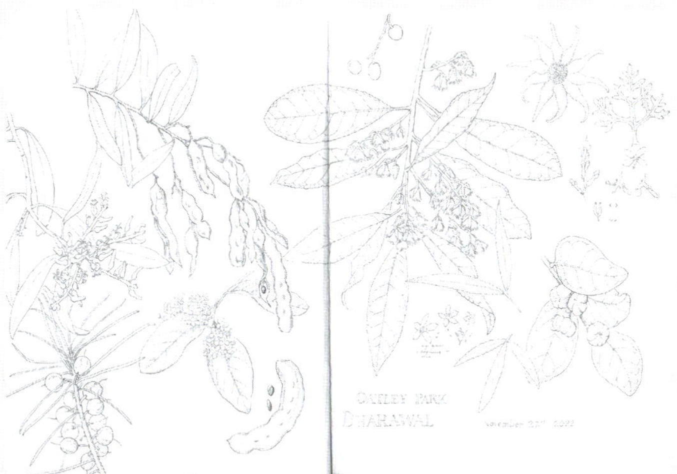

The double-page spread after most of the flowers had been drawn first in pencil, then ink, apart from those that I added later to fill in gaps and balance colour. The flowering tree *Elaeocarpus reticulatus* was probably my favourite, with its frilly white flowers and stunning blue berries. This composition created itself totally organically, as I placed one element down after another. It was a very refreshing process.

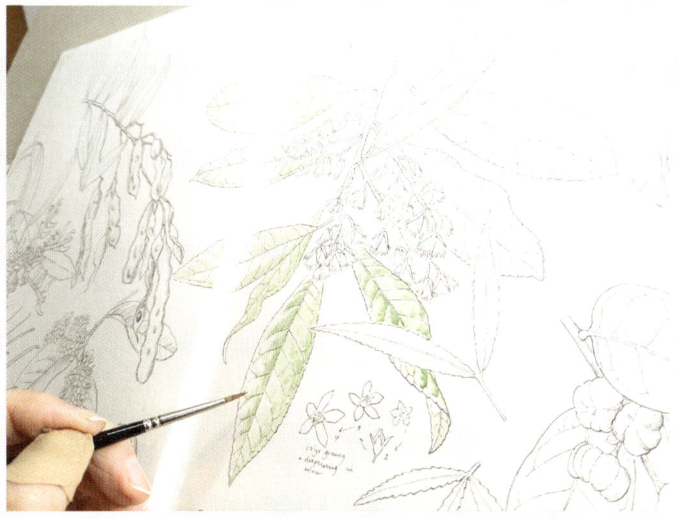

The first layers of watercolour being added to the pen and ink drawings. Watercolour was added as small washes, being careful not to overload the cartridge paper. I was careful to observe how the paper was acting as I added paint – if it started to buckle, I knew it had reached its limit.

technique evolved as the work progressed – this work was truly the product of a holiday mindset.

Pen and Ink with Watercolour

It was great fun to explore a technique that I did not have much experience with. I love the immediacy and strength given by pen and ink with watercolour wash. As I moved across the page, I became more confident using it.

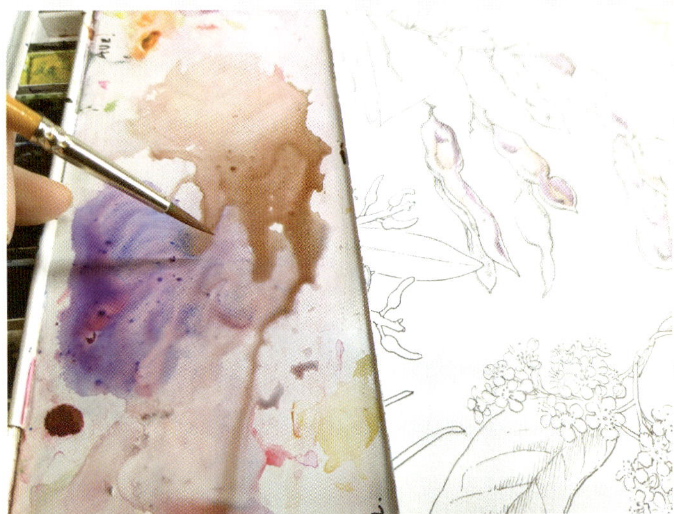

Mixing browns and violets for the seed pods of *Acacia fimbriata*. Unlike many of my projects, I did not have names for all these species until I had drawn them. Some were familiar from my childhood, but others were not.

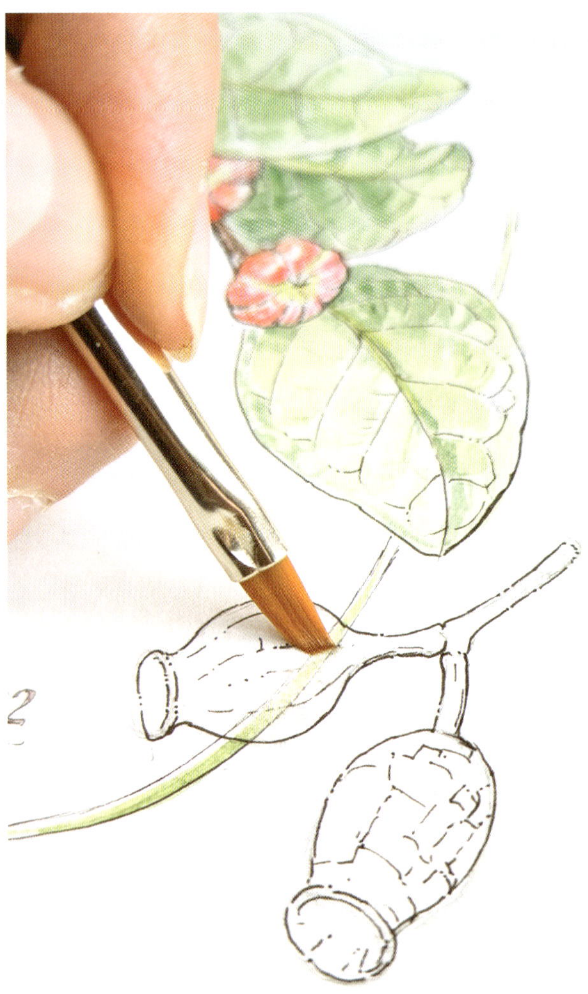

Here I used a flat shader brush with stiff bristles to lift some of the watercolour and ink from a blade of grass, so that I could draw some eucalyptus pods over it; this was a last-minute addition.

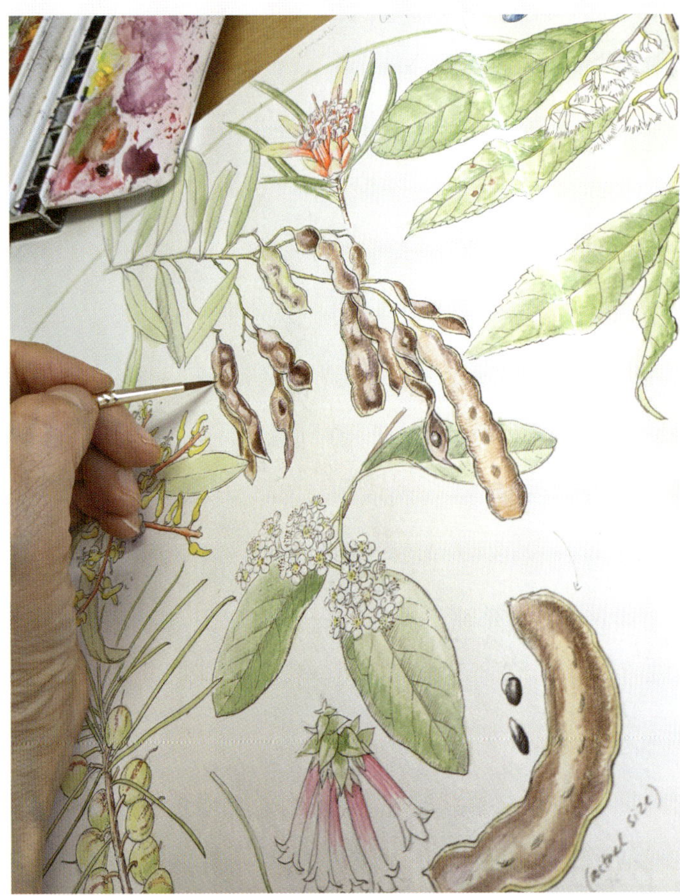

Adding more layers of watercolour. Once I had familiarised myself with the new technique, I became more confident at adding further layers of paint as well as alternating paint with extra layers of ink where needed.

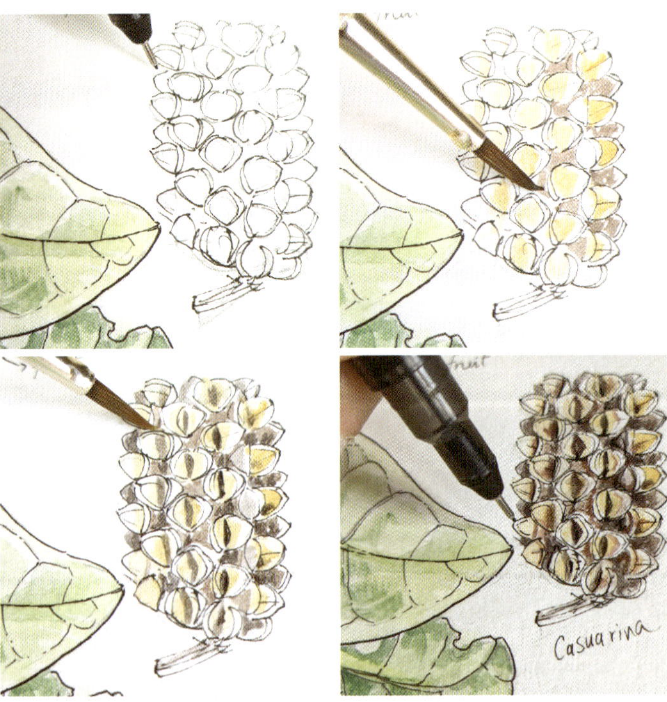

By the time I added the final elements, such as the *Casuarina* seed pod, my drawing style on this page had loosened up considerably. I no longer needed to make very detailed under-drawings in pencil, but added more detail in both pen and watercolour as I was building up the layers.

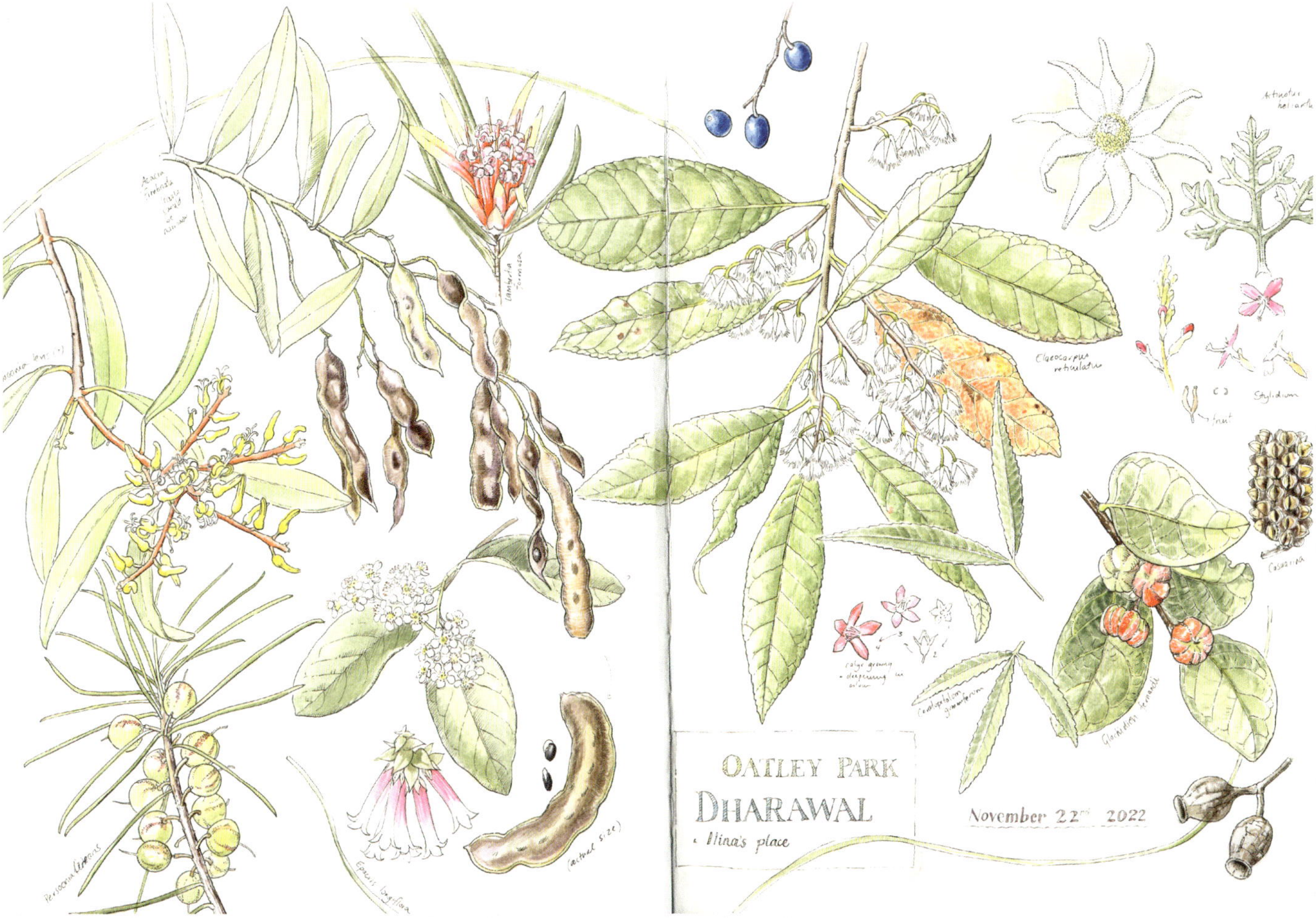

The finished piece, complete with name label and date. As I visited this reserve at least six times and there were dozens of amazing plants, I could fill at least six more double-page spreads. 'Oatley Park' is the official name of the nature reserve, but it is actually on Dharawal Aboriginal Land. As this page will always remind me of the wonderful walks I enjoyed there with my sister, I also included her name.

Drawing and painting in the field in your botanical sketchbook may take a degree of organisation and effort, but once you are there it is one of the best activities you can do. It combines two of my favourite things: being outdoors and observing and drawing plants. What more could you ask for? It will provide you with total immersion in nature, so I hope you will give it a try.

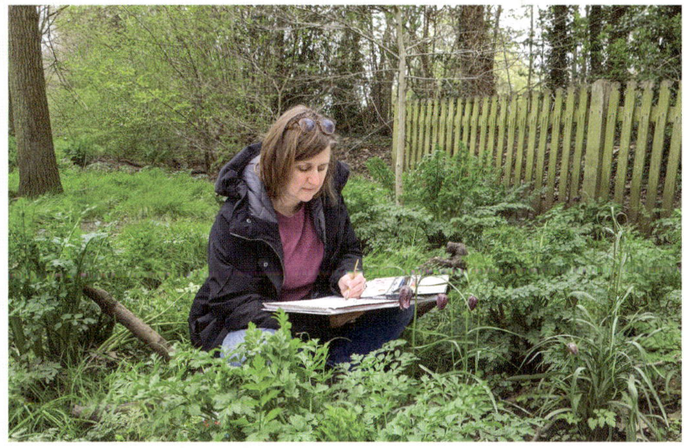

Happy days outdoors: keeping company with beautiful plants and the sounds of scurrying water rats and singing birds.

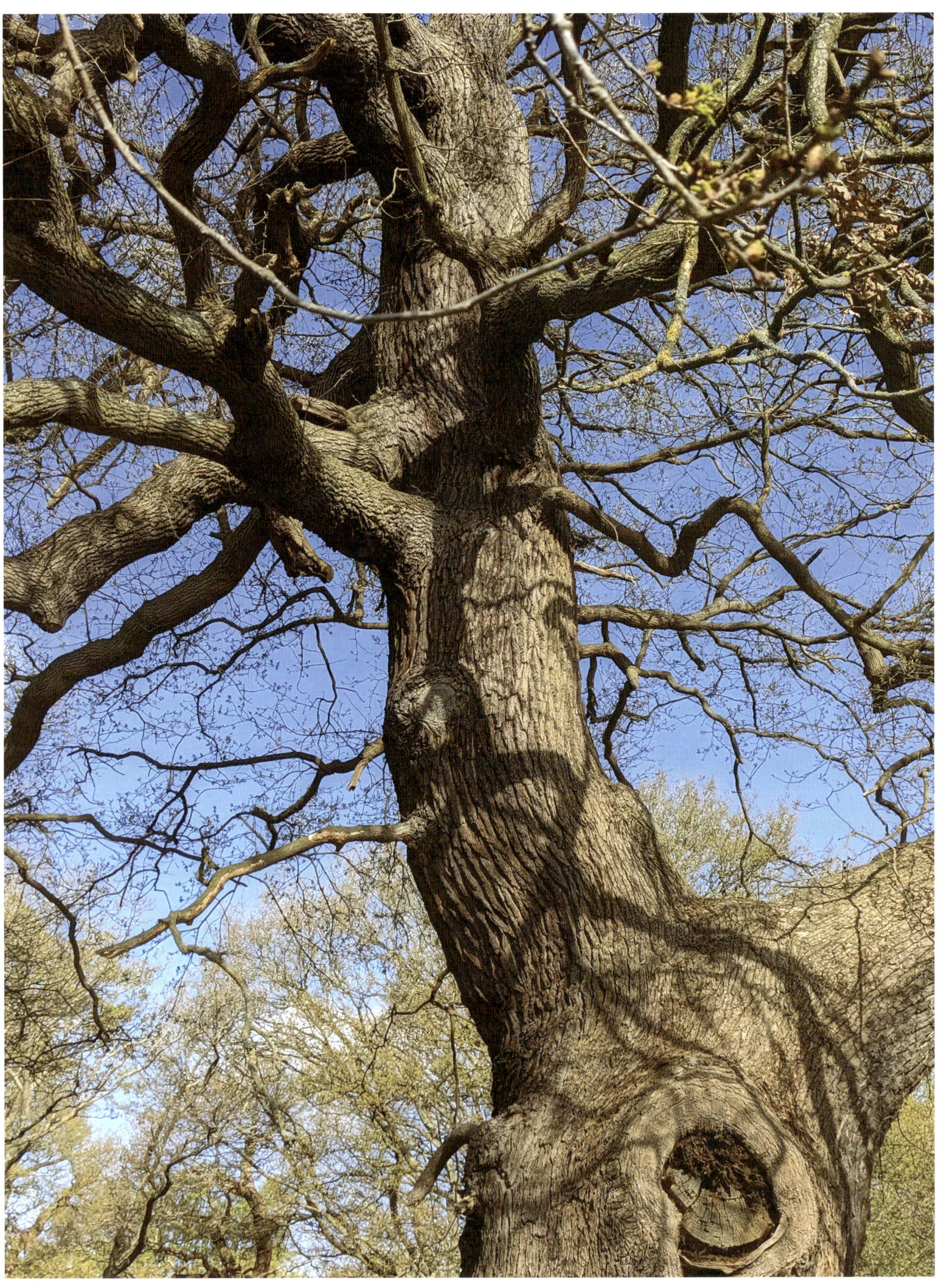

CHAPTER 7

CAPTURING TREES THROUGHOUT THE SEASONS

For those who are fortunate enough to live in an area with some greenery, trees may be their constant, silent companions. When they are always in your field of vision, either directly or peripherally, it is easy to take for granted their shapes, colours, and seasonal changes. By recording these aspects in a botanical sketchbook, you can deepen your engagement with them whilst depicting a year in the life of a particular species.

Trees are a great subject to observe and record in detail because they can be studied and drawn as they grow through the year. Artistically they offer everything, from large forms down to the tiniest of details. As well as the variety of form and size, the leaves, flowers and fruits also provide an interesting range of colours. Deciduous trees in particular offer a seasonal progression of budding, bursting into leaf, flowering and fruiting, before dropping their leaves to reveal a bare, woody skeleton.

Study page for a field guide, featuring various trees in the Fagaceae family. Each specimen was drawn from life in pencil, before trying small amounts of green watercolour mixes over the top of the drawings.

Magnificent trees give every artist something to draw no matter what the season.

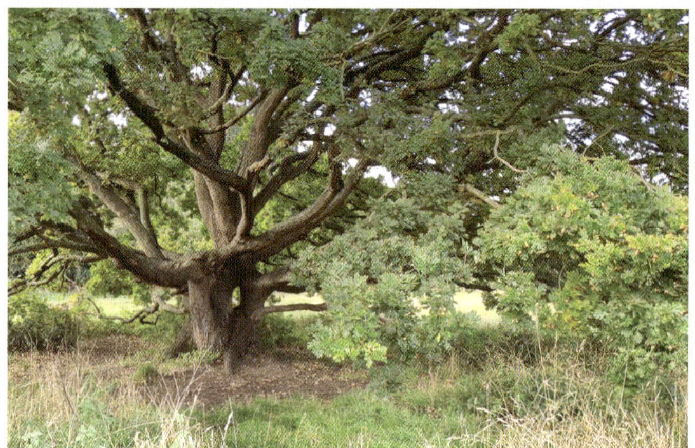

The beautiful *Quercus robur* oak that grows near my home. With its low branched trunk and spreading branches, it is a perfect specimen for getting up close to.

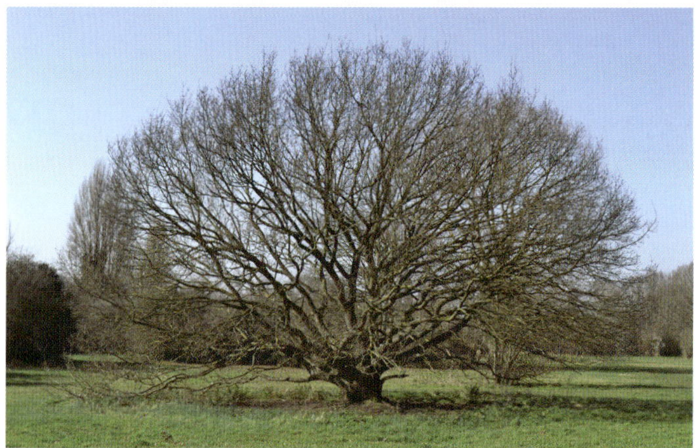

The leafless skeleton was drawn from a photograph. It was too cold to sit outside and draw, and the photograph was sufficient for such a small-scale drawing.

For this project I decided to focus on an oak tree (*Quercus robur*) that I pass almost every day. It was already a familiar subject, but I looked forward to getting to know it even better by making studies of it and its parts over the course of a year.

Winter and Early Spring

My first drawings were made in the late winter when the leafless skeleton of the tree could be seen. By walking around the tree and observing it at different times of the day, I found a view that showed its large, spreading habit at its best. This aspect also happened to be one that was well lit from the left, which is my preferred side for the light source. The low angle of the winter sun defined the tree's trunk and branches well. Working from a photograph was the easiest option in this case, as it was a bit too cold to sit and draw outside. The photograph also allowed me to view the tree's form at a reduced size. I drew the leafless tree first in pencil, later adding some mixed brown and dark grey watercolour to the pencil drawing to make it stronger.

At the same time as the photo was taken, I cut a small portion of branch from the lower reaches of the tree, choosing branchlets that contained small buds. Back in the studio I drew these directly on to the page, angling the branch across the page in a naturalistic way, mimicking the direction of the branches as they appeared on the tree. This provided the framework for the composition of the whole page. I drew a grouping of three buds, as well as drawing another section of branch that overlapped the first.

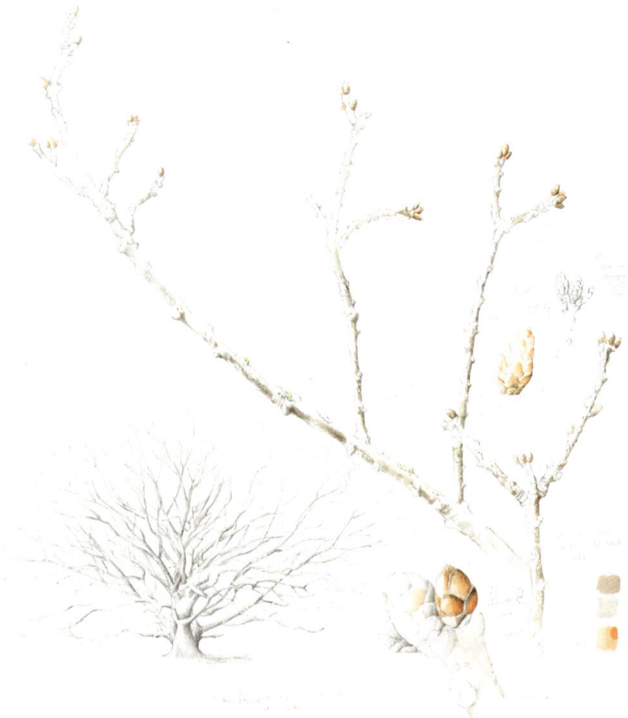

The start of the *Quercus robur* sketchbook page, drawn in the A3 Daler Rowney 'Ebony' spiral-bound cartridge paper sketchbook. Placing the small branch bearing buds diagonally across the page created multiple spaces in which to add detail as the work progressed.

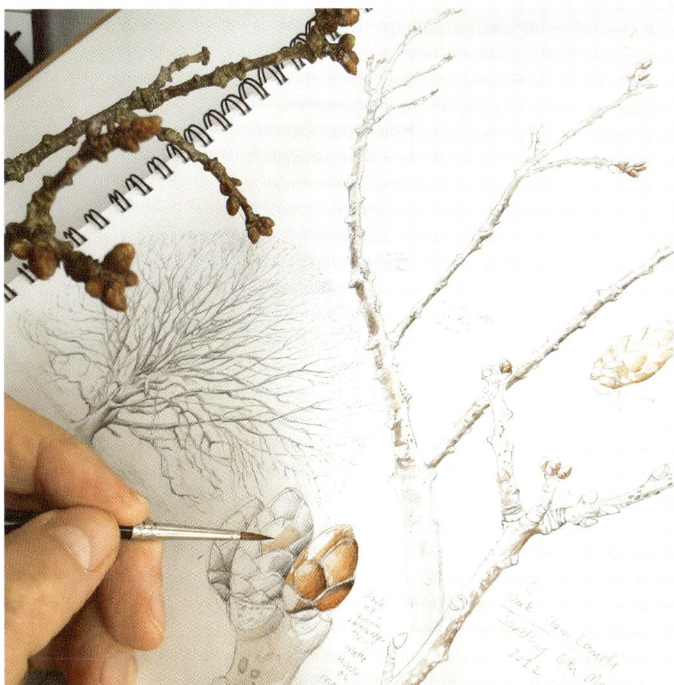

Painting the rich red-browns of the oak's leaf buds.

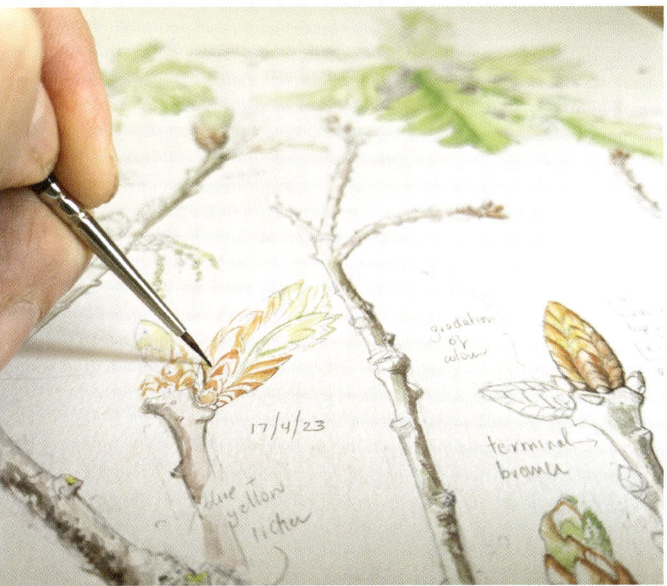

The oak branches already drawn on this page created empty spaces and negative shapes, which I used to slot in my drawings of the buds. Framed by the grey-brown branches, the warm red-browns of the buds, with their hint of fresh greens to come, added variety to the page.

More buds were added over the following weeks as I watched them develop throughout early spring. It was so interesting to see the buds becoming more elongated, and the smallest tips of fresh, bright green leaves emerge. At this stage it was vital to keep a close watch on the tree. Although I had seen it in bud for many successive years, I had not recorded the exact timing of its budding and opening. I checked on the tree almost daily to make sure I did not miss the vital moments.

Recording and Adding Colour

The next step was to add colour to the pencil drawings. It is always best to mix colours whilst observing the material directly in situ. By matching from life, your colours will be more accurate than when using a photograph viewed on screen or printed. In this case, I particularly loved the rich red browns of the bud scales.

Once I was happy that my colours matched the subject, I added watercolour by erasing some of the graphite, a little at a time, and replacing it with paint. It is not necessary to remove all the pencil when adding colour to a sketchbook page. In fact, it is that combination of the two media that gives sketchbook studies some of their charm. The addition of colour really started to bring the page to life. It can be helpful to add written notes to your page at this stage, for future reference, including such information as the names of the pigments used to mix your colours.

Tree Flowers and Spring Leaves

Finally, the first leaves began to unfold from the bud scales. Some clusters of bud scales produced miniature leaves in bright-yellow green, whilst others on the branch produced hanging catkins of yellow male flowers. As it was difficult for me to draw these details at the tree, I collected a few small branchlets to study at home. My drawings had to be completed promptly, as the delicate parts of these branchlets withered very quickly.

During the first year of this study, I missed the opportunity to draw the male flowers under magnification. Fortunately, I had recorded the date on which the oak tree produced male flowers and was able to visit it at the same time the following year. I could now fill in the gap with some additional drawings of the flowers.

The final piece added to this page was a branch of the newest, fully opened spring leaves. These I drew in situ. I located a suitable branch of leaves situated at the right height for me to observe and draw them whilst sitting in a portable chair. It was wonderful to be able to sit with the tree for the few hours that it took to draw the leaves. There was a beautiful feeling of the promise of spring as I sat with the sun on my back. The only drawback was the breeze, which flung the branch around from time to time! The female flowers could just be seen as tiny buds on the

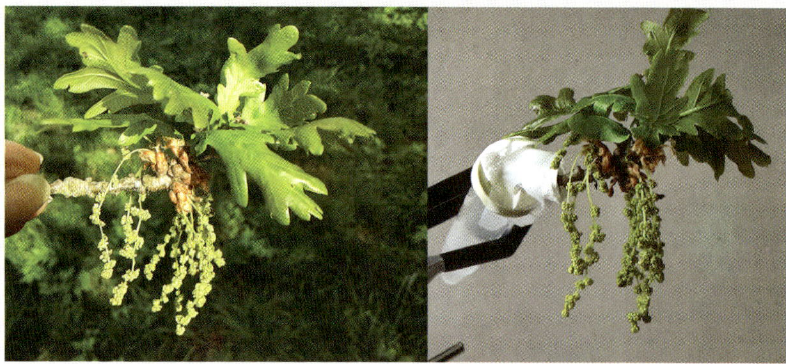

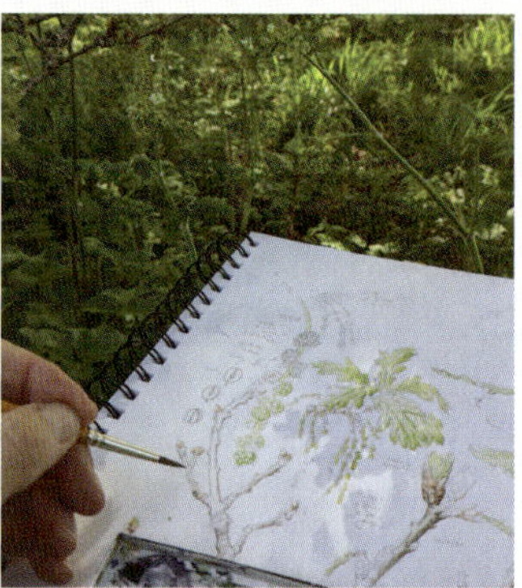

A small branch with emerging leaves and male flower catkins, which I took back to set up in the studio. The leaves withered very quickly, so I decided to draw the next stage of spring leaves directly from the tree.

Dating entries in a sketchbook helps me to return at the right time to fill in elements that have been missed the previous year.

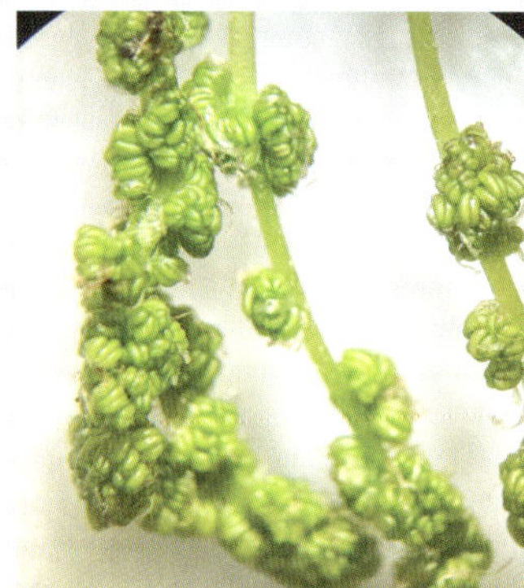

Male catkins and flowers observed and drawn in the second year of the oak sketchbook. These flowers are about to open.

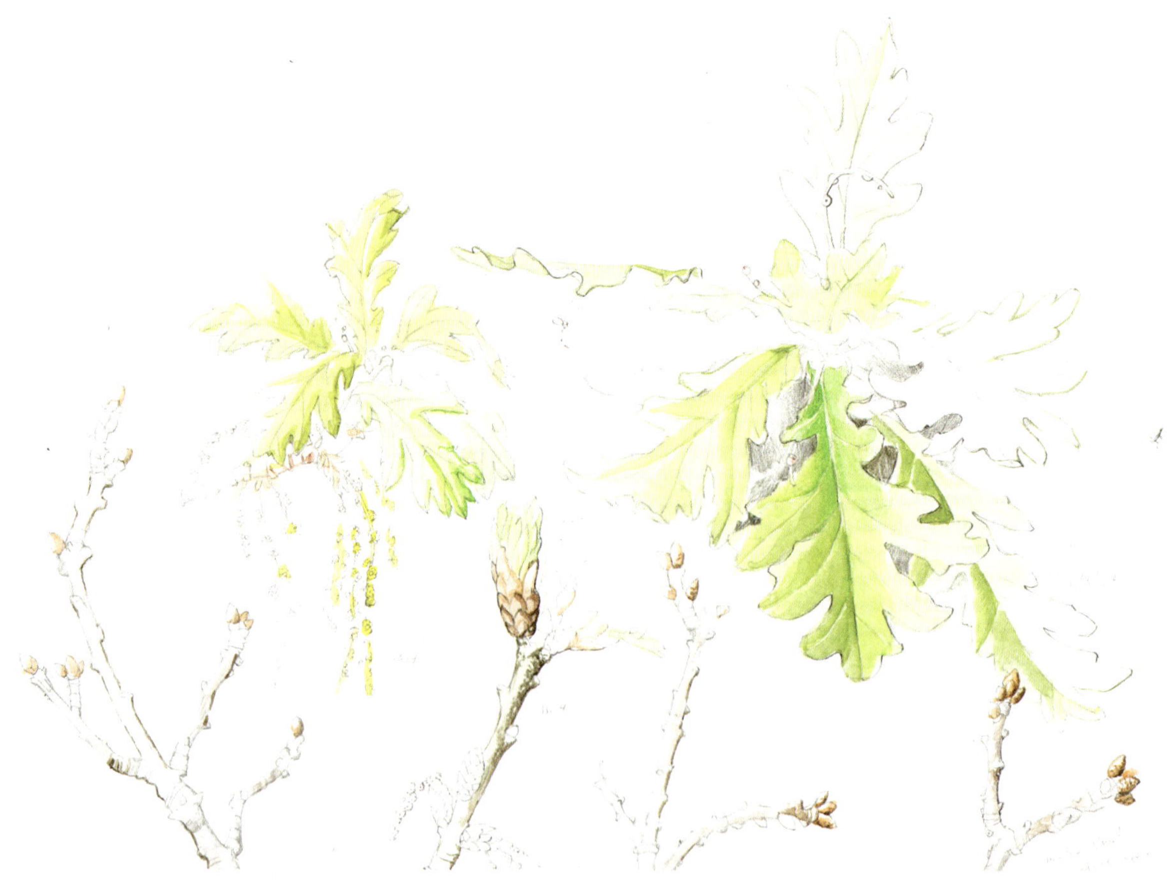

The oak sketchbook page with the addition of freshly opened leaves and male catkins in spring.

inflorescent branches emerging from the leaves with the promise of acorns to come.

Once the shapes and details were drawn in pencil, I added watercolour to some parts of the drawing. As the leaves were such a bright, light green, I decided to darken the negative spaces behind the leaf margins to make the leaves themselves stand out on the white paper. This both emphasised the outlines of the leaves and added depth to the image.

At this stage I decided to leave the page alone and to add the next studies to a new page of the spiral-bound sketchbook.

Because I had recorded all the relevant dates in my sketchbook in the first year, I knew when to return the following spring, to collect fresh material from which to draw male catkins and their flowers. I knew exactly what to expect this time and took a few catkins away to study and draw under the microscope. All the new details were added in the space I had left vacant on the sketchbook page.

The finished first page of the *Quercus robur* sketchbook study. There is only one thing left to squeeze in here: a study of the pistillate (female) flowers.

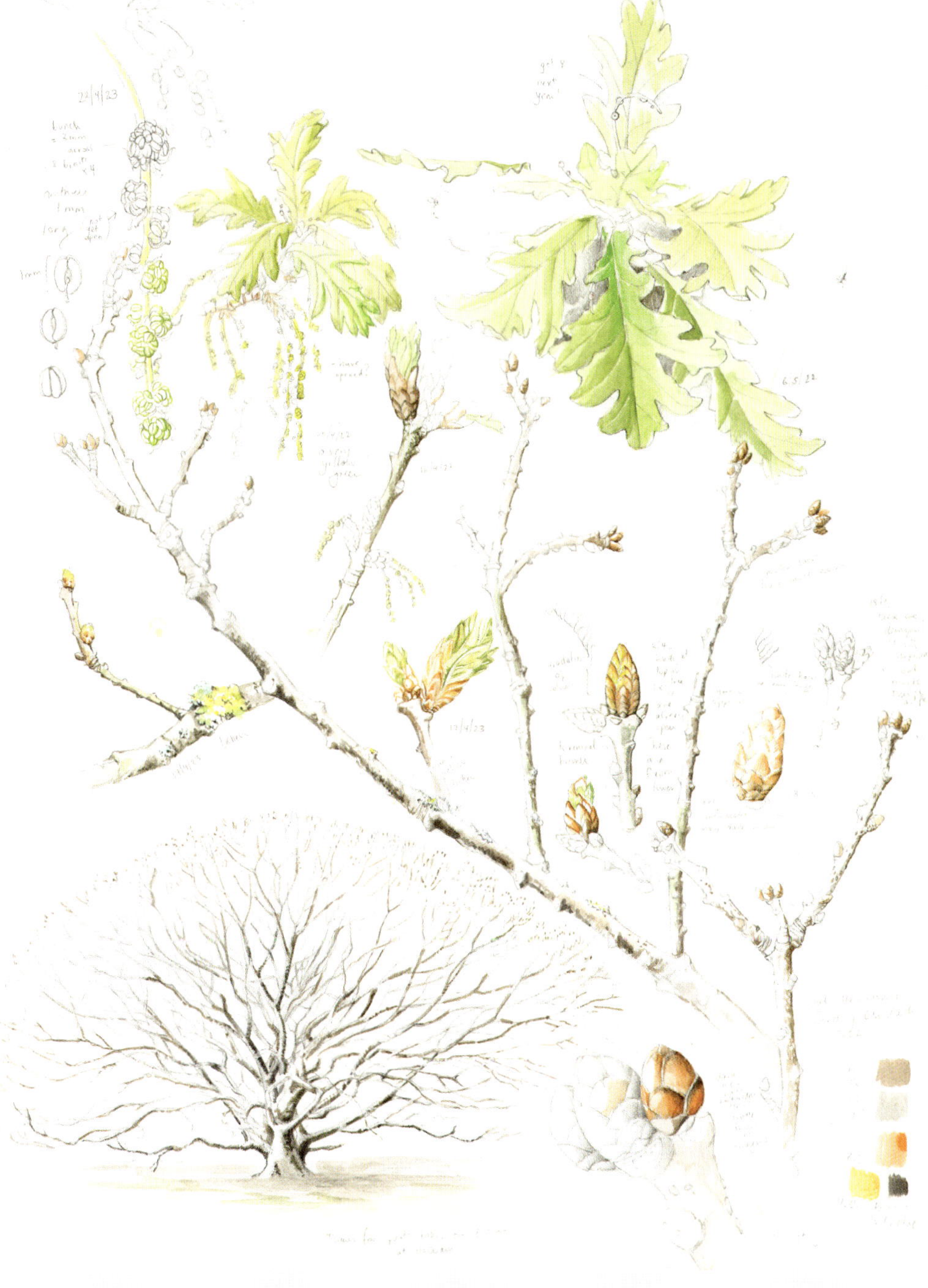

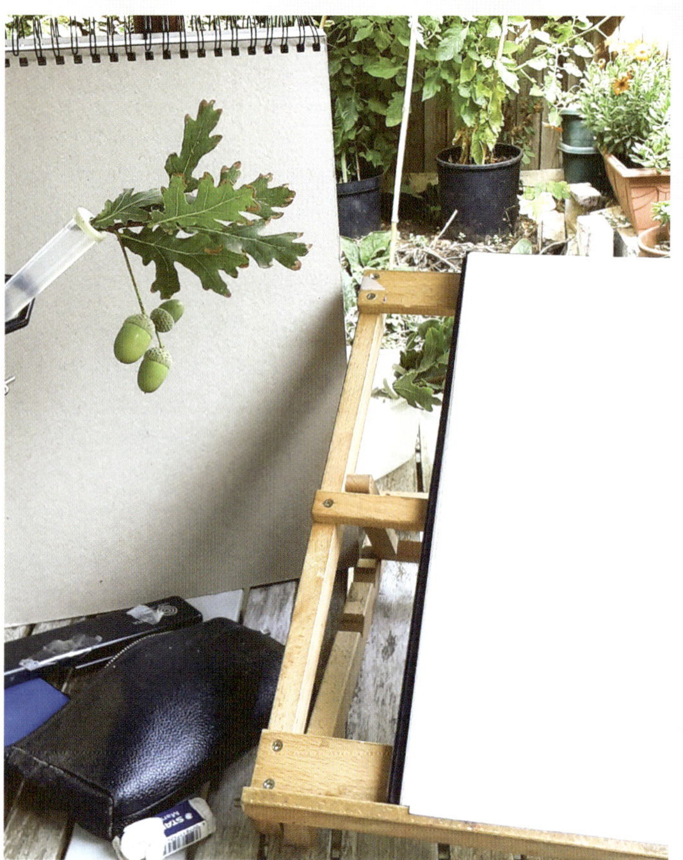

After setting up the branch so that it replicates a natural position, the specimen can be placed close to the drawing page, which is propped up here on a wooden desk easel.

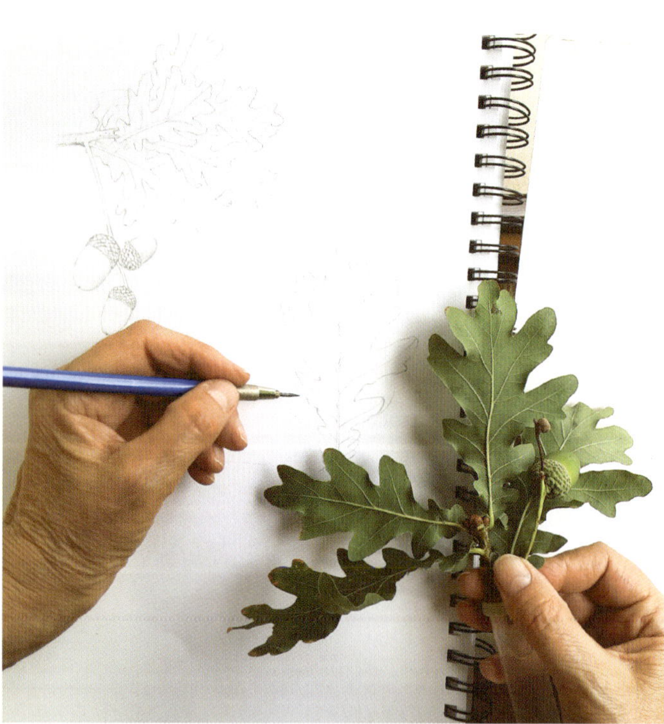

As well as drawing the leaves attached to the branch, I took one leaf that looked 'typical' and drew it from both sides, noting the venation pattern as well as the different colour and texture of both the adaxial (upper) and abaxial (lower) surfaces.

Summer and Autumn: Acorn Time

In my earlier drawings I had observed a good number of female flowers, indicating that this could be a good fruiting season for the tree. Sure enough, a few months later it was beginning to develop lots of healthy-looking green acorns. I was now ready to start depicting the next phase of the oak's seasonal cycle.

As there was abundant material, I cut two small branchlets with leaves and acorns attached and took them home to draw. I was careful to note the positions in which these were held on the tree, so I could recreate them in the sketchbook. In this case I used my retort stand, placing the branchlets in a florist's tube filled with water and fixing it in the clamp.

Changing Sketchbooks

At this point I decided to change from the spiral-bound sketchbook to the sewn-bound Fabriano 'Venezia' book.

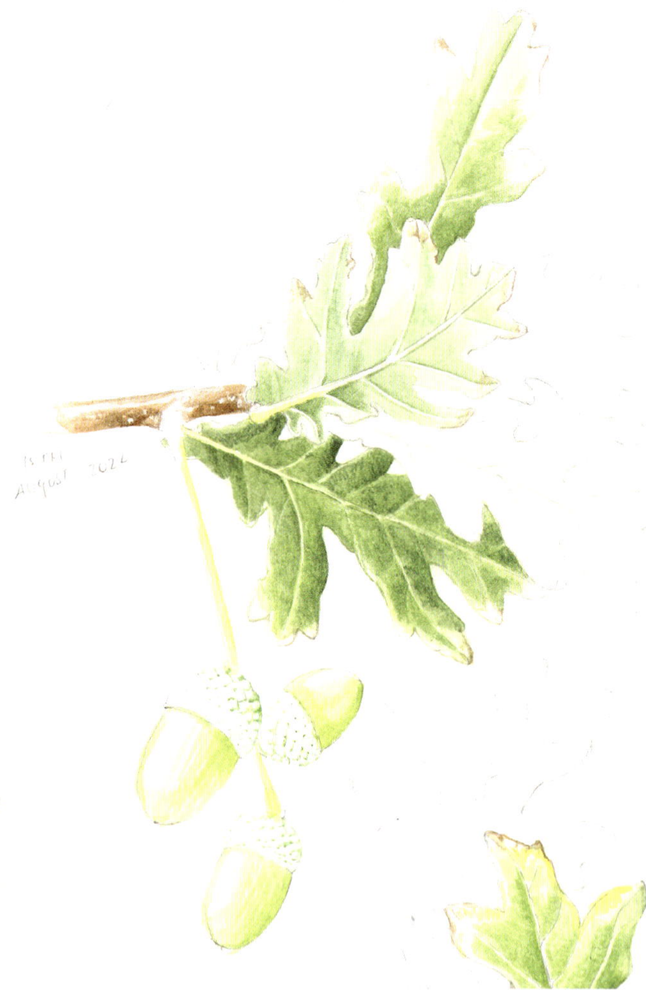

Copied over from the spiral-bound sketchbook, the very first sprig of leaves and acorn I added to the new double-page spread was the green one from August.

I had a very strong vision about how I wanted this study to look, imagining a series of drawings spreading across a horizontal page. The Fabriano 'Venezia' sketchbook seemed better suited to this approach, as I could work across the double-page spread. There was also something about the creaminess and texture of the paper that I felt was better suited to the work. As I envisaged working more with colour, it seemed a good idea to choose a heavier paper that would be able to take a little more paint.

Acorns and Colour

As the weeks and months passed, I was delighted to see my tree covered in ripening acorns. This was proving to be a 'mast' year for it – the term is used to describe a year when oaks and other trees produce a particularly abundant crop of their fruits. How lucky! I was curious to record the different colours of the acorns as they ripened, as I had never studied this before.

Picking up where I had left off in the spiral-bound sketchbook, I started the double-page spread by copying over the sprig of leaves and green acorns at the left side of the page. I continued visiting the oak tree later to observe acorns at different stages. On one day in September, I was very pleased to find acorns at several different stages of ripeness. This was reflected in their colours changing from green to yellow, turning slowly orange and then brown. I picked one of each colour and, after photographing them, took them home so that I could capture them as soon as possible.

I added more sprigs of leaves into the sketchbook showing the ripening acorns changing from yellow through to dark brown. Picking the occasional acorn and taking it home in its cap to draw and paint, I noticed that any acorns I carried in my pocket emerged looking very different from when they went in. This is because some of the bloom, which is like a light dusting on the surface of the fruit, was rubbed off in my pocket. The result was an accidentally polished acorn that was much shinier than it had been on the tree! My colour studies of the acorns at different stages proved to be very useful, as they formed the basis of my colour palette for the branchlets.

The leaves aged alongside the ripening acorns, darkening in colour and becoming richer in texture. There appeared to be some premature yellowing of some of the leaves on the side which caught the most sun. The unusually hot and dry summer may have caused this, and for a while I was very worried about the tree's survival, but thankfully it seemed to pull through.

I became reluctant to cut more of the tree's branchlets, even though there were plenty of branches, so I worked from a combination of photographs and observation from life. I did, however, collect some fading autumn leaves with their beautiful bright colours. These leaves were clearly ready to drop, as they fell as soon as they were touched.

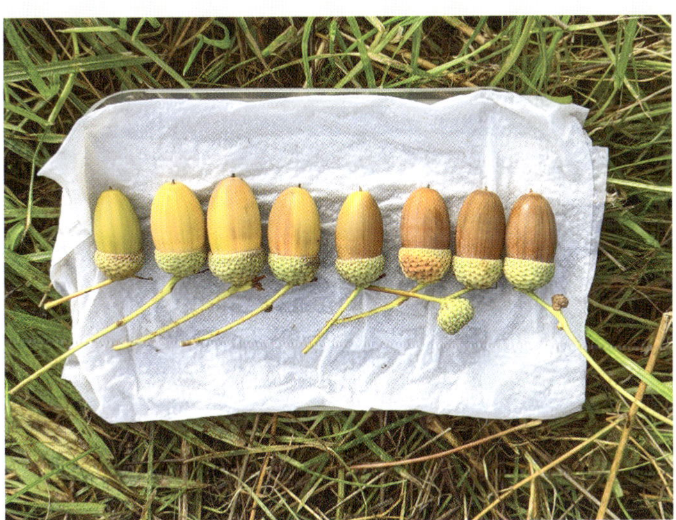

The range of acorn colours I observed on one visit to the *Quercus robur* tree in September was amazing.

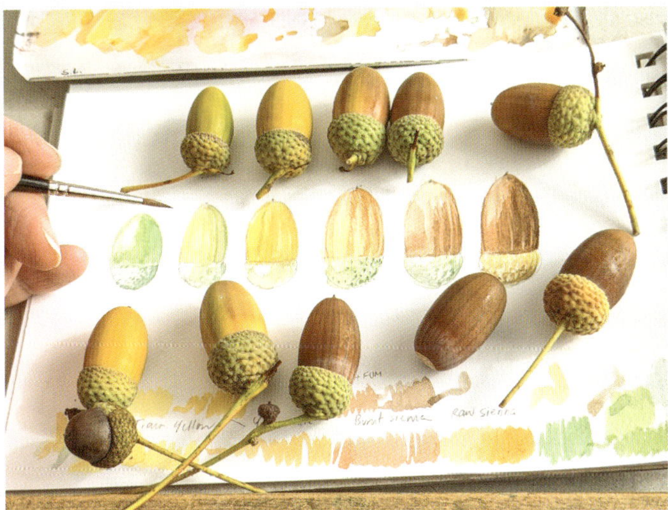

As soon as I had the acorns in the studio, I drew them and added the colours that I could record from life. The scaly caps of the acorns remained blue/grey for some time, before they too started to turn brown with age.

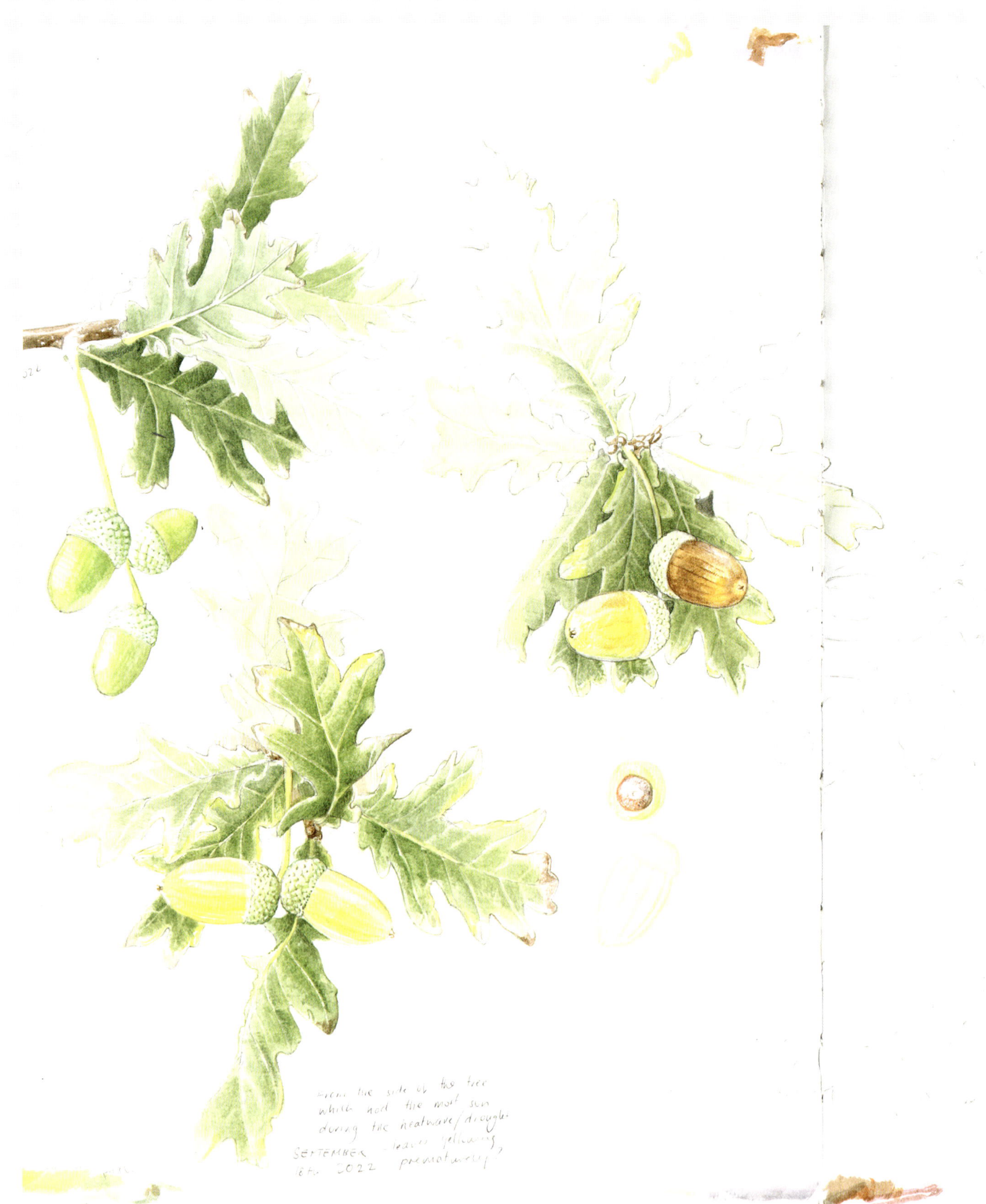

The *Quercus robur* sprigs with their ripening acorns spread slowly across the double page.

The Last Acorn

Returning to the tree nearly every week, I realised it was becoming increasingly difficult to find acorns intact with both seed and cap. As the season wore on, they naturally dropped from their caps or were collected by both squirrels and people! I drew and painted the final acorn in the last week of October. Of course, there were probably plenty more above my eye level, but this was the last one I could see. Hanging loosely in its cap, ready to drop at the slightest touch or breeze, it was a beautiful rich, deep brown colour.

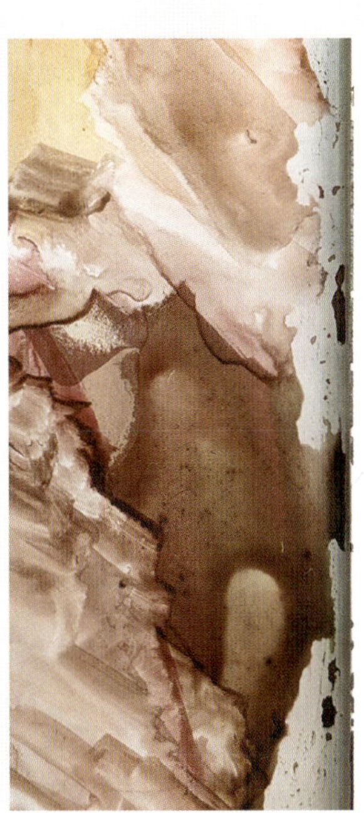

Mixing colour for some of the most mature acorns.

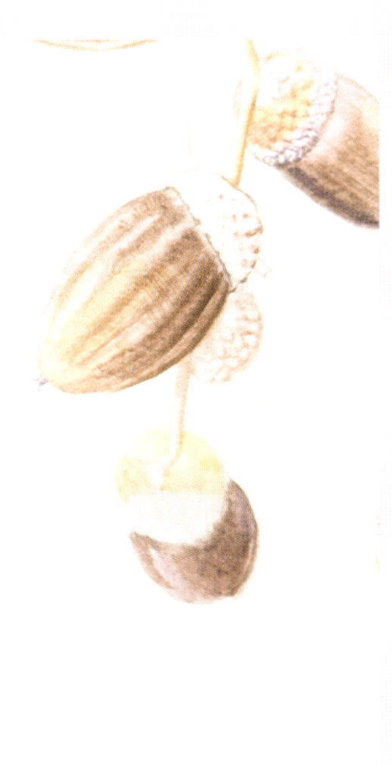

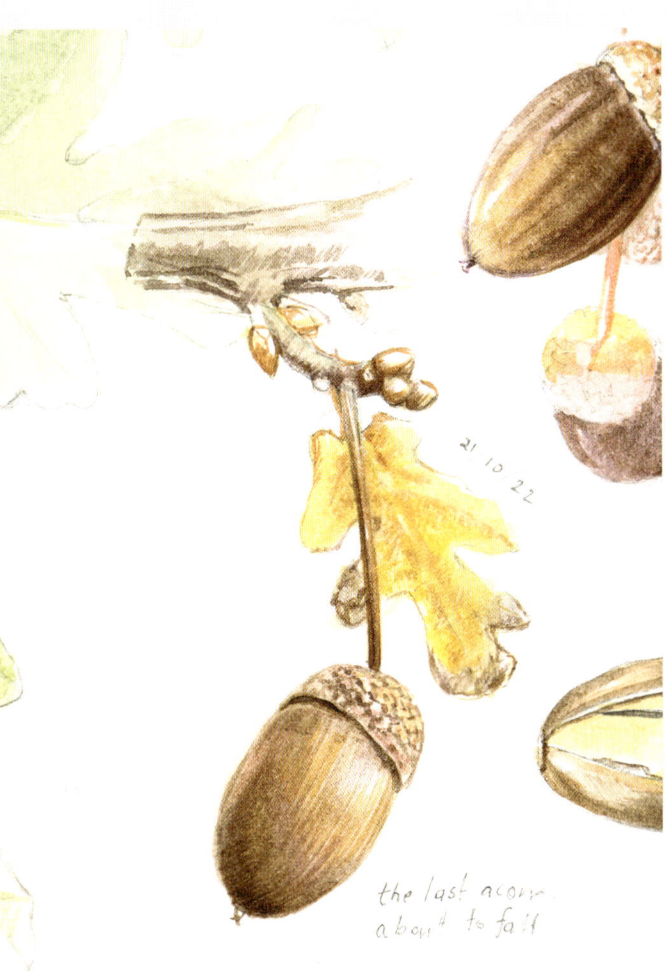

The last acorn. I tried to capture the way it hung precariously within its cup, ready to fall at any moment.

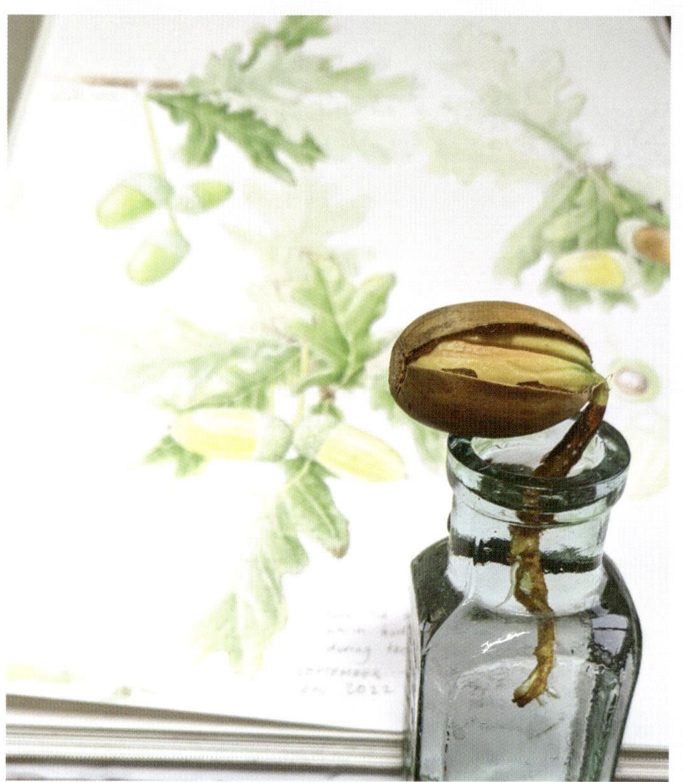

Sprouting an Acorn

Finally, I searched in the ground beneath the tree for sprouting acorns. It was very exciting to find some and, as they were abundant, I took a few home to study. Some I lay on a bed of soil in a pot, with their roots downwards. These failed to grow, but the one that I suspended in water (using some sticks that I had wired together) started to sprout. I checked on it every few days and drew the developments as the shoot began to grow upwards, and the roots downwards. When I went away for a few weeks, I asked family members to take reference photos for me. I took the sprouting acorn out of the water for brief periods in order to observe and draw its roots.

After about a month the shoot was 30cm high and showing full leaves. Its growth then paused, and it began to look a little sickly and etiolated. After some weeks I planted it into a pot, which I placed outside. I had lost my view of the roots but had ensured its survival.

The sprouting acorn that I had collected from the ground kept growing after I had placed it in water.

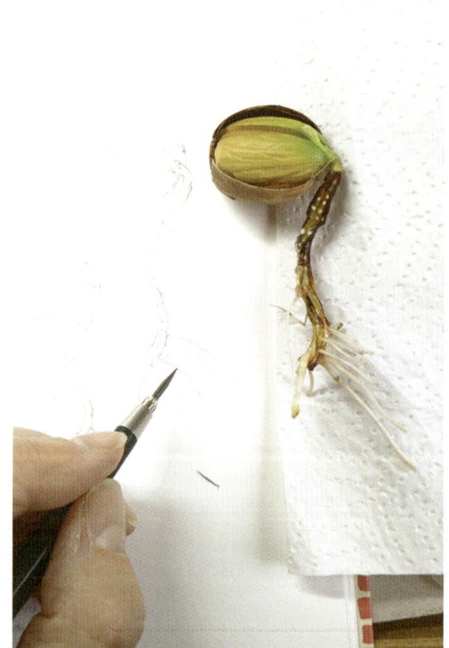

When I wanted to draw the sprouting acorn's roots, I had to carefully lift it out of the small bottle vase. It was fascinating to see the first side-roots bud and then grow.

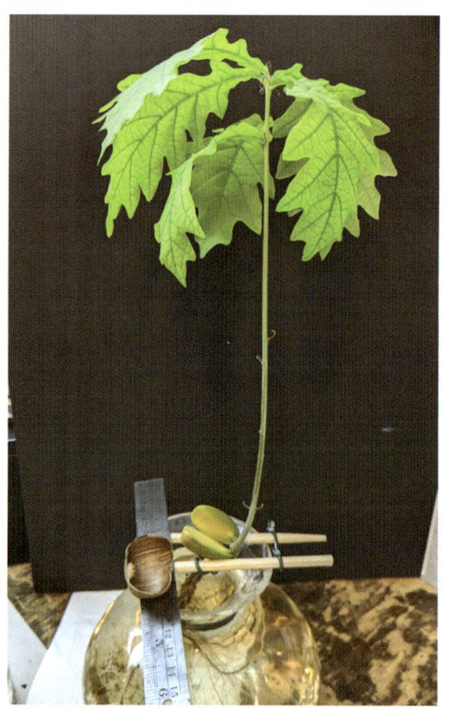

The sprouting acorn was transplanted to a larger vase, where it was kept suspended above the water on a makeshift support.

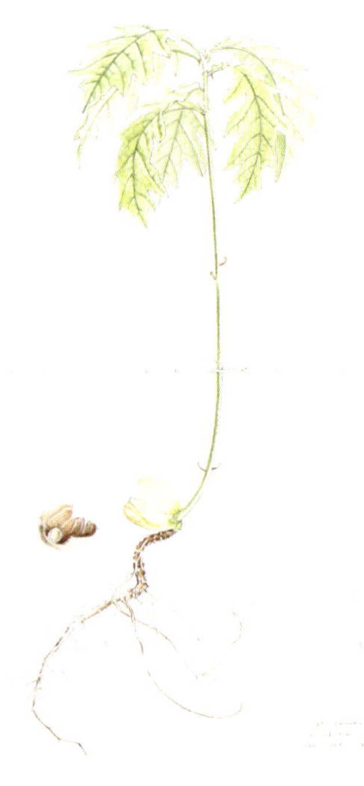

There was no more room on the double-page spread for the oak seedling; it needed its own page. The seedling also needed a new, bigger home, so I planted it out into a pot.

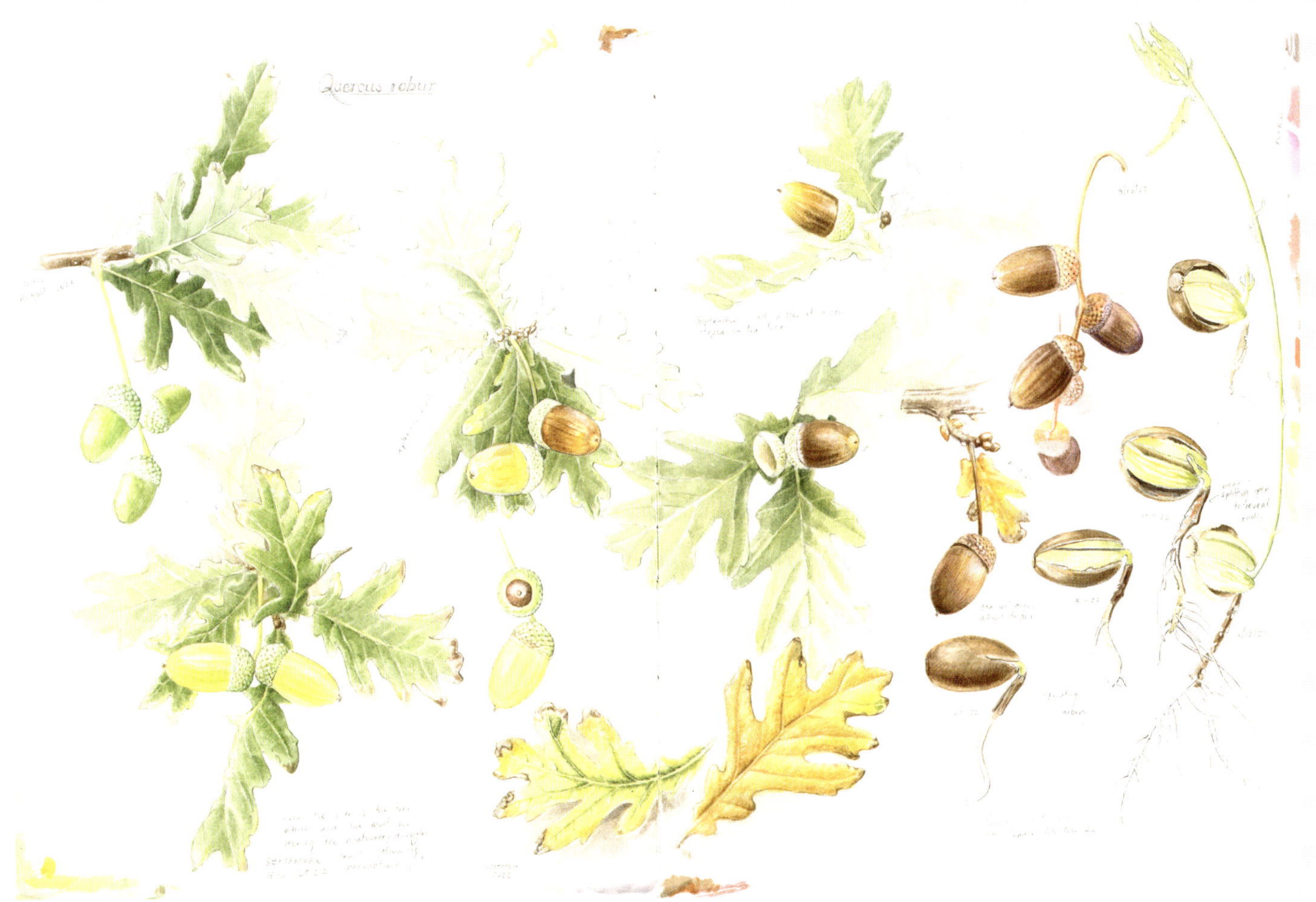

The final double-page spread of *Quercus robur*'s leaves and acorns, complete with sprouting acorn to signify the beginning of another cycle.

I was very pleased with this study, as it came out almost exactly as I had imagined. From fresh green growth to sprouting acorn, the double-page spread certainly tells a story. I hope I have done parts of this beautiful tree justice.

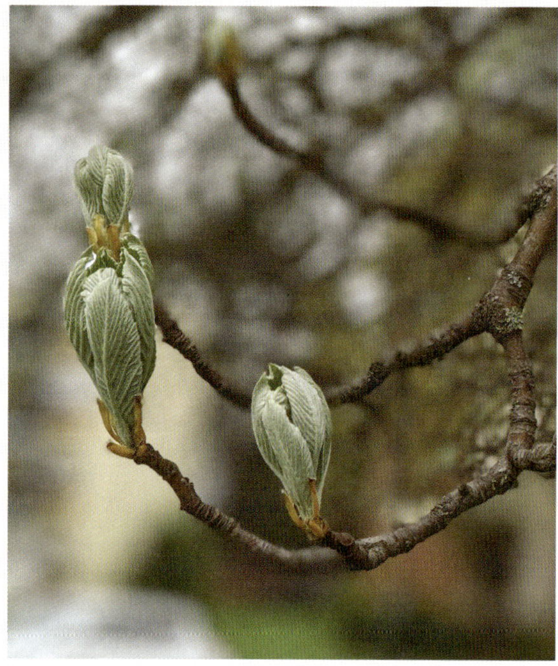

The new budding leaves of the whitebeam tree, covered in white hairs, resemble ice cream cones.

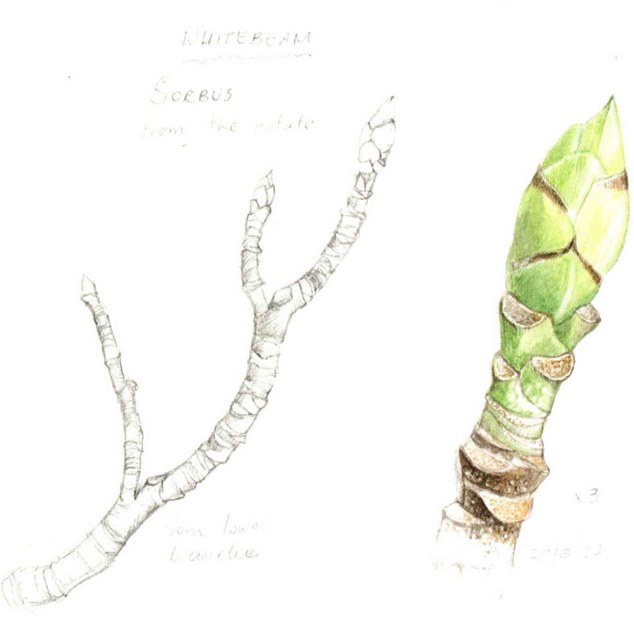

The whitebeam winter branch with its distinctive terminal bud scales.

Another lovely neighbourhood tree, this whitebeam *Sorbus alba* is probably around 60 years old. It has a neat and compact shape, reminiscent of the classic tree that a child might draw, with its upright trunk and rounded crown. I walked past this tree for many years on my way to the bus stop before deciding to draw and paint it. I love that something so simple and beautiful could draw my attention and cheer me up even on the most ordinary of days.

Spring Buds and Leaves

I began drawing the winter buds of the *Sorbus alba* before moving on to the very first emerging leaves. As with the oak, the buds scales of trees are unique for each species and are useful for identification when the tree is dormant. I enlarged the terminal bud to three times life-sized, using my proportional dividers to multiply each measurement from the specimen accordingly.

As I moved on to the emerging first leaves, I began to understand why the tree's common name is 'whitebeam'. The white appearance of the underside of the leaves is created by thick woolly indument (hairs), which is especially dense in the compact form of the newly emerging bud leaves.

Using References in the Studio

Once the whitebeam tree's leaves have emerged, it makes incredibly fast progress. The flower buds emerge at the same time as the new leaves, from the centre of each cluster. It is very hard as an artist to keep up with this tree – before I knew it, I was collecting a small branch with fully open flowers for drawing.

Photographing each branchlet before cutting it was particularly important here, to capture the position of the inflorescences in relation to the leaves. This allowed me to create a similar set-up in the studio on my plant stand.

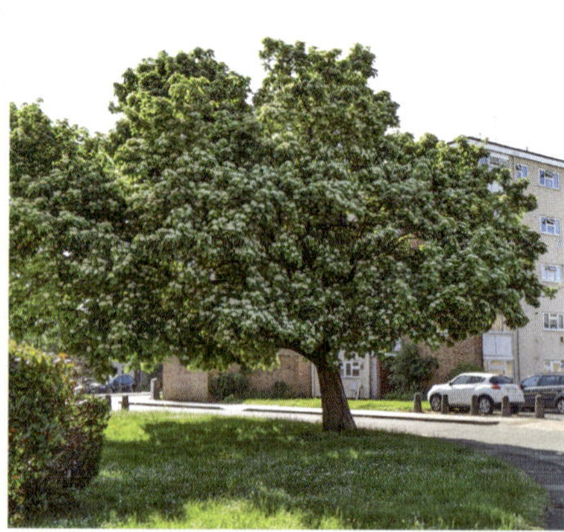

The whitebeam in full flower. It is such a stunning tree, I love to walk past it at any time of year, but especially when it is in full flush.

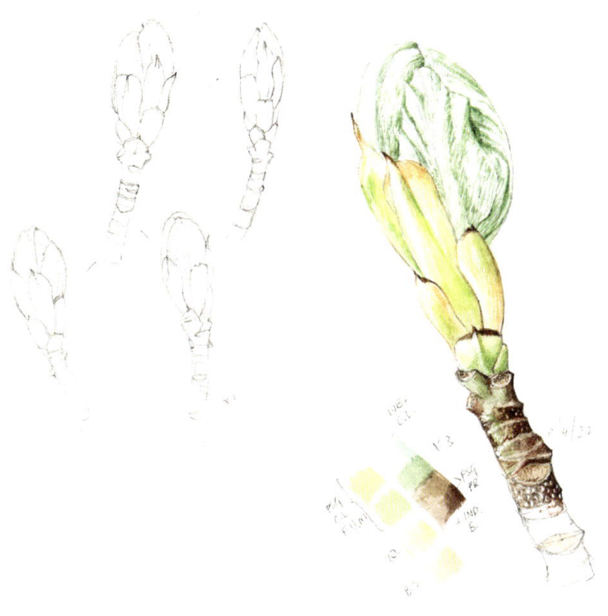

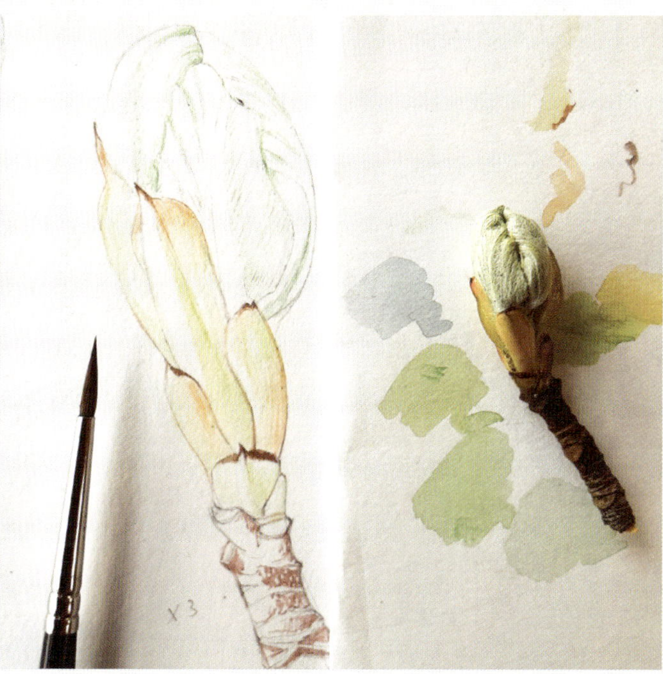

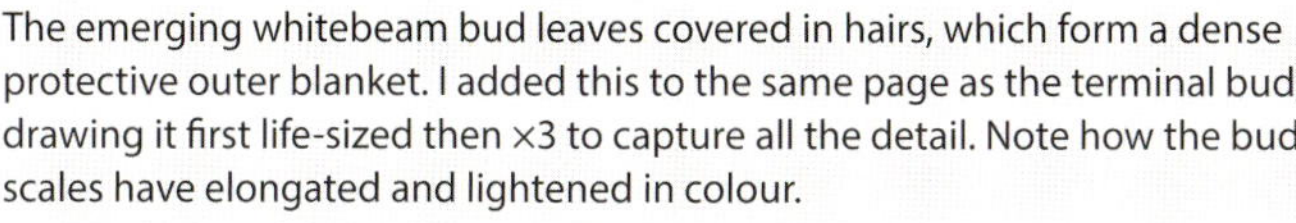

The emerging whitebeam bud leaves covered in hairs, which form a dense protective outer blanket. I added this to the same page as the terminal bud, drawing it first life-sized then ×3 to capture all the detail. Note how the bud scales have elongated and lightened in colour.

Matching colour directly to the emerging leaves of the whitebeam.

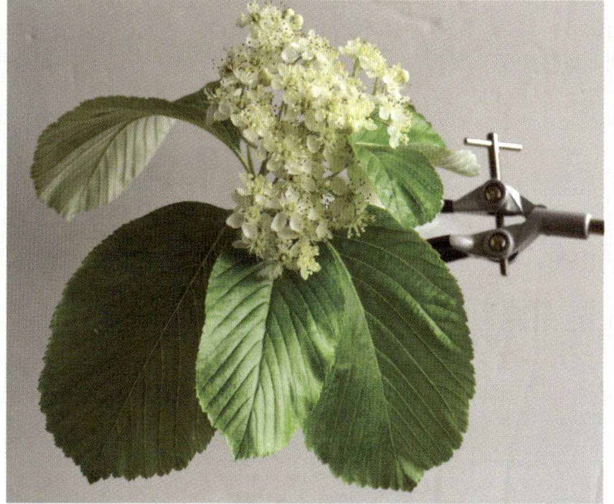

Setting the whitebeam branchlet up on the retort stand, I rotated it and moved it up and down until I was satisfied that its position was sufficiently naturalistic, and showed the leaves and inflorescence to their best advantage for drawing.

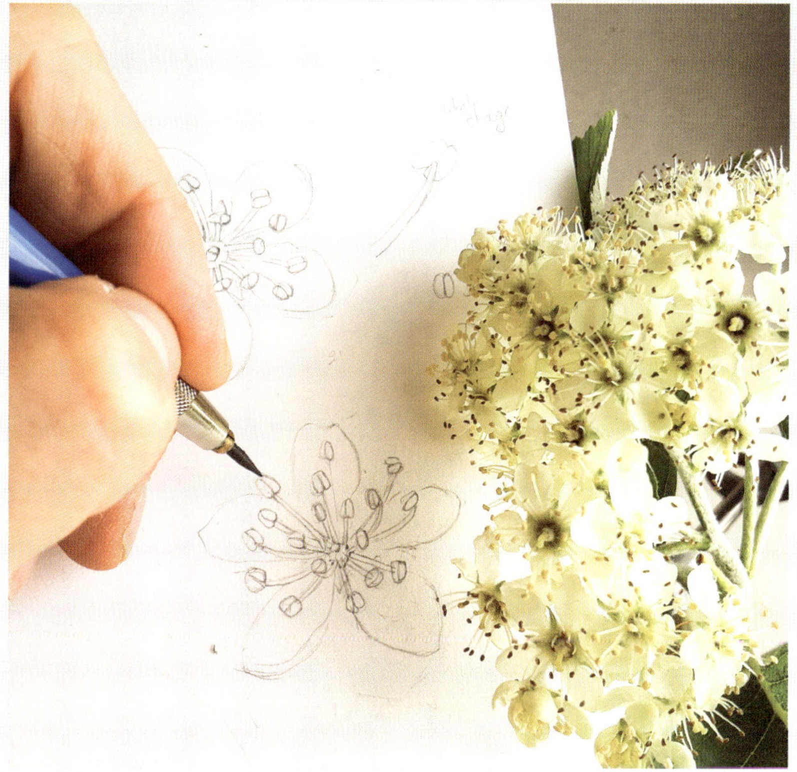

Another reason for choosing this specimen was to capture an inflorescence with flowers that had not gone over – in other words, flowers with anthers that were still intact.

When attached to the tree, flowering branches are busy transporting a lot of sap and sugars to the flowers, so it is very likely that a specimen will wilt quickly after cutting. As soon as I had the branchlet back in the studio, I put it into a florist's tube filled with water. I placed the tube in the stand and, with reference to my photos, attempted to replicate its natural position there.

Using my proportional dividers, I drew the flowers at a magnification factor of times two and three, to capture all their details. However, I still wanted to find out more about the structure of the flowers, so I made spirit specimens by putting some of them into a jar containing clear alcohol. I planned to look at them later under a microscope.

Summer Leaves and Berries

I had been looking forward to berries arriving on this tree and I was surprised to see them appear and ripen long before the leaves changed colour. The shiny red berries contrasted beautifully with the colour of the upper surfaces of the leaves, which were still rich green. They also looked attractive alongside the pale white/blue of the undersides of the leaves.

In the same way that I set up my flowering specimen in the spring, I positioned the cut branchlet in a florist's tube held in the clamp of my retort stand. In truth, I am not

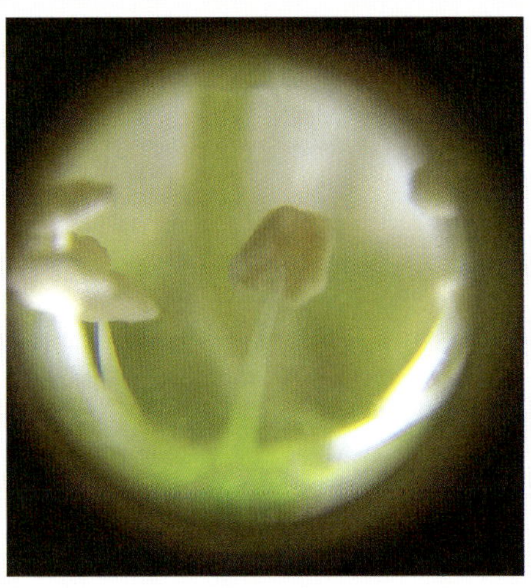

Not having a microscope to hand, I used my phone camera to zoom in on the flower's details. I also tried using a macro attachment for the phone lens. It did not take great photos but it did give me a better view of the attachment of filament to anther.

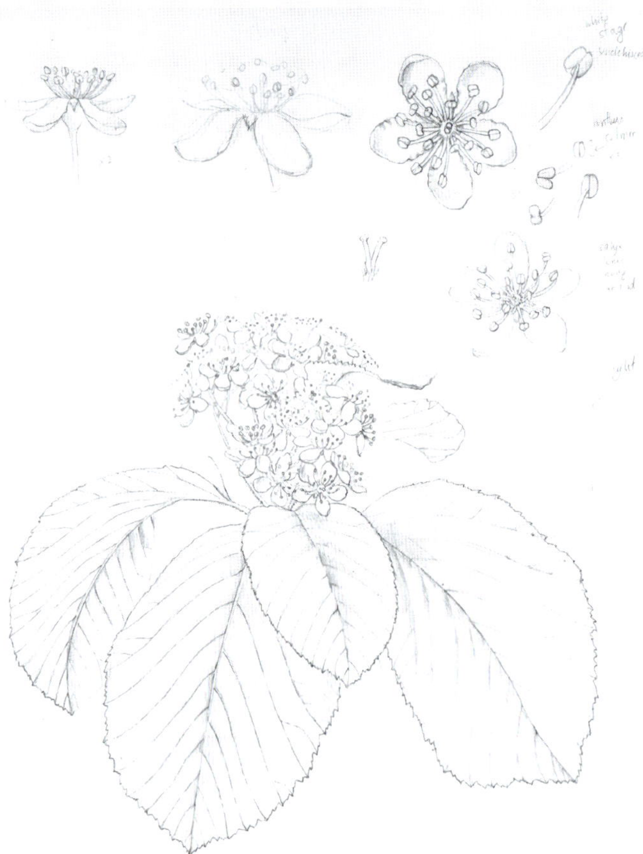

The final sketches for the first two whitebeam pages in the A3 watercolour sketchbook, showing the flowering branchlet and details of the flowers.

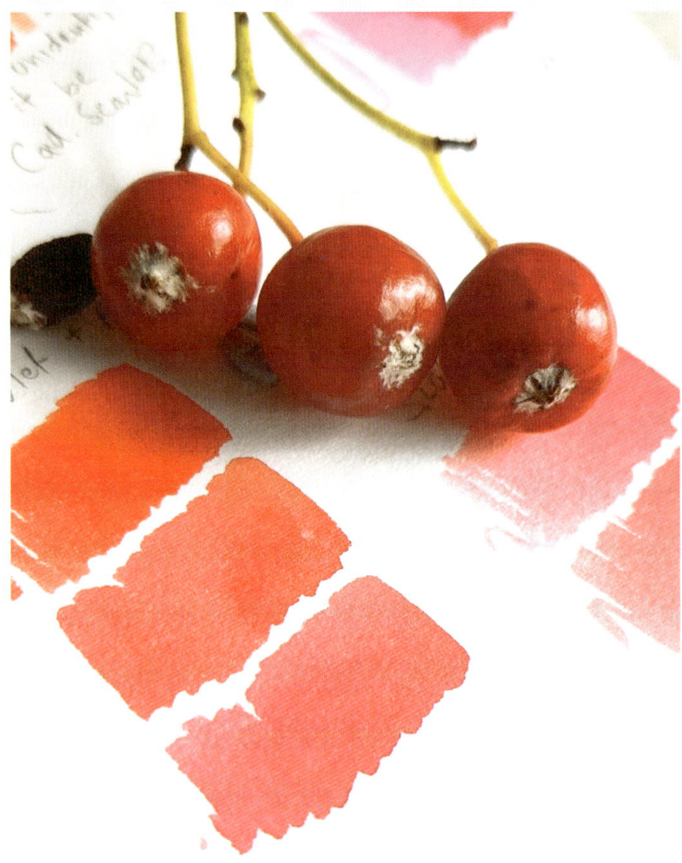

Loose colour studies of single whitebeam berries were made in the colour sketchbook before cutting and drawing/painting a branchlet with berries attached.

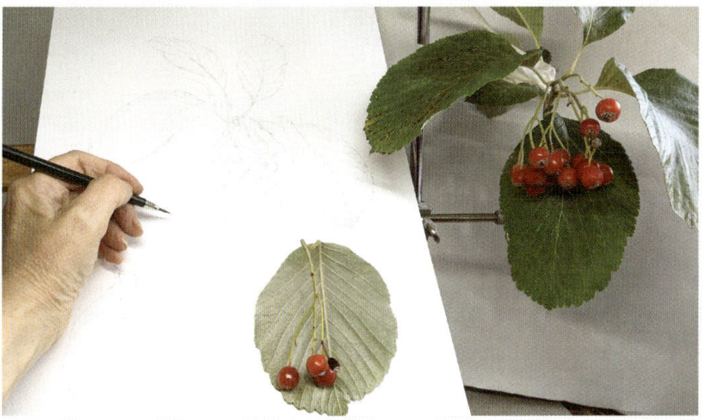

The fruiting branch set up on the stand alongside the second study page of *Sorbus alba*. I also turned a leaf over to record the very different surface texture and colour of the other side, which contrasted nicely in texture and colour with the berries.

convinced that this specimen truly replicated the branch when it was still attached to the tree. The heavy berries seem to hang more droopily than they had previously. Still, it was very useful to draw the specimen up close as I could capture the complicated branching pattern of the infructescence and see how the berries' colours changed as they were at different stages of ripeness. It was also fun to record the way the light fell on the leaves.

Because I had so many berries, I was able to take a few and draw and paint them separately. This allowed me to document several things. By drawing a longitudinal section of the fruit, I could see its shape more clearly than I could while it was still hanging on the branch. It became clear that the berry's widest point is towards its apex – it is not a perfect sphere at all. This fruit contained one black seed and the remains of another, aborted seed. Finally, the remains of the calyx (the parts of the flower that make up the sepals) were quite persistent on the fruit. Their hairiness clung to the top of the fruit long after the petals had dropped off and the ovary had ripened.

Autumn Berries and Leaves

Finally, in October the leaves began to show various bright and beautiful shades of autumnal colours. The leaves were an incredibly intense yellow while they were still on the tree, but I noticed that, as soon as they fell, their colour began to fade. I brought some leaves home as quickly as I could and decided to capture the colours straight away. Laying a leaf down on a page of my small colour-study sketchbook, I threw colour on to the paper rapidly and confidently. I was then able to replicate these colours quite easily, as I took another leaf and added it to the sketchbook page where I had already captured the summer leaves and berries.

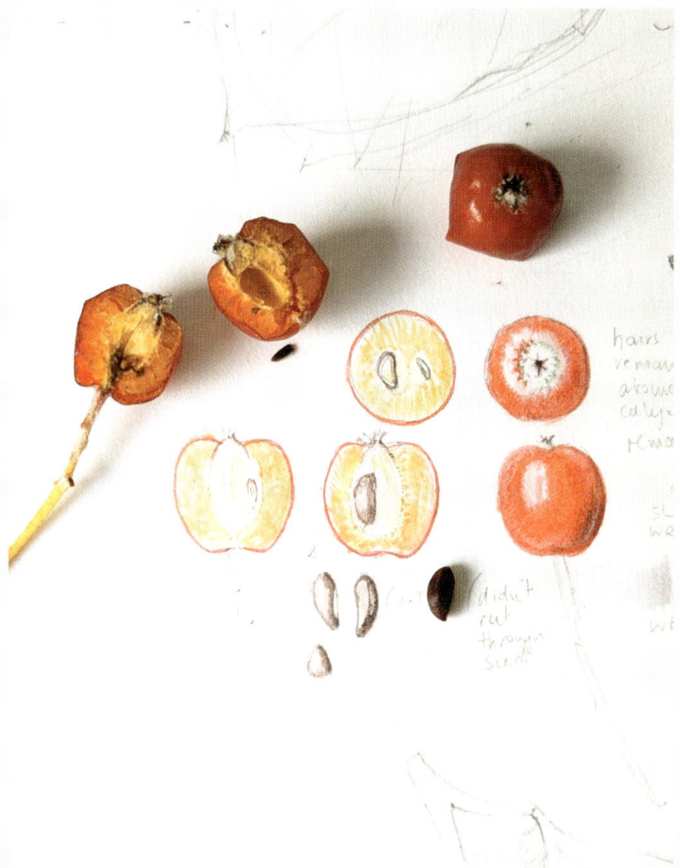

Investigating the whitebeam's fruits, cutting them to show the colours and position of the seeds inside. There was an abundance of material on this tree.

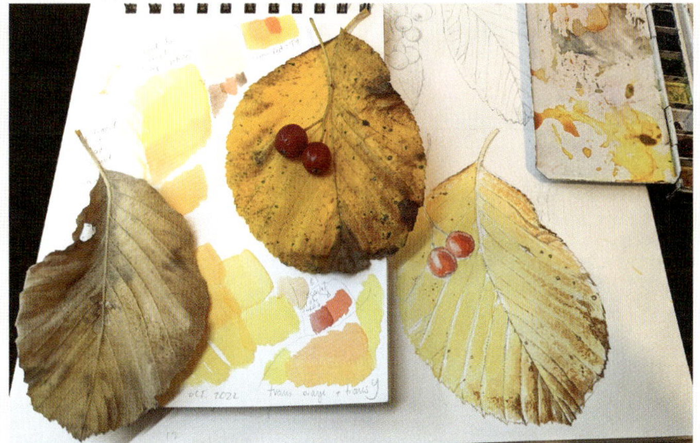

Capturing colour as quickly as possible, I laid down concentrated washes of yellow; first in the colour-study sketchbook, and then on a drawn version of the whitebeam leaf on the same page as the studies from the summer.

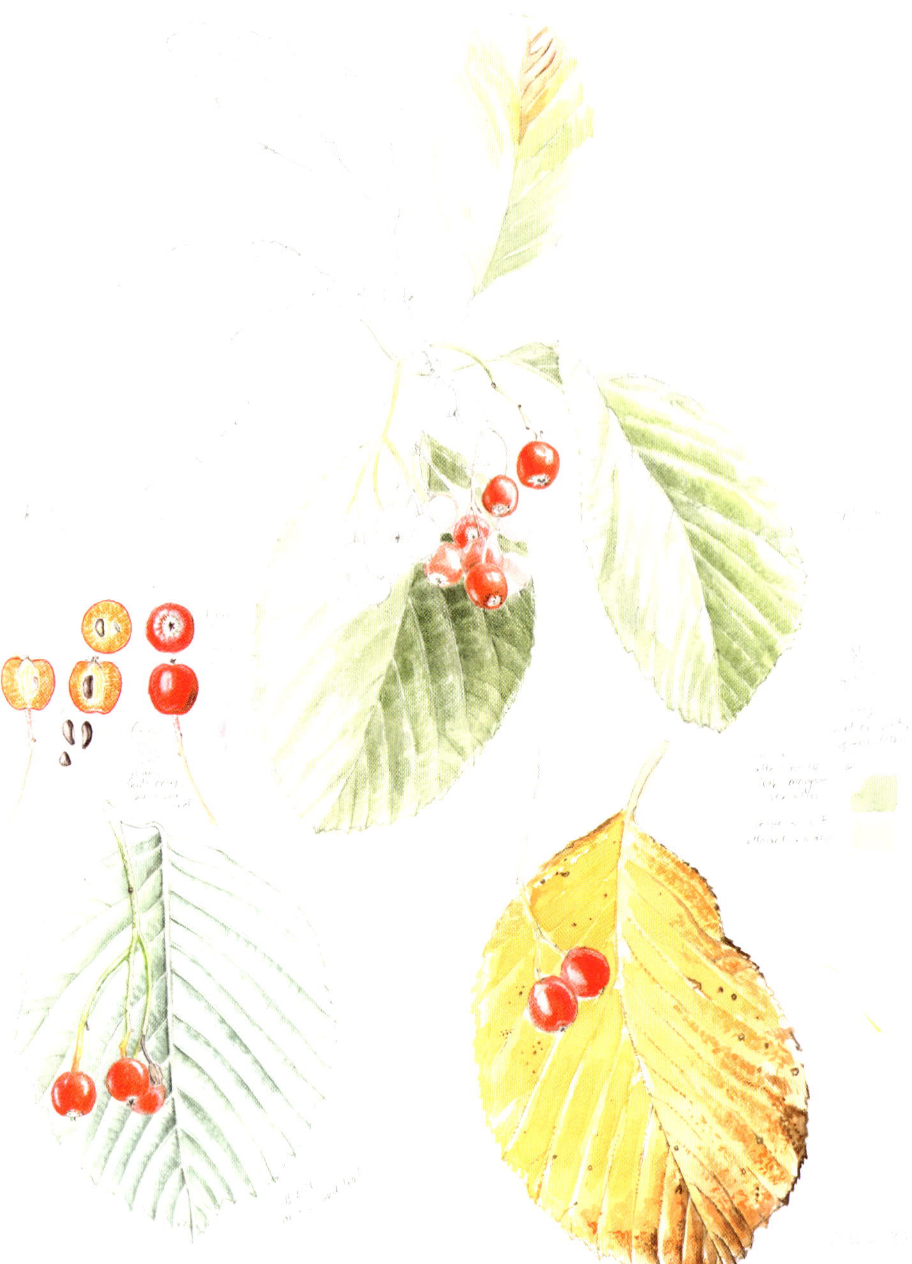

There are many more observations still to be made about this tree. I did not begin the whitebeam studies with any specific intention in mind. One of the strongest outcomes for me has been an increased confidence with mixing and applying colour. I am looking forward to autumn again when I can revisit painting some of those stunning leaves. I would also like to draw and paint parts of the tree again to make more of a feature of the while leaf underside, as well as capture the whole tree both with and without leaves.

CONNECTING WITH TREES THROUGH ART

Having studied, watched and investigated the oak and the whitebeam throughout their entire growing season, I have formed a strong bond with them both. As each new season begins, I have come to recognise exactly what is going on with them. They are not 'my' trees, of course, but when I walk past them now, I do refer to them as 'mine'. Through art, I have made a special connection with them – I hope you too can find a couple of trees to bond with in the same fashion!

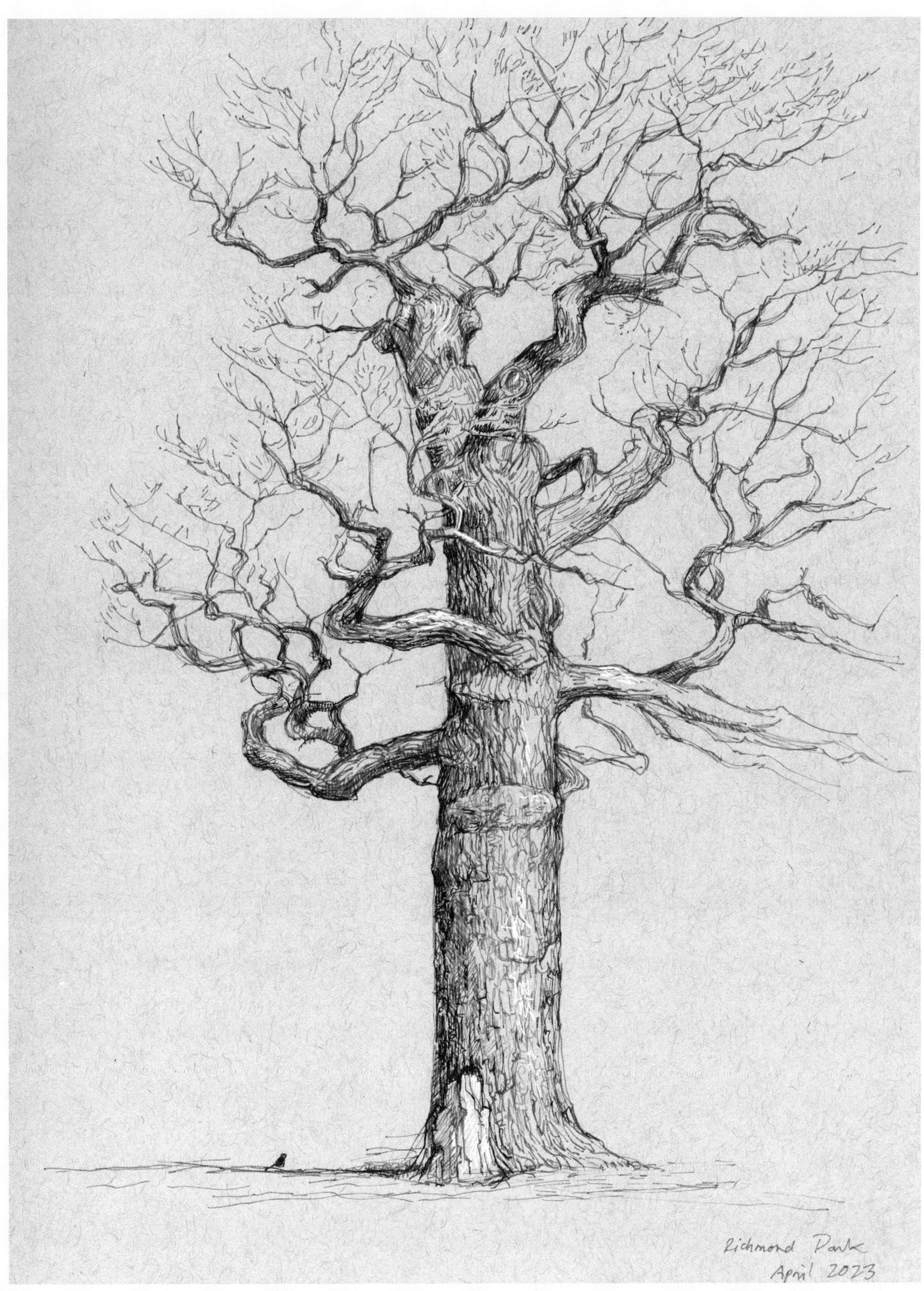

Leafless oak trees in winter make excellent subjects for pen and ink drawing, such as this one on tan-toned paper. This was drawn from a photograph, but I would like to try drawing many more winter trees outdoors next winter, if I can bear the cold.

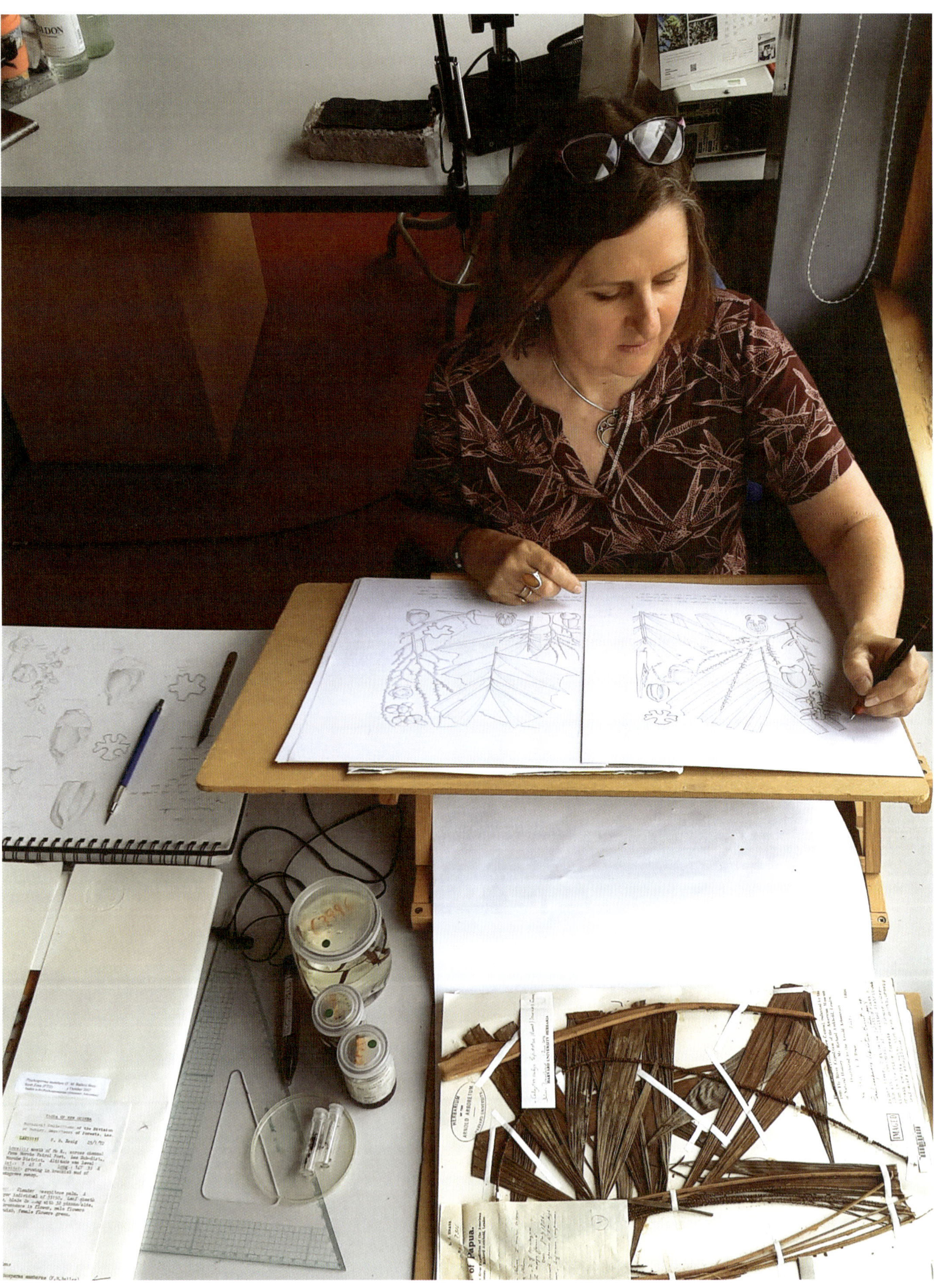

CHAPTER 8

SCIENTIFIC BOTANICAL SKETCHBOOK

Drawing for scientific botanical illustration requires a special set of skills. The key is to understand botanical structures and to draw them with a high degree of accuracy. The scientific botanical illustrator must also possess a good knowledge of botany and plant anatomy. Behind every polished scientific illustration are complex and rigorous preparatory drawings that fill the sketchbooks of every scientific botanical illustrator.

I have worked as a scientific botanical illustrator for around 30 years, producing pen and ink illustrations of plants for publication in books and journals. These illustrations are usually commissioned by a botanist, who will describe in words what I am describing in visual form. The illustrations may be describing a new species of plant to science, or illustrating an identification guide such as a regional flora.

Many of my watercolour pieces, which may not be destined for publication, are also created with the same level of scientific accuracy and explanation in mind. I have filled many sketchbooks with the working drawings for these pieces. They are the most technical of all my collection, with the highest level of accuracy and the greatest attention to detail.

I have not always been very organised about keeping my scientific drawings together in a sketchbook, and once worked on loose sheets of paper. However, I soon realised that it was vitally important to keep all my drawings in one place, to make my work easier. If I needed to check a drawing during a later stage of the project, it was possible to pinpoint the exact date and page of the drawing.

Since then, I have filled many sketchbooks with scientific drawings of plants for various projects. Each page documents the investigative process of drawing for botanical accuracy and detail.

Below I will share with you some of the unique challenges and best working practices for a scientific botanical illustrator's sketchbook. Whether you are pursuing a career in botanical illustration or would simply like to elevate your plant drawing skills, this chapter will show you some of the special techniques that I use and the type of sketchbook studies they create.

PREPARATORY WORK

Drawings for scientific illustration are detailed and complex. The term 'working drawings' is perhaps more suited to this type of botanical sketchbook than any other, as it can be a difficult process that demands hard work and precise concentration. I often make more drawings than is strictly necessary, as this gives me and the botanist more choice as to which elements to include in the final piece. Once the complicated work of drawing plants in scientific detail has been done in the sketchbook, the drawings can be selected and composed into a final piece.

The final piece will typically be a pen and ink illustration to be published in a scientific journal, or sometimes a watercolour piece if I am painting scientific studies. Scientific illustrations are often created using digital rendering software; however, illustrators using these digital tools still often use pencil and paper to make the initial drawings from plant specimens.

The most detailed and disciplined of my studies are to be found in my scientific botanical sketchbooks. Drawings made for scientific illustration require a particular approach, with an emphasis on observation, accuracy and attention to detail.

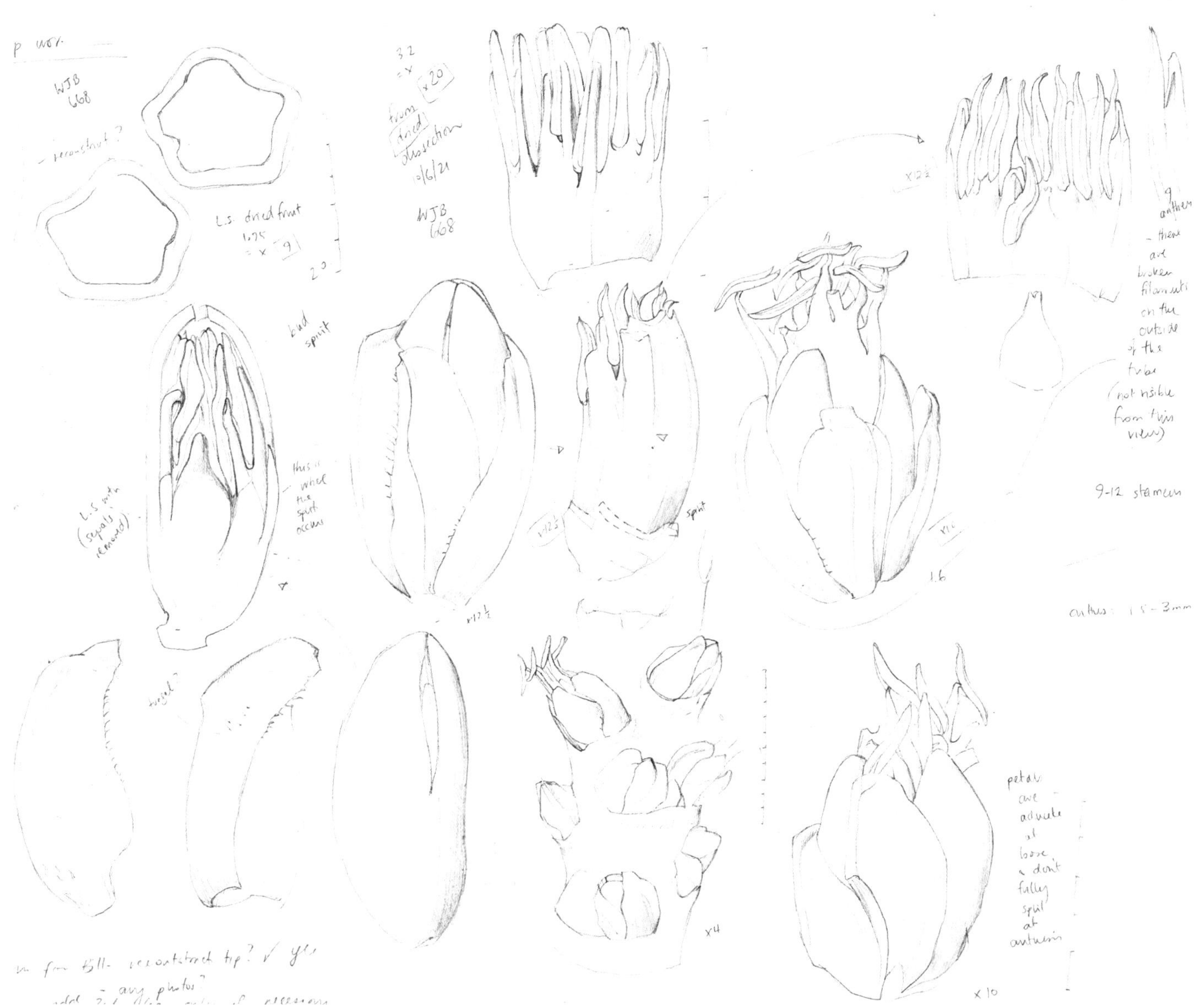

Scientific sketchbook drawings of the flowers of a new species of *Calyptrocalyx* palm from New Guinea. After being given initial directions by the botanists, I followed my own instincts on what to draw. My drawings are often in response to questions that arise along the way. In this case, the question was 'How are the stamens and their filaments arranged?'

What to Include

When you are a professional working for a commissioning botanist, the question of what to draw is easily answered, as you will be given specific instructions on what parts to include. Even with this guidance, I usually draw more than requested. Not only does this help me to understand the plant myself, it also gives the botanist a choice of sketches to take through to the final illustration. I always take lots of notes from my discussions with the commissioning botanist and ask plenty of questions.

If you are not working for a botanist, however, you need to be your own botanist. For whatever reason you decide to take a scientific approach to your sketchbook study, it is useful to do some research on your plant subject. You can either draw first and research later; research first, then draw; or take an approach that is a combination of both (the most usual). It is impossible to learn all there is to know about botany in one go, but you can learn about each plant you investigate and draw as you come to it. In this way, you will slowly build up a knowledge of botany and botanical terms.

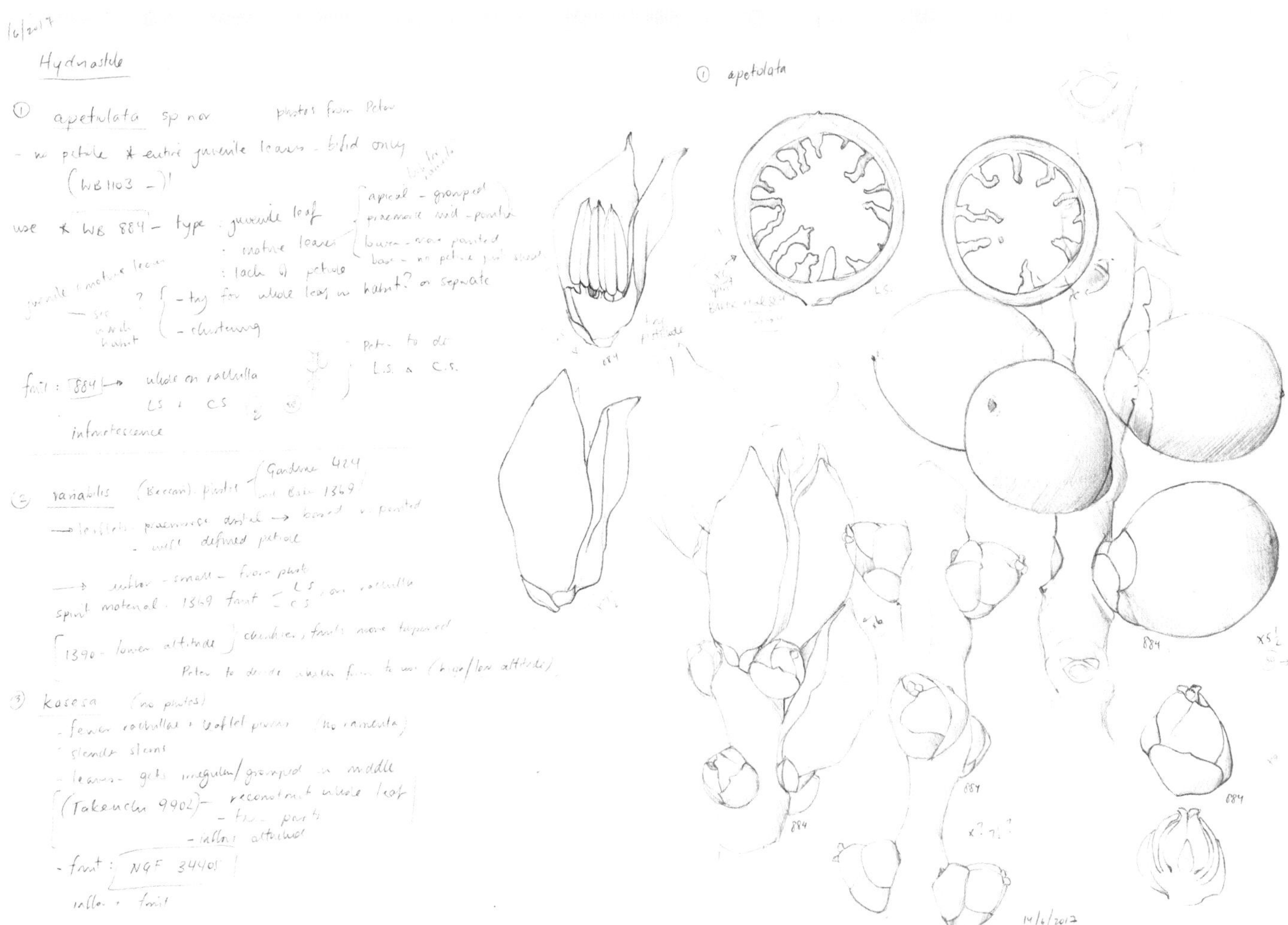

A classic page from my A3 spiral-bound botanical sketchbook: on the left, many notes taken from discussions with the commissioning botanist; on the right, sketches of flowers and fruit of one of the palm species being described in the genus *Hydriastele*. The two were allowed to overlap in order to save space, as I wanted to keep all the drawings of that specimen on one page for easy reference.

Research

As a starting point, research your plant species and where it belongs in the plant classification system. Which plant family does it belong to, and what characteristics should it therefore display? Look at examples of scientific illustrations of the plant and its relatives to see what the convention is for drawing that plant. The daisy family *Asteraceae*, for example, has its own special terminology for its flowers' parts, as do grasses. Learn a little at a time.

Integral to this process is curiosity. As you begin to draw, questions will arise about your plant and your sketchbook studies will attempt to answer them. For example, 'What are these hairs I see on the leaf? Let's take a closer look'; or 'Are these stamens attached to the base of the petals?' As well as asking myself these questions about plant anatomy, I also find myself driven by the aesthetic appeal of part of a plant. As you dissect a flower and lay its parts out, you may find those parts forming beautiful patterns and want to keep dissecting and drawing.

It may take more than one attempt to create an accurate drawing, but with each subsequent attempt, our understanding and drawing will improve. I believe there is no such thing as a wasted drawing. Every drawing you make – even those that do not look great – teaches you something and is worthwhile practice as you hone your skills.

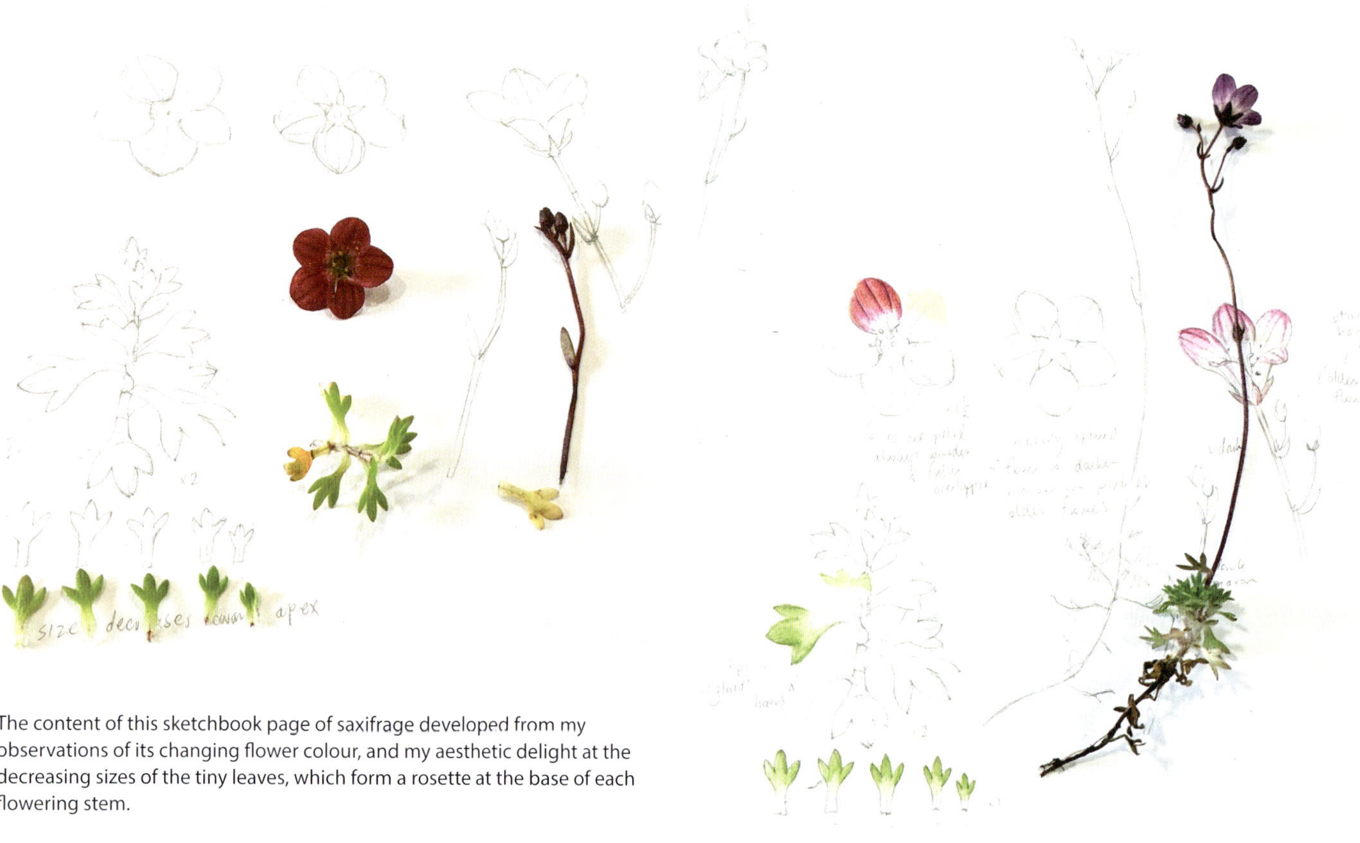

The content of this sketchbook page of saxifrage developed from my observations of its changing flower colour, and my aesthetic delight at the decreasing sizes of the tiny leaves, which form a rosette at the base of each flowering stem.

This single stem containing roots, leaves and flowers was added after the flowers and individual leaves had been drawn, so it had to be squeezed in between two flower drawings.

The Sketching Process

Far from simply being a means to an end, the drawing process helps both botanists and botanical illustrators to understand their subject. When I start drawing in my scientific sketchbook, it can take time for my understanding of a plant to 'click'. When it does, my drawings flow more easily. Shapes must be confidently defined, as must attachments between parts and small but important anatomical details.

On each page of my scientific sketchbook, my thought process is clear as I move from one part to another. Objects are drawn from different angles until I have captured exactly what I wanted. They are erased, edited and corrected numerous times until the shapes are just right. Specific parts are zoomed into and enlarged to find out more. Often, a scientific botanical illustrator will discover aspects of a plant that the botanist may not have been aware of. The discussion between illustrator and commissioning botanist is a two-way and collaborative one. The botanist tells the illustrator what to look for, and the illustrator shows the botanist what they have found.

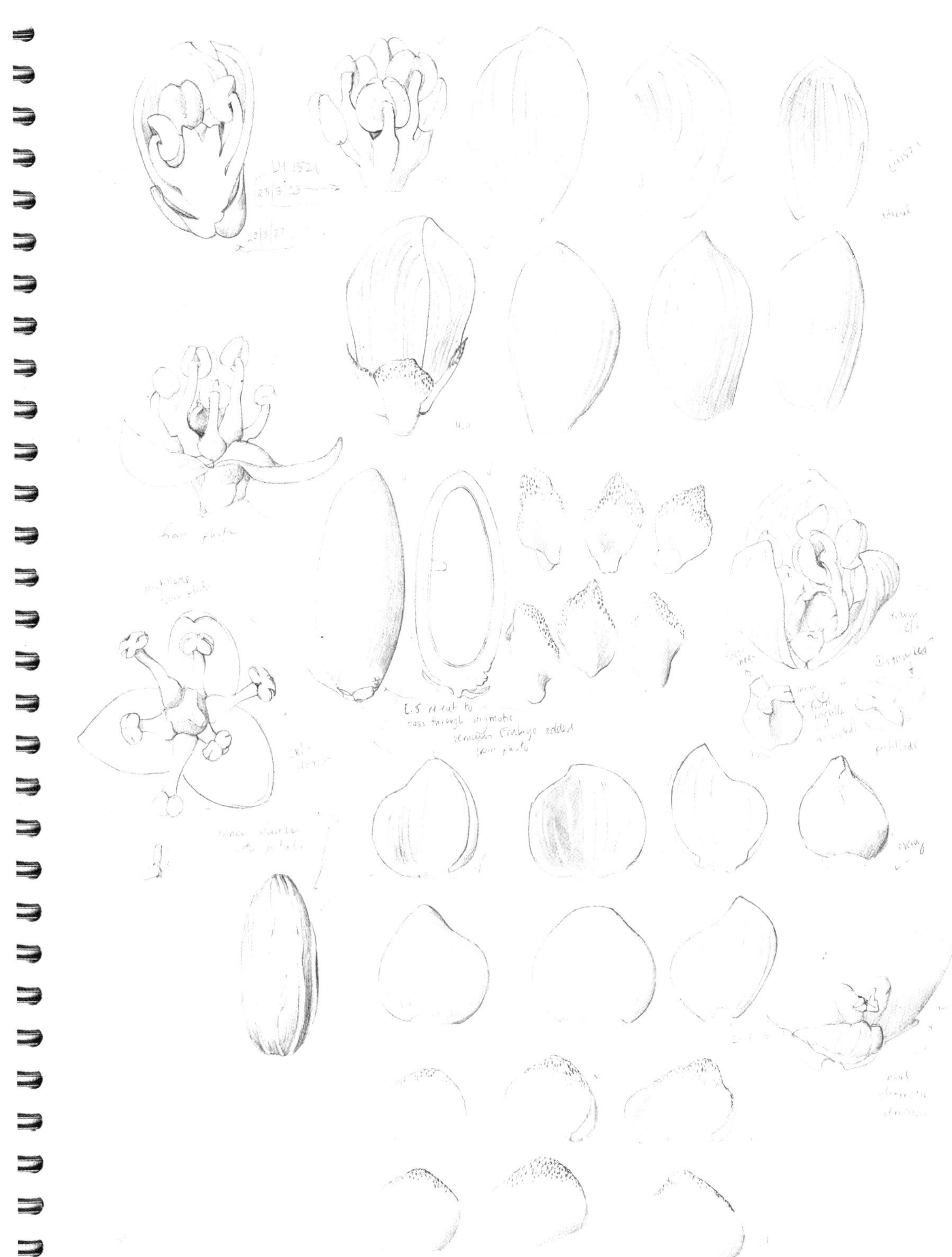

When creating this sketchbook page for a new genus of palm from Vietnam, *Truongsonia*, I carefully drew its flower much enlarged from a specimen. Beginning with the whole flower, the next steps were to carefully remove each part, working from the outside of the flower inwards until only pieces remained. This is called destructive sampling, as the specimen is destroyed as the observations progress. There was very little material in this specimen, so each drawing had to be confidently completed before moving on to the next stage; the dissected flower cannot be put back together again. This study took up a whole page in my A3 Seawhite sketchbook.

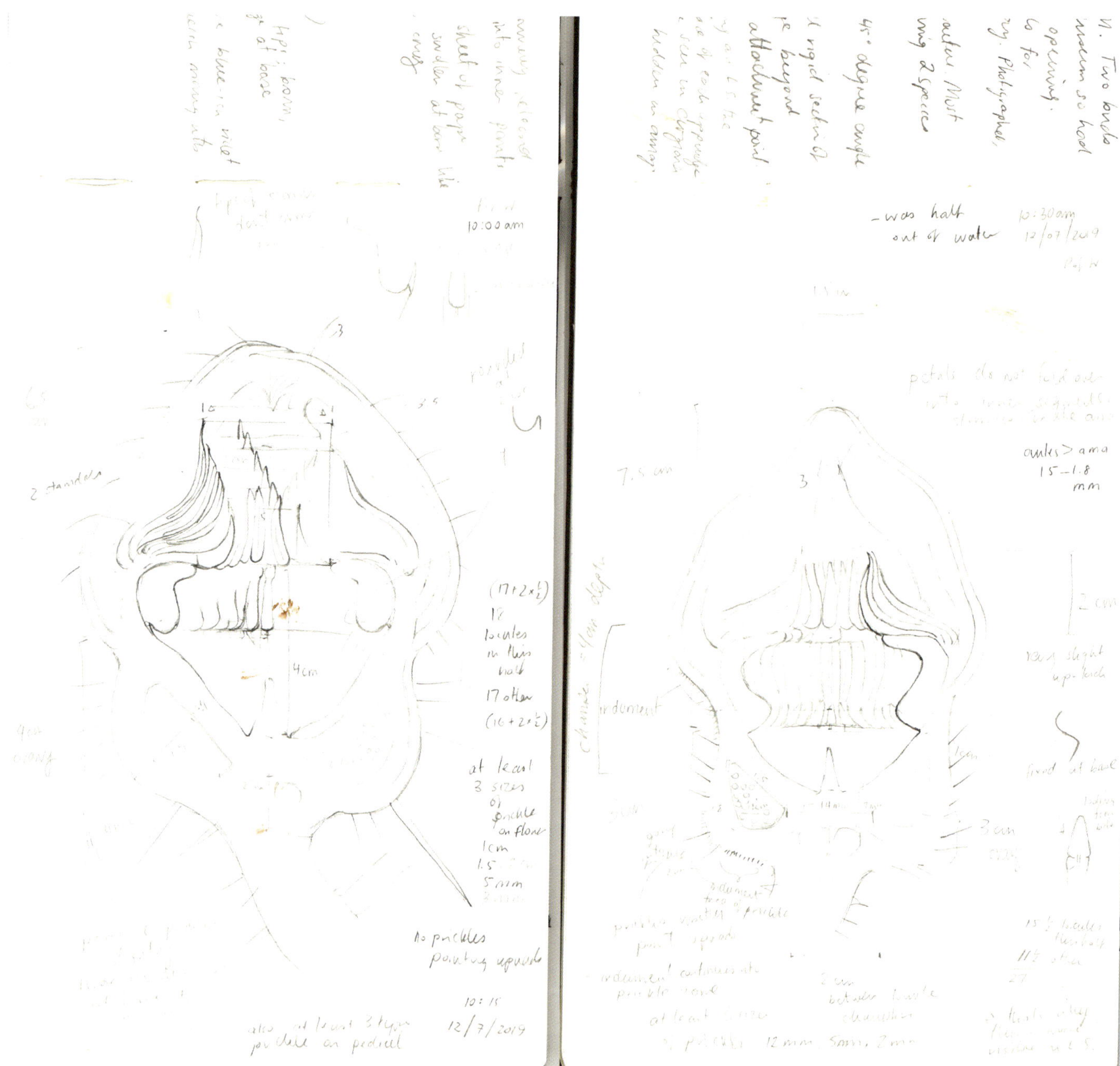

Drawing informs science: botanists and artists both agree that drawing is the best tool for understanding plant structure better. While working on the flowers of the giant water lily genus *Victoria*, I acted as both botanist and illustrator. By drawing dissected flower buds of *Victoria amazonica* (left) and *Victoria cruziana* (right), I discovered a new way of telling the species apart, based on the shape of the carpellary appendages. It was only when emphasising their shape with an outline that I realised how different they were. Both buds were drawn on the same day in my portable, pocket-sized Moleskine A5 sketchbook.

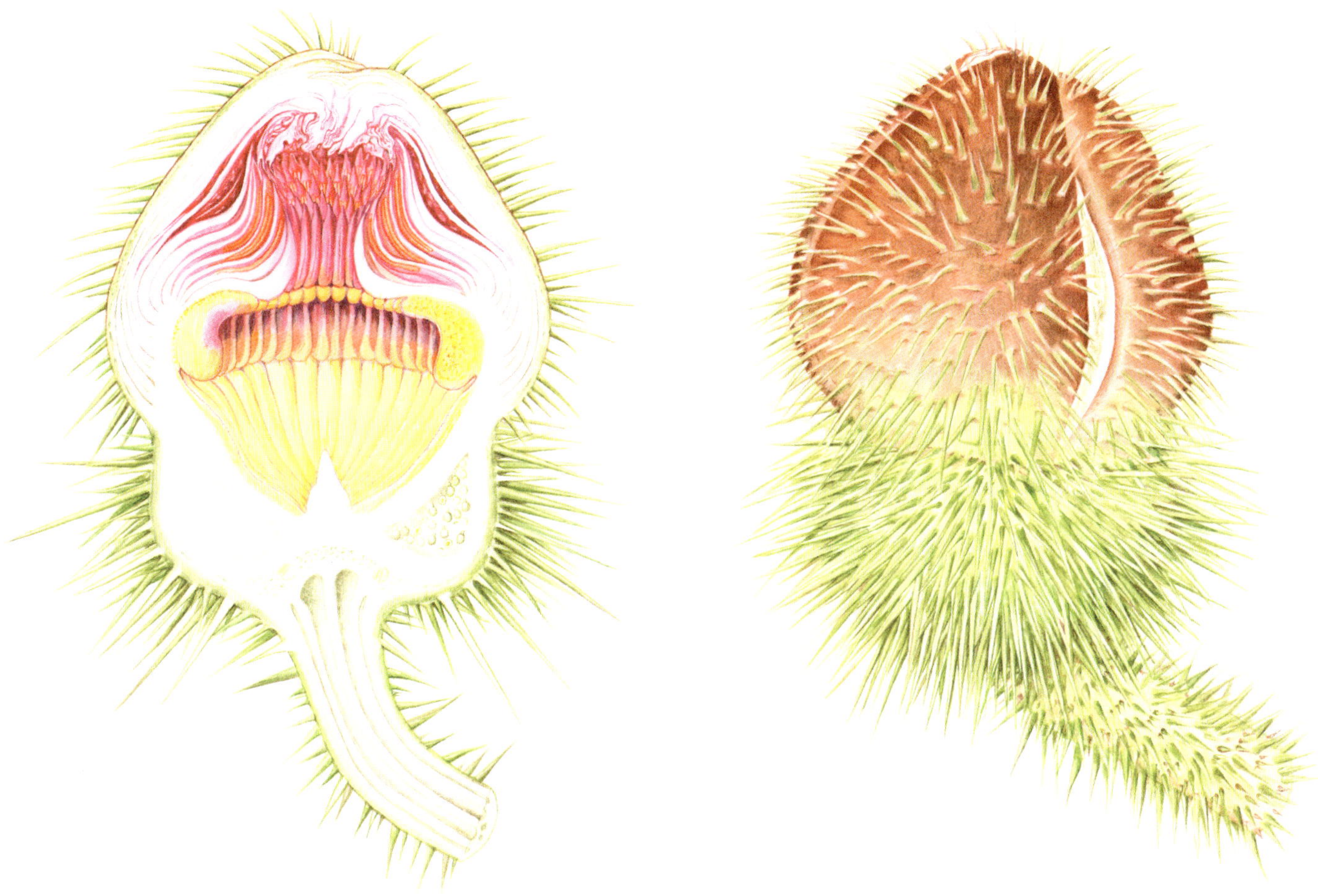

While most scientific illustrations intended for publication are made in pen and ink, they can also be made in watercolour. This watercolour painting of *Victoria amazonica* buds is also intended to be scientifically accurate and informative by showing the flower bud both whole and in longitudinal section. The longitudinal section reveals diagnostic details about the flower's inner parts, their arrangement, and their colours.

WORKING FROM HERBARIUM SPECIMENS

As many scientific botanical illustrators are created from preserved specimens, it is worth exploring how this influences the process of sketching for scientific illustrations. Most of the plant material I draw for botanists comes from herbarium specimens collected from around the world. Specimens containing parts of a plant (or, if small, an entire plant) are cut in the field and given a unique collection number. They are then placed into a herbarium press, where they are dried with sheets of paper and circulated air until they are completely dry and flat. This method of collection is an excellent way of preserving plant parts. There can be a degree of deformation in the specimen, such as shrinkage, for example, but usually a specimen retains enough information to allow a botanist to study it for many decades, even centuries.

For the illustrator, one of the main benefits of drawing herbarium specimens is that they do not grow or change. As they are flat, there is little need to consider perspective or foreshortening of parts. The challenge lies in bringing the specimens 'back to life'. This can be done in a limited way by using drawing skills to visually 'unfold' specimens. Physical unfolding would damage the specimen, so special drawing techniques must be used.

Leaves and larger plant parts may be presented to the illustrator folded many times. They cannot be unfolded physically, as this would damage the precious specimen. Instead, they are 'unfolded' using drawing, by measuring each part in turn and recreating the intact specimen on the sketchbook page.

Enlarging and Reducing

If a specimen is very large, I may draw a very small-scale model of it before deciding which size to draw it for the final piece. This can be done either with a ruler or dividers, or both.

Other parts of herbarium specimens that find their way into the botanical sketchbook are those that need to be shown at an enlarged size. Measurements are taken directly from the specimen with either a ruler or dividers, and transferred to the paper at a larger size. Dividers are especially useful for transferring measurements from herbarium specimens. Proportional dividers allow an instant enlargement or reduction to be made without any calculation, as they can be set to a fixed proportion. The measurement on one end will be reflected as an enlargement or reduction on the opposite end.

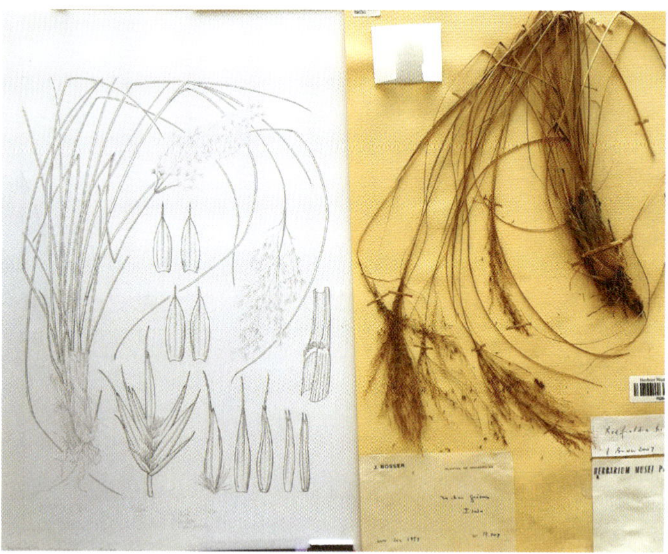

A pen and ink illustration of a grass species sits on the desk easel alongside the herbarium specimen from which it was drawn. The small floral details were captured first in the sketchbook before being placed around the main subject on the final piece.

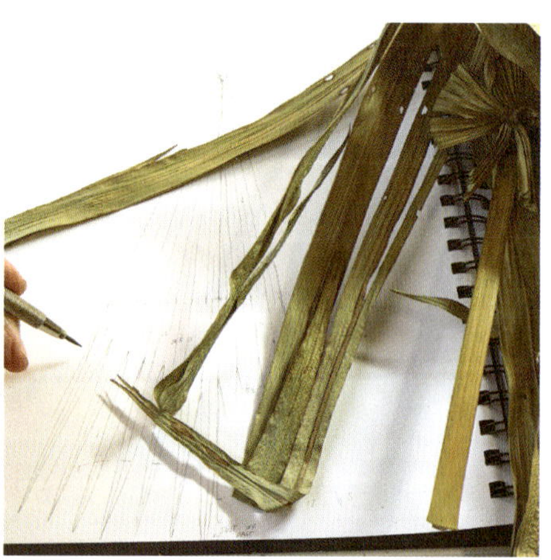

This large fan leaf of *Saribus pendulinus,* illustrated for its description as a new species, was first drawn at a very small, diagrammatic scale so that I could see its full, unfolded shape. I then drew it large enough to see the leaf's veins and how they were arranged. This was done by measuring each folded part of each leaflet with a ruler, then transferring a reduced-size version on to the paper.

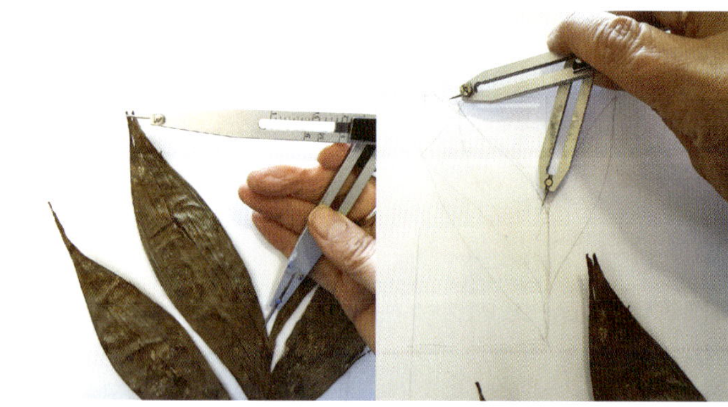

Measuring the length of a palm leaflet using proportional dividers. Proportional dividers can be set to a size (for example, ×2 or ×3) using a sliding screw in their centre. By flipping the dividers from one end to another, it is possible to transfer to the paper an enlarged or reduced measurement to the specified ratio. Here the dividers are set to '2', giving a transferred measurement of one half.

Taking Care of Specimens

When working with preserved specimens it is important
to be very mindful of their precious nature and treat them
with great care so as not to damage them. The number of
leaves, flowers, fruits or seeds on a specimen may be very
limited. For this reason, you must draw very carefully,
especially when making destructive sampling. If you are
dissecting the only flower on a specimen, for example,
you must draw the whole flower carefully and thoroughly
before you destroy it by dissecting it. Destructive sampling
may only be done with permission from the owner of
the specimen.

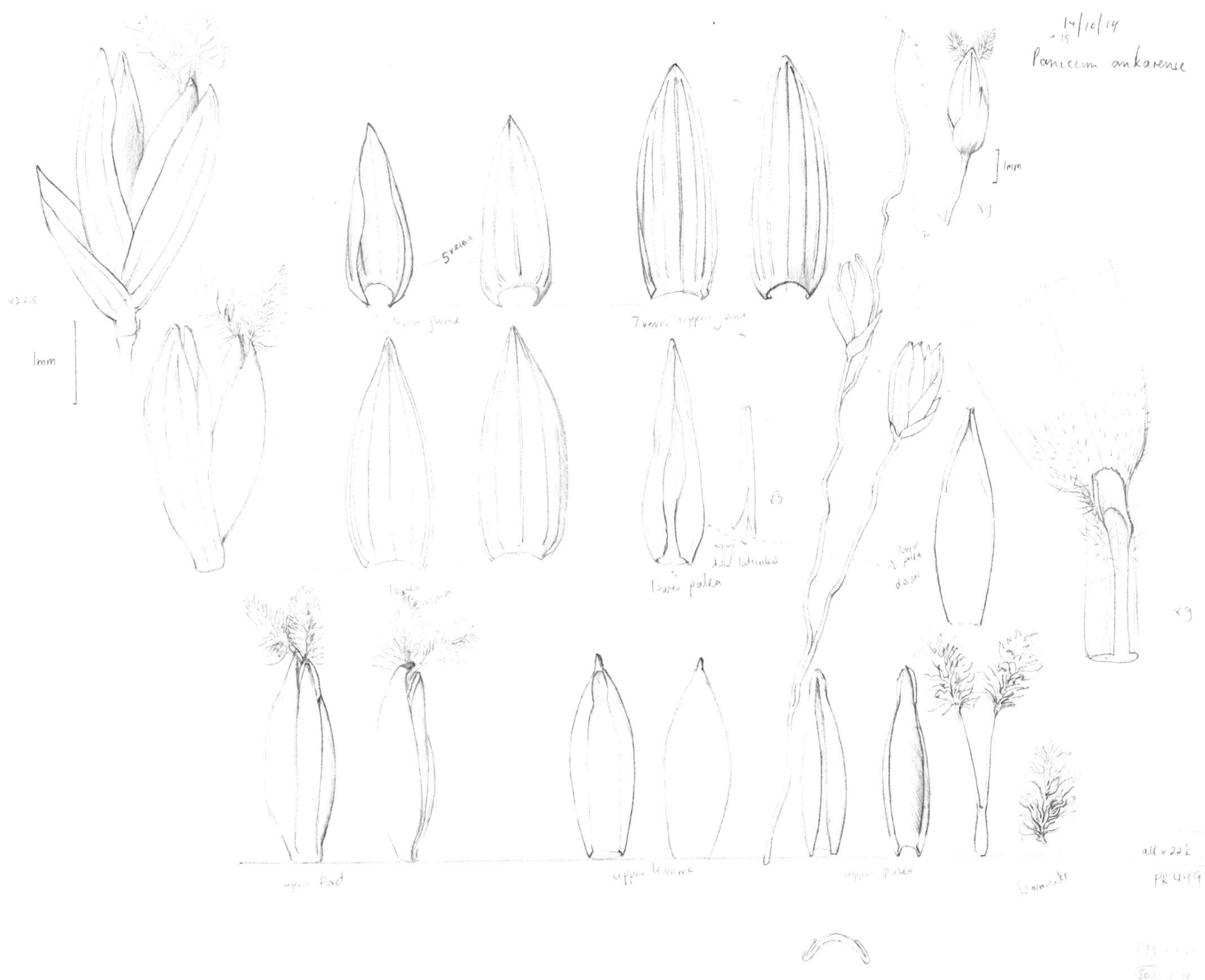

The grass spikelets of *Panicum ankarense* were drawn intact before each layer in turn was removed and draw to one side in a
systematic fashion. The parts have their own terminology: lower and upper glume, lemma, palea. It helped to write down the names
of each part as it was removed and drawn from the front (ventral view) and back (dorsal view). Destructive sampling may only be
done with permission from the owner of the specimen. The specimen's collection number was also included and each part drawn at
the same scale for ease of size comparison.

A good example of this is the drawing of the grass spikelet (the flowering part of a grass). The drawing starts with a whole spikelet in which there are several layers of parts that wrap around each other. Each layer is removed one at a time and drawn as soon as it is removed, before moving on to the next part. As the spikelet cannot be put back together, there is only one chance to capture the sequence of parts.

WORKING FROM FRESH SPECIMENS

Working with fresh plant material is easier in some ways than working with preserved materials, as it has not been distorted by pressing and drying. However, it must be worked on quickly before it begins to dry and shrivel. The artist also has control over what to investigate, especially if there is an abundance of plant material available.

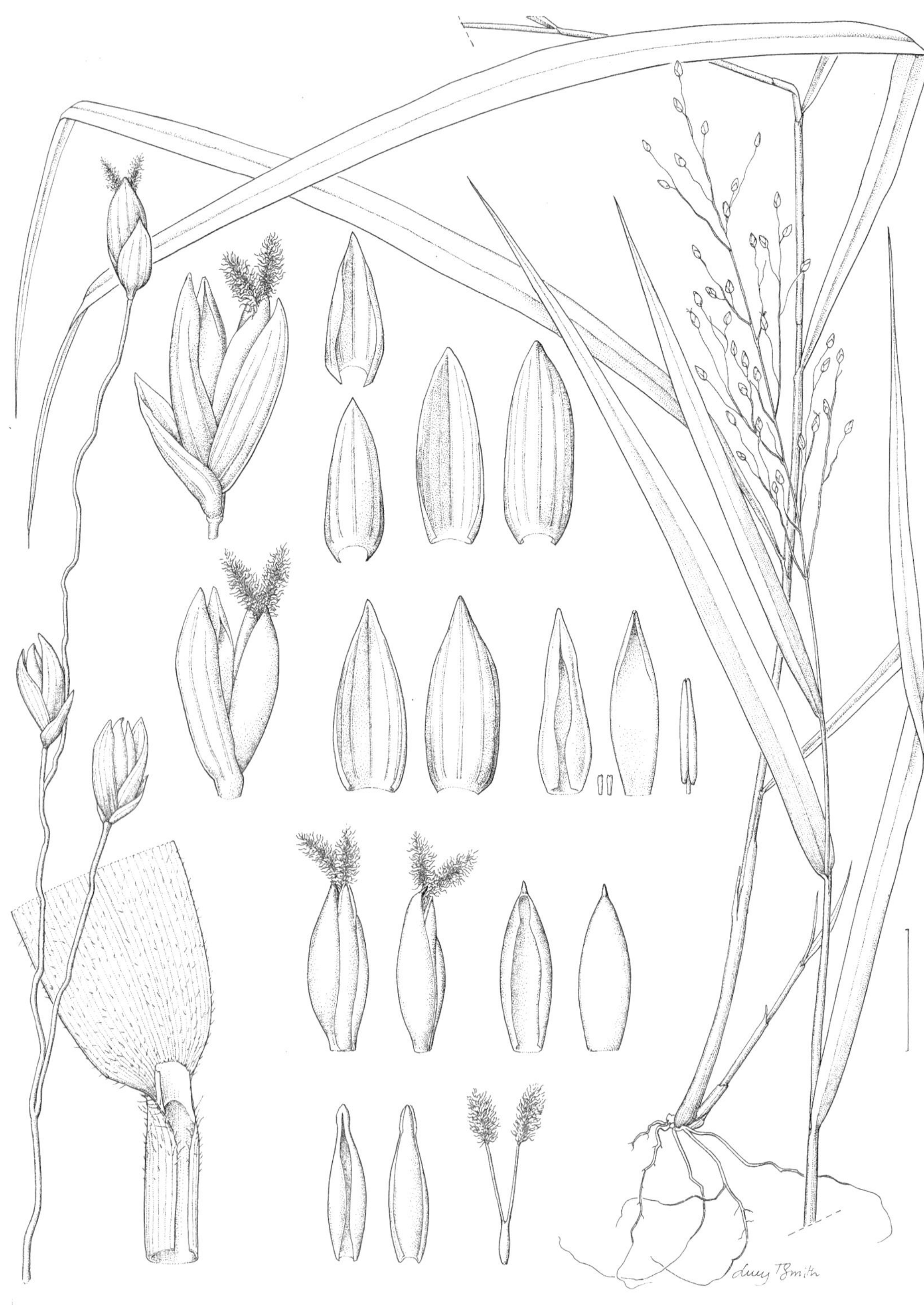

The finished pen and ink illustration of *Panicum ankarense* shows most of the dissected parts from the sketchbook pages, ordered slightly differently and slotted into the spaces created by the drawings of the larger parts of the grass composed within the picture frame.

Once fresh plant material has been cut, it can be kept in a bag or container in a refrigerator. Small parts can be placed in a petri dish lined with wet paper towel and covered when not in use. It is very useful to photograph freshly cut material as soon as possible, in order to capture the state of the flower at that stage. If possible, be prepared to have more than one flower available for cutting, so that you can replace a deteriorating specimen with a fresh one (provided they are at the same stage of growth).

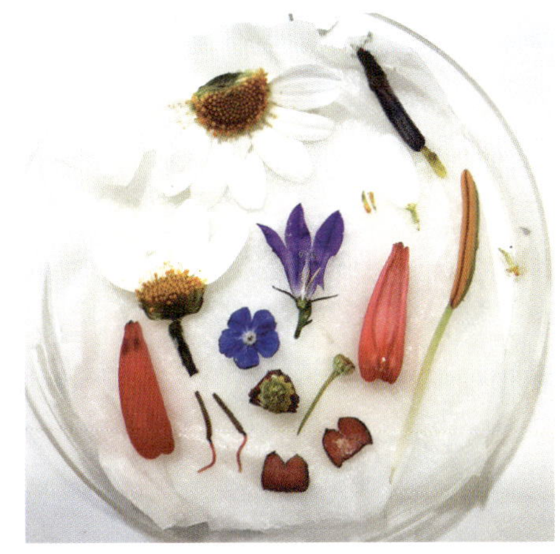

An assortment of recently dissected flowers is kept fresh by placing on a damp piece of paper towel in a petri dish.

WORKING FROM WET SPECIMENS

Material from herbarium specimens can be rehydrated to make it easier to study and dissect. For example, flowers that are loose on the specimen or able to be cut away, can be soaked or boiled in water. As the brittle parts re-absorb the water, they become soft and pliable again and can be pulled open to draw the structures inside. This rehydrated, wet material is best viewed submerged and floating in water so that it maintains its three-dimensional form.

Some plants and plant parts may also be collected and transformed into 'spirit specimens', by placing them immediately into alcohol. If they are kept permanently in the solution, they will retain the three-dimensional physical character that can be lost to pressing. Seeds, fruits, and some very small plants preserve well after being treated in this way. As colour is lost, they are most suitable for monochrome work such as pen and ink.

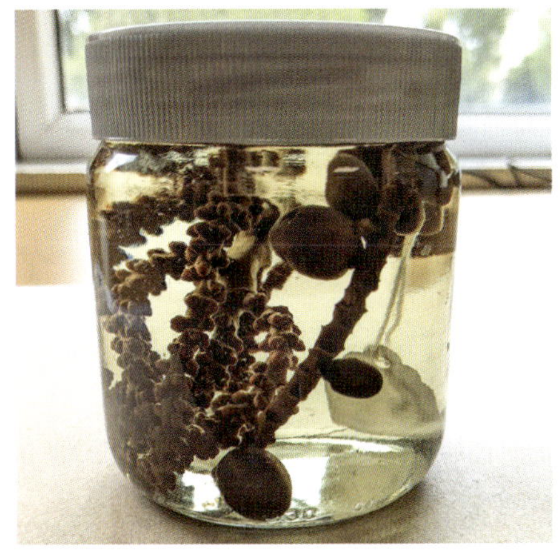

A spirit specimen of palm flowers and fruits. The alcohol solution has removed all colour from the specimen and turned it to a dull brown, but the three-dimensional form is intact. These specimens are much easier to draw than flattened, dried herbarium specimens.

Like rehydrated herbarium material, spirit specimens are best viewed floating in water in a petri dish or similar vessel. This makes drawing a challenge, however, as the specimen is likely to move around. The water should be just deep enough to cover the specimen, but not so deep that it can easily float away. You can pin down a wet specimen by fashioning an underwater 'cradle' from a small amount of Blu Tack, or try weighing it down with a paper clip. Some of the most difficult drawings I have had to make were of tiny flowers drawn and dissected underwater. It can be impossible to get the parts to stay still long enough to observe them properly. Some were so small that even the thinnest of forceps points looked as delicate as hammers under the microscope lens.

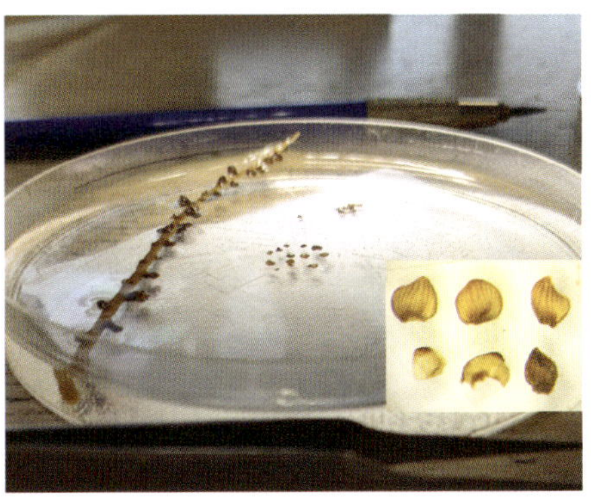

The tiny flowers of *Truongsonia lecongkietii*, a new genus and species of palm, floating in water in a petri dish; inset is the view under the microscope.

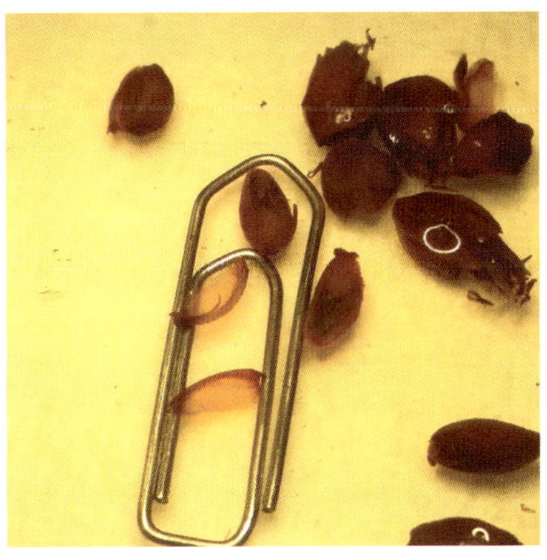

Examining specimens under water presents the unique problem of how to stop them moving and floating away. A paperclip can be used to hold them still long enough to draw. One of the flowers is emerging slightly above the water's surface, creating a distracting light reflection. Too much water will encourage movement and floating, while too little water will create too many of these reflections.

When there is fresh material available, why not make your own preserved specimens? They can prove very useful for checking various details – for example, the number and position of veins on a leaf, or the distribution of hairs on a surface – long after the fresh material has withered and died. Pressed herbarium specimens are also useful for projects where the correct identification of wild plants is required. As well as being useful for future reference, they also become 'voucher specimens', a source of back-up information behind the illustration.

Pressing and drying

Large parts of plants should ideally be pressed and dried using a plant press. Smaller parts can sometimes be pressed easily in the back of a sketchbook, with a piece of paper towel or something similarly absorbent placed around the specimen to avoid it leaching moisture or colour on to the pages. You can even mount your specimen parts on the same page as your sketchbook study. Either glue them to the page or keep them separate in a small packet, which you can make by folding tracing paper, or use ready-made small cellophane or plastic sleeves.

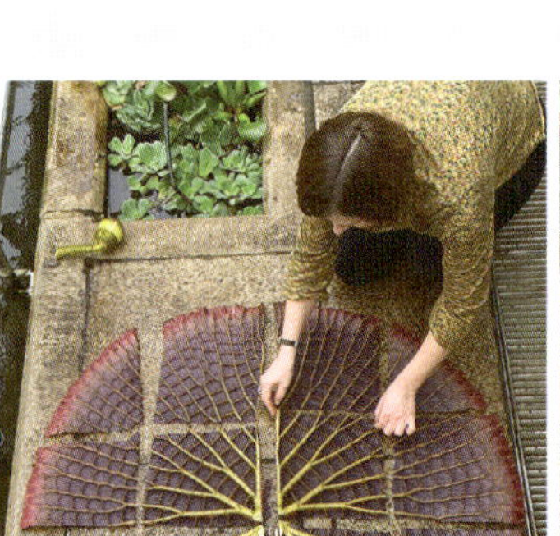
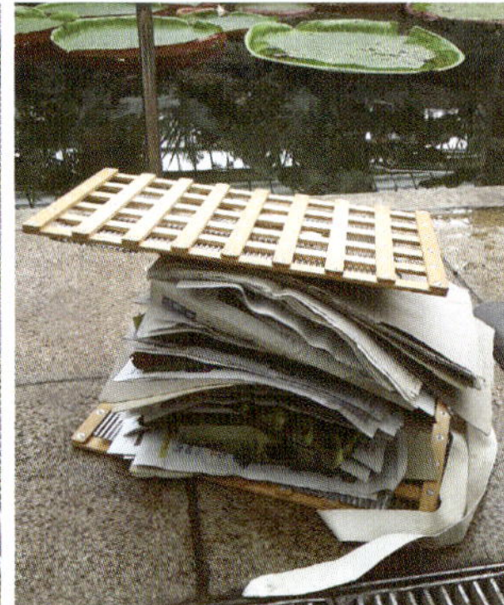
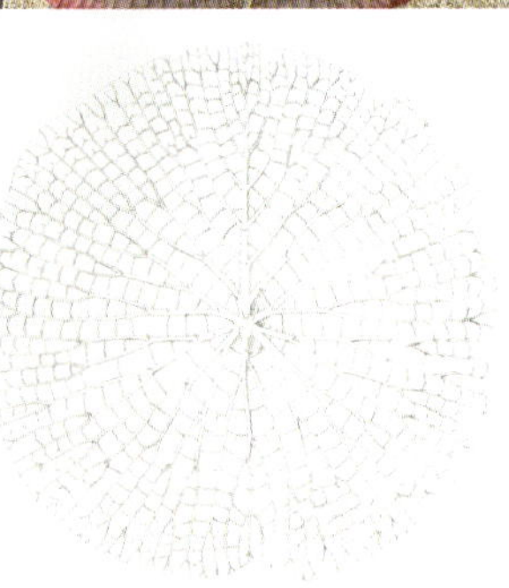
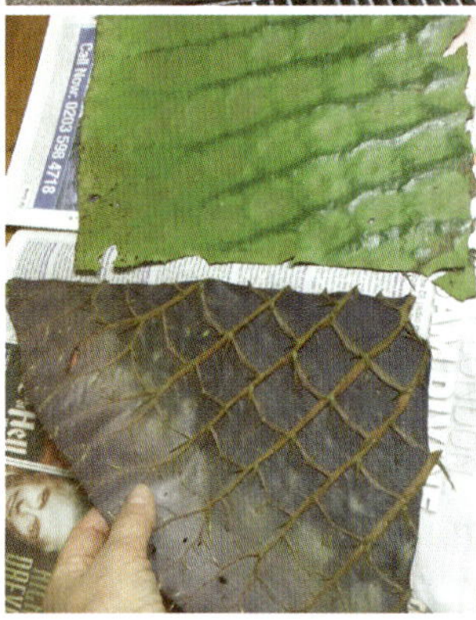

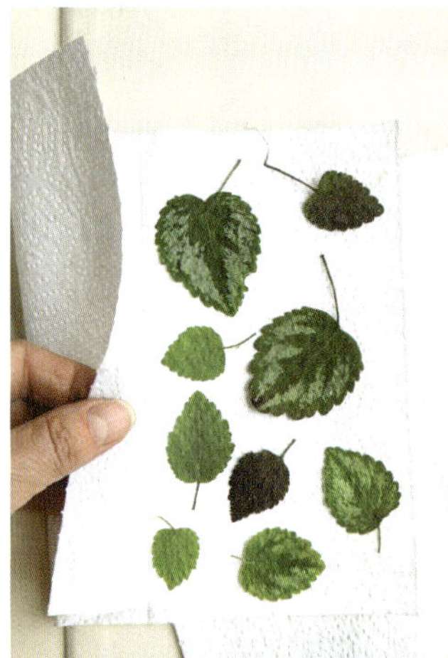

Most botanical artists' own specimens will be a bit smaller than a giant water lily leaf! I pressed a few *Lamium galeobdolon* leaves and a dissected flower, drying them between the back pages of my sketchbook on absorbent paper towel. The book was placed under a pile of heavier books and the paper changed once a day until the leaves were fully dry and pressed.

Making a reference specimen in preparation for drawing a life-sized giant *Victoria amazonica* giant water lily leaf. First it was cut into fourteen pieces that would fit in the plant press. The press was kept in a well-ventilated environment and the pressing papers wrapped around each piece were regularly changed until, days later, the three-dimensional ribs and blade had been reduced to a flat, dry specimen. As the sketches of this leaf were made primarily from photographs, the dried specimen was an important source of information for the venation patterns. It also serves as a voucher specimen for the artwork, which was a life-sized painting of the leaf.

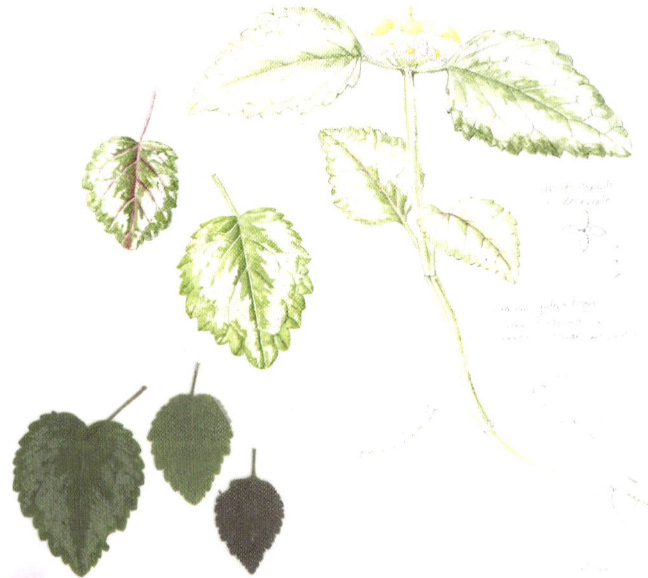

Three of the *Lamium galeobdolon* leaves were placed into a small packet made by folding a piece of tracing paper. This was then taped to the underside of the *Lamium galeobdolon* page, for future reference. The packet protects both the leaves and the drawing on the facing side of the page. Having the leaves with the drawing will allow me to refer to them when drawing more information, such as hairs.

Spirit specimens

If you do not have time to examine in detail freshly collected flowers, or do not have immediate access to a microscope or drawing space, you can make spirit specimens. Simply take a jar and fill it with some form of clear alcohol. Before placing the plant material into the jar, label it with your name, the date and place collected, and the name of the plant if you know it. Jewellers' tags can be written on and attached to the specimen, otherwise write on a piece of paper and add that to the jar.

In all cases it is vital to remember that you must not collect or preserve parts of plants from any areas where they are protected.

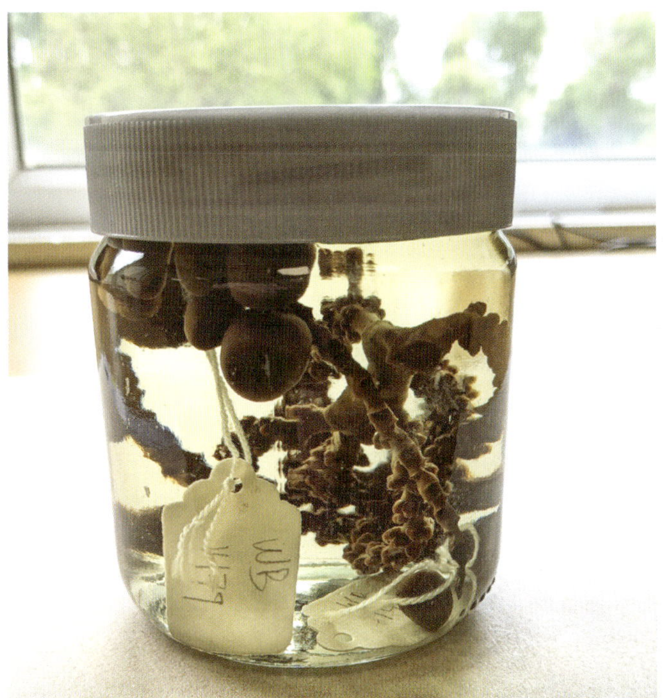

Jewellers' tags are useful for labelling both pressed and spirit specimens. If placing any kind of written tag into alcohol, use pencil to write the collecting name and number, as pen will dissolve in the alcohol and the writing will be removed.

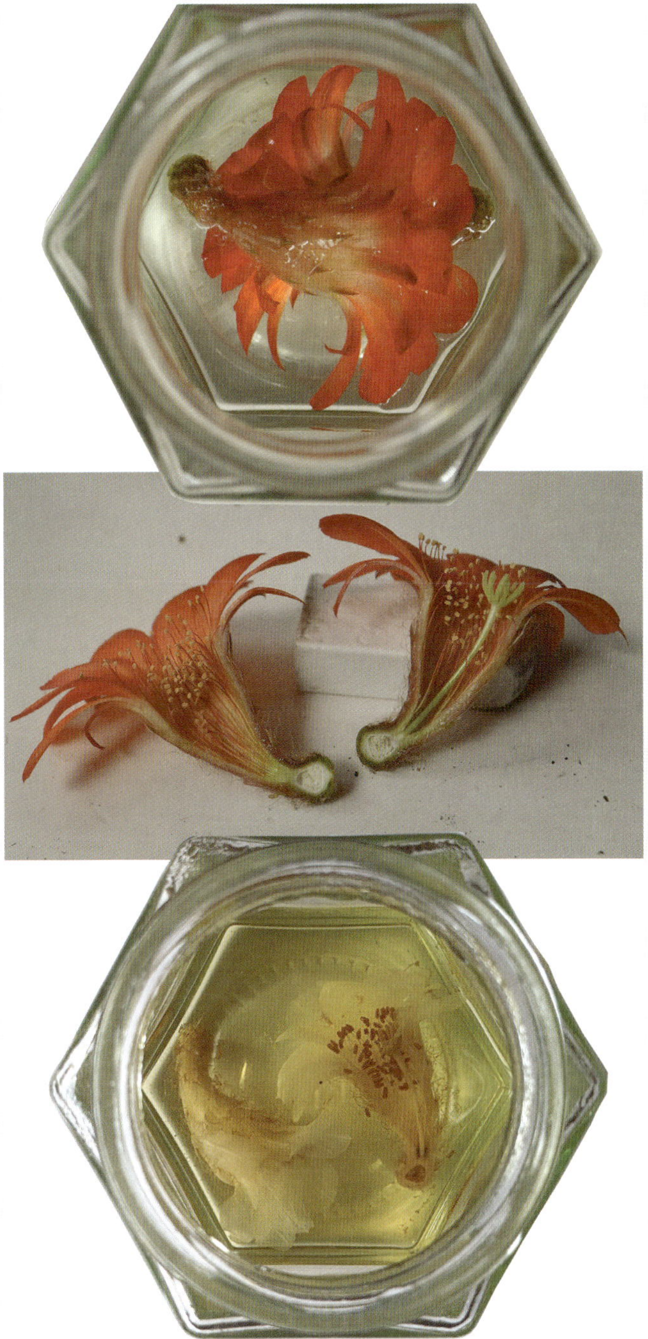

After being drawn, dissected and painted from life, this cactus flower was placed into a jar containing clear alcohol. The alcohol has removed the colour, but preserved the flower's form, allowing it to be studied in the future.

MAGNIFICATION AND MEASUREMENTS

Many parts of the plants that need to be drawn cannot be seen easily with the naked eye, and therefore it is not possible to produce informed or informative drawings of the details without magnifying them. Drawing something at a scale that is larger than life can be done with the aid of magnifying glasses and microscopes. A hand-held magnifying glass is useful for examining specimens, but a desk-mounted magnifier is even better as it allows for hands-free examination while drawing.

Some of the details for scientific botanical illustration are so small that they can only be seen and drawn using a microscope. These details may include, for example, hairs, glands, veins and tiny flower parts. A stereo microscope with a zoom magnification function is best for viewing

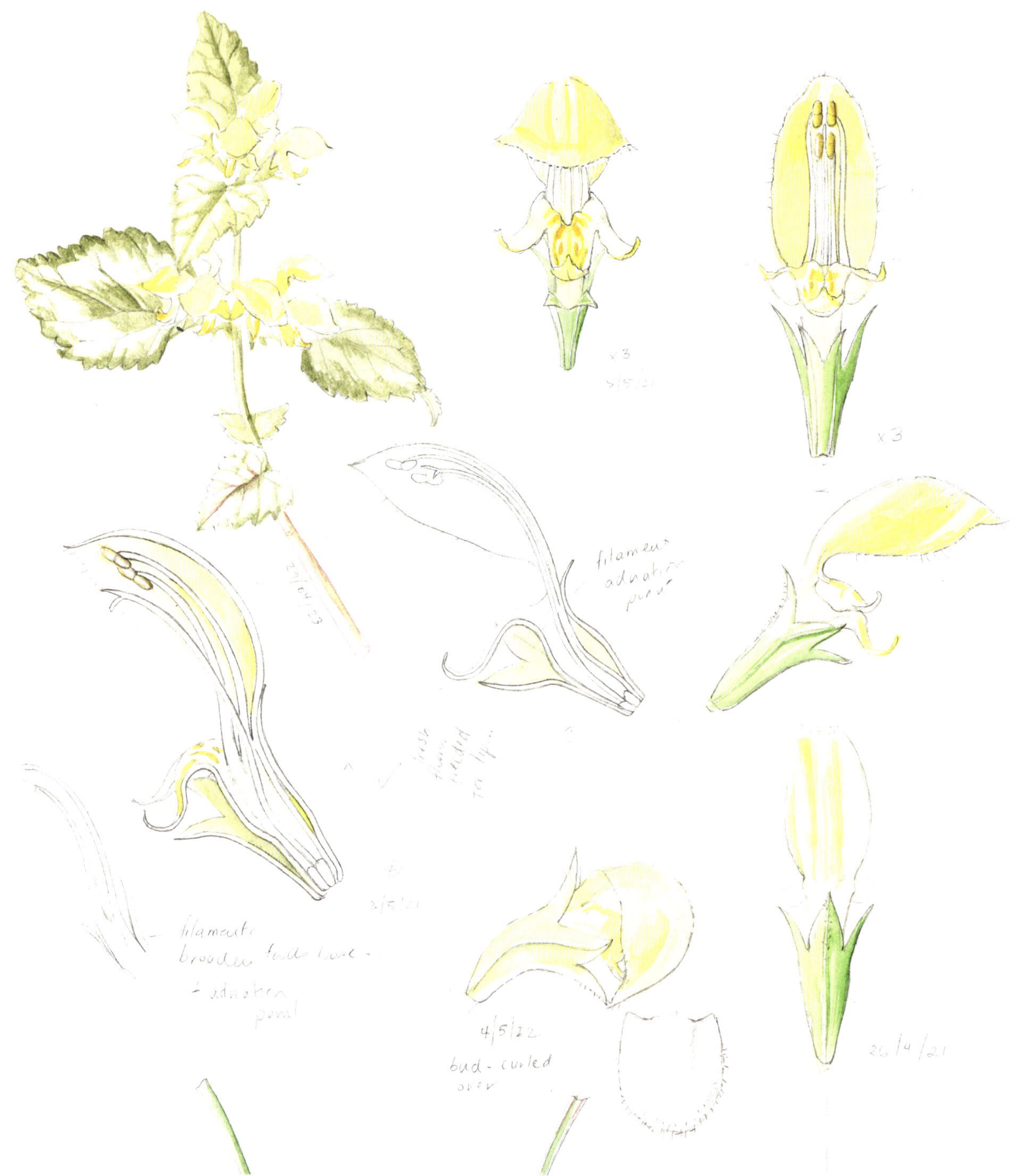

Flowers of *Lamium galeobdolon* were studied with a hand-held magnifying glass and enlarged ×3 using proportional dividers for this sketchbook study.

and drawing botanical specimens. Some include the ability to capture photographs, and some can be plugged into a computer where the subject can be viewed on the screen.

The stereo microscope I use has the advantage of a camera lucida (also known as a 'drawing tube') attached to it. This uses mirrors to project an image of the paper laid beneath it into one of the two microscope eyepieces. When viewing your subject through both eyepieces, you see a double image, simultaneously viewing the specimen and the area beneath the camera lucida (which is held to one side). By placing your drawing paper in the camera lucida zone, a type of 'tracing' can be done over the projected image. This makes the initial drawing process quicker and enables you to record the exact magnification at which the drawing was made. After outlining the basic forms, I like to turn off the camera lucida and continue the drawing by eye.

In the absence of a camera lucida, drawing can be assisted by taking measurements under the microscope lens with a ruler. The specimens may also be laid out on graph paper. For objects that are reasonably flat, a piece of graph paper placed under the subject will allow you to read off measurements and even draw up a corresponding enlarged grid. You can also use proportional dividers to measure your subject while looking at it under the scope, transferring the enlarged measurement across. A clear ruler held against or over a specimen will allow measurements to be observed and read off.

Most digital microscopes allow for image capture and will usually have a built-in scale indicator as well. If you are using an old microscope without image capture, photographs can be taken down the lens. Using a phone camera, position the lens over the eyepiece until the subject comes into view, then focus and shoot.

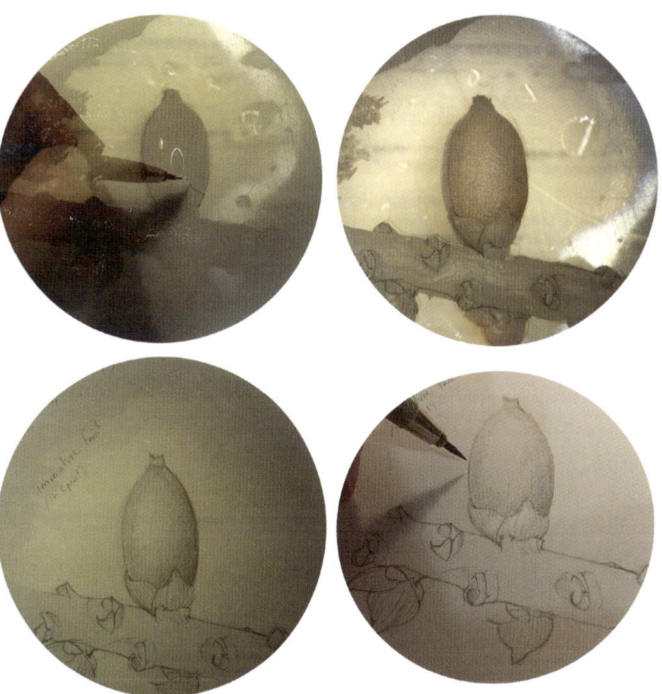

A palm fruit as seen through the camera lucida lens: first, my hand and pencil drawing the ghosted image of the specimen on to the sketchbook page. Once the basic form has been captured, I toggle the camera lucida off and continue working on the sketchbook drawing without it.

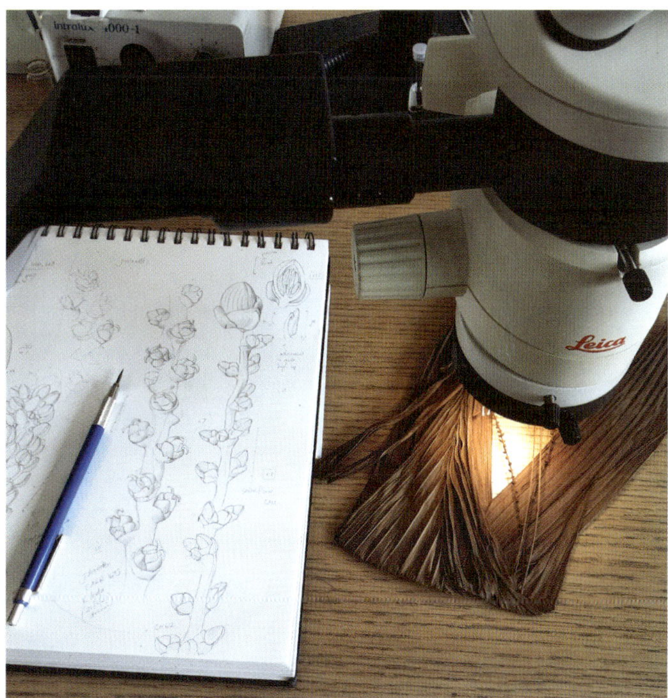

The camera lucida arm extends to the left of the stereo microscope so that I can make my left-handed drawings. The illuminated specimen, a rachilla of dried palm flowers, can be seen under the scope. The enlarged drawing of the rachilla is on the sketchbook beneath the camera lucida.

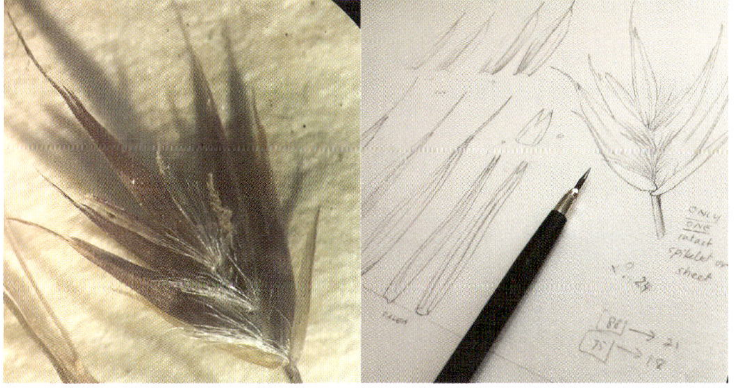

This grass spikelet was the only one that was intact on the herbarium sheet, so it had to be drawn with care. The drawing on the right shows the intact spikelet, followed by dissected parts of florets from other parts of the specimen. The magnification factor of '×24' has been written under the drawing.

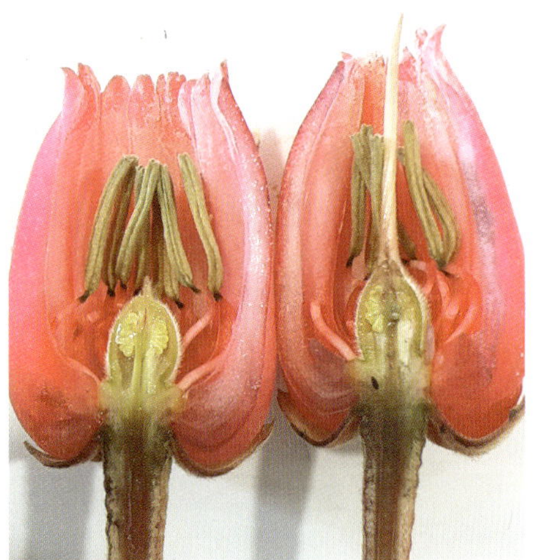 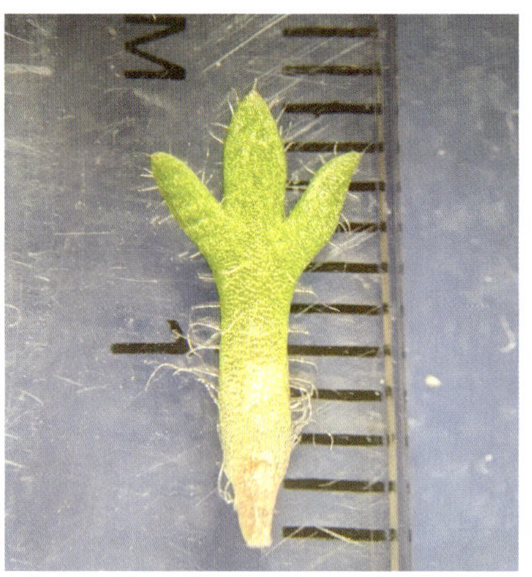 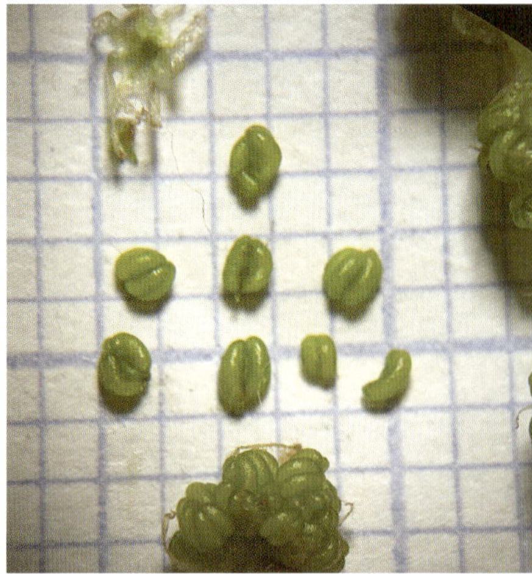

The ability of phone cameras to zoom in at high magnification can help you to see very small details inside flowers and other plant parts. This photograph of a dissected *Crinodendron hookerianum* flower was taken with a phone camera. The ovules within the ovary, which measure just 0.8mm, can be clearly seen.

This small saxifrage leaf was placed on a clear plastic ruler and photographed through the microscope lens with a phone camera to record its size. The photo makes perfect drawing reference, as the leaf structure and its hairs are clearly visible.

Dissected flowers from freshly collected male catkins of *Quercus robur*, viewed under the microscope lens and photographed by pointing a phone camera down one of the eyepieces. Laying a whole flower and another with dissected parts on 1mm graph paper allowed me to read off the measurements and draw the elements at a larger scale.

Tips for drawing scientific sketchbook studies:

- Be methodical if you can, so that you and any botanist reviewing the drawings can understand how the dissection progressed.
- Use clear, sharp, single pencil lines in your drawing, with minimal shading.
- When dissecting a specimen into multiple parts, lay them out in a logical progression, lined up on a horizontal line ruled across your page.
- When drawing vertical parts, rule a vertical perpendicular line to keep them upright rather than leaning to one side or the other.
- Date your drawings: if you need to check them later, they will be easier to find.
- Record all specimen numbers. This information must be included on the finished illustration and will also allow you to find the specimen later if any part of the drawing needs revision.
- Always make a note of scale, showing a multiplication factor ('×2'), a line showing the height and/or width of the object, or a scale bar – or all three if you wish to be very thorough.
- Use as few magnification factors as you can, especially between parts that are being compared.
- If possible, keep as many of your drawings of the same subject on one page, as this will make it easier to review them for inclusion in the final piece.

While photographs of microscopic material are very useful for reference, it is still important to physically examine the material first. Carefully prodding and poking the specimen will clarify different layers of tissue and help you to distinguish clear boundaries between forms and attachments.

Measurements are taken either with dividers or a ruler (or both). Proportional dividers are especially useful, as they allow you to scale up or down instantly. Each part of the plant is measured one section at a time, then that line is transferred to the sketchbook page until the whole specimen has been drawn.

Always make a note of the scale at which you draw something. For example, if I am drawing life-size I will either write '×1' or nothing at all. If drawing at double the size, my notation will be '×2'. If drawing at half life-size my notation will be '×½' (or ×0.5). If you prefer, you can write the measurements of the object instead; sometimes I do both.

PLANNING THE COMPOSITION

When drawing a complex scientific botanical illustration, there are many elements to fit on to a single page. To work through compositional ideas, it is useful to make thumbnail diagrams with different options. Sketch out several smaller boxes in roughly the same proportions as the finished piece. Imagine how the various elements for

Mixed specimens – details from two different species of *Ptychosperma* palm, *Ptychosperma macrocarpum* and *Ptychosperma mooreanum* – included on one sketchbook page. Specimen numbers and names have been recorded, and a line drawn between the two to ensure there is no confusion between them.

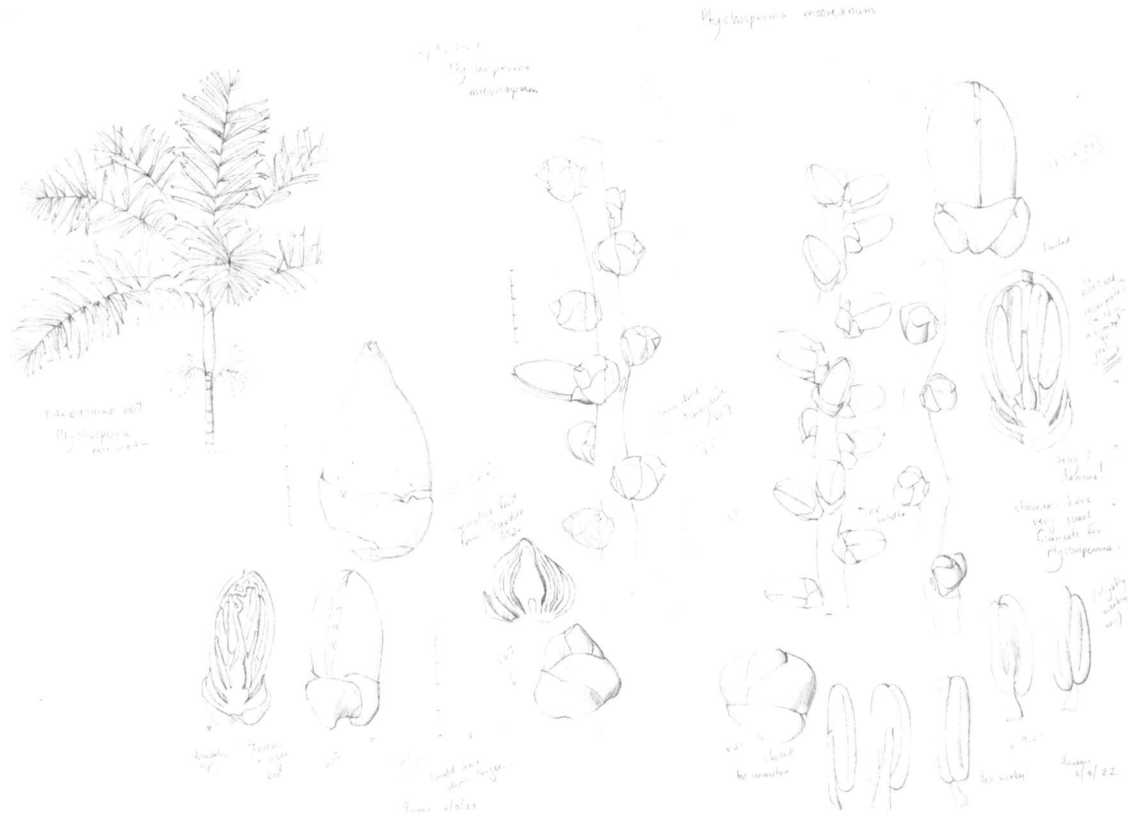

your illustration will fit into the box by sketching in their shapes, as roughly or as detailed as you like.

Some of my final compositions use a mixture of this planned method and a more organic, less planned approach. I often draw the larger elements of my illustration in pencil directly on to the final page, making them as large as possible while leaving room for the smaller elements such as flowers, fruits, seeds and dissections to come. I call these negative spaces left around the central objects 'windows'. Once you have drawn all the elements that you will need in the sketchbook, you can think about where to fit them around the spaces that are left (including overlaps if you wish). This can be done physically, by photocopying the drawings, cutting them out and moving them around the page. Alternatively, you can do it by scanning the drawings and trying out different compositions in a digital illustration or photograph editing program.

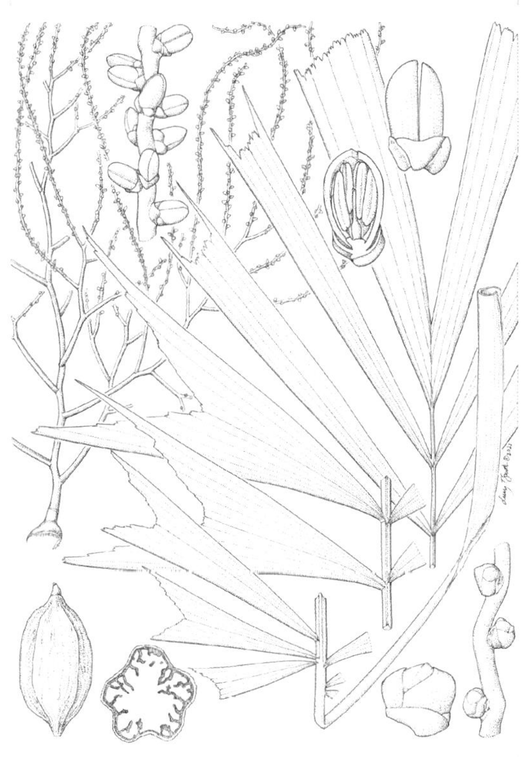

This illustration of *Ptychosperma mooreanum*, published in *Palms of New Guinea,* is typical of the careful, tidy composition of a finished scientific illustration in pen and ink. The clarity and calm nature of the composition was able to be planned thanks to all the hard work that went into the messier, preparatory work in the scientific botanical sketchbook.

TRANSFERRING DRAWINGS FROM THE SKETCHBOOK

The drawings in my scientific botanical sketchbook are copied on to the final piece of paper where they will be inked. I use a lightbox to do this, tracing each element carefully on to its assigned place in the final composition. As there is potential for errors to creep into the drawing, I check each traced line drawing very carefully against the original, refining the traced parts to match the sketchbook.

In the sketchbook drawings, enough shaded tone is included to inform me about how to model form in pen and ink. In pen and ink, my method for doing this is stippling (using tiny dots). I sketch in some of this tonal work but refer to the sketchbook page for most of the information while I am inking. My goal in the sketchbook drawings is to do all the work involved in observing and recording the plant details, so that the inking process is only a matter of interpreting those drawings into another media. The hard work and planning should already have been done by the pencil drawings.

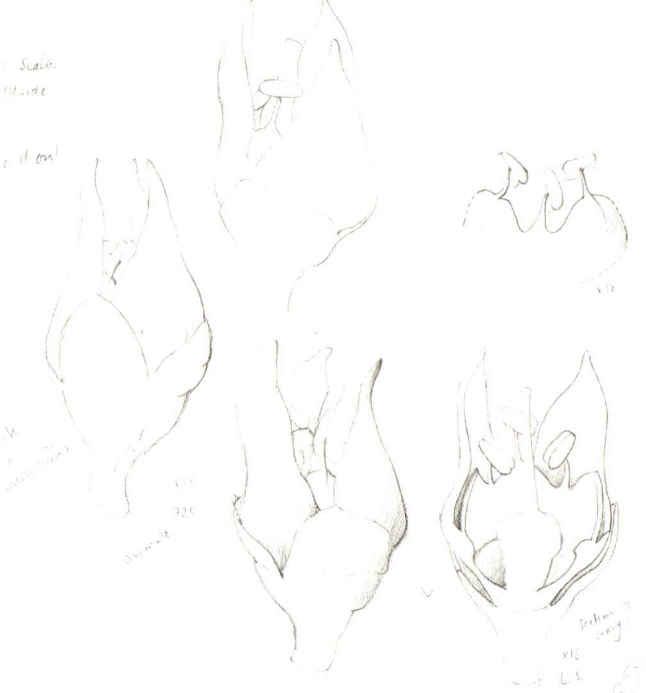

When inking in the finished botanical illustration, I constantly refer to the detailed drawings in my sketchbook. I check that details have been traced correctly and follow the tonal shading guidelines that have been determined in pencil, interpreting them in pen and ink techniques such as stippling.

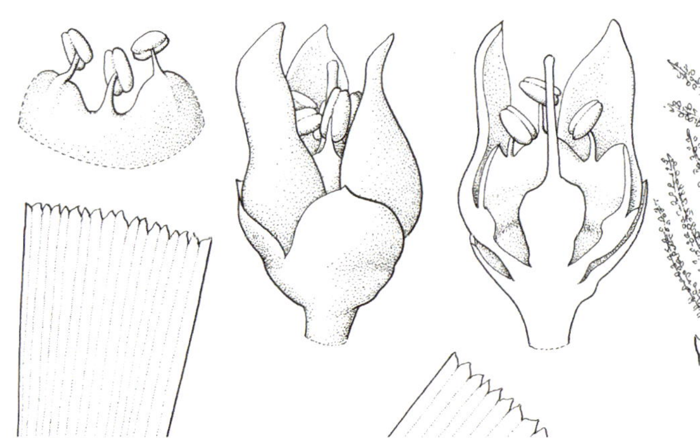

The *Licuala* palm flowers rendered in pen and ink, using different sizes of Rotring technical pen. Stippled dots have been added to show tonal values.

Drawing of a *Licuala* palm flower in the sketchbook, showing clear lines and tonal shading in pencil. The small flowers, which measured only 2mm in height, were drawn at a magnification of ×18. I made a note wondering whether to cut through the ovary on this flower, but on further investigation discovered that I could not find any detail there.

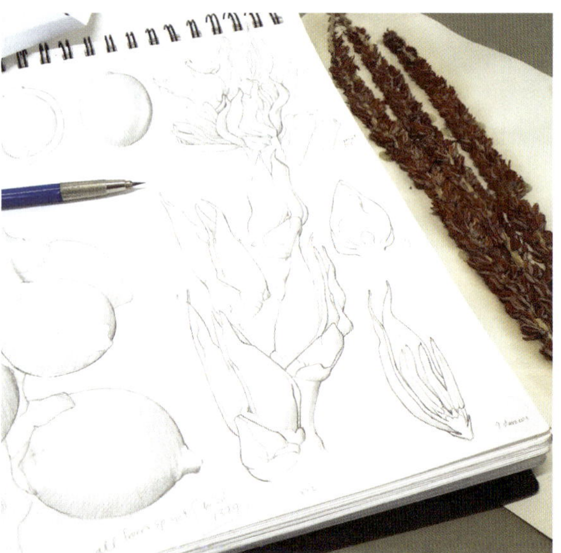

Drawings of a palm specimen include details of the flowers. The flowers are borne on a branch called a rachilla, and in this species they are found in triads (groups of three) containing two staminate (male) and one pistillate (female) flower. The brown, dried specimen is visible to the right of the sketchbook. As well as referring to the sketchbook drawings while inking the final piece, I sometimes have the specimen to look at as well.

Even if you are not planning to make scientific botanical illustrations, there is plenty to learn from the rigour and discipline demanded by the practice. Do not be intimidated by the word 'scientific'. The process of drawing for scientific investigation requires some knowledge of botany, all of which can be learned a little at a time as you work your way through projects. The most important attributes you can possess are a thirst for understanding plants and your own curiosity. However, I should add a word of warning here: once you start looking in this deep way into your plant material, you may not be able to stop.

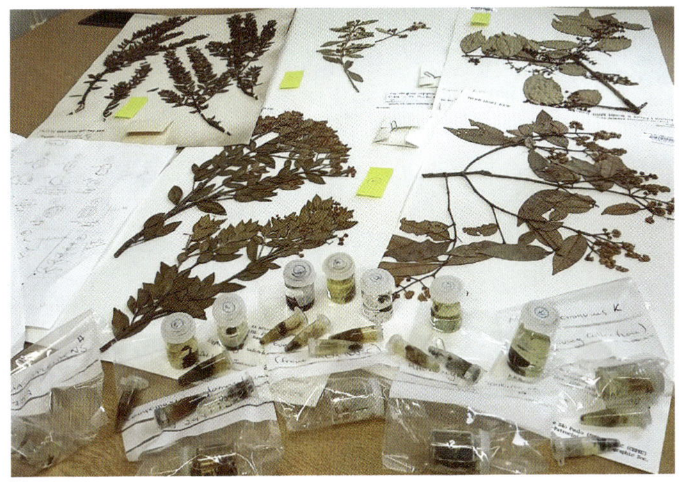

The scientific botanical sketchbook is a crucial intermediary tool. It helps turn this…

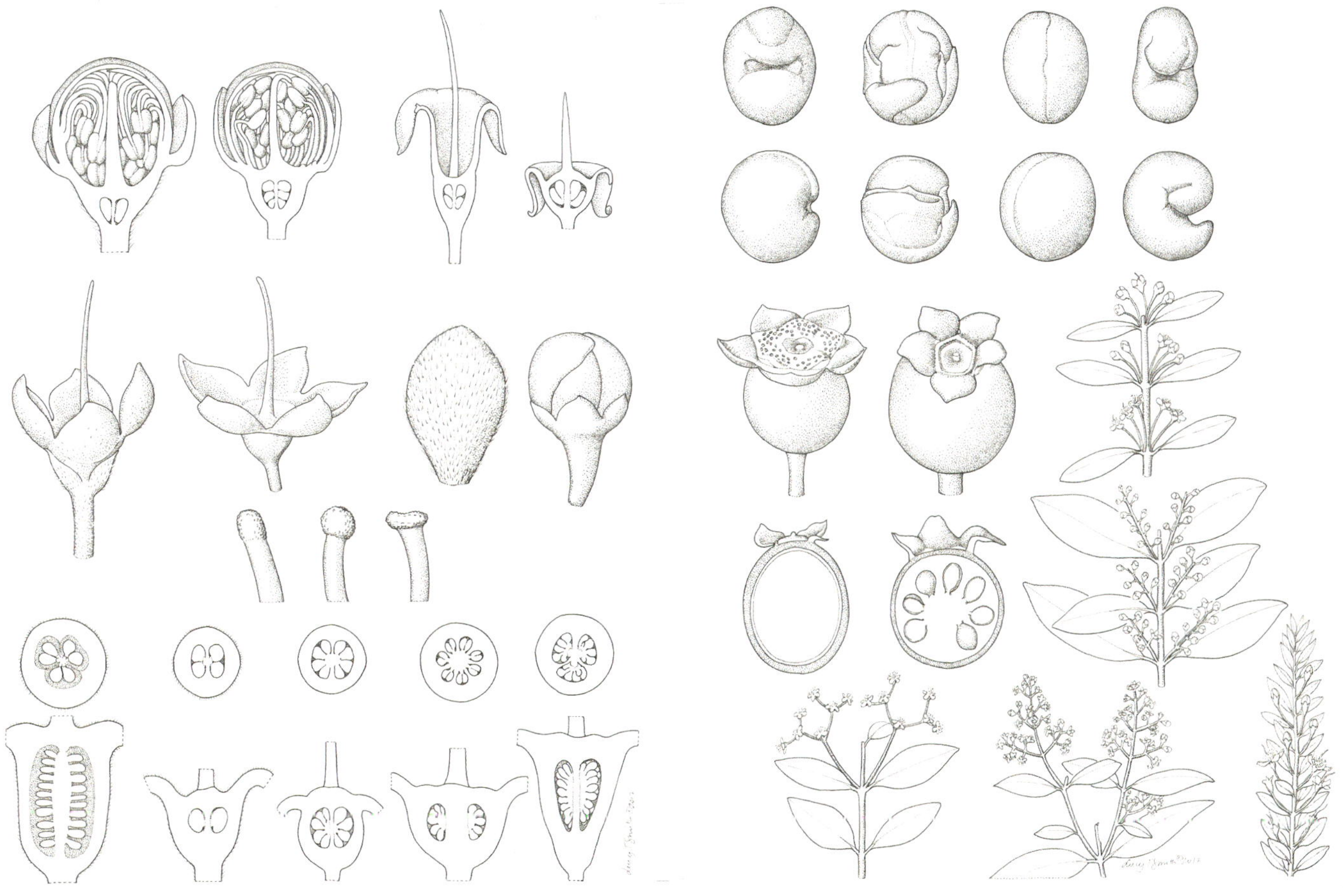

… into these!

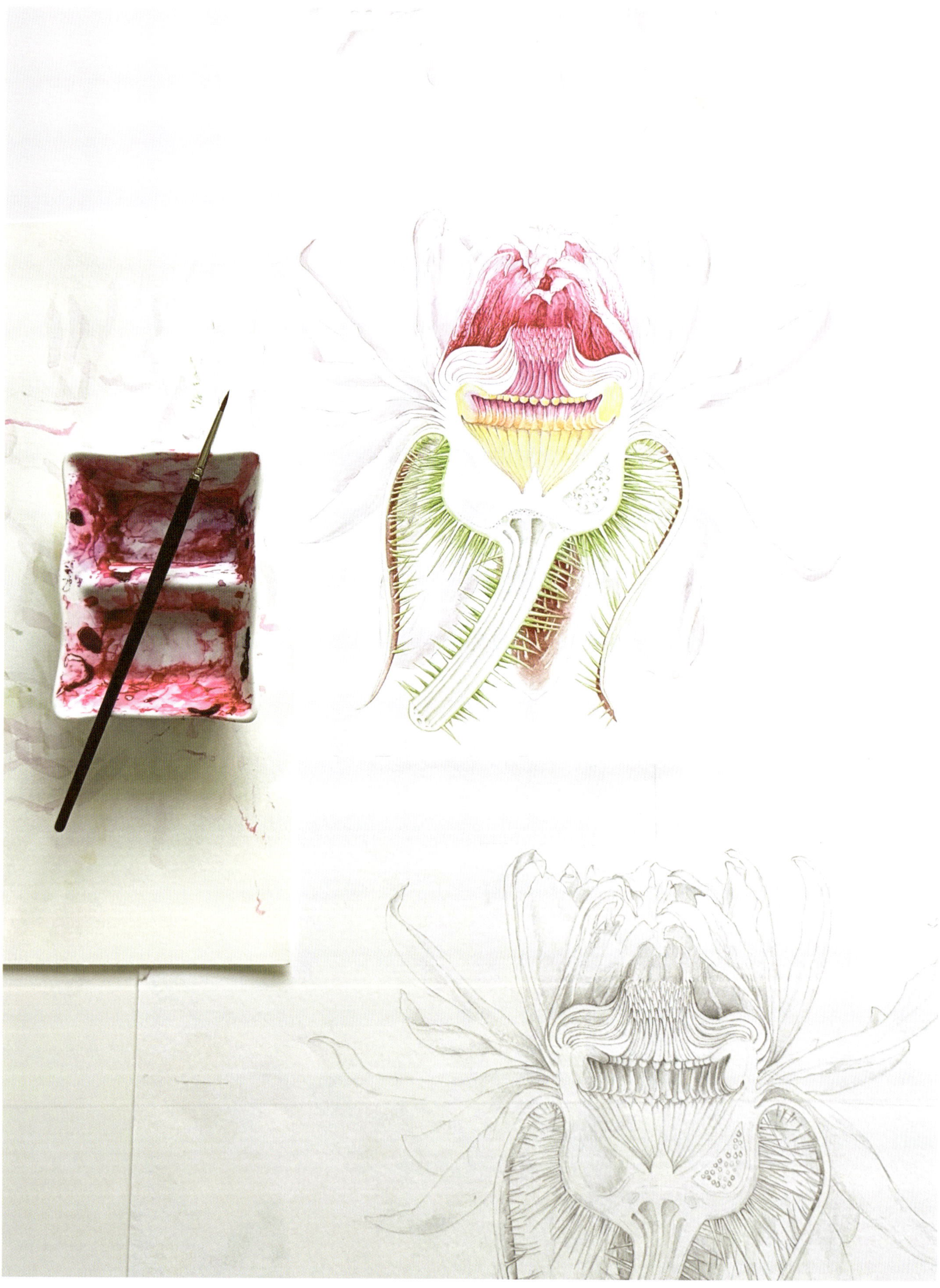

CHAPTER 9

HOW SKETCHBOOK STUDIES INFORM THE FINISHED WORK

When you look at a finished and perfect piece of botanical art or illustration, you are not just looking at a pretty picture. It will be the result of a huge amount of invisible preparatory work, which is usually hidden from view. The pages of my botanical sketchbooks demonstrate the extent of this preparatory work, which involves thinking, observing, understanding, sketching, drawing, painting and making notes. It is a process that is analytical and creative, being both an exploration and a means to an end.

You may be wondering what happens with the working drawings in my botanical sketchbooks. How do they end up in finished pieces? There are many examples of my sketchbook studies included here. This final chapter will show some finished artwork in a variety of styles and techniques. They are all pieces that began life as drawings and colour studies in the botanical sketchbook. In the past, most people did not get to see the background work, but increasingly it is being included in the displays in art galleries exhibiting botanical art.

Some sketchbook studies are begun with a finished piece already in mind. Others are made without a clear idea of where they might lead or end up. Other studies prove to be useful in creating more than one piece of finished work. There are a number of ways in which botanical sketchbook studies can contribute to finished compositions.

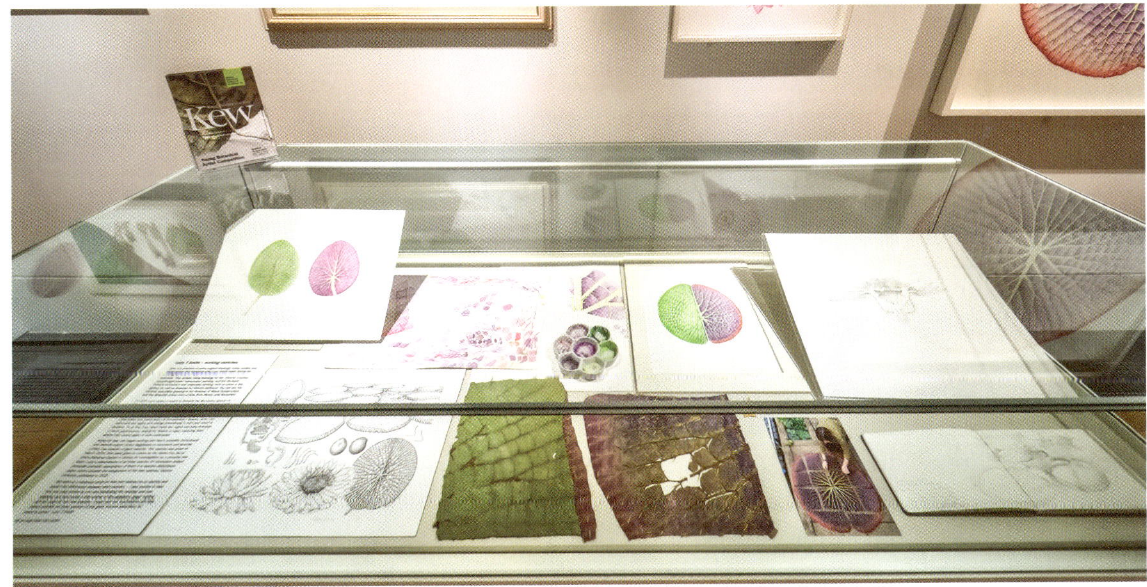

Working drawings and studies from my project illustrating the giant *Victoria* water lilies, displayed in a cabinet at the Shirley Sherwood Gallery of Botanical Art, Kew Gardens in the *Wonderful World of Water Plants* exhibition (2023). This selection of drawings, colour studies and specimens demonstrates the background work that goes into the final pieces of artwork on the gallery wall. The theme to this cabinet is the water lily leaves and the sketches and research work behind them.

Finished illustrations cannot always be painted immediately from the fresh plant specimen, such as this ephemeral night-opening *Victoria amazonica* flower. Complex subjects also require heavy drawing and editing – in these cases, botanical sketchbook studies are an invaluable reference source for the final work.

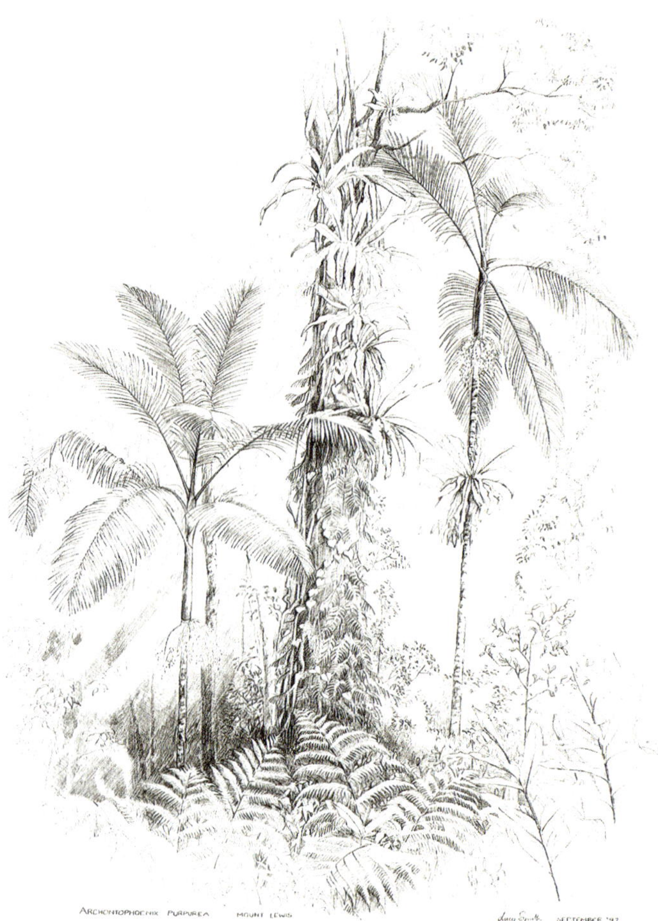

Sketch of *Archontophoenix purpurea*, a study for the watercolour and gouache painting of this palm from North Queensland, made from field sketches and notes and photographs. I removed this and other sketches from my sketchbook and framed them for inclusion in an exhibition. They were sold, leaving me with just old copies of the sketches.

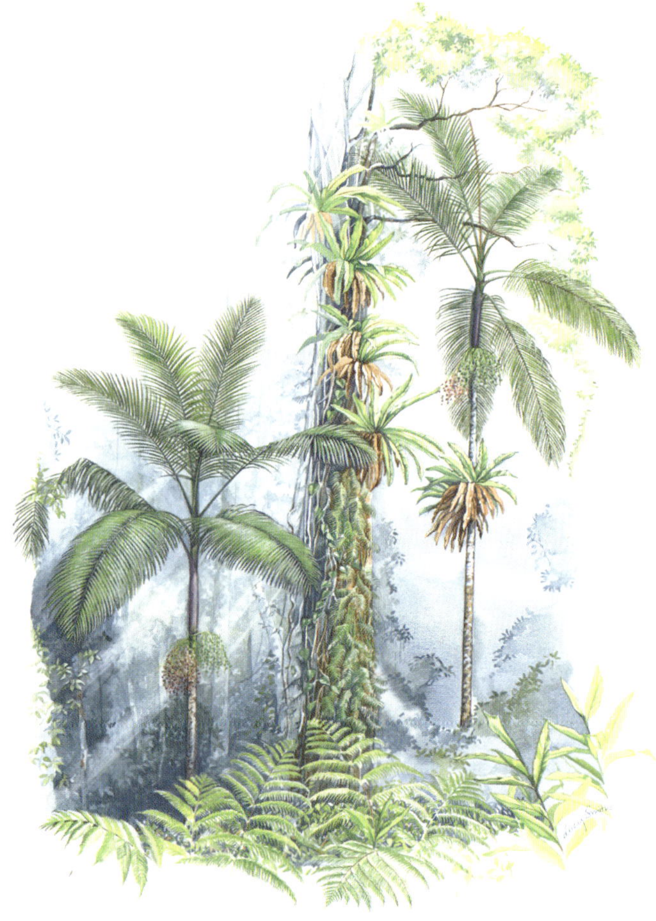

Watercolour and gouache painting of *Archontophoenix purpurea*, a rare palm endemic to one location: Mount Lewis in Queensland, Australia. The final work was exhibited at the Pinnacles Gallery, Townsville, Australia in 1999.

THINKING ABOUT COMPOSITIONS

Composition is one of the most important design elements of an illustration. The drawings in my sketchbook help me to visualise the shape and size of elements so that I can work out where they will fit within a larger composition. Thumbnail sketches contribute to the processing of ideas about movement and balance. Good composition balances all the elements in an artwork visually, while laying out parts of a plant in a logical order that can be read with minimal explanation.

Sometimes, ideas for the composition of a final piece present themselves as I am drawing parts of plants in the sketchbook. If these organic compositions work well, they can be transferred straight over to the final piece. On other occasions, the elements in the sketchbook have been drawn without a final composition in mind. Whichever way final compositions evolve, all the elements can be taken from the sketchbooks and copied over to the finished piece of watercolour, pen and ink or other working surface.

TRANSFERRING DRAWINGS FROM THE SKETCHBOOK

The main method I use for transferring my sketchbook studies to other working surfaces is tracing with a lightbox. The sketch is laid on the surface of the lightbox and the piece of paper to which the drawing is being transferred is placed on top of that. The light shining through both pieces of paper allows me to trace an outline on to the upper piece of paper.

In the past, lightboxes were large, chunky pieces of equipment, but now it is possible to buy LED light pads, which are flat and lightweight. Because they are so slim, they can be slipped between the pages of the sketchbook. Once positioned under the sketchbook page, the paper on to which the drawing is to be transferred can be placed over the page. The drawing shows through and can then be traced over. I usually use a 2H pencil, taking care not to let the tip dig into the paper and leave a groove that cannot be erased.

When transferring drawings that are in an awkward location in the sketchbook, for example, too close to the spiral binding of a page, or in the crease of a sewn-bound book, there are two options. First, if you have access to a photocopier, you can make a copy of the drawing. You can darken the drawing at the same time by adjusting the setting of the photocopier. The copied drawing can then be placed on the lightbox for tracing.

An added advantage of using a photocopier for this step is that you can enlarge or reduce the sketchbook drawing to a different size if that is what you require for the final piece. You may also wish to cut out the photocopied drawings and place them on the final page, moving them around to see where they might fit best in the final composition.

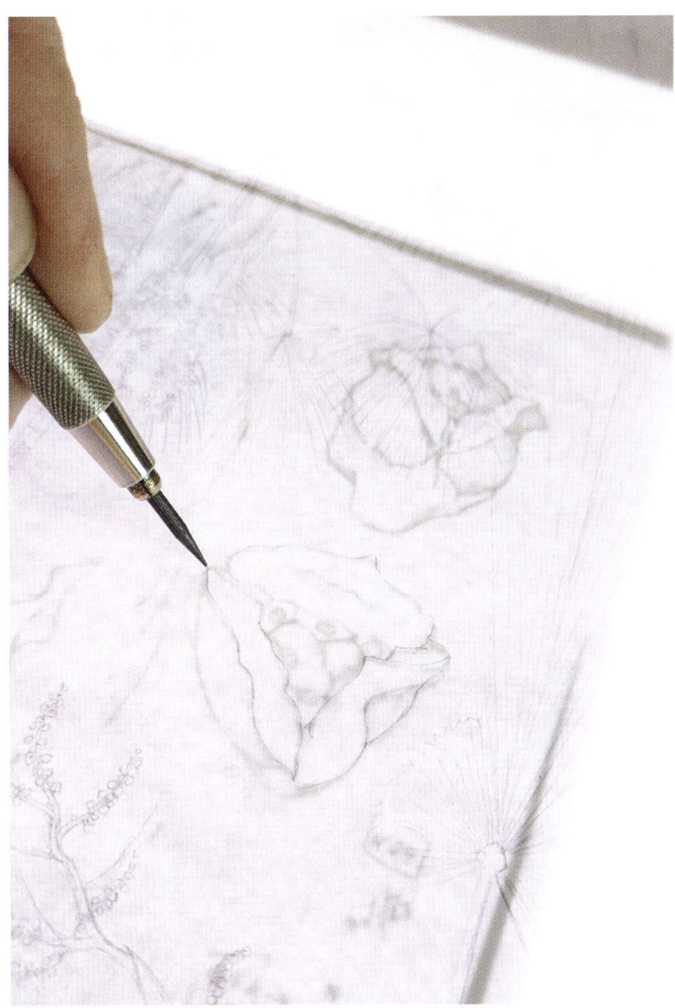

Tracing the drawings of *Saribus pendulinus* flowers from the sketchbook on to Bristol board paper for inking in the final composition. This newly described species is one of 250 I have illustrated for *Palms of New Guinea*. I prefer to use a flat LED lightbox as it is slim enough to slip between the pages of the sketchbook when tracing.

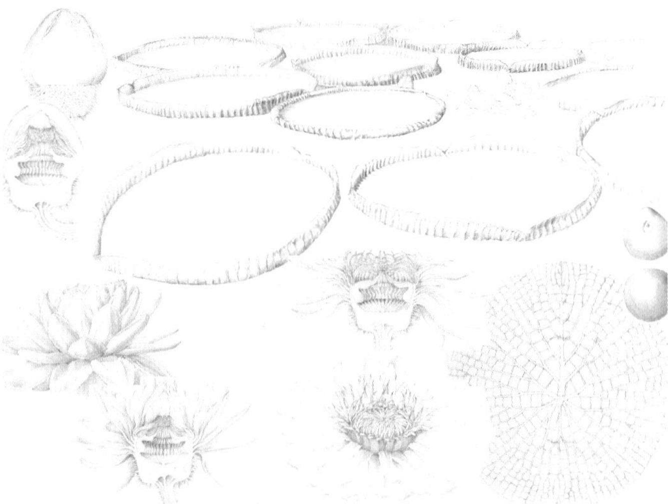

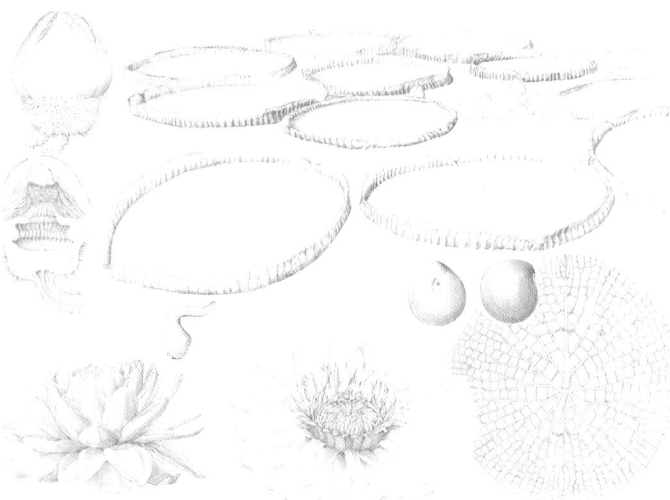

The first version of the draft scientific illustration of *Victoria boliviana*. All my sketchbook drawings were scanned and placed into the final compositional format, which was A3 in size (29.5 × 42cm). It became apparent that this composition was too crowded, and some elements would have to be removed.

A later version of the draft scientific illustration of *Victoria boliviana*, showing most of the elements that were included in the final composition. Once I was happy with the composition, I printed a life-sized version and traced it on to Bristol board for inking.

The other option when transferring your drawings is to use tracing paper. This may be necessary if your sketchbook drawing is in an awkward place on the page, as above, or if the surface on to which you are transferring the drawing is too thick for the light from a lightbox to shine through. Place the tracing paper over your sketchbook drawing and trace the outline of the drawing on to it. Use a harder pencil such as 2H for this as you will find that that the graphite comes off a lot more intensely than on cartridge paper. Once you have the outline, turn the tracing paper over and cover each line with a layer of a softer pencil, such as HB. The tracing is now ready to transfer. Place the tracing paper correct side up again on your new surface and draw down the outline on to your other piece of paper using a highly sharpened 2H pencil.

Finally, sketchbook pages can be scanned, and the elements cut out and rearranged digitally using illustration software such as Adobe Photoshop. Once the final arrangement has been composed on-screen, it can either be printed out to size for direct tracing or simply used as reference and the original drawings traced. I used this method when illustrating three species of giant *Victoria* water lilies for a scientific paper. I wanted to design a single illustration for each species that would encapsulate all their important comparative features. Planning the complex compositions was made much easier by arranging and rearranging scanned copies of my sketchbook drawings digitally in Photoshop. Each element could be re-sized and moved around repeatedly.

Whichever way you choose to transfer your sketchbook drawings, a degree of re-drawing on the final surface will be required. Errors in the drawing can creep into the transferred drawing. Lines can be misinterpreted, as can overlaps and joins. Take the time to carefully re-draw the transferred drawing, making constant reference to the original sketchbook drawing, and to the plant, if you still have it to hand.

SAME DRAWINGS, DIFFERENT APPLICATIONS

Sometimes, the studies made in my sketchbook for a specific project are used in more than one way for finished pieces. For example, a piece drawn for a pen and ink scientific illustration may find its way into a watercolour painting, and vice versa. For me, this is about getting great value out of my sketchbooks. The *Tahina spectabilis* example of a finished piece informed by sketchbook drawings (*see* below) certainly achieved this, as it resulted in three very different pieces of artwork.

Below are some of my favourite examples of finished pieces of artwork and the sketchbook studies that informed them, shown from concept and preparation work through to the end.

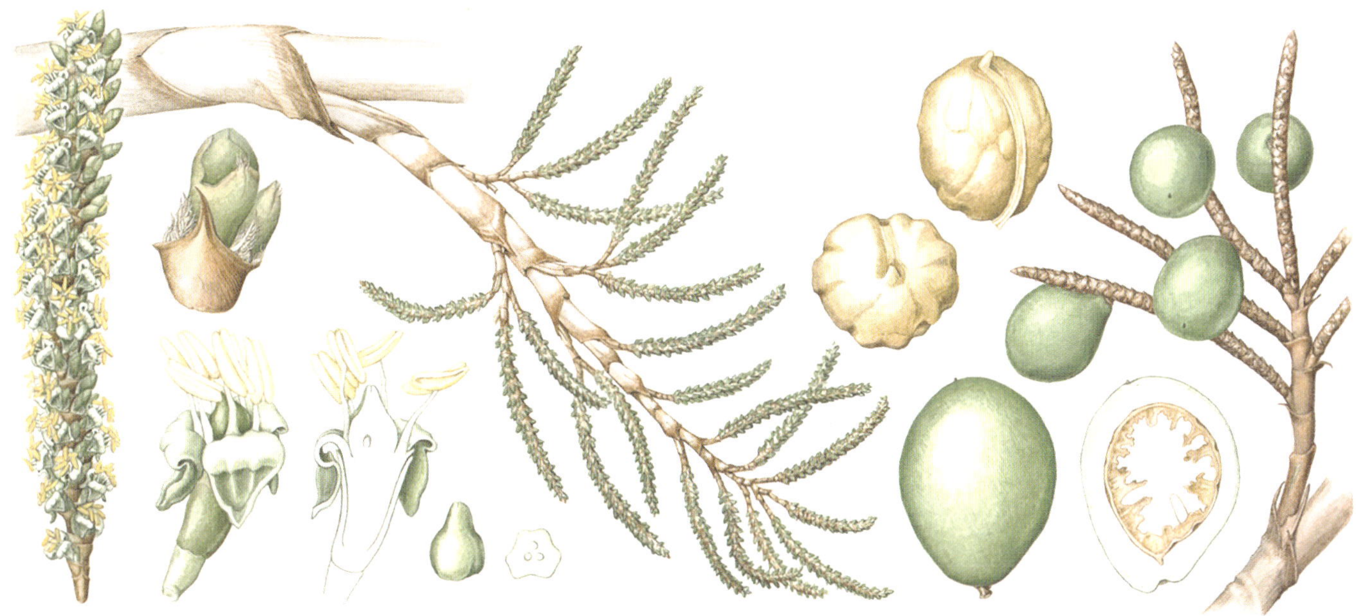

Detail of the flowers, fruits and seeds of *Tahina spectabilis*, a very large and rare palm from northwestern Madagascar. It was described as a new genus and species to science in 2008.

I was very fortunate to be working with the palm botanists at Kew when this incredible palm was discovered and described as new to science. They gave me the opportunity to draw it several times, from different types of reference material, and I was able to create three different series of illustrations from that material.

Part 1: Description of a New Genus and Species

In 2007, a new and unusual palm was spotted growing in a remote location in northwestern Madagascar. Some plant material was collected and sent to the botanists at Kew for study. The specimens came from a huge tree, but the material was surprisingly sparse. One leaf had been cut down to fit into a herbarium press. There were no fresh flowers, fruits or seeds available to collect, so some old inflorescence and fruit parts were gathered from the ground beneath one of the plants. Some dried fruits and seeds were collected, and some photographs were taken for reference.

It was suspected that this palm was not just a new species, but a new genus as well. However, the botanists needed to prove this by examining the specimens and publishing an illustrated description of the palm.

The small amount of dried flowering material was crucial for the botanists to try to identify the palm and its nearest relatives. Destructive sampling in the form

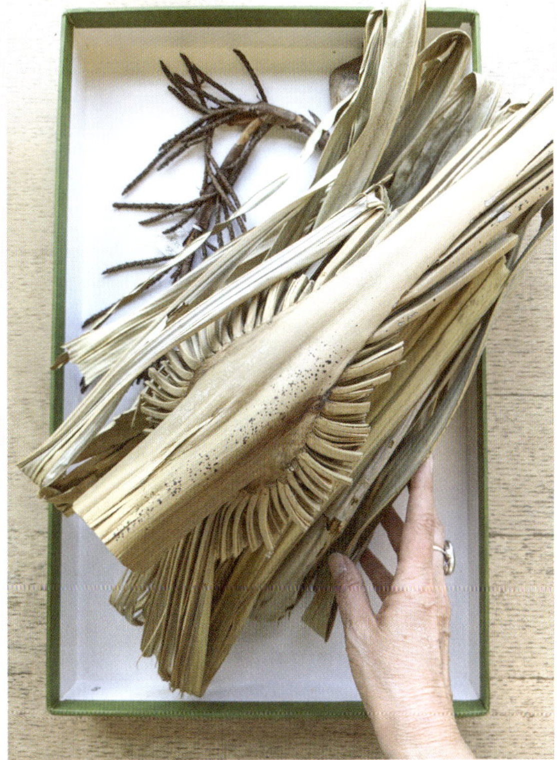

One of the first specimens of *Tahina spectabilis* was a large leaf with many of its segments cut off and the remainder folded and dried. It was kept loose rather than mounted on a herbarium sheet, so I was able to examine it from all sides and draw it from two angles, showing the folding pattern of the leaflets and the mid-rib at the centre of the fan leaf.

My first dissections and drawings of the precious *Tahina* specimen material were made with the botanists watching. The fruit and seed (left) were dried. The brittle bud (right) was the only intact flower specimen in existence. The drawings are not very detailed, as the material was in a poor state, but I gleaned what I could from the specimens.

of dissection was needed for my drawings, so this was done under supervision by the botanists. I first drew the flower buds still attached to the inflorescence, before carefully removing one to be drawn on its own. Its outer bracts were then removed and drawn, and so on, until the bud was in pieces. Scientific observations such as form and measurements were made by the botanists during each step.

Using descriptions of the palm as well as DNA evidence, the botanists were confident enough to publish a description of the palm and give it a name: *Tahina spectabilis*. My two pen and ink illustrations were included in the scientific paper, which was published in the *Botanical Journal of the Linnean Society of London*, Volume 156(1), 2008.

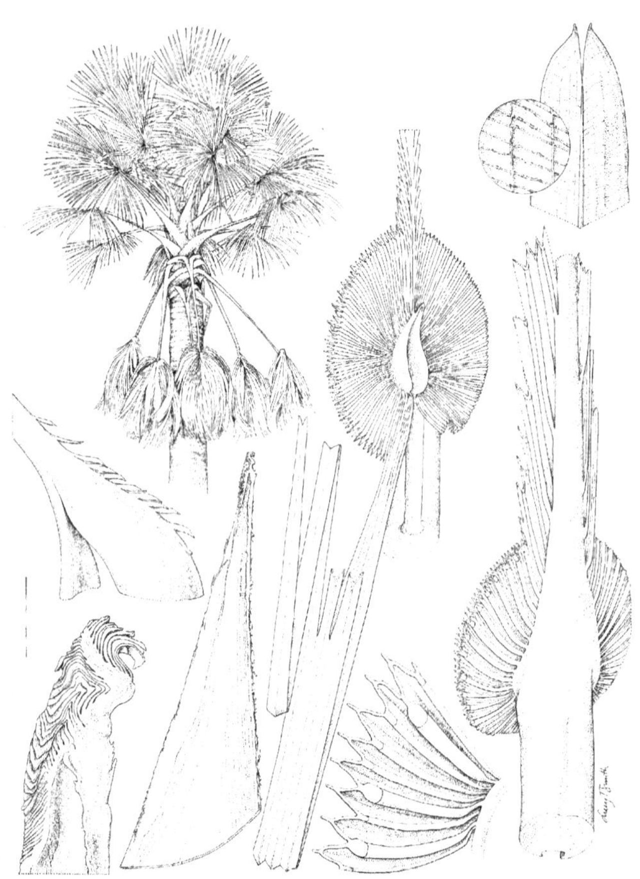

The first illustration of the *Tahina spectabilis* consisted of drawings made mostly from a photograph of the palm and a single leaf collection.

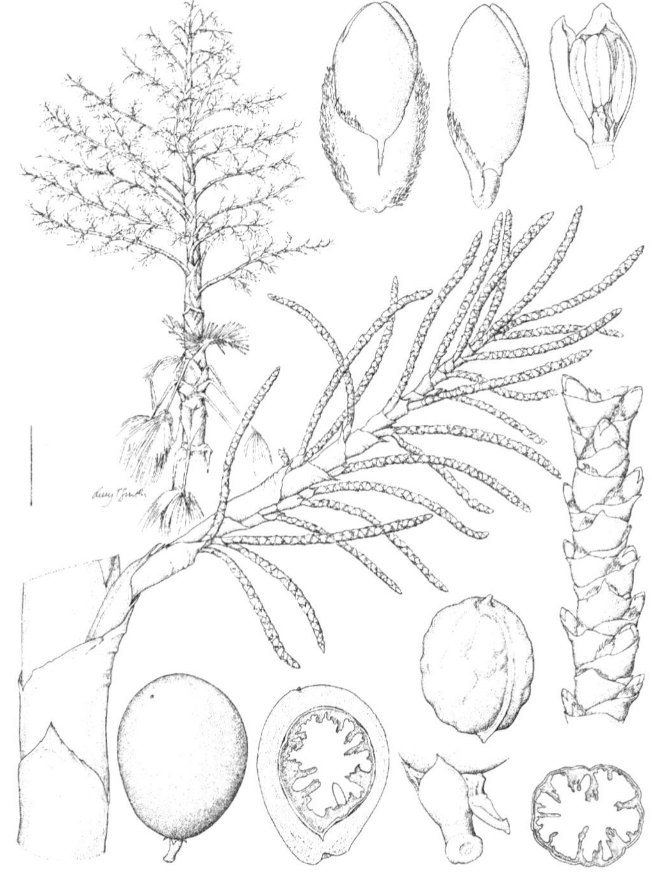

The second illustration of *Tahina spectabilis* also relied on photographs and the scant specimen containing some dried buds, fruits and seeds.

Part 2: lllustrations for the Book *Genera Palmarum*

Around the same time, the book describing every genus of the palm family (*Genera Palmarum*) was being updated and published as a second edition, with the addition of several new genera that had been described in the intervening years. The description of the new genus *Tahina* occurred when the book was already being prepared for publication, but there was no way it could be left out. There was an issue, however, in that the illustrations in the original book focused in detail on the flowers and fruits of each palm genus. The poor existing specimens of the recently discovered *Tahina* did not match the requirements of the publication.

Thankfully, a few months after the first specimens of *Tahina spectabilis* had been collected, field botanists made a new expedition to the location in Madagascar and found a newly flowering plant. They quickly made a spirit specimen of the flowers, fruits and seeds and sent them to the botanists at Kew. It was a great relief for me to be able to draw from better-quality material; my later drawings show that I had been able to capture so much more information about the flowers of *Tahina spectabilis* than before.

For the finished illustration, I was asked to use the same technique as the artist Marion Ruff Sheehan, who had illustrated the first edition of *Genera Palmarum*. This involved using pen and ink wash, and the illustrations contained flower and fruit drawings and dissections that were more detailed than in most scientific papers. It was the new specimens, preserved both in dried form and in spirit, that allowed me to make the drawings and dissections required.

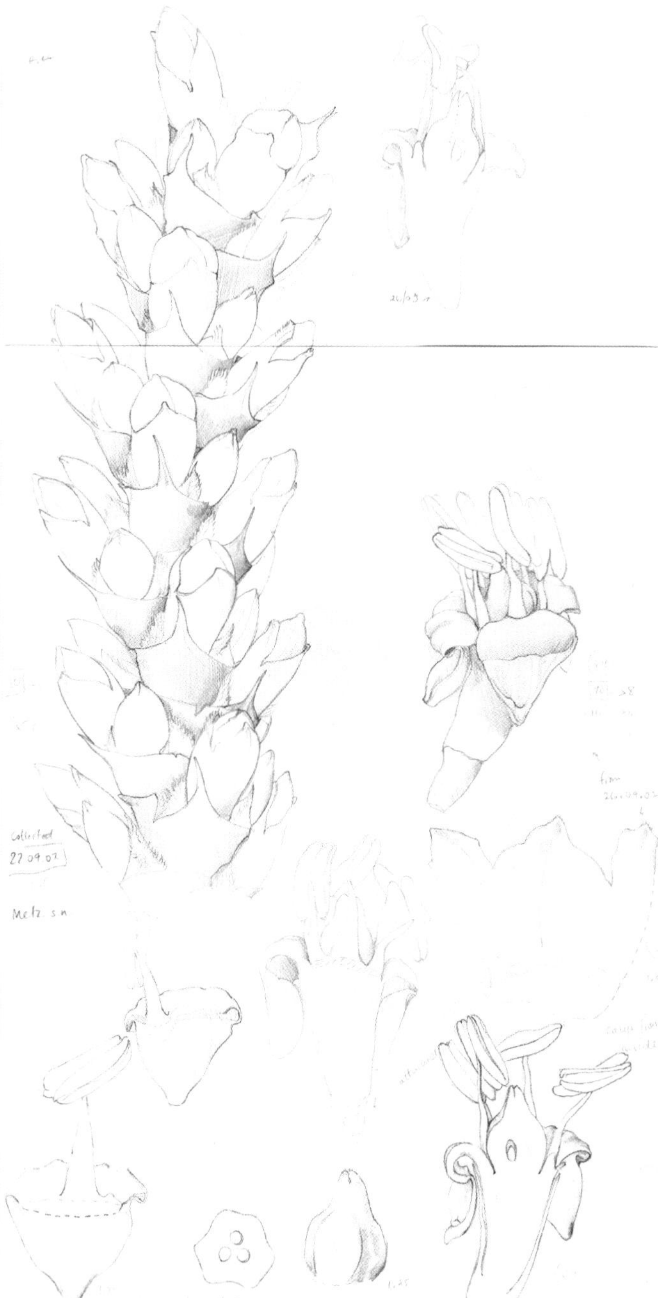

In September 2007, spirit specimens of the flowers of *Tahina spectabilis*, preserved beautifully in three dimensions, became available. Now I could draw the flowers thoroughly, observing and drawing how they were arranged on their rachilla as well as dissecting a single flower both longitudinally and in its parts. The quality of the drawing is much higher thanks to the improved quality of the material. While I was drawing the flower buds under the microscope, I realised the drawing would go off the page, so I attached another piece of paper to make space for them.

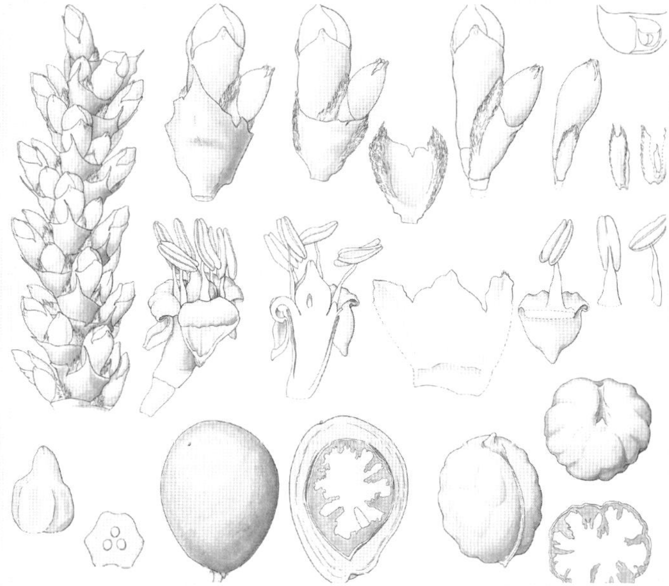

Illustration of *Tahina spectabilis* for *Genera Palmarum* (second edition, published 2008). I had to use an unfamiliar technique of pen line and wash to match the style of the book's previous illustrator. It is a much more detailed explanation of the flowers and fruits of the palm.

Part 3: A Painting Commission

The third and final part of this illustration story is a private commission to create a painting of this magnificent palm tree. The brief was open, but the commissioner liked the previous work I had done showing Australian palms in their natural habitats. He was also inspired by the exciting story of the palm's discovery to science. I decided to make the most of all the previous work I had done on this plant and tell the whole story of that discovery by depicting the palm in its natural habit, and to include some of the details I had been privileged to draw. I had not attempted combining palm, habitat and details into a single composition before. The new composition would combine my previous drawings and photographic reference of the palm taken in the field.

I tried various compositions in thumbnail form, considering whether to scatter the detail elements around the main subject. Eventually, I decided to keep the details separate from the picture plane of the main piece. I worked backwards from the size of the final piece and its height and width proportions.

Unfortunately, I was not able to see this palm in the wild in person, so I had to rely on a series of excellent photographs that were supplied to me. First, I worked on drawing up the main part of the composition, showing two of the palms in their natural habitat. This species flowers from its growing tip, producing a huge, branched inflorescence. Once it has flowered and fruited, the whole plant dies. The photographs given to me allowed me to combine in my drawing a flowering plant alongside one that was still growing.

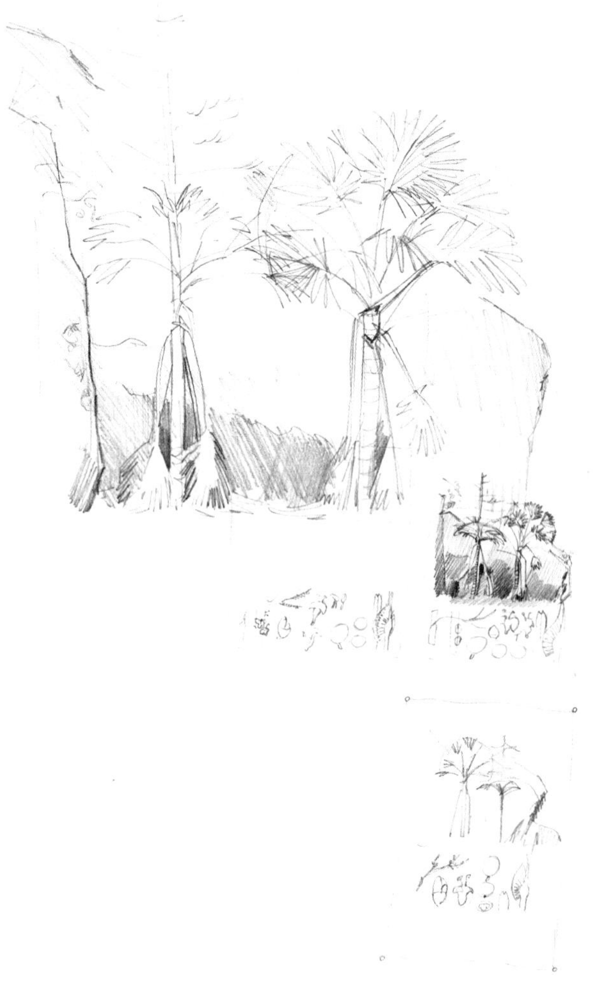

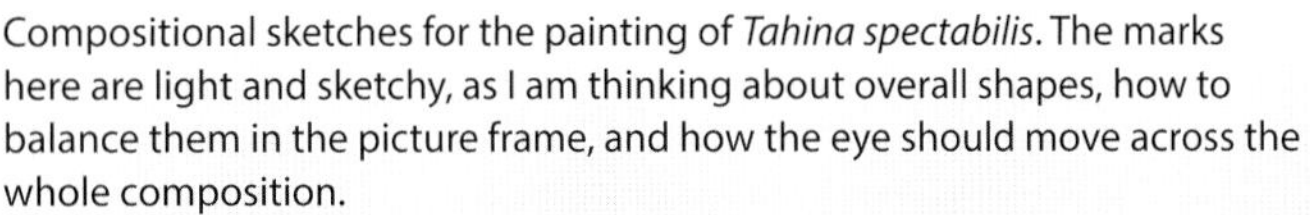

Compositional sketches for the painting of *Tahina spectabilis*. The marks here are light and sketchy, as I am thinking about overall shapes, how to balance them in the picture frame, and how the eye should move across the whole composition.

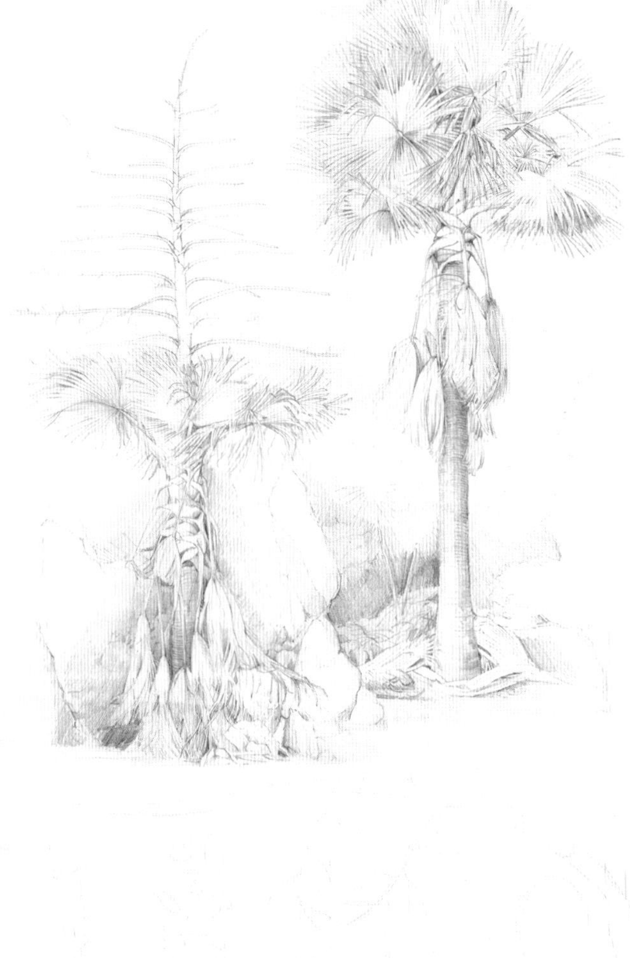

Unfortunately, I have not seen the magnificent *Tahina* palm myself in its Madagascan habitat, but I was supplied with excellent photographs from people who had. I wanted to include the palm at two different stages of its life: growing and producing its inflorescence before collapsing and dying.

The placement of the main drawing left me
a horizontal rectangular area at the bottom
of the composition for the flower and fruit
details. As always, I considered the placement
of the existing elements I had drawn up and
added in a few fresh elements drawn from
more photographs. I then looked at how the
two parts worked together, making sure that
the eye moved smoothly from the main image
down into the details. This was the first time
I had combined details with a main subject in
this way, so I put a lot of thought into creating a
balanced composition. Once I was happy with
the final composition, I traced my sketches on
to illustration board to create the painting in
watercolour and gouache.

The commissioner of the painting was very
happy for the finished image to be made into
prints, many of which have gone back to the
palm's home of Madagascar. There, they have
been used to raise both funds and awareness to
help protected this endangered species.

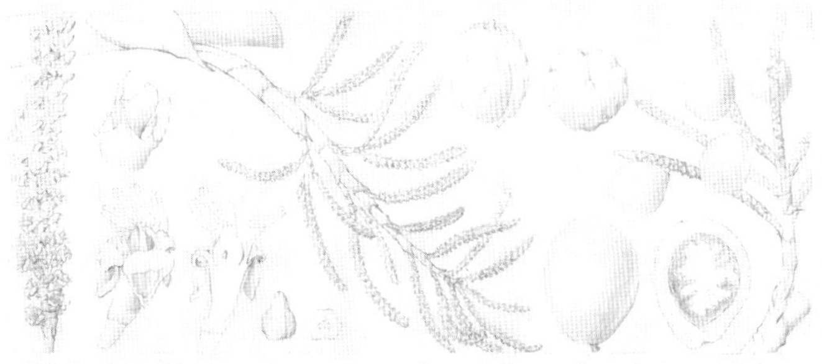

I was able to select details from some of my existing drawings of the *Tahina*
palm, as well as making some new ones from specimens and photographs.

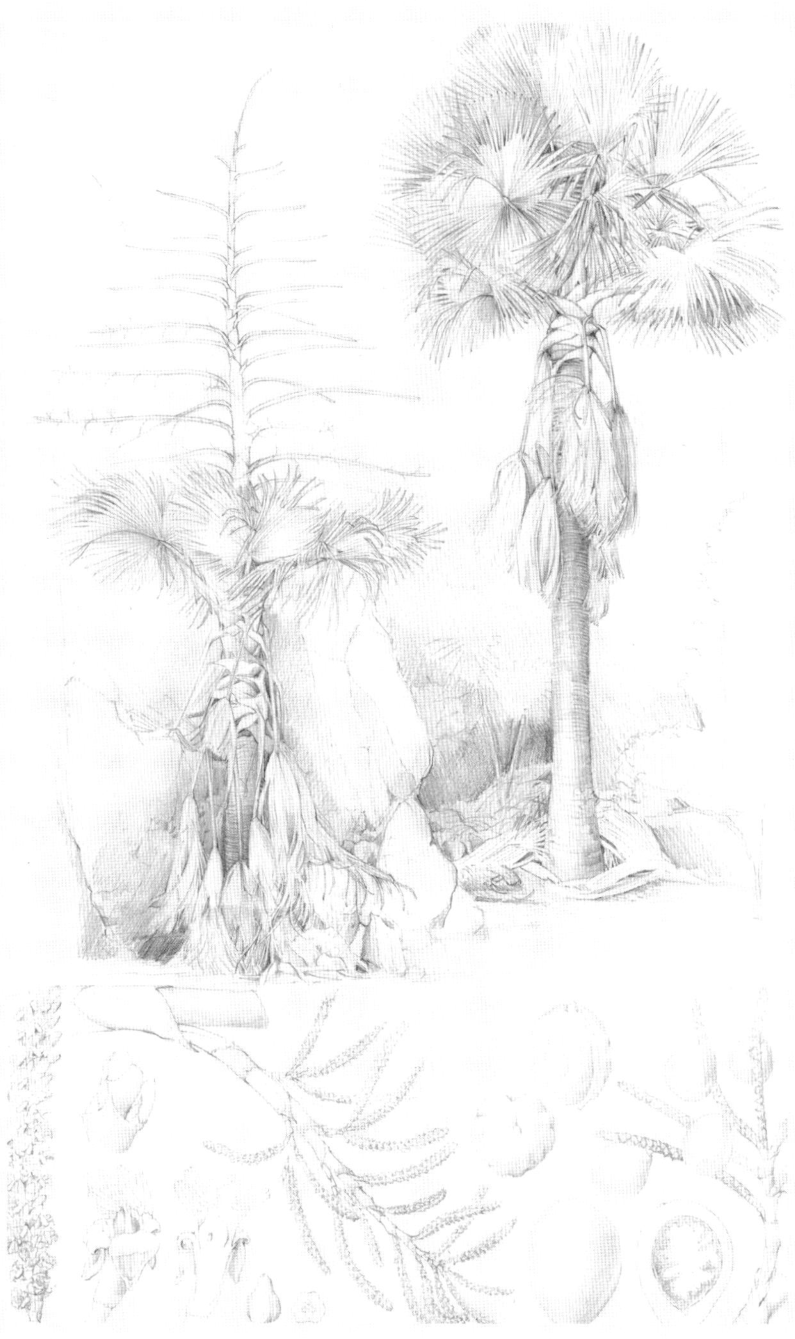

Deciding on the composition by scanning both drawings and looking at them on screen.
Once I had moved one of the seeds at the last minute, I was ready to move on to the
final painting.

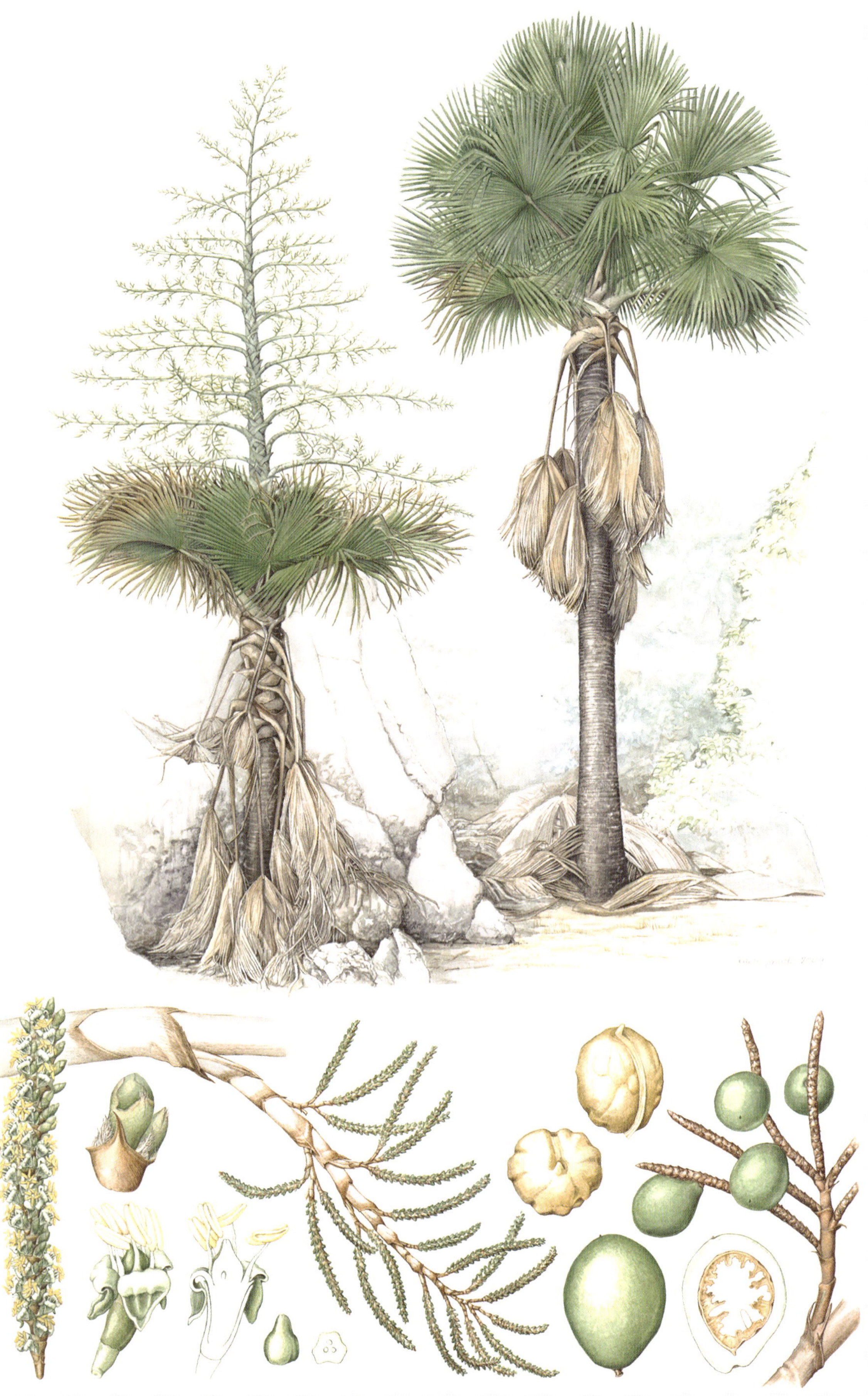

The final piece, *Tahina spectabilis*, completed using watercolour and gouache on illustration board. The original is in a private collection and a number of prints have also been made from it. Many have gone to Madagascar to help raise awareness of the endangered status of the palm.

This project started as an illustration for Kew's *Curtis's Botanical Magazine*. *Gustavia longifolia* is a beautiful plant that grows in South America. Cultivated in the Tropical Nursery at Kew, it was believed to have died in its pot until it suddenly began to produce characteristic large leaves from its tip, and flower buds from its trunk. There was some urgency to capture the flowers before they finished, as this was a rare opportunity to observe the plant flowering in cultivation.

Sketching in the Glasshouse

To draw the plant from an optimal viewpoint I sat on a stepladder, making several drawings of it in situ – not in its natural habitat as such, but in a large pot in a nursery! I observed that the flowers, which were perched on top of elegantly curving pedicels, opened for a day before their petals and stamens promptly fell off and on to the floor.

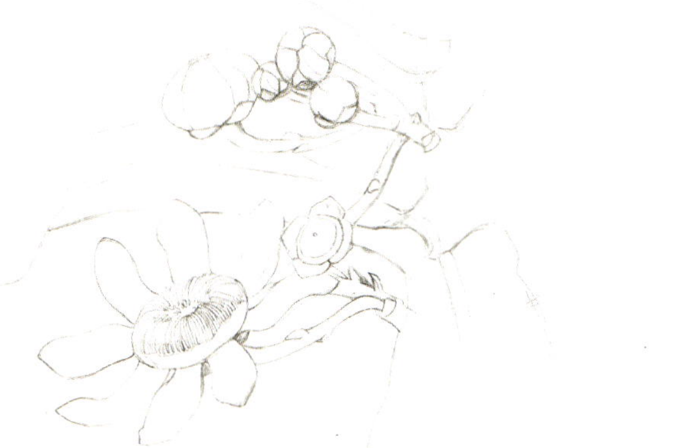

One of several views of the *Gustavia longifolia* flowers budding from the plant's stem. The upper perianth segments (petals), and the stamens, which form a dense layered ring, drop away from the rest of the flower very soon after opening.

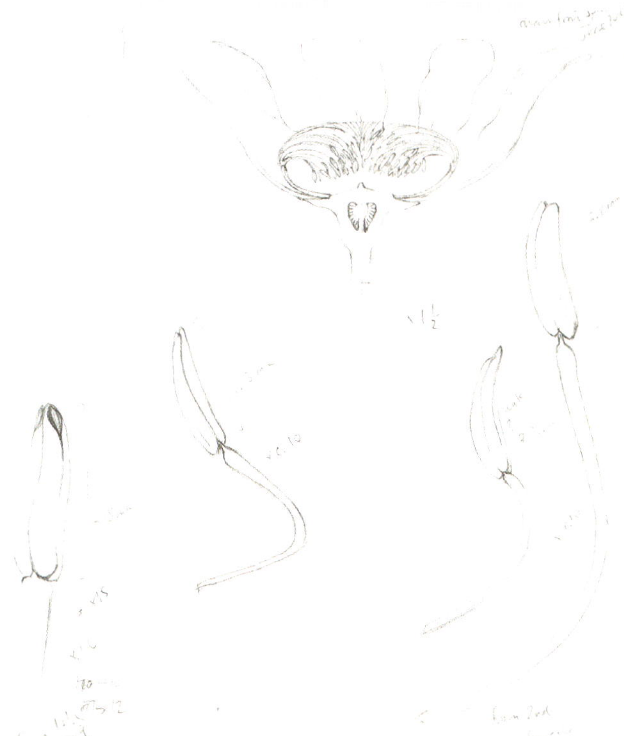

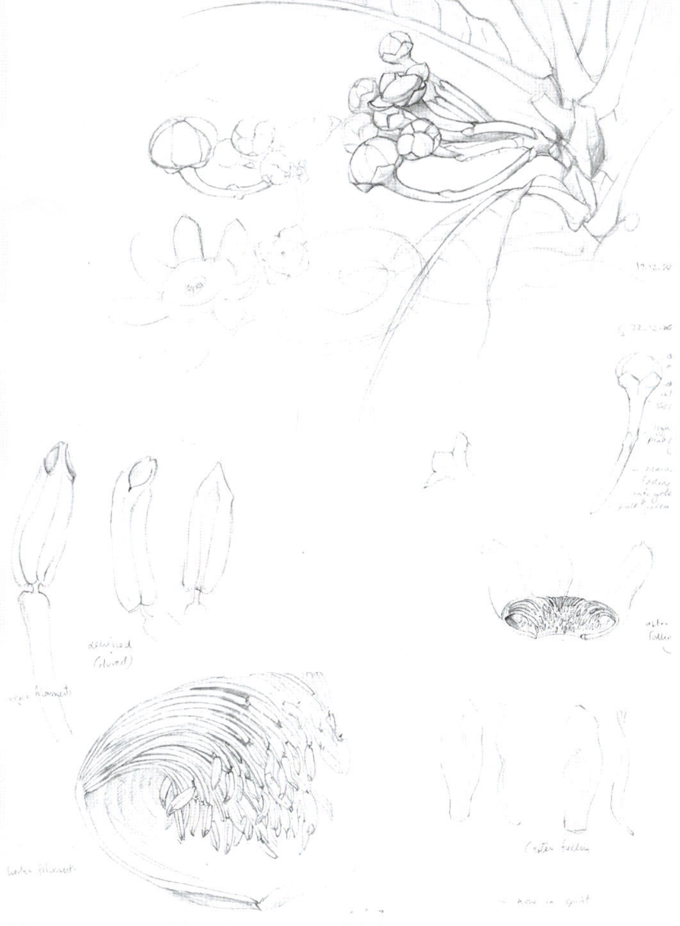

Gustavia longifolia is buzz-pollinated: its anthers open only in response to the specific vibration of a buzzing bee. This is replicated in cultivation by a tuning fork, which vibrates on a similar frequency when struck. The filaments are attached to the stamens at their base (above), curving over strongly towards the centre of the flower where the anthers hang upside down (right).

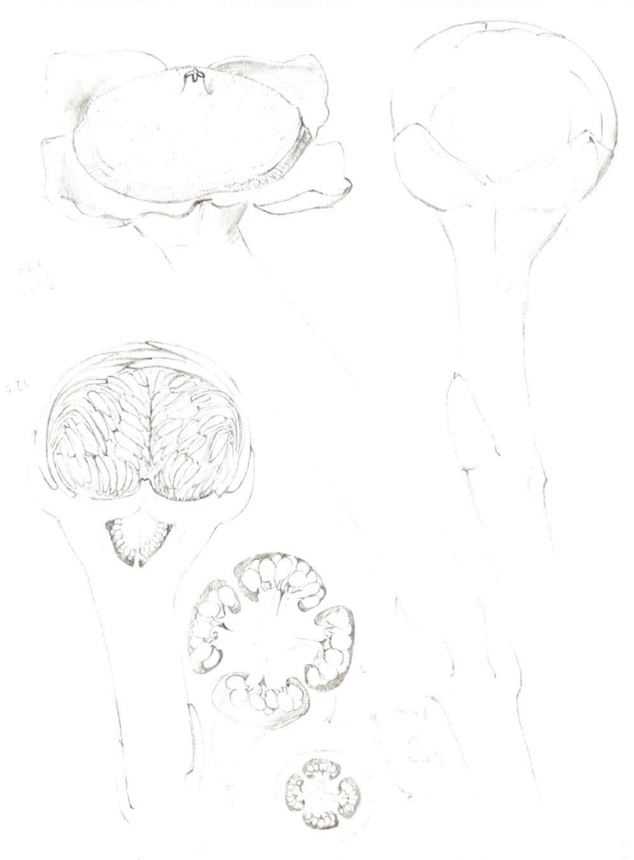

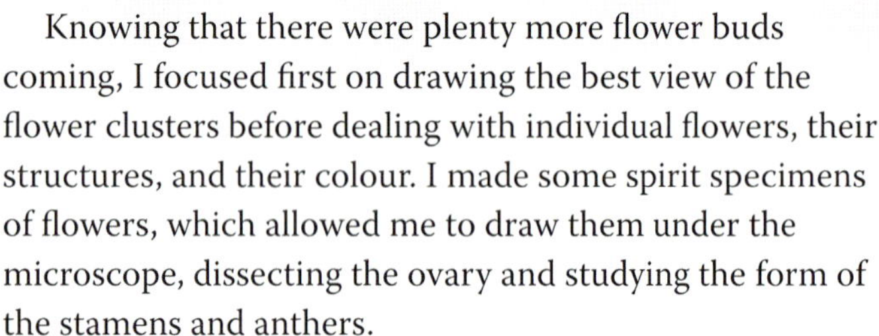

Longitudinal and transverse sections of an unopened flower bud allowed me to illustrate the structure of the flower's ovary and see how its ovules were attached inside the locules.

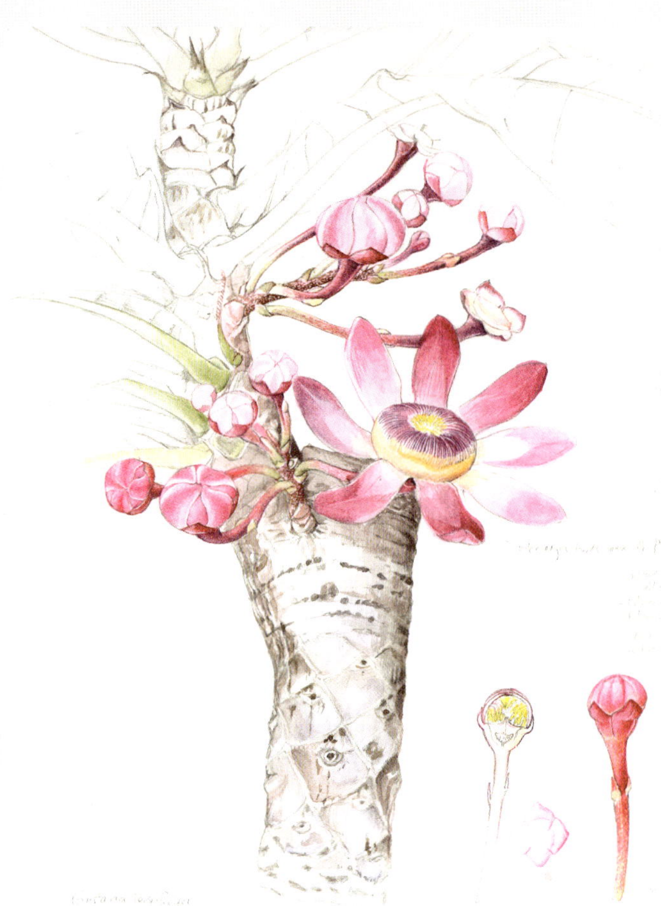

The drawing used for the final piece of *Gustavia longifolia*. Adding colour to this sketch brought the page to life. I had drawn the open flower but not painted it, and waited for the final bud to open so that I could capture its colour before the flowering event finished. I like the position of the inflorescences, as they show flower buds at all stages of development, including those whose petals and stamens have fallen off.

Knowing that there were plenty more flower buds coming, I focused first on drawing the best view of the flower clusters before dealing with individual flowers, their structures, and their colour. I made some spirit specimens of flowers, which allowed me to draw them under the microscope, dissecting the ovary and studying the form of the stamens and anthers.

Capturing Flower Colour

Finally, it was time to capture the colour of the flowers, which I planned to add to my existing drawings. Unfortunately, I was unable to get to the nursery for a few days during this crucial time. My contacts there told me that flower after flower had opened and fallen off. Suddenly there was only one flower bud left! The horticulturists were carefully watching the plant for me and called one morning to say that the final flower had opened. Dropping everything, I rushed to Kew with my drawings and watercolours and was able to capture the beautiful pinks and maroons of that last flower.

Finished Illustrations in *Curtis's Botanical Magazine*

The finished watercolour based on the sketch was painted on watercolour paper at the size of a *Curtis's Botanical Magazine* plate, 12.5 × 21cm. As the flowers were now all gone, I relied heavily on my sketch and colour studies.

The other sketches I had made of the flower were used for an accompanying diagnostic pen and ink illustration. Around the same size as the colour plate, it included as much work from the sketches as I was able to use. Reducing one of the large single leaves to fit on the plate, I drew and inked in the flower buds on their inflorescence, and some of the flower details and dissections. My aim was to make sure that the two illustrations complemented each other successfully.

The finished watercolour piece
of *Gustavia longifolia* appeared
in *Curtis's Botanical Magazine* in
Volume 7(4), 2010.

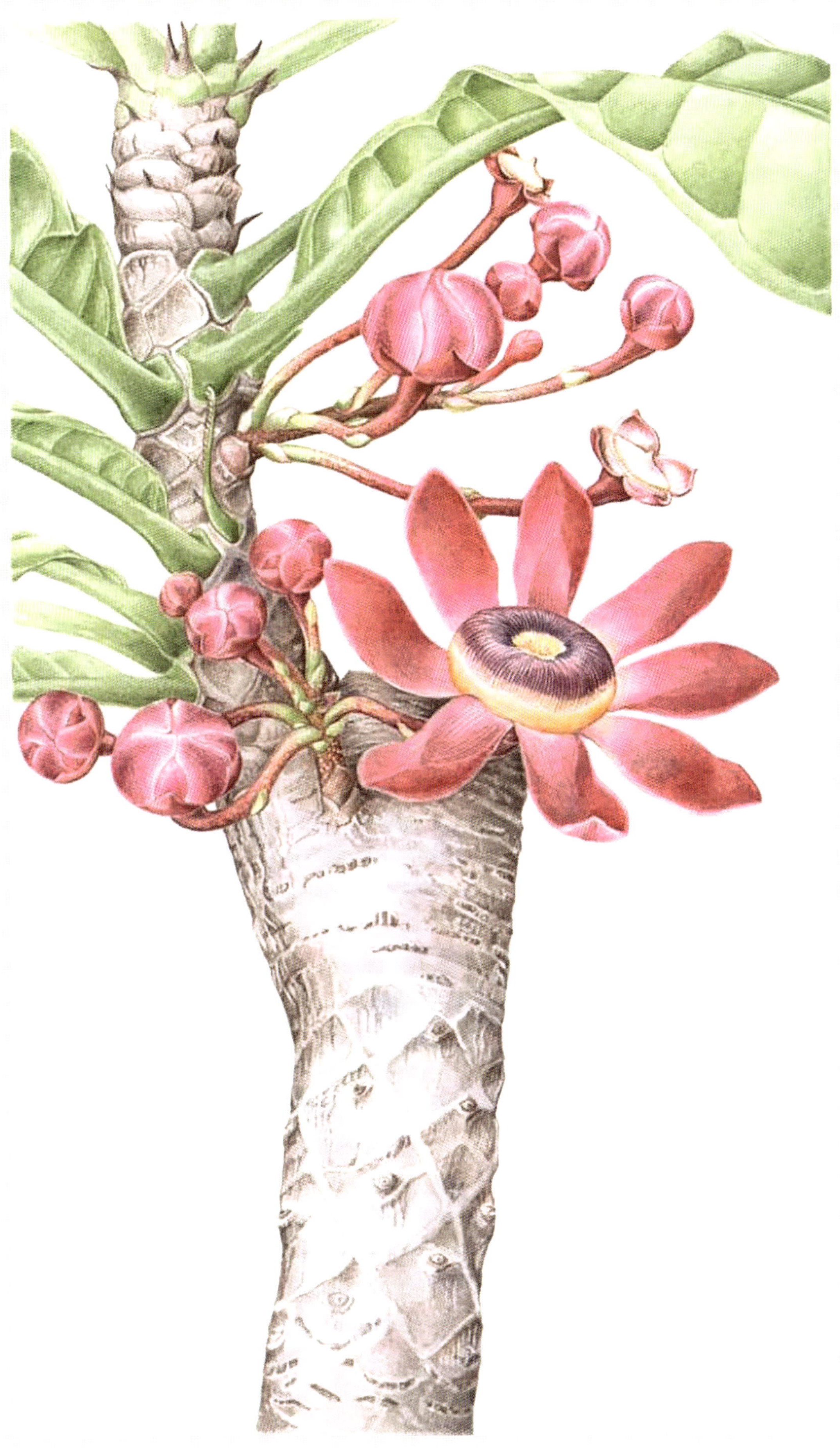

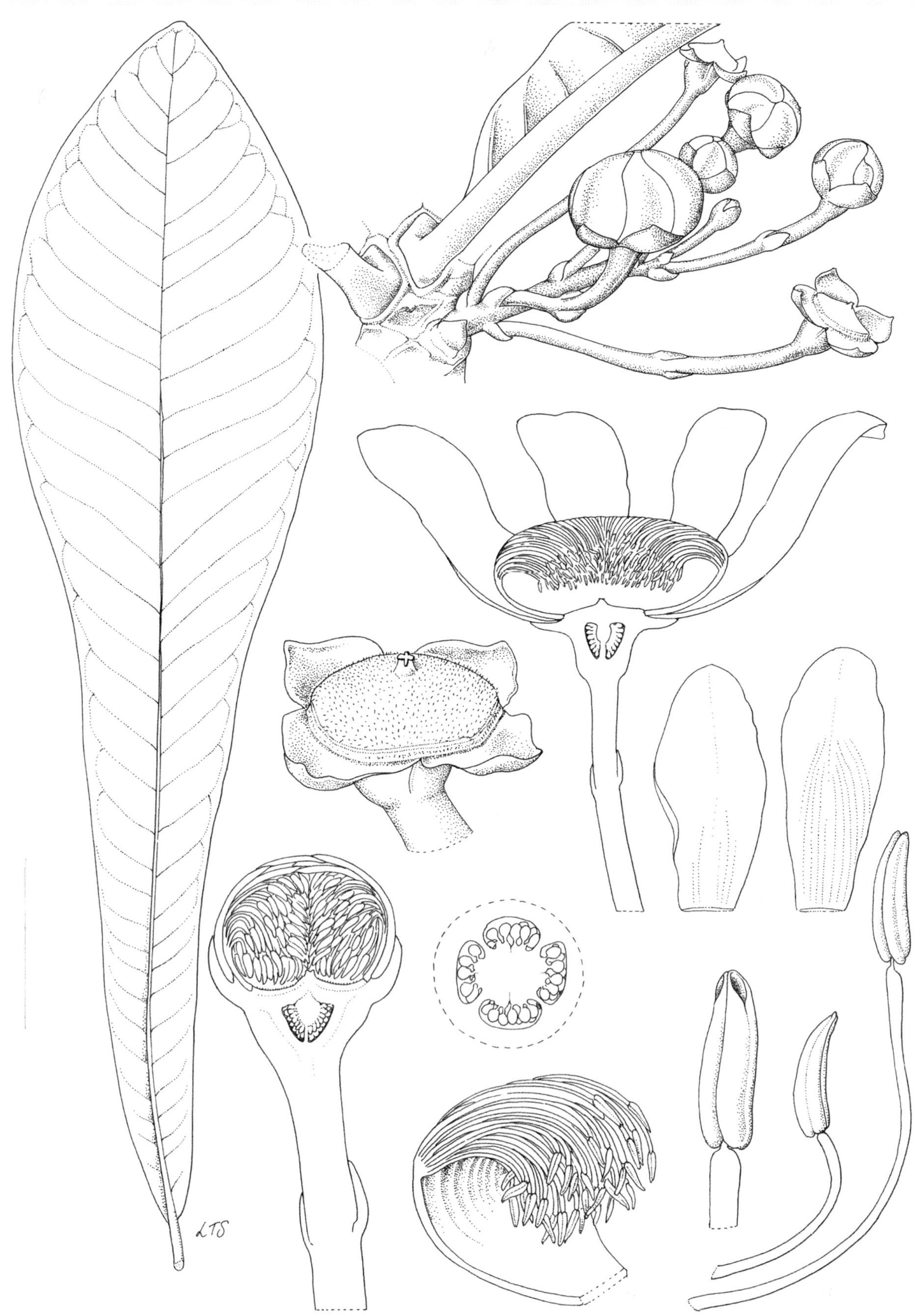

Pen and ink illustration of *Gustavia longifolia* showing more scientific details of the plant's flowers, published alongside the watercolour piece. I was pleased to incorporate many of the sketches I had drawn into these final artworks.

I drew many detailed sketchbook studies in pencil for my project illustrating the flowers and leaves of the giant *Victoria* water lilies. Originally intended for use as watercolour paintings, the drawings were also adapted for use in diagnostic pen and ink illustrations, to appear in the scientific paper about the genus that I co-authored. Three main illustrations were required, one for each species. Each image needed to encapsulate as many diagnostic features as possible of the species, in formats that would also allow for easy comparison between the three.

There were so many elements to include in these illustrations that I knew digital illustration software would be the best way to design them. First, I scanned each pencil drawing separately. After creating an A3-sized template for each illustration in Photoshop, I added each element such as the habit of the plant in the water, the flower buds and open flowers, to the digital page. Several iterations of each composition were tested before a successful layout was found.

Once I was satisfied with the composition, I printed out a copy of the layout at actual size. I traced the composition on to Bristol board in 2H pencil, before inking over the pencil with Rotring technical ink pens sizes 0.15, 0.18, 0.25 and 0.35. The flowers were so complex that there was no way I could have drawn them straight on to the finished piece of watercolour paper.

All the original drawings I made of the giant *Victoria* water lilies have been used in various ways: as drawings to understand and document the species' characters and differences; traced on to watercolour paper and painted in colour; and finally used for diagnostic pen and ink drawings. The paintings and drawings are designed so that the three species can be easily and clearly identified as different from each other. I certainly have made the most of my sketchbook drawings in this case.

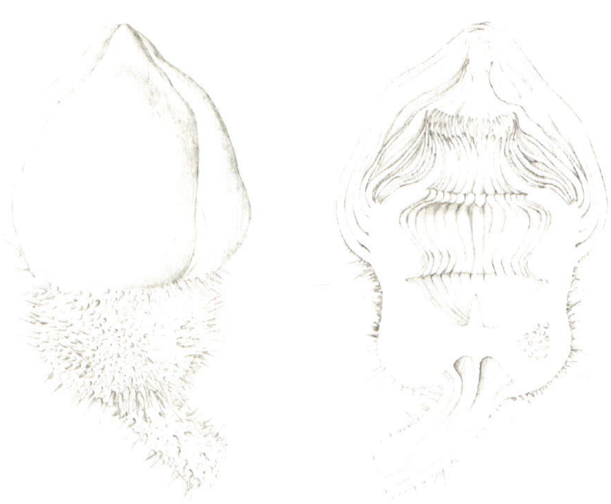

For each of the species of *Victoria* I made life-sized drawings of the buds, both whole and cut in longitudinal section. This is the bud of *Victoria cruziana*.

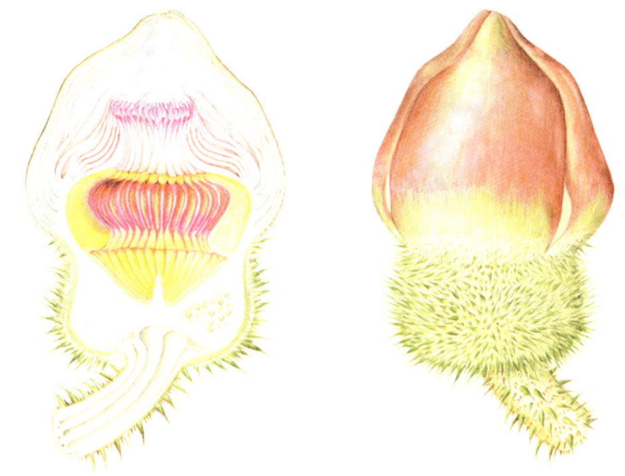

The same drawing, traced on to watercolour paper and painted in colour. I took the opportunity to change the order of the whole bud and section, as I thought the colours looked more balanced this way around.

1

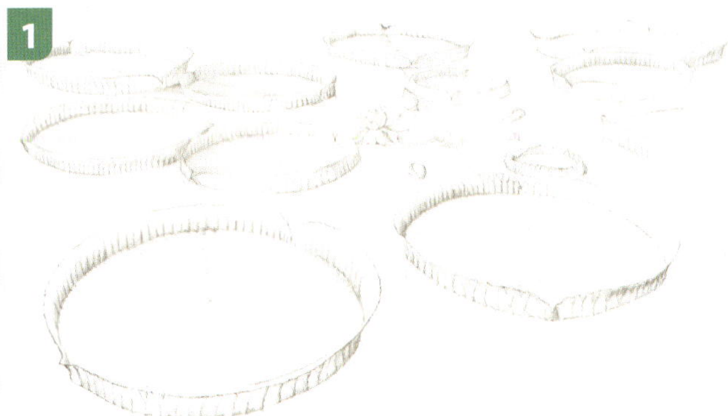

The habit of *Victoria cruziana* was sketched from a combination of my own photographs and drawings made from life. This was to be the main subject of the diagnostic illustration, around which the other elements could be placed.

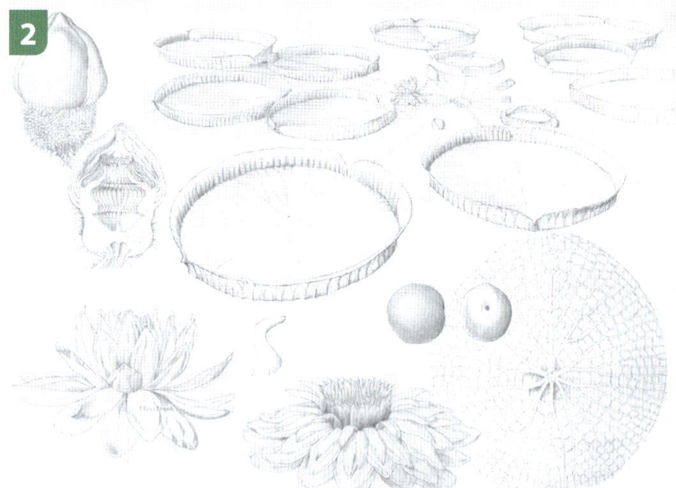

One of the draft compositions using cropped scans of multiple elements that had first been drawn in the sketchbook. By saving each element as a layer in Photoshop, they could be moved around the illustration area until a satisfactory composition was found. The final composition was printed out at the correct size, traced and re-drawn on to a piece of Bristol board using 2H pencil.

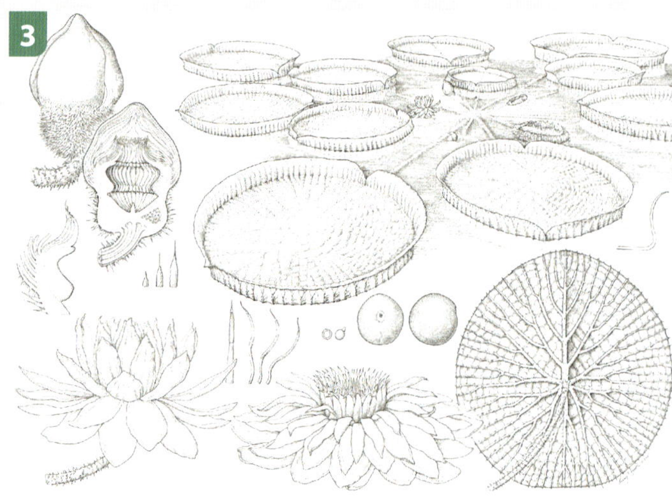

The final diagnostic illustration of *Victoria cruziana*, rendered in pen and ink. It is now ready to be scanned and labelled digitally for publication.

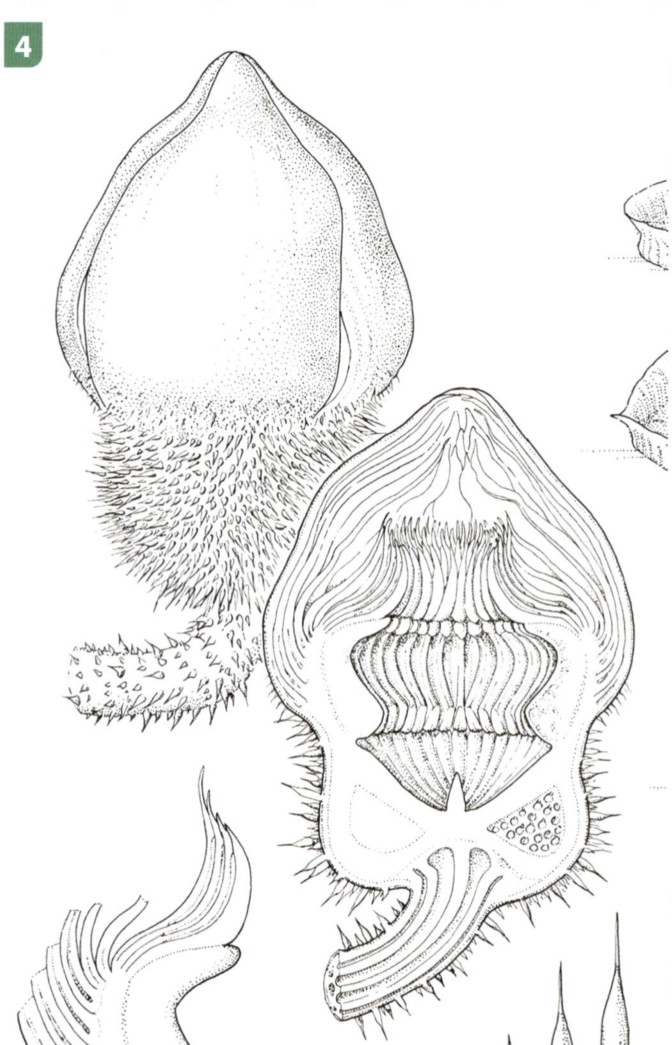

The buds of *Victoria cruziana* rendered in ink in the final scientific illustration of the species. These were drawn much smaller than the original sketchbook drawing and overlapped so that they would fit into the composition.

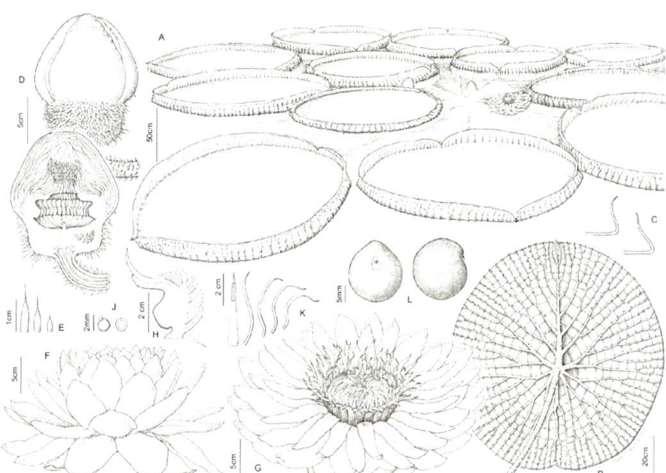

The diagnostic illustration of the new water lily species *Victoria boliviana*. Each of the three illustrations published in *Frontiers in Plant Sciences* (Volume 13, 2022) was designed to allow easy comparison across all three species.

PALMS OF NEW GUINEA

Examples of sketchbook pages for the project on the palms of New Guinea are dotted through this book. There are at least five full A3 sketchbooks for this project, which I have been working on for more than two decades. Below are four of the finished pen and ink illustrations made from those sketches.

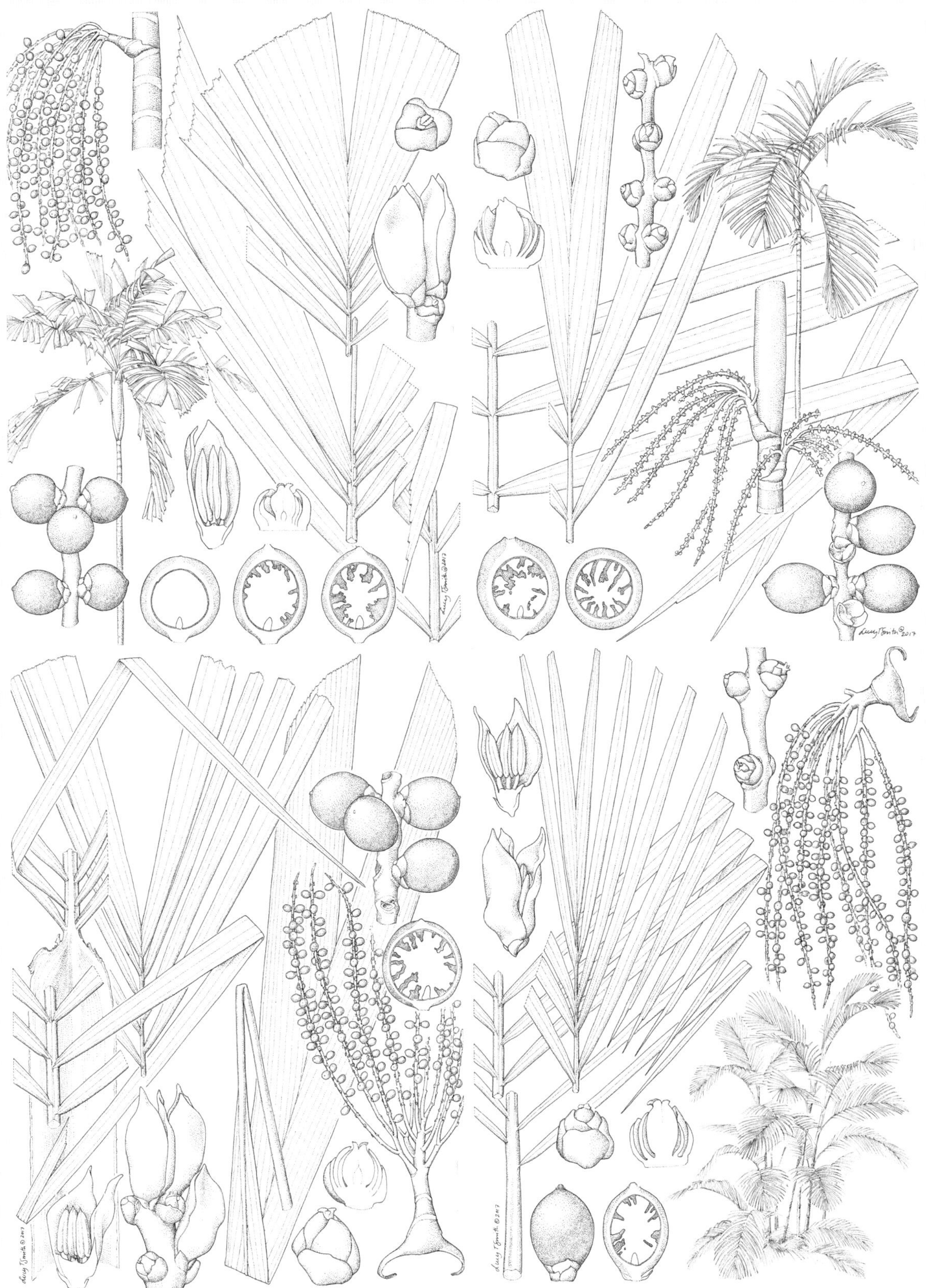

Many sketchbook pages have been used to do preparatory work for 250 pen and ink drawings for *Palms of New Guinea*, a 23-year long project I have illustrated, published by Kew Publishing in 2024. Behind every one of the 250 pieces is at least one sketchbook page covered in notes, scribbled calculations and detailed dissection drawings. The sketchbooks mark a passage of time and document the development of the project. I will always look back on them with happiness and a sense of fulfilment.

FINAL WORDS

Every Picture Tells a Story

Every finished piece of botanical artwork drawn, inked or painted to perfection and hanging on a gallery wall, or published in a journal or book, is the product of much preparatory work. From humble beginnings in the pages of a botanical sketchbook, big ideas and even bigger artworks can grow. I hope that the chapters of this book have given the reader a glimpse into the work that botanical sketchbooks do.

Focus and Connection with Nature

Drawing and painting plants in a sketchbook allows you to narrow your focus and appreciate the beauty and diversity of plant life. I can open a page of one of my sketchbooks and be happily transported, for example, to the memory of a sunny afternoon spent sitting under an apple tree or a Transylvanian meadow buzzing with insects. I will never regret time spent with nature, nor time spent drawing. No time spent with my botanical sketchbook is ever wasted, whether I am happy with the result or not.

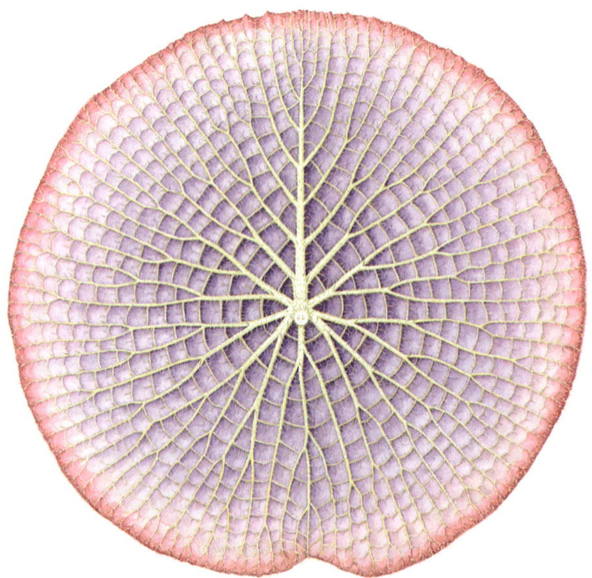

Out of the page and on to the wall: measuring 120 × 120cm, the life-sized watercolour painting of the underside of a *Victoria amazonica* leaf is the product of research, observation, understanding and drawing carried out in the botanical sketchbook. The original is now in the collection of Dr Shirley Sherwood.

Stops and Starts, Successes and 'Failures'

There are plenty of pages in my botanical sketchbooks that are almost empty, containing barely started or half-drawn and abandoned pages. I do not call these pages 'failures'. Not every page in your botanical sketchbook will be a masterpiece, and that is the whole point of it. While you may choose to share the pages of your sketchbook with other people, it is primarily a space for you and your work alone. Every time you draw or paint, you learn something about your plant subject and about technique. There is no such thing as a wasted drawing.

Nurturing Creativity

A great deal of my botanical artwork is highly ordered and organised, drawn for specific professional purposes. That part of my sketchbook practice is essentially for maintaining high standards of observation and organisation. This can also inspire creative paths that I wish to follow in my own time. I also like to open my botanical sketchbooks and draw simply for enjoyment and exploration. This is where I go to relax and remember all the reasons why I love to draw and paint plants.

There does not have to be an agenda behind nor an outcome from your botanical sketchbook studies, but those studies may spark ideas that you had not anticipated. This is the creative process in action. Until you pick up a pencil, pen and paintbrush and start *doing*, ideas exist only in your head. The physical process of experiencing plants by touching with your hands, observing with your eyes, and moving a pencil across the page is where ideas start to take concrete shape.

Starting Your Botanical Sketchbook

I hope that you have enjoyed seeing inside my botanical sketchbooks and learning about some of my approaches and the stories behind them. More importantly, I hope you will be inspired to open your own botanical sketchbook and give some of the ideas a try. Whether you are drawing and painting plants for the very first time, or are an experienced sketchbook user, there is always more to learn. With plants as a subject matter, you should never be short of material to work from.

I wonder, what will be the thing about plants that grabs your attention and compels you to stop and try to capture it?

My final words must be: sit, observe, draw, paint, but most of all, enjoy!

First published in 2024 by
The Crowood Press Ltd
Ramsbury, Marlborough
Wiltshire SN8 2HR

enquiries@crowood.com
www.crowood.com
This impression 2025

© Lucy T Smith 2024

All rights reserved. No part of this publication may
be reproduced or transmitted in any form or by
any means, electronic or mechanical, including
photocopy, recording, or any information storage and
retrieval system, without permission in writing from
the publishers.

British Library Cataloguing-in-Publication Data
A catalogue record for this book is available from the
British Library.

ISBN 978 0 7198 4337 2

Lucy T Smith has asserted her right under the Copyright,
Designs and Patents Act 1988 to be identified as the
author of this work.

Author's website: www.lucytsmith.com

Dedication and Acknowledgements

Dedicated to my mother and father for a love of nature, art
and books, and to my husband and daughter, sisters and
friends for their love and support.

Thanks to botany and horticulture colleagues past and
present for sharing their knowledge and passion with me.
Special thanks to the Royal Botanic Gardens Kew where,
in my work as a freelance botanical artist, I have been
privileged to access amazing plants. And finally, to all my
botanical art students whom I have had the pleasure to
teach – you have taught me so much too.

Thanks to the following for providing images:
Paul Pudi, page 42; Laurence Hill, pages 98, 101, 102
and 106; Aaron Davis, pages 111, 115 and 134; and Mary
Beth Sutter, page 155.

Cover design by Sergey Tsvetkov
Graphic design and typesetting by Peggy & Co. Design
Printed and bound in India by Parksons Graphics Pvt Ltd